The Classical and Christi.

MW01258111

There has been a considerable amount of literature in the last 70 years claiming that the American founders were steeped in modern thought. This study runs counter to that tradition, arguing that the founders of America were deeply indebted to the classical Christian natural-law tradition for their fundamental theological, moral, and political outlook. Evidence for this thesis is found in case studies of such leading American founders as Thomas Jefferson and James Wilson, the pamphlet debates, the founders' invocation of providence during the revolution, and their understanding of popular sovereignty. The authors go on to reflect on how the founders' political thought contained within it the resources that undermined, in principle, the institution of slavery, and explores the relevance of the founders' political theology for contemporary politics. This timely, important book makes a significant contribution to the scholarly debate over whether the American founding is compatible with traditional Christianity.

Kody W. Cooper is UC Foundation Assistant Professor of Political Science and Public Service at the University of Tennessee, Chattanooga.

Justin Buckley Dyer is Professor of Government and Jack G. Taylor Regents Professor at the University of Texas at Austin.

The Classical and Christian Origins of American Politics

Political Theology, Natural Law, and the American Founding

KODY W. COOPER
University of Tennessee at Chattanooga

JUSTIN BUCKLEY DYER
University of Texas at Austin

CAMBRIDGE
UNIVERSITY PRESS

CAMBRIDGE
UNIVERSITY PRESS

University Printing House, Cambridge CB2 8BS, United Kingdom

One Liberty Plaza, 20th Floor, New York, NY 10006, USA

477 Williamstown Road, Port Melbourne, VIC 3207, Australia

314–321, 3rd Floor, Plot 3, Splendor Forum, Jasola District Centre, New Delhi – 110025, India

103 Penang Road, #05–06/07, Visioncrest Commercial, Singapore 238467

Cambridge University Press is part of the University of Cambridge.

It furthers the University's mission by disseminating knowledge in the pursuit of education, learning, and research at the highest international levels of excellence.

www.cambridge.org
Information on this title: www.cambridge.org/9781009098113
DOI: 10.1017/9781009106030

First published 2022

A catalogue record for this publication is available from the British Library.

ISBN 978-1-009-09811-3 Hardback
ISBN 978-1-009-10784-6 Paperback

For Cormac James, Belén Elizabeth, Perpetua Rose, Campion Thomas,
Felicity Clare, Sebastian Sixtus, Zélie Grace, and Bosco Joseph Paul

—KWC

For Lincoln Christine

—JBD

Contents

Figures

Acknowledgments

As Benjamin Franklin observed in the 1737 edition of *Poor Richard's Almanack*, "there is no better relation than a prudent and faithful Friend." Our friendship stretches back to childhood and extends through our time together in graduate school at the University of Texas at Austin and now to this joint intellectual project we have labored over for the past several years. Each of us is blessed to have in the other such a prudent and faithful friend, and we are grateful for the time we have spent thinking, talking, debating, and writing together.

We are jointly appreciative for the sage advice and friendly criticism from J. Budziszewski, Jeffrey Tulis, Paul DeHart, Kevin Stuart, Matthew Wright, Nicholas Drummond, Allen Hertzke, and Glenn Moots. Three anonymous reviewers also provided helpful criticism and feedback on various parts of this project. On the publishing side, Robert Dreesen and the editorial team at Cambridge University Press have been a pleasure to work with.

Parts of this book grew out of material previously published in *Politics & Religion*, *American Political Thought*, *Duquesne Law Review*, and *Federalist Society Review*. We acknowledge permission to build on that material here. As a coauthored project, we have also amassed our own individual debts.

Kody thanks Shilo Brooks and everyone at the Benson Center for the Study of Western Civilization at the University of Colorado–Boulder for research support necessary to complete final revisions and edits, and he especially thanks the other 2021 Summer Fellows at the Benson Center: Jeremy Fortier, Christie Maloyed, Lisa Gilson, David and Allison Levy, Owen Anderson, Paul Ulrich, and Laura Jenkins for their helpful feedback on the project. He also extends a special thanks to Jedd and Cassie Martin for their warm Colorado hospitality and joyful embrace of the chaos that comes with hosting a family of nine for a month. This project would not have come to completion without you! Kody is grateful as well for the support from the University of Tennessee at

Chattanooga, including support from the Ruth S. Holmberg grant, the Summer Writing Stipend, and the warm advice and encouragement from colleagues at the Department of Political Science and Public Service. Finally, he is thankful for the unconditional love and unfailing support from his family.

During the final stages of this book's production, Justin returned from the University of Missouri to the University of Texas at Austin, where he had completed his PhD. He thanks his colleagues, new and old, for their support. Mizzou's Kinder Institute on Constitutional Democracy was a wonderful place to pursue answers to the questions raised in this book, and he remains ever grateful to Rich and Nancy Kinder for making that interdisciplinary and interideological project possible. Over the last several years, he has been invited to share parts of this research at the Natural Law Workshop at the UC Berkeley School of Law, at the Symposium on Truth and the Law at Duquesne University School of Law, and at various meetings and events organized by the James Wilson Institute. For the opportunity to do so, he thanks John Yoo, Steve Hayward, Janice Rogers Brown, Bruce Ledewitz, Heidi Li Feldman, Hadley Arkes, and Garrett Snedeker. For research assistance and help with graphic design and cover ideas, he thanks Bailey Martin and Allison Smythe, respectively. Finally, he is grateful for the steadfast love and encouragement of his wife, Kyle, and their children, Bennett, Pierce, and Lincoln.

I

Introduction

Classical and Christian Origins

When John Adams wrote to his wife, Abigail, on July 2, 1776, to report news of the signing of the Declaration of Independence, the British North American colonists were not yet living in our secular age.[1] America's Declaration of Independence came a century before Friedrich Nietzsche first declared, through the mouth of a madman, that God is dead. Even then, the madman's announcement turned out to be premature, for as he realized, "[t]his tremendous event is still on its way, wandering; it has not yet reached the ears of men."[2] The event still on its way was not so much the death of God as the death of the theological tradition that underpinned core liberal concepts we often take for granted, such as basic human dignity, natural rights, the reality of goodness, the reliability of reason, and moral agency grounded in free will. As Kyle Harper has noted, the full realization of this tremendous event "would unravel in future time, and its consequences would be unsettling."[3]

The inauguration of our secular age, grounded in reductive materialistic presuppositions that harken back to the ancient worldview of Epicurus, has created a discrepancy between the framing assumptions of our public life and basic concepts we routinely take for granted. One example of this discrepancy was provided in an essay published in *The Atlantic* titled, "There's No Such

[1] See generally Charles Taylor, *A Secular Age* (Cambridge, MA: Harvard University Press, 2007).
[2] Friedrich Nietzsche, *The Gay Science*, trans. Josefine Nauckhoff (New York: Cambridge University Press, 2001), 120.
[3] Kyle Harper, "Human Rights and Human Dignity: The Long View" (lecture at the Kinder Institute on Constitutional Democracy, University of Missouri February 19, 2015); see also Kyle Harper, "Christianity and the Roots of Human Dignity in Late Antiquity," in Timothy Samuel Shah and Allen D. Hertzke, eds., *Christianity and Freedom* (New York: Cambridge University Press, 2016), 123–48.

Thing as Free Will."[4] Philosophers and theologians, of course, have debated the question of free will for millennia. What was new was the confidence with which the article pronounced that neuroscience had settled the debate. Chemistry and physics, according to the author, can explain every thought, every hope, and every dream (and this would of course include our thoughts about free will or anything else). This is an old assertion, purportedly supported by new evidence, and the implications are indeed unsettling, for it would mean that freedom and moral responsibility are illusions. As a character in C. S. Lewis' *That Hideous Strength* contends, such a state of affairs would mean that "[s]ocial relations are chemical relations."[5] On this view, politics and law are, and can only be, applied chemistry. One unsettling implication is that the analytic distinction between freedom and tyranny, consent and coercion, persuasion and propaganda, and ultimately sanity and insanity, begins to break down. So, too, does the very notion of a moral law that governs free, rational creatures.

Nietzsche considered free will to be the "foulest of all theologians' artifices,"[6] and there has been a related debate in the United States for some years about whether what Edward Corwin famously called the "higher law" background of American constitutionalism is just the foulest of all political theorists' creations.[7] Is natural law, an idea that presumes within it the concept of free will and much else that modernity has purportedly rejected, something to be taken seriously? Writing around the same time that Corwin was teaching at Princeton and leading the American Political Science Association, Columbia University psychologist Edward Thorndike drew out the full logic of the modern materialistic outlook, which poses a unique challenge to the natural-law tradition. "The life of a dog or a cat or a chicken obviously consists largely of and is determined by appetites, cravings, wants, desires and the like and their gratification or satisfaction" and so "also does the life of man."[8] If Thorndike was right – if our lives are determined by our appetites, cravings, and desires – then there seems to be no way for us to speak intelligibly about making choices or about being morally responsible for our actions in any meaningful sense. Our lives and identities could then be reduced to our biochemical composition, and we would at any moment be the obedient servants of our passions and appetites, since it could not be otherwise. Reason, accordingly, would not be the rightful ruler of our desires but would be merely calculative. Thomas

---

[4] Stephen Cave, "There's No Such Thing as Free Will," *The Atlantic* (June 2016). Accessed February 16, 2022, from www.theatlantic.com/magazine/archive/2016/06/theres-no-such-thing-as-free-will/480750/

[5] C. S. Lewis, *That Hideous Strength* (New York: HarperOne, 2003), 252.

[6] Friedrich Nietzsche, "Twilight of the Idols," in Walter Kaufmann, ed., *The Portable Nietzsche* (New York: Penguin Books, 1977), 499.

[7] See Edward S. Corwin, *The "Higher Law" Background of American Constitutionalism* (Indianapolis, IN: Liberty Fund, 2008).

[8] Edward Thorndike, *Human Nature and the Social Order* (New York: Macmillan, 1940), 96.

Hobbes gave voice to this conception of reason, which served as "scouts and spies" to "find the way to the things desired."[9]

The American founders, chronologically caught between the neo-Epicurean materialism associated with Hobbes and the nihilistic atheism of Nietzsche, bear little resemblance to either. When John Adams wrote exuberantly to Abigail with news of the Declaration of Independence, he exclaimed:

Yesterday, the greatest Question was decided, which ever was debated in America, and a greater perhaps, never was or will be decided among Men. A Resolution was passed without one dissenting Colony "that these united Colonies, are, and of right out to be free and independent States ....." ... You will see in a few days a Declaration setting forth the Causes which have impel'd Us to this mighty Revolution, and the Reasons which will justify it, in the Sight of God and Man.[10]

The Declaration's appeals to human and divine tribunals, to the "opinions of mankind" and to the "Supreme Judge of the World" were not simply rhetorical; they offer justifications in the "Sight of God and Man." Thomas Jefferson later commented during the semicentennial celebration of the Declaration that it was a beacon of liberty to the world, an inspiration to all peoples and future generations to secure the "blessings and security of self government" and a rejection of aristocratic claims that natural inequality was divinely ordained.[11] For Adams and Jefferson, both the meaning and practical influence of the Declaration had a deeply theological context.

The Declaration points to questions that are ancient but not antiquated. Who is this "Supreme Judge of the World"? Who or what is "Nature's God" whom the Declaration identifies also as the Creator who endows human beings with unalienable rights? Prominent scholars argue that the revolutionary significance of the natural-rights tradition invoked by the Declaration is that it is subtly (and intentionally) subversive of traditional biblical theology. In this framing, Nature's God stands as an alternative to, and an emancipation from, the God of Abraham, and the early modern natural-rights theories developed by Hobbes, Locke, Montesquieu, and others are seen as part of a larger project to pour the new wine of secular liberal individualism into the old wineskins of the classical Christian natural-law tradition. Thomas Pangle describes this project as one involving a "titanic strategy of propaganda, whereby Holy

---

[9] Thomas Hobbes, *Leviathan*, ed. A. R. Waller (Cambridge: Cambridge University Press, 1904), 45.

[10] John Adams, *Revolutionary Writings*, ed. Gordon Wood (New York: Library of America, 2011), 91.

[11] Thomas Jefferson, "Letter from Thomas Jefferson to Roger C. Weightman, June 24, 1826," Declaring Independence: Drafting the Documents, Library of Congress. Accessed June 28, 2021, from www.loc.gov/exhibits/declara/rcwltr.html

Writ is to be reconceived and in a sense rewritten so as to be subsumed in a vast secular revolution."[12]

The suggestion that the Declaration is also part of this vast secular revolution, conceived by philosophers and implemented by strategic propaganda, provokes various questions about the American founding along theological, historical, and political lines. Theologically, does the biblical account of God's causal relation to the world radically set apart the God of Abraham from the God of Nature? Historically, did Americans in the founding era publicly invoke the aid of the latter rather than the former? Politically, what did it matter? The focal point of analysis in the scholarship addressing this question has been the God of the biblical account of creation in contrast with the philosophers' pantheistic God, a deity indistinguishable from the rational organizing principles of an eternal and uncreated universe. On this account, as Matthew Stewart recently argued, the "Declaration of Independence – precisely where it superficially seems to invoke the blessing of the established religion – really stands for an emancipation of the political order from God."[13]

This basic narrative about the American founding has become conventional scholarly wisdom in many circles. In contrast, the thematic chapters in this book argue, in different ways, that the background assumptions of American public life during the American founding were derived from and compatible with the Christian natural-law tradition that developed from the long engagement of Christianity with classical political philosophy, hitting its highwater mark in medieval scholasticism and retaining its influence through the dominant theological traditions in the North American colonies. Those background theological and philosophical assumptions included the following:

(1) Natural law has a lawgiver.
(2) The Lawgiver is the divine creator who is separate and distinct from creation. As such, nature is not divine, and the God of Nature is not a pantheistic God.
(3) Practical reason grasps the moral content of the natural law as goods proper to human beings as rational animals and the practical necessities associated with the pursuit of such human goods.
(4) The natural law is prescriptive, imposing moral duties or obligations, not merely descriptive, offering hypothetical imperatives.
(5) The natural law emanates from the nature of God in which there is a unity of power and goodness. God's sovereign authority, in which moral obligation is grounded, is therefore not a result of superior physical strength alone but also is connected to God's goodness.

---

[12] Thomas L. Pangle, *Political Philosophy and the God of Abraham* (Baltimore, MD: Johns Hopkins University Press, 2003), 6–7.
[13] Matthew Stewart, *Nature's God: The Heretical Origins of the American Republic* (New York: W. W. Norton, 2014), 7.

(6) Sovereignty in a rightly ordered political community is modeled after the pattern of divine sovereignty, in which power and goodness are unified. Power alone does not confer sovereign authority.

(7) The rule of law means that the sovereign is subject to and bound by a higher moral law. Might does not make right. Absolute sovereignty understood as the imposition of the sovereign's will is analytically indistinguishable from tyranny.

(8) Sovereignty originally resides with the whole people, but sovereignty remains subject to a higher law. The people do not exercise an unbounded absolute sovereignty based on will alone. As such, consent is a necessary but not sufficient condition for the rightful exercise of government power.

(9) God sustains and provides for creation both through the natural law and through other exercises of divine providence that include revelation in Scripture and divine interpositions in human events.

(10) Natural law is itself one aspect of God's providence. Reason is epistemologically distinct from revelation, but reason nonetheless remains a form of participation in God's eternal law.

Taken together, these tenets provide a basic outline of the Christian natural-law tradition, and each tenet was included among the framing assumptions of American public philosophy in the colonies in the eighteenth century. They were taught as part of the moral philosophy curriculum in the colonial colleges, affirmed by each of the dominant theological traditions in the colonies, and appealed to in public life during the revolutionary and constitutional eras. It is not the case, of course, that every individual participant in public affairs affirmed each of these tenets. Some of the founders privately expressed skeptical or religiously heterodox opinions, particularly about the divine provenance of Hebrew and Christian Scripture. Yet, as Mark Hall has demonstrated, only a very small number of founders espoused the more radical deists' creed of a distant and disinterested creator who lets the world run on its own accord.[14]

Rather than a general philosophical deism, specific ideas that developed within Christian theology underpinned the natural-law tradition that the founders affirmed. Of course, the promise of natural law is that it can be understood and affirmed based on our common human nature, and therefore it provides a common moral standard or measure that transcends parochial differences and partisan interests. Yet that very epistemological claim – that each human being has access to moral knowledge based on a common created human nature – rests on contested ontological and theological premises about the foundations of moral knowledge and moral obligation that have practical implications for how we understand sovereignty and the rule of law. The

---

[14] Mark David Hall, *Did America Have a Christian Founding? Separating Modern Myth from Historical Truth* (Nashville, TN: Nelson Books, 2019), 3–19.

framing assumptions of the founding era provided answers to those questions that had developed from the long Christian engagement with the natural-law tradition. Indeed, the Christian natural-law tradition was a dominant force shaping the public philosophy of the American founding, and the evidence has been hiding in plain sight. That is the animating argument of this book.

1.1 CONTRIBUTION AND DISTINCTIVE APPROACH

The interconnections between theology, natural law, and the American founding have been the subject of scholarly study going back a hundred years. These are old topics, yet they remain fresh and relevant today. Twentieth-century scholars analytically grouped natural-law doctrines into two basic traditions. "The older and once dominant traditional natural law," James McClennan observed, "encompassing the classical and Christian schools, subscribed to the view that a Divine Being, ruler of the universe through an eternal and universal law, is the supreme lawgiver, and that natural law is an emanation of God's reason and will," a tradition since supplanted by "the modern natural rights concept, which is essentially a secular, individualistic assertion of the claims of man in a world naturalistically conceived."[15] Utilizing this basic dichotomy, there has been a considerable amount of scholarship in the last seventy years claiming that the American founders were steeped in modern thought where such thought is said to embody a rejection of both Aristotelian political philosophy and classical Christianity, including the Christian natural-law tradition. On this interpretation, the political philosophy that undergirds the Constitution represents a rupture with ancient and medieval ideas about the nature of political order and instantiates distinctly modern ones.[16] At the same time, there has also been a body of scholarship underscoring the pervasive influence of classical sources directly upon American founding thought.[17] From multiple angles, a number of scholars in recent decades have also argued for the biblical – for the Hebraic and Christian – roots of the American political

[15] James McClennan, *Joseph Story and the American Constitution: A Study in Political and Legal Thought* (Norman: University of Oklahoma Press, 1971), 70.
[16] See, e.g., Frank M. Coleman, *Hobbes and America: Exploring the Constitutional Foundations* (Toronto: University of Toronto Press, 1977); Walter Berns, "Judicial Review and the Rights and Laws of Nature," *Supreme Court Review* 49 (1982): 49–82; Paul A. Rahe, *Republics Ancient and Modern* (Chapel Hill: University of North Carolina Press, 1994); Thomas L. Pangle, *The Spirit of Modern Republicanism: The Moral Vision of the American Founders and the Philosophy of Locke* (Chicago: University of Chicago Press, 1990); Michael P. Zuckert, *The Natural Rights Republic* (Notre Dame, IN: University of Notre Dame Press, 1997); Gary L. McDowell, *The Language of Law and the Foundations of American Constitutionalism* (New York: Cambridge University Press, 2010).
[17] See, e.g., Eric Nelson, *The Greek Tradition in Republican Thought* (New York: Cambridge University Press, 2004); David Bederman, *The Classical Foundations of the American Constitution: Prevailing Wisdom* (New York: Cambridge University Press, 2008).

order.[18] There is therefore a real dispute as to how we should understand and interpret the American founding and its significance. Most scholars have adopted a multiple traditions solution to the problem, arguing that the American founding is, as one scholar recently put it, a blended scotch with no single origin.[19] But this leaves open questions concerning the degree of influence and whether some traditions are more fundamental than others.

A careful analysis of the founding period reveals that ideas central to American founding thought are not only compatible with but presuppose classical natural law and natural theology. One strong piece of evidence for this is the colonists' consistent rejection of absolute and arbitrary power both in theology and in politics. The classical political tradition begins with the rule of law, but the characteristic doctrine of modern political philosophy and the modern state is the arbitrary rule of will. Early modern philosophers who broke from the classical tradition conceived of the sovereign as unlimited by the people below or by God above. As the supreme fountain of all law, the sovereign could not be constrained by the law.[20] The American founding's reaffirmation of the rule of law, combined with its emphasis on republicanism and consent as the necessary efficient cause of government, was a rejection of the modern turn to arbitrary power. Put another way, both the divine right of kings and the modernist doctrine of the absolutely sovereign state were conceived as a rejection of the classical natural-law tradition's assertion that the king is established by law and is under law. The rule of law in this sense found an example and archetype in the Christian doctrine that God rules through the wisdom of his eternal law, not through power alone. To the revolutionary generation in America, it seemed that the Crown had rejected the rule of law in favor of arbitrary and absolute sovereignty, and so the Continental Congress argued in the Declaration of Independence. As the American colonists rejected arbitrary rule and reaffirmed the rule of law, they did so from within the conceptual framework of the Christian natural-law tradition.

1.2 NATURAL LAW AND THE RULE OF LAW

Over and against the notion that sovereign power stands above the law, the American founders embraced the idea that those who exercise political authority should be ruled by law. These arguments were embedded in a theological

---

[18] See, e.g., Donald Lutz, *The Origins of American Constitutionalism* (Baton Rouge: Louisiana State University Press, 1988); Russell Kirk, *The Roots of American Order* (Wilmington, DE: ISI Books, 2003); Barry Alan Shain, *The Myth of American Individualism* (Princeton: Princeton University Press, 1996).

[19] Robert P. Kraynak, "The American Founding as a Blended Scotch: A Reply to Thomas West," *American Political Thought* 9(1) (2020): 115–43.

[20] See generally Francis Oakley, *The Watershed of Modern Politics: Law, Virtue, Kingship, and Consent (1300–1650)* (New Haven and London: Yale University Press, 2015).

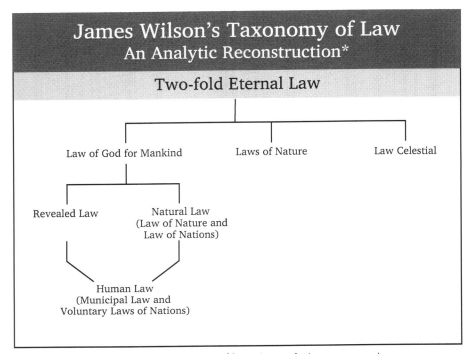

FIGURE 1.1. James Wilson's taxonomy of law: An analytic reconstruction.
Source: James Wilson, *The Collected Works of James Wilson*, eds. Mark David Hall and Kermit L. Hall (Indianapolis, IN: Liberty Fund, 2007), vol. 1, 497–98.

context and are fully comprehensible only in light of the persistent influence of the classical Christian natural-law tradition and its emphasis on the rule of law in theology and in politics. According to the natural-law tradition that was a common cultural inheritance of the founding generation, God created everything in existence and provided the rules by which each part of his creation would be governed. Nature, in one of its eighteenth-century usages, referred simply to the whole of creation, and the predominant view in the founding era was that each part of creation is purposeful. In continuity with a typology of law that developed from the medieval Christian natural-law theories of Thomas Aquinas and Richard Hooker, early modern jurists such as William Blackstone and James Wilson asserted that the purposes of creation emanated from God's twofold eternal law. The eternal law is the divine reason that both structures God's own actions and by which God governs creation, hence its twofold dimension. Beneath the eternal law are the laws that govern angels and spirits made just; the laws of inanimate matter; and the laws that apply to embodied, rational human beings. The analytic reconstruction in Figure 1.1 found with more commentary in Chapter 7, shows how James Wilson described this typology of law in his early lectures at the College of Philadelphia. It is remarkable for being an otherwise unremarkable replication of Christian natural-law theory by one of America's most influential constitutional framers and one of the founding era's most eminent jurists.

1.3 WHAT IS NATURAL LAW?

Founding era thought developed out of the perennial natural-law tradition, which identifies natural law as the moral law for human beings known to reason through rationally apprehended goods, rationally discerned moral obligations, and the freedom of the will to choose to obey or disobey this law. It is *natural* because it rooted in reason, which is the highest aspect of our nature, and it is *law* because it imposes moral obligation. To act in accordance with our nature means to act consistently with the way we are designed to function. It is proper to human nature to act according to reason, that is, for reason to order our passions and appetites to appropriate ends. When reason rules, it does so by identifying what is good according to our nature (i.e., the kinds of things we are and are designed to be) and pursuing it. These, then, are the foundational questions of ethics: What kinds of things are good for human beings? How do we attain these goods through our actions? Natural law, however, is not a law of necessity, and human beings may, individually and in societies, deliberately act against their natural moral obligations to the detriment of their own happiness or flourishing.

That some things are good and that we ought to pursue what is good in our day-to-day lives, are axiomatic. These truths are foundational to practical reason in the way that axioms are foundational to mathematics. This is what we mean by "self-evident." If you know what it means to be parallel, then you will agree that parallel lines do not touch. If you do not apprehend the truth of this axiom, however, no one will be able to prove it to you. In the same way, ethics will rest on some very basic axioms that are indemonstrable and underived. From those axioms we reason about how to live well, but in order to apprehend the axioms – to understand what is noble and just, as Aristotle says – we must first be brought up in good habits, because vice mars our moral vision.[21] Happiness is the term Aristotle used to describe the result of a life well lived, but we cannot achieve happiness on our own. This is why Aristotle famously said that man is by nature a political animal – not because men spontaneously engage in politics but because living well as human beings requires them to live in political communities. A man who can flourish on his own, Aristotle thought, would be either a beast or a god.[22]

[21] Aristotle, *Nichomachean Ethics*, ed. and trans. Roger Crisp (Cambridge: Cambridge University Press, 2000), 6.
[22] Aristotle, *Politics*, trans. Benjamin Jowett (Kitchener, Ontario: Batoche Books, 1999), 6.

With Aristotle, we are not yet at the natural-law tradition, but we are close. Other theorists soon identified the principles that lead to human happiness as law. As the Roman statesman and philosopher Cicero wrote in the voice of Laelius, "[t] here is a true law, a right reason, conformable to nature, universal, unchangeable, eternal, whose commands urge us to duty, and whose prohibitions restrain us from evil."[23] There is nothing distinctly Christian about what the ancient tradition taught, but many Christians thought it was for the most part correct: our universe is imbued with purposes; human beings should act according to reason; we are by nature political animals; these principles do impose themselves on us as law. Christians, however, have qualified or at least emphasized a few things about the ancient tradition. First, the natural law has a lawgiver. It is the product of the mind of God, part of the divine reason, or what Aquinas, Hooker, and James Wilson each called the eternal law. Second, law is an ordinance of reason made for the common good by someone with authority, and it is made known to those who are morally obligated to obey.[24] Natural law fits this description. It is an ordinance of reason made by God for the care of the human community and promulgated through the deep structure of the human psyche. Human law, to be truly law (and not simply an act of violence or coercion), must also fit this description: It must be reasonable, made for the common good by someone with authority to make law, and made known. If it is not, then it is defective as law to the degree that it deviates from the natural archetype.

The seventeenth-century English common lawyer Thomas Hale offered this short summary of the law of nature: "It is the Law of Almighty God by him to Man with his Nature discovering the morall good and morall evill of Moral Actions, commanding the former, and forbidding the latter by the secret voice or dictate of his implanted nature, his reason, and his conscience."[25] These broad claims informed the Anglo-American legal tradition and influenced the way the American founders thought about law. To take just one example, consider the often-cited excerpt from twenty-year-old Alexander Hamilton's defense of the American revolution against criticism from the royalist Episcopalian Bishop Samuel Seabury. Drawing his argument largely from Blackstone's *Commentaries*, the young Hamilton asserted that "Good and wise men, in all ages . . . have supposed that the deity, from the relations we stand in, to himself and to each other, has constituted an eternal and immutable law, which is, indispensably, obligatory upon all mankind, prior to any human

[23] Marcus Tullius Cicero, *The Political Works of Marcus Tullius Cicero*, trans. Francis Barham (London: Edmund Spettigue, 1841–42), vol. 1, 270. Accessed June 30, 2021, from http://oll .libertyfund.org/titles/cicero-treatise-on-the-commonwealth-5

[24] Thomas Aquinas, *Summa Theologica*, trans. Fathers of the English Dominican Province (Chicago: Encyclopedia Britannica, 1952), I–II.90.4.

[25] Matthew Hale, *On the Law of Nature*, ed. David S. Sytsma (Grand Rapids, MI: Christian's Library Press, 2015), 41.

institution whatever" and that from this law are derived the natural rights of mankind.[26] The classical natural-law tradition was in the intellectual air that both the future Federalists and the future Republicans breathed. It was Thomas Jefferson, after all, who in the first draft of the Declaration of Independence appealed to the "laws of nature & of nature's god" and affirmed the "sacred & undeniable" truth that "all men are created equal" and "from that equal creation they derive rights inherent & inalienable among which are the preservation of life, & liberty, & the pursuit of happiness."[27]

Although Jefferson was not personally fond of Blackstone, whom he later called a "honied" Tory,[28] the first two paragraphs of the Declaration of Independence echoed some of the major theoretical themes in Blackstone's *Commentaries*. As Carli Conklin notes, "Blackstone's discussion of the pursuit of happiness was both preceded by, and informed by, his discussion of the laws of nature and of nature's God."[29] The various strands of the natural-law tradition come together in Blackstone's account of God's one paternal precept: "that man should pursue his own true and substantial happiness."[30] James Wilson also insisted, in his celebrated lectures on law at the College of Philadelphia in the early 1790s, that God's "will is graciously comprised in this one paternal precept – Let man pursue his happiness and perfection."[31] Wilson's comment makes sense within the larger theological and philosophical world of the American founders. Wilson began his lecture on the general principles of law and obligation by observing the pervasive order, proportion, and fitness of the universe. Everything, including God, is governed by law, Wilson insisted.[32]

One implication of the theological idea that God is governed by law is that God's actions are neither arbitrary nor capricious. There is instead a unity of power and goodness in the simplicity of the divine nature such that God's

[26] Alexander Hamilton, "The Farmer Refuted," in Harold C. Syrrett, ed., *The Papers of Alexander Hamilton, Volume I: 1768–1778*, (New York: Columbia University Press, 1961), 87.

[27] Thomas Jefferson, "Rough Draft of the Declaration of Independence," in Justin Buckley Dyer, ed., *American Soul: The Contested Legacy of the Declaration of Independence* (Lanham, MD: Rowman & Littlefield, 2012), 7.

[28] Thomas Jefferson, From "Thomas Jefferson to James Madison, 17 February 1826, Founders Online," National Archives. Accessed July 17, 2021, from https://founders.archives.gov/documents/Jefferson/98-01-02-5912. For discussion and sources, see Carli Conklin, "The Origins of the Pursuit of Happiness," *Washington University Jurisprudence Review* 7 (2015): 201, n. 21.

[29] Conklin, 201, n. 22. Cf. William Blackstone, *Commentaries on the Laws of England in Four Books*, ed. George Sharswood (Philadelphia: J. B. Lippincott, 1893), vol. 1, 28–43. Accessed June 30, 2021, from http://oll.libertyfund.org/titles/blackstone-commentaries-on-the-laws-of-england-in-four-books-vol-1. Conklin notes that Blackstone uses the phrase "the law of nature and the law of revelation" and later "the law of nature, and the law of God."

[30] Blackstone, *Commentaries on the Laws of England in Four Books*, vol. 1, 41.

[31] James Wilson, *The Collected Works of James Wilson*, ed. Mark David Hall and Kermit L. Hall (Indianapolis, IN: Liberty Fund 2007), vol. 1, 523.

[32] Ibid., 1: 464.

sovereignty is bounded by his own goodness and reason. This is why Wilson was at pains to emphasize in his lectures that "from almighty power infinite goodness can never be disjoined."[33] God's rightful authority – and our obligation to obey – is not simply a product of superior power. So, too, it is with human authority, which models itself after the divine original. The rule of law in human affairs means the rule of one with authority to legislate for the good of the community. To the extent that a ruler abuses this authority and legislates to the detriment of the common good, then his decrees cease to be lawful.

In practice, of course, maintaining and even identifying the rule of law is a complicated business. The question of who wields lawful authority and how one came to lawfully wield that authority was central to the American revolution, and each possible answer to those questions relied on contested claims about history, tradition, policy, and the role of consent in establishing political authority. The Americans claimed in the Declaration of Independence that governments "derive their just powers from the consent of the governed," a claim that has an intellectual pedigree going back to the ancient and medieval world.[34] Consent itself is not a modern innovation, as is sometimes suggested, unless one holds that consent, unbounded by morality, may establish absolute sovereignty in place of the rule of law. This view did have advocates in the early modern period, and the American founders associated the view with Thomas Hobbes. In the passage from Hamilton's criticism of Bishop Samuel Seabury quoted earlier, the immediate context for Hamilton's appeal to God's immutable and eternal moral law was a rejection of what he took to be the political teaching of Hobbes. According to Hamilton, Seabury taught that man is free of the restraints of law and government in the state of nature, but that in society the weak must submit to the strong. "There is so strong similitude between your principles and those maintained by Mr. Hobb[e]s," Hamilton observed, insultingly, "that, in judging from them, a person might, very easily *mistake* you for a disciple of his."[35]

Hamilton took Seabury to task for his alleged enmity "to the *natural rights* of mankind." Ignorance of natural rights was no excuse in such an enlightened age, but such ignorance did, Hamilton insisted, extenuate one's guilt. His advice to the illustrious Seabury: "Apply yourself, without delay, to the study of the law of nature." To the introductory student of natural law, Hamilton recommended Grotius, Pufendorf, Locke, Montesquieu, and Burlamaqui along

---

[33] Ibid., 1: 503.

[34] For a discussion of the compatibility of consent-based theories of political obligation and ancient and medieval political philosophy, see Francis Oakley, *The Watershed of Modern Politics: Law, Virtue, Kingship, and Consent (1300–1650)* (New Haven and London: Yale University Press, 2015), 172–239; Mark C. Murphy, *Natural Law in Jurisprudence and Politics* (New York: Cambridge University Press, 2006), 91–132; Leo Strauss, *Natural Right and History* (Chicago: University of Chicago Press, 1953), 120–64, particularly 141.

[35] Hamilton, "The Farmer Refuted" (1775), 86–87. Italics in original.

with "other excellent writers on this subject."[36] For good measure, he drew at length from the works of William Blackstone, whom all young lawyers read. The "law of nature," Blackstone taught, "being coeval with mankind and dictated by God himself, is, of course, superior in obligation to any other. It is binding over all the globe, in all countries, and at all times. No human laws are of any validity, if contrary to this; and such of them are valid, derive their authority, mediately, or immediately, from this original."[37] The theoretical framework of natural law was pervasive in colonial America, and it was firmly embedded in the broader tradition of Anglo-American constitutionalism. The idiom of natural law and natural rights filled the pamphlets and sermons, speeches and treatises, courtroom debates, and legal arguments of a generation of statesmen and lawyers in America.[38]

These appeals to natural law explicitly rejected the modern view of absolute sovereignty, frequently associated with Thomas Hobbes, which held, in contrast, that God's sovereignty is a consequence solely of his superior physical power. While there is an ongoing scholarly debate about the true nature of Hobbes's teaching, historically there was a set of propositions associated with Hobbes that we may call Hobbist without wading into the ongoing debate about Hobbes' true philosophy.[39] According to what we refer to as Hobbism, there is no standard of goodness outside of God's will. God's sovereignty is therefore absolute in the sense that it is unbounded by anything other than arbitrary will.[40] Of course, many readers, beginning with Hobbes' own contemporaries, accused him of harboring a thinly veiled atheism that renders even these superficial pronouncements about God's sovereignty as a distraction from the underlying point of his political philosophy, which was the establishment of the absolute sovereignty of the human ruler. According to Hamilton's barb against Seabury, the world depicted by Hobbes is one in which "[m]oral obligation, according to him, is derived from the introduction of civil society; and there is no virtue, but what is purely artificial, the mere contrivance of politicians, for the maintenance of social intercourse."[41] The reason Hobbes affirmed such an "absurd and impious doctrine," Hamilton concluded, is "that he disbelieved the existence of an intelligent superintending principle, who is the governor, and will be the final judge of the universe."[42] Note that Hamilton

---

[36] Ibid., 86.

[37] Ibid., 86–88; cf. Blackstone, *Commentaries on the Laws of England in Four Books*, 1, 40–41.

[38] See, e.g., R. H. Helmholz, *Natural Law in Court: A History of Legal Theory in Practice* (Cambridge, MA: Harvard University Press, 2015), 127–72.

[39] For an argument that Hobbes understood himself to be more in continuity with the classical natural-law tradition than Hobbism as we describe it here, see Kody W. Cooper, *Thomas Hobbes and the Natural Law* (Notre Dame, IN: Notre Dame University Press, 2018).

[40] Our use of the term "Hobbism" is both analytical and historical because voluntarism and absolutism in theology and politics are common features of "Hobbism" or "Hobbist" teaching as interpreted by seventeenth-century English readers of Hobbes.

[41] Hamilton, *Papers of Alexander Hamilton*, 87.   [42] Ibid., 87.

connected a rejection of God's providence with a rejection of a classical view of moral obligation under the natural law.

By analogy to God's absolute sovereignty (whether or not God exists), the human sovereign would be absolute and unbounded by anything other than arbitrary will. Modern sovereignty, on these Hobbist terms, renders the rule of law and the distinction between good and evil meaningless. Both are synonymous with the will of the sovereign. By connecting belief in natural law with a belief in an "intelligent superintending principle, who is the governor, and will be the final judge of the universe," Hamilton was not original. Instead, he was channeling a larger tradition of reflection on natural law that stands against the modern, Hobbist view of sovereignty. The shared background assumptions of that tradition included a belief that God created the universe and created the natural laws that direct the universe to its ultimate end or perfection. These laws include both the physical laws that govern the inanimate and nonrational parts of creation and the moral law of human nature. The latter clarifies what constitutes genuine human well-being and thereby helps man to pursue his own happiness, or flourishing, by living a life of virtue.

Along these lines, Blackstone wrote that "when the supreme being formed the universe, and created matter out of nothing, he impressed certain principles upon that matter, from which it can never depart, and without which it would cease to be."[43] Blackstone then went on to draw an analogy between the laws of physical nature and the moral law of human nature, writing that,

> God, when he created matter, and endowed it with a principle of mobility, established certain rules for the perpetual direction of that motion; so, when he created man, and endowed him with free will to conduct himself in all parts of life, he laid down certain immutable laws of human nature, whereby that free will is in some degree regulated and restrained, and gave him also the faculty of reason to discover the purport of those laws.[44]

Conklin notes that Blackstone was clear "that the immutable laws of nature that pertain to the physical world (inanimate or animate, irrational creation) and the immutable law of nature that pertains to man (animate, rational creation) are put in place by a Creator God to govern all creation."[45]

This same theological framework is preserved in the Declaration of Independence, even in Jefferson's original rough draft that declared the "sacred and undeniable" truth that "all men are created equal" and that "from that equal creation" men derive "inalienable" natural rights. The final document, after extensive drafting and editing, appeals to the "Laws of Nature and of Nature's God" and identifies that God as the "Creator" of nature and the

[43] Blackstone, *Commentaries on the Laws of England in Four Books*, vol. 1, 38.
[44] Ibid., 39–40.
[45] Carli N. Conklin, *The Pursuit of Happiness in the Founding Era: An Intellectual History* (Columbia: University of Missouri Press), 59.

"Supreme Judge of the world," who governs his creation through an overarching "Divine Providence." These appeals to natural law occur in a larger theological context. Although Jefferson and some of the principal founders – including other members of the Committee of Five who wrote the Declaration, especially Benjamin Franklin and John Adams – held unorthodox religious beliefs, all of these men publicly and privately affirmed a shared natural theology: that there is a Creator who has imbued the world with discernible natural laws, both physical and moral, and who governs the affairs of men with his sustaining and intervening providence. Michael Pakaluk, following Avery Cardinal Dulles, refers to this natural theology as the "deist minimum" that in late eighteenth-century America was combined with providentialism and was "held by Christians of all denominations (and also by Jews and philosophical theists), who nonetheless might differ on what additional doctrines were revealed."[46] This combination of the deist minimum with providentialism and a doctrine of the divine creation of nature served as a workable and stable public theology that made sense of the Declaration's assertions.

1.4 THE CHRISTIAN NATURAL-LAW TRADITION

The classical Christian natural-law tradition that developed from the Christian engagement with classical philosophy broadly affirms that God created the world and governs it through his sustaining and intervening Providence; that in God's nature the unity of goodness and power renders intelligible the rule of law; and that, by analogy to God's rule, the rule of law in the human community is distinguished analytically from the absolute and arbitrary will of the sovereign, which is tyranny. One did not have to be a Christian to affirm these things, but the tradition dominant in the American founding was a distinctly Christian tradition that grew out of the Christian engagement with classical philosophy and the particular permutation of that tradition in the jurisprudence of England.

As Mark Hall has helpfully outlined, there are various senses in which one might describe the American founding as "Christian." It could be that the founders *identified* as Christians, or that they were *sincere* Christians, or that they were *orthodox* Christians, or that in some sense they *acted like* Christians. Each of these may or may not be true for some founders to various degrees – but our argument does not rest on any of these claims. Hall defends another sense in which one might claim the founding to be Christian that corresponds to our argument here: the founding was *influenced* by Christian ideas.[47]

---

[46] Michael Pakaluk, "Telling the Truth about God and Man in a Pluralist Society," in Christopher Wolfe, ed., *The Naked Public Square Reconsidered* (Wilmington, DE: ISI Books, 2009), 92.

[47] Mark David Hall, *Did America Have a Christian Founding?* (Nashville, TN: Nelson Books, 2019), xxi–xxii.

One challenge in making this argument is defining, even provisionally, what it means for an idea to be Christian. Those who identify as Christian contest the meaning of Christianity among themselves, and their disagreements turn in part on different ecclesiological claims. Without entering the fray of sectarian disputes, we would posit as broadly acceptable a use of the term Christian that includes the ideas summarized in the Apostle's Creed, the Nicene Creed, and the Athanasian Creed. To take one example, assumption 2 from our list of background assumptions earlier in the chapter, which affirms the existence of a Creator that is distinct from creation, is the first proposition affirmed in the Apostles' and Nicene Creeds. Like the other background assumptions regarding God's power, goodness, the natural law, and so forth, Christians believe the existence of a Creator distinct from creation is in principle knowable by reason unaided by revelation in Scripture. But the proposition remains *Christian* both in the sense that Christians believe (by faith) that it has been revealed to be true by God and in the sense that the proposition was fleshed out and illuminated in a distinctively Christian philosophical tradition. One aspect of the development of that tradition is the insistence that we are all created equal in some fundamental moral sense, an idea that changed the world and deeply influenced the American project.[48] "Christianity, which has made men equal before God," Tocqueville noted in his introduction to *Democracy in America*, "will not flinch to see all citizens equal before the law."[49] The same observation about the Christian provenance and development of ideas could be made for each of the other assumptions listed earlier. (We also discuss the classical Christian approach to knowledge by faith and reason later in this chapter.)

None of this is to suggest that the political institutions created in the American founding era were necessary deductions from Christian tradition or from classical natural-law principles. Enactments of the American constitution makers were, rather, prudential judgments about which natural-law theory permits a wide degree of freedom. Even so, such judgments can be informed by Christian ideas without being necessitated by them. Illustrative is the national arrangement of church–state relations in the early republic, which at once affirmed principles of institutional separation and nonestablishment, the

---

[48] See Tom Holland, *Dominion: How the Christian Revolution Remade the World* (New York: Basic Books, 2019). "That all men had been created equal, and endowed with an inalienable right to life, liberty and the pursuit of happiness, were not remotely self-evident truths," Holland writes. "That most Americans believed they were owed less to philosophy than to the Bible: to the assurance given equally to Christians and Jews, to Protestants and Catholics, to Calvinists and Quakers, that every human being was created in God's image. The truest and ultimate seedbed of the American republic – no matter what some of those who had composed its founding documents might have cared to think – was the book of Genesis" (400).

[49] Alexis de Tocqueville, *Democracy in America*, trans. Gerald E. Bevan (New York: Penguin Books, 2003), 21. See also Larry Arnn's foreword to Robert Reilly, *American on Trial: A Defense of the Founding* (San Francisco: Ignatius, 2020), especially x–xi.

rights of conscience and free exercise, religious pluralism, nondiscrimination, and the public duty to give thanksgiving to God. In our view, such an arrangement is in continuity with, even if it is not necessitated by, the Christian natural-law tradition.

In eighteenth-century America, the way in which this tradition was expressed in British and (later) American jurisprudence was not modern, if by "modern" we mean a pared-down natural-law theory that is detached from a providential God and that prioritizes will over reason in governing the political community. The founders rejected such a modern, Hobbist view of absolute sovereignty and, by their positive pronouncements, affirmed a Christian view of natural law. What they specifically affirmed was that God created the world and imbued various aspects of his creation with discernible laws to direct creation to its proper end. For human beings, the moral laws of human nature, known by reason, point the way to happiness or flourishing in this life. God's right of prescribing these laws, and our obligation to obey, is rooted in God's power *and* goodness, and the natural law therefore is not merely an imposition of arbitrary will. Similarly, human rulers are bounded by a real moral good when they make decrees to govern the human community. Good is not merely what is dictated by the will of the sovereign.

Another way to look at this is to consider the question posed in Plato's *Euthypho*: Do the gods love things because they are good, or are they good because the gods love them? Reframed within the monotheism of the Abrahamic faiths and in the context of natural law, the question is whether the sheer fact of God's willing makes something a moral obligation, or whether God's will conforms to an objective standard of goodness. There are two horns to this dilemma. If we say that goodness is a product of arbitrary will (that is, lacking any reason outside of the sheer fact of will), then the concept of goodness is emptied of its meaning. Goodness is merely nominal, referring to whatever God happens to desire, which makes even saying that God is good an empty tautology. On the other hand, if we say that there is a real, objective standard of goodness to which the will of God must conform, then that standard of goodness, not God, would be the ultimate reality – an untenable theological position in orthodox Christianity. The Christian answer to this dilemma is to emphasize the unity of will and goodness in God's nature. In his *Laws of Ecclesiastical Polity*, for example, the sixteenth-century Anglican theologian Richard Hooker insisted that "[t]hey err therefore who think that of the will of God to do this or that there is no reason besides his will" and yet maintained nonetheless that "the freedom of the will of God [is not in any way] abated, let or hindered, by means of this; because the imposition of this law upon himself is his own free and voluntary act"[50] What Hooker and others in

---

[50] Richard Hooker, "Laws of Ecclesiastical Polity (1594–97)," in *The Works of That Learned and Judicious Divine Mr. Richard Hooker with an Account of His Life and Death by Isaac Walton*, rev. R. W. Church and W. Paget, 7th ed. (Oxford: Clarendon Press, 1888), vol. 1, 204.

the Christian tradition taught – that moral obligation comes from both the will and goodness of God – navigates the two horns of the *Euthyphro* dilemma.

These theological questions have practical implications for political philosophy. On the one hand, a theology that roots moral obligation in the arbitrary will of God alone suggests that God's superior strength is the source of his authority, setting the pattern for human rule founded on force, the strong doing what they will and the weak suffering what they must. On the other hand, a theology that affirms a standard of goodness outside of God's will lacks any authoritative prescription. It can do no more than establish hypothetical, rather than categorical, imperatives. Power without goodness does not entail authority, and goodness without authority does not entail law. The unity of power and goodness is necessary for the establishment of the rule of law founded on the idea of an authority who may legitimately legislate for the common good. The rule of law, understood in these terms, sets apart the Christian view of natural law from the modern, Hobbist understanding of absolute sovereignty. Liberty in the Christian conception is the freedom to do that which is right – the freedom, in other words, to obey the rule of law. Liberty is not license, the absence of restraint, or the ability to do what one wants. The rule of law forever stands against the imposition of will on the world, an idea that is captured in the distinctively American and Christian hymn, *America the Beautiful*:

> *America! America!*
> *God mend thine every flaw*
> *Confirm thy soul in self-control,*
> *Thy liberty in law!*

There is also another distinguishing feature of the Christian natural-law tradition: It separated analytically the law of nature from the law of revelation. We see this clearly in the reconstructed typology of law from James Wilson cited earlier, and it informed the various theological traditions of the American founders. By analytically separating the natural law and the revealed law, the Christian natural-law tradition provided a framework for the development of an ecumenical conception of citizenship and the disestablishment of state churches. The rejection of the Christian natural-law tradition in modern political philosophy led in the other direction: to the reunification of church and state and the suppression of religious dissent. So it is, for example, in the Hobbist vision of the Leviathan and in the Rousseauian vision of the General Will.

1.5 MORAL EDUCATION IN THE FOUNDING ERA

These very ideas and distinctions about reason and revelation, the rule of law, God's nature, and the right ordering of will and reason were a regular part of moral education at the colonial colleges. In an important but overlooked study from the 1930s, James Walsh documented the importance of scholastic disputations in the curriculum at the colleges of Yale, Harvard, Princeton, Philadelphia, and Rhode Island during the era in which the founders were educated. As Walsh notes, the recurring discussions in the colonial curriculum were "of freedom of the will, of the natural law, of conscience, of happiness as man's last end, of the necessity for revelation, the occurrences of miracles, and of man's rights and duties."[51] One thesis that students at the College of Philadelphia had to defend, publicly and in Latin, on commencement day was: *Natural law prescribes all things not by words but, with reason as a guide, in accord with the fair and good.*[52] The modern view of absolute sovereignty stems from a rejection of each of the ideas packed within this one thesis and insists that there is no such thing as good outside of the will of the sovereign power.

As Paul DeHart has demonstrated, dominant strands of colonial education cut against the modern embrace of absolute sovereignty by affirming that moral obligation is rooted in both the goodness and the will of God, not arbitrary will alone.[53] Presidents at the colonial colleges often taught moral philosophy, a subject that embraced both natural theology and natural law. From the published writings and lecture notes we have from the most prominent college presidents during the time in which many of the founders were educated, we see that the ultimate ground of moral obligation was something they considered and addressed. Despite denominational differences, their answers were the same. Samuel Johnson, president of the Anglican King's College (later Columbia University) from 1754–1763, taught that the "*Obligation* we are under, as moral *Agents*, to practice accordingly, implieth some *Law*, binding us, under certain Penalties, to such Actions as are morally Good, and to forbear the contrary."[54] The law commands us to do what is good, but the sheer fact of God's command does not make something good. Good is antecedent to the command.

Thomas Clapp, president of the Congregationalist Yale College from 1745–1766, similarly taught that

Moral Virtue is a Conformity to the *moral Perfections of God*; or it is an Imitation of God, in the moral Perfections of his Nature, so far as they are imitable by his Creatures.

---

[51] James J. Walsh, "Scholasticism in the Colonial Colleges," *New England Quarterly* 5(3)(1932): 506.

[52] Ibid., 522. The original Latin text reads: *Lex naturalis non vebis, ast, ratione duce, omnia ex aequo & bono determi nat.* The English translation was provided by Dennis Trout.

[53] Paul DeHart, "The Nature and Foundation of Moral Obligation in Founding Thought," draft chapter for *Revolutionary God: Classical Theism and the Foundations of the American Political Order* (manuscript in progress dated March 25, 2022). For the structure of the following section, we are indebted to this illuminating chapter shared privately with the authors.

[54] Samuel Johnson, *Elementa Philosophica* (Philadelphia: Franklin and Hall, 1752), 6.

And the moral Perfections of God are the *sole* Foundation and Standard of all that Virtue and Goodness and Perfection which can exist in the Creature.[55]

Underscoring this point, Clapp asserted that God's moral perfection provides the basis for our obligation to heed his commands. The *"Obligation* which every rational Creature and moral Agent is under" is accordingly "to be confirmed to the *moral Perfections of God.*"[56] Developing this point at length, Clapp was clear that moral obligation arises

principally, from the infinite and absolute Perfection of the divine Nature: For as God is the most perfect Being, so the most *perfect State* of any other Being must consist in being *like to him*. As he is the only self-existent Being, the original Standard of all Perfection and all Creatures derive their several Degrees of Perfection from *him*, he must be the *only* Rule and Pattern for *them*; and their highest Perfection must consist in being like to the original and *all-perfect* Standard.[57]

It is only in a "secondary Sense" that obligation arises "from the *declared Will or Law of God*: That is, as the *Will* and *Law* of God declare what the *divine Perfections* are; and what Temper and Conduct in *us*, is a Conformity to them."[58] According to Clapp, the "divine Perfections are the *primary*, the *ultimate* and *sole* Foundation and Standard of all moral Virtue and Obligation." In a secondary sense, but only in a secondary sense, then, the "Law or Will of God is the *next* and *immediate* Rule to us, as it declares what these Perfections are; and what Temper and Conduct in us, is a Conformity to them." Importantly, "*Reason* is a Power or Faculty in us whereby we are, in some Measure, able to *understand* this Law."[59] Moral obligation applies to "every rational Creature," that is, every creature who can rationally apprehend his duty. Moral guilt, according to Clapp, presupposes moral knowledge. The idea of human reason as a "measured measure" has deep roots in the Christian tradition that can be traced from patristics like Augustine and scholastics like Thomas Aquinas to the Americans.[60]

A final example is taken from the colonial colleges: John Witherspoon, president of the Presbyterian College of New Jersey (later Princeton University) from 1768–1794, taught in his lectures on moral philosophy that the "Nature and will of God is so perfect as to be the true standard of all excellence, natural and moral; and if we are sure of what he is or commands, it would be presumption and folly to reason against it or put our views of fitness

[55] Thomas Clapp, *An Essay on the Nature and Foundation of Moral Virtue and Obligation; Being a Short Introduction to the Study of Ethics* (New Haven, CT: B. Mecom, 1765), 3. Italics in original.
[56] Ibid., 8. Italics in original.   [57] Ibid., 9. Italics in original.   [58] Ibid., 12. Italics in original.
[59] Ibid., 40. Italics in original.
[60] See Russell Hittinger, *The First Grace: Rediscovering the Natural Law in a Post-Christian World* (Wilmington, DE: ISI Books, 2014), 41 and 289, n. 60.

in the room of his pleasure."[61] In emphasizing the perfect will of God, however, Witherspoon was careful to reject the idea that moral obligation is rooted in will alone: "to say that God, by his will, might have made the same temper and conduct virtuous and excellent which we now call vicious seems to unhinge all our notions of the supreme excellence even of God himself."[62] In contrast, Witherspoon asserted that "[f]rom reason, contemplation, sentiment, and tradition, the Being and infinite perfection and excellence of God may be deduced; and therefore what he is and commands is virtue and duty."[63] As a result,

we ought to take the rule of duty from conscience enlightened by reason, experience, and every way by which we can be supposed to learn the will of our Maker and his intention in creating us such as we are. And we ought to believe that it [the rule of duty] is as deeply founded as the nature of God himself, being a transcript of his moral excellence, and that it is productive of the greatest good.[64]

1.6 THE THEOLOGICAL FRAMEWORK OF NATURAL LAW

The idiom of natural law and natural rights deployed by the Americans in the Imperial Crisis of the 1760s and 1770s is only fully intelligible within the colonists' shared theological framework, reflected in the moral philosophy curriculum of the colonial colleges, that emphasized God's ongoing providential role in ruling creation according to the pattern of his own goodness, a rule that human beings could participate in through the exercise of their God-given faculty of reason. This framework was Christian in the sense that it developed from the Christian engagement with classical philosophy, even as it was taught as part of natural rather than revealed theology. As Witherspoon noted in his introductory lectures, the field of moral philosophy involved "an inquiry into the nature and ground of moral obligation by reason, as distinct from revelation,"[65] a subject that included natural knowledge of God's character and

---

[61] John Witherspoon, *Lectures on Moral Philosophy* (Princeton: Princeton University Press, 1912), 28.

[62] Ibid., 28.   [63] Ibid., 29.

[64] Ibid., 1. Even more strongly, Witherspoon expressly rejects the proposition that virtue and moral obligation are founded exclusively upon "The will of God": "By this is not meant what was mentioned above, that the intimations of the divine will point out what is our duty, but that the reason of the difference between virtue and vice is to be sought nowhere else than in the good pleasure of God, that there is not intrinsic excellence in anything but as he commands or forbids it. They pretend that if it were otherwise there would be something above the Supreme Being, something in the nature of things that would lay him under the law of necessity or fate. But notwithstanding the difficulty of our forming clear conceptions on this subject, it seems very harsh and unreasonable to say that the difference between virtue and vice is no other than the divine will. This would take away the moral character even of God himself. It would not have any meaning then to say he is infinitely holy and infinitely perfect." See 26–27.

[65] Ibid., 1.

providential work. Even this distinction between reason and revelation, how-ever, was one that developed within and was refined by the Christian engage-ment with classical philosophy that reached a medieval high-water mark in the synthesis of Thomas Aquinas. In Aquinas's formulation, the truths knowable by unaided reason were called the *preambula fidei* – the preambles to faith.

The distinction between unaided and aided reason continued and was pre-supposed by the Christian traditions most influential to the colonists, including both the Anglican and Calvinist traditions. Both accepted the traditional Christian distinction between truths known by reason and truths known through the direct revelation of God in Scripture and in the historical incar-nation of Jesus Christ. Calvin, for example, opened his *Institutes of the Christian Religion* with a discussion of our twofold knowledge of God. We know God as Creator through reason, but we become aware of God as Redeemer only through revelation.[66] Natural law in this framework is con-nected to our knowledge of God the Creator, not God the Redeemer, and God's revealed plan for redemption presupposes moral guilt and natural moral knowledge. The same framework is retained in the Anglican tradition of Richard Hooker, who divides the law for mankind into the Law of Reason and the Law of Revelation.[67] Meanwhile, although a small minority in America, Roman Catholics in the founding generation such as Maryland's Charles Carroll were educated in the Catholic vein of the Christian natural-law tradition, which retained the direct influence of Aquinas's teachings.

The idiom of natural law and natural rights was also Christian in the sense in which Christianity might be juxtaposed to a modern political philosophy that denies God's ongoing providential role in the world, including God's onto-logical relevance to natural law and natural rights; holds notions of the good to be nominal and not real; and replaces the classical conception of the rule of law with the absolute sovereignty of the state. This constellation of beliefs is what some readers of Hobbes derisively called Hobbist, and the association of these beliefs with Hobbes is what led John Quincy Adams to declare, in his retro-spective account of the American founding, that "[t]he theory of Hobbes is directly opposite to that of Jesus Christ" because "it extinguishes all the rights of man, and makes force the cornerstone of all human government."[68] For the last half century, however, prominent scholars have recast the American founding itself as fundamentally Hobbist. Frank Coleman, for example, argued in the 1970s that "American constitutionalism is the product of a revolutionary movement in political thought whose direction and nature is embodied in

---

[66] See John Calvin, *Institutes of the Christian Religion*, trans. Henry Beveridge, bk. 1, "Of the Knowledge of God the Creator," 35–205, bk. 2: "Of the Knowledge of God the Redeemer," 207–459.

[67] Hooker, *Laws of Ecclesiastical Polity*, vol. 1, 150.

[68] John Quincy Adams, *Social Compact Exemplified in the Constitution of the Commonwealth of Massachusetts* (Providence, RI: Knowles and Vose, 1842), 23.

Hobbes's major works and that Locke and Madison must be relegated to the conservative role of disseminating and implementing the constitutional ideas of Hobbes."[69] On Coleman's account, the distinguishing feature of the classical tradition was its affirmation of the rule of law. Hobbes, however, rejected the rule of law by "declaring the priority of the states (the office of the sovereign) to the law and by refusing to affirm an inner content of the law." Accordingly, "[t]he authority of the law is dependent neither on its reasonableness nor on its agreement with custom, but on its source as the will of the sovereign."[70] Coleman concludes that on these Hobbist premises, "The liberty of the individual does not consist in obedience to the rule of law, but in those things the law neglects to regulate."[71] In this Hobbist account, liberty and license are the same.

Many other scholars have followed suit in identifying American founding thought with Hobbes, often connecting the dots through esoteric readings of alleged intermediaries such as John Locke. Yet the basic primary sources push strongly in the other direction. Far from declaring the priority of the sovereign to the law and "refusing to affirm an inner content of the law," as Coleman averred, the founders came down decisively on the other side of the question, reaffirming the rule of law. "We have heard the impious doctrine in the old world," Madison wrote in *Federalist* no. 45, "that the people were made for kings, not kings for the people." But "as far as the sovereignty of the States cannot be reconciled to the happiness of the people, the voice of every good citizen must be, Let the former be sacrificed to the latter."[72] So Madison had been taught, presumably, in the course of his classical and Christian education under teachers that included John Witherspoon. Indeed, the curriculum at the colonial colleges in the period in which the founders were educated was distinctively scholastic. Classical natural law remained an accepted theological inheritance across the various Christian sects in the North American colonies, and the Bible profoundly shaped the worldview of the founding generation.[73]

As Daniel Dreisbach and others have documented, the "Bible, more than any other written word, informed the world of the founding fathers and the society around them."[74] Scholars often take a cue from a famous letter in which Thomas Jefferson describes the "American mind" as a blend of "Aristotle,

---

[69] Frank Coleman, *Hobbes and America: Exploring the Constitutional Foundations* (Toronto: University of Toronto Press, 1977), 3.

[70] Ibid., 93–94.   [71] Ibid., 94.

[72] Clinton Rossiter, ed., *The Federalist* (New York: Penguin, 2003), 285–86.

[73] On colonial education, see James J. Walsh, *Education of the Founding Fathers of the Republic* (New York: Fordham University Press, 1935). On the role of the Bible in shaping the intellectual world of the founders, see, more recently, Daniel L. Dreisbach, *Reading the Bible with the Founding Fathers* (New York: Oxford University Press, 2016); Carl J. Richard, *The Founders and the Bible* (Lanham, MD: Rowman & Littlefield, 2016).

[74] Dreisbach, *Reading the Bible with the Founding Fathers*, 5.

Cicero, Locke, &c" – the ancients and moderns in an odd amalgamation.[75] But Donald S. Lutz's survey of the political literature of the founding era (with a sample that excluded most political sermons) showed that the founders cited the book of Deuteronomy more often than Montesquieu's *The Spirit of the Laws* and nearly twice as often as all of Locke's writings combined.[76] The founders appealed to the Bible over and over again in political tracts and speeches.

It is not simply that Christianity was culturally influential, a relic of America's Puritan past. Most of the founders were actually religious believers of one sort or another, judging at least by what they wrote and spoke. "Almost all agreed," Dreisbach notes,

> [t]hat there was a Supreme Being who intervened in the affairs of men and nations. They believed God was the author of the rights of men; and the rights God had granted to humankind, no man should take away. Most believed that man was a fallen creature and, therefore, should not be entrusted with unrestrained power over other human beings.[77]

Although the founders differed on ecclesiastical and soteriological questions, they had a shared natural theology that remained a common inheritance of Christendom. About the laws of nature and of nature's God, they agreed, even as a very small minority privately mocked the idea of miracles or supernatural revelation. And while it is true that a belief in divine providence, natural law, and natural rights, coupled with a grim view of human nature, might be held on grounds independent of any belief in biblical revelation, it remains that those beliefs were deeply embedded in a culture that was shaped by Christianity. Even those who had an idiosyncratic view of Christianity or remained philosophically or religiously skeptical nonetheless operated within a Christian milieu.

Pascal began his famous poem *Memorial* with the words: "God of Abraham, God of Isaac, God of Jacob / not of the philosophers and of the learned."[78] Many modern scholars of the American founding would readily follow Pascal's dichotomy and count the founders among the learned deists who followed the God of the philosophers, not the God of the Bible. In the context of the American founding, however, this is a false dichotomy. A better distinction is one shared by Catholic, Anglican, and Reformed Christian theology, that is, between natural knowledge of God the Creator and revealed knowledge of God

---

[75] Thomas Jefferson, "From Thomas Jefferson to Henry Lee 8 May 1825." Accessed June 30, 2021, from https://founders.archives.gov/documents/Jefferson/98-01-02-5212

[76] Donald S. Lutz, "The Relative Influence of European Writers on Late Eighteenth-Century American Political Thought," *American Political Science Review* 78(1) (1984): 189–97.

[77] Dreisbach, *Reading the Bible with the Founding Fathers*, 12.

[78] Blaise Pascal, *Pensées*, trans. A. J. Krailsheimer (New York: Penguin Classics, 1995), 285.

the Redeemer.[79] With very limited exceptions, the founders were not deists or pantheists, but they did primarily appeal in public life to God the Creator, known by reason, and to cognate concepts such as providence, natural law, and natural rights. For the last half century, scholars have labored to show that America was not founded as a Christian nation, and we would agree with this in the senses we outline earlier and in the sense that the United States was not founded as a sectarian confessional state. Yet scholars have also downplayed or denied the degree to which the animating ideas of the American founding were deeply indebted to the Christian natural-law tradition. The founders did not unite the offices of church and state, nor did they require assent to specific doctrinal beliefs to hold national public office or maintain good standing as a US citizen, but this is precisely because they were shaped by, and they acted upon, ideas that developed through the long Christian engagement with natural-law philosophy.[80]

1.7 A ROADMAP

Each of the chapters in this book can stand alone, but collectively the chapters proceed chronologically and point to overlooked ways in which the Christian natural-law tradition framed and structured the political thought of the founding era despite much conventional scholarly wisdom to the contrary. We begin in the next chapter with the transatlantic British constitutional crisis of the 1760s and 1770s. The debate sparked by the Stamp Act of 1765 gave birth to rival colonial and imperial interpretations of the constitutional order. Chapter 2 uncovers the shared theistic natural-law foundations of the interlocutors and reassesses the interaction of three themes of the debate: economic, constitutional, and foundational, the latter involving first principles and an appeal to natural law and natural rights. We examine a number of the leading patriotic lights in the debate with some emphasis on James Otis and John Dickinson and find substantial evidence that the founders presupposed and leveraged a classical and Christian natural-law theory in the pamphlet debates.

The Declaration of Independence represents the culmination of the pamphlet debates, and the Declaration's original draftsman, Thomas Jefferson, represents a certain challenge to our thesis, namely, that some of the principal founders were theologically heterodox and philosophically skeptical. Because Thomas

---

[79] This analytical distinction is sometimes overlooked because Christians claim to know God as both Creator and redeemer through the virtue of faith – but this does not undermine the distinction.

[80] The record of church–state relations at the state level is more complex than at the national level. See Carl Esbeck and Jonathan Den Hartog, eds., *Disestablishment and Religious Dissent: Church-State Relations in the New American States* (Columbia: University of Missouri Press, 2020).

Jefferson is foremost among the heterodox and skeptical founders, we use him as a case study and show that even Jefferson affirmed a creational metaphysic and a natural-law theory of morality that has surprising continuities with classical natural law. The third chapter sheds new light on Jefferson's metaphysics and philosophical anthropology as well as John Locke's philosophical anthropology and theory of property. The chapter shows how Jefferson's Lockean natural-rights republicanism has surprising continuities with important aspects of the Christian natural-law tradition.

Chapter 4 builds on the discussion of the pamphlet debates and the theological underpinnings of Jefferson's natural-rights republicanism by entering into the specific debate over the normative justifiability of the revolution. Applying Christian principles of just war and just law, as developed by Thomas Aquinas, we put forward an analytic argument that the revolution was in principle justified from the perspective of classical Christian natural-law theory. We argue, in other words, that the American Revolution was not only framed by its participants in terms that were consistent with the Christian natural-law tradition but that the argument for revolution was in fact consistent with that tradition. In making this case, the chapter explores the criteria within the classical Christian natural-law tradition for assessing the justice of commencing war (*jus ad bellum*) and offers a reassessment of the revolution in light of these principles.

Although an examination of the justice of the colonists' actual conduct of the war (*jus in bello*) in light of the natural-law principles of just war remains beyond the scope of this book, Chapter 5 looks at the conduct of counter-intelligence and diplomacy during the war in detail. What we argue in this chapter is that the theme of divine providence, which plays a central role in the Christian natural-law tradition, structured the understanding of key participants in the revolutionary diplomatic and intelligence corps. Entering into a debate critical for our overall thesis, we contend that American revolutionary providentialism rejected the mere general providence associated with some eighteenth-century English deists and rather adopted a vision of God as particularly provident and agential in the victory of the United States. This chapter highlights the providentialist self-understanding of major actors in American counterintelligence and Franco-American diplomacy, including John Jay, the Culper Spy Ring, Silas Deane, Benjamin Franklin, and Pierre Beaumarchais.

We then turn our attention in Chapter 6 to the postrevolutionary 1787 U.S. Constitution and the contested meaning of popular sovereignty in light of the classical Christian natural-law tradition we have thus far explored. Some Americans in the nineteenth century criticized the Constitution for not explicitly grounding itself in the divine economy of law. Their worry was that the document suggested the radical sovereignty of man in rejection of divine authority, a thesis that shares much in common with modern interpretations of the U.S. Constitution offered today. We recount the modern, positivist theory of sovereignty with particular emphasis on Rousseau's democratic sovereign. In examining the constitutional convention and constitutional debates, we find that the framers rejected a positivist account of "We the People." Rather, their creational metaphysic, rooted in the Christian natural-law tradition, entailed what we call "secondary sovereignty," a vision of human persons acting collectively as secondary causes under God, the first cause. Drawing on Orestes Brownson's account of the nature of sovereignty under the U.S. Constitution, we argue that the idea of secondary sovereignty provides a better account of the authority of the written constitution than a modern account that understands constitutional authority merely in terms of the will of the popular sovereign.

Next, in Chapter 7, we explore James Wilson's lectures on law delivered in 1790–1791 just after the ratification of the Constitution. If Thomas Jefferson presents one challenge to our thesis, James Wilson presents another. One of only six men to sign both the Declaration of Independence and the Constitution, Wilson was among the more outwardly orthodox and pious of the founders. In his lectures on law, he developed an ostensibly classical and Christian vision of American jurisprudence, yet some interpret Wilson to be subtly and esoterically subversive of the classical tradition he seemed to represent. Prominent political theorists have recently argued that Wilson was a theistic rationalist who subscribed to a modern Enlightenment conception of natural law that subtly subverted the main tenets of orthodox Christianity. By focusing on contested aspects of Wilson's celebrated lectures, we show that his representative writings on jurisprudence in the first years after the ratification of the Constitution is continuous with and deeply indebted to the classical Christian natural-law tradition.

Finally, in conclusion, we consider what relevance our argument has for contemporary debates about Christian nationalism, integralism, and the powerful renaissance of identity politics today. Joshua Mitchell has called the latter our "Godless Great Awakening," a politicized and atheistic Christian heresy in which Christianity's deepest insights about sin, death, and human longing are distorted and transferred to the civic realm.[81] That progressive brand of identity politics now sits alongside various resurgent strands of Christian nationalism. Each can be seen in its own way as a departure from the classical and Christian origins of American politics and the natural-law tradition that shaped American founding thought. That tradition remained, even in the eighteenth century, one of the dominant influences on the American founders, and it helps account for the ideas that drove the revolution and

---

[81] Joshua Mitchell, "A Godless Great Awakening," *First Things* (2020, July 2). Accessed July 17, 2021, from www.firstthings.com/web-exclusives/2020/07/a-godless-great-awakening. For Mitchell's fuller argument about the logic of identity politics, see Joshua Mitchell, *American Awakening: Identity Politics and Other Afflictions of Our Times* (New York: Encounter Books, 2020).

undergirded the Constitution of 1787. As we approach the Semiquincentennial of the United States, our society is now in the middle of a vibrant, dynamic, and ongoing reassessment of the role, meaning, and legacy of the ideas that led the colonists to assume among the powers of the earth the separate and equal station to which, they claimed, they were justly entitled "under the Laws of Nature and of Nature's God."

2

God and Nature's Law in the Pamphlet Debates

"The Revolution was in the Minds of the People," John Adams reflected in a letter to Thomas Jefferson in August 1815,

and this was effected, from 1760 to 1775, in the course of fifteen Years before a drop of blood was drawn at Lexington. The Records of thirteen Legislatures, the Pamphlets, Newspapers in all the Colonies ought be consulted, during that Period, to ascertain the Steps by which the public opinion was enlightened and informed concerning the Authority of Parliament over the Colonies.[1]

Adams went on to recommend a number of prominent Massachusetts statesmen, lawyers, and preachers as pamphleteers of particular importance, including James Otis, John Dickinson, and James Wilson.[2] Those pamphlets are a window into the theoretical frame of the American mind in the decades leading to the Declaration of Independence. The shared background assumptions of those pamphlets include the existence of a providential God whose governance of the world was an essential premise in their natural-law theories of morality and law. Most of the leading lights of the patriotic pamphleteers held their natural-law principles within a Christian frame, and the pamphlets they wrote in the 1760s and 1770s cast light on the ideas the colonists put forward, with one united voice, in the Declaration of Independence.

---

[1] John Adams to Thomas Jefferson (24 August 1815), *The Papers of Thomas Jefferson*, Retirement Series, 1 October 1814 to 31 August 1815, ed. J. Jefferson Looney (Princeton: Princeton University Press, 2011), vol. 8, 682–84.

[2] John Adams, "To Antoine Marie Cerisieir, 14 January 1783," Founders Online, National Archives. Accessed July 7, 2021, from https://founders.archives.gov/documents/Adams/06-14-02-0111-0003

2.1 TWO STAGES AND THREE THEMES OF THE
PAMPHLET DEBATES

A great transatlantic political contest in the decades preceding the revolution was animated by essays, tracts, newspaper articles, speeches, sermons, and pamphlets debating the justice of various enactments of Parliament, the nature of the English Constitution, the first principles of politics, and, ultimately, whether the North American colonies should separate from England. As Bernard Bailyn points out, "the pamphlets are the distinctive literature of the Revolution ... [which] reveal, more clearly than any other single group of documents, the contemporary meaning of that transforming event."[3] Clearly then, they provide an important window into the revolutionary American mind.

The pamphlet debates proceeded in two stages, and each stage had three principal themes of argument. In the first stage, roughly in the mid- to late 1760s, the debates focused on the utility and justice of the measures enacted under the Grenville, Rockingham, and Chatham administrations (1763–1768), including the Sugar Act of 1764, the Stamp Act of 1765, the Declaratory Act of 1766, the Townshend Acts of 1767–1768, and the nature of parliamentary authority and representation. In the second stage during the years leading up to war, debate was punctuated by flashpoints such as the Tea Act and the Coercive Acts. In this state, the patriot pamphleteers pivoted to defend a dominion theory of the English constitution, holding that the colonies were not subject to parliamentary oversight even as they remained within the dominion of the English Crown. Each stage had three key themes of argumentation: one over the economic health of the imperial center and the colonies, one over the constitutional arrangements or fundamental customs of the empire, and one regarding appeal to first principles.[4]

2.1.1 The First Stage

The first stirrings of the opening stage of the debate can be traced to the aftermath of the Seven Years War and the government of George Grenville, prime minister from 1763 to 1765. The empire had spent over 80 million pounds to win the war, more than doubling the national debt. In the years after the war, over half of British expenditures were payments in service of the debt. Partly due to maladministration and partly due to rampant colonial smuggling, many of the laws of trade were ineffective. Consider the example

[3] Bernard Bailyn, *The Ideological Origins of the American Revolution* (Cambridge, MA: Belknap Press, 1967), 14.
[4] For a helpful discussion to which the following account is indebted, see Ian R. Christie and Benjamin Lebaree, *Empire or Independence, 1760–1776: British-American Dialogue on the Coming of the American Revolution* (New York: Phaidon Press, 1976).

of molasses, which was supposed to be governed by the Molasses Act of 1733. It was believed by the Treasury and testified to in the House of Commons that the Americans, mostly unlawfully, imported around 8 million gallons of this commodity per year without paying duties on it, suggesting a revenue shortfall of around 200,000 pounds per year. The growing awareness of the evasion of duties combined with the burgeoning national debt and concern to provide for the ongoing defense of the sprawling empire spurred the Commons under the Grenville administration to seek reform of trade regulation and to raise new revenues from the colonies.[5] Hence, the Sugar Act, passed in April 1764, was prefaced with the stated purpose of "defraying the expences of defending, protecting, and securing the said colonies and plantations" and "more effectually preventing the clandestine conveyance of goods to and from the said colonies."[6] The act imposed new duties on a range of goods in addition to molasses, such as indigo and madeira wine, and it banned American export of a range of goods such as coffee, hides and skins, whale fins, lumber, and iron to anywhere but Britain or other colonies. The act was to be enforced by customs agents and certification procedures and cases adjudicated by a court of vice admiralty in Halifax, Nova Scotia.

Before the Sugar Act was passed, the House had approved a resolution calling for stamp duties to be placed on the colonies, but action was delayed until 1765. Passed by Parliament in February 1765, the Stamp Act was again prefaced with the purpose of defraying the costs of protecting the colonies, and the Sugar Act was cited as a precedent for further revenue measures, which were "just and necessary." This act required a range of public and private business to be conducted by official documents with attendant duties, including a wide range of legal and court documents, attorney licenses, liquor licenses, university certificates, wills, deeds, newspapers, and even playing cards.[7]

From the imperial perspective articulated variously by men such as Thomas Whately, Soame Jenyns, and William Knox, Parliament's regulatory and tax policies were entirely within the authority of the Crown and Parliament. Imperial arguments tended to focus on the forecasted economic benefits of the policy for the empire and on the constitutional authority of Parliament to pass them. Whately's defense of the trade regulations placed them in the tradition of the Navigation Acts going back to 1651, which had required trade to be conducted in British ships and enumerated goods that could be traded only within the empire.[8] Whately provided an articulation of the mercantilist and

---

[5] Ibid., 28–31.
[6] "The Sugar Act, 1764," The Avalon Project, Yale Law School. Accessed July 1, 2021, from https://avalon.law.yale.edu/18th_century/sugar_act_1764.asp
[7] Ibid.
[8] Thomas Whately, "The Regulations Lately Made …," in Gordon S. Wood, ed., *American Revolution: Writings from the Pamphlet Debate* (New York: Library of America, 2015), vol. 1, 227.

economic nationalist logic of imperial policy. The colonies were the source of a favorable balance of trade and therefore the principal source of Great Britain's economic and military power, and he argued that the regulations would foster British manufacturing prowess over and against rival European powers:

> To encourage the Consumption of our own Produce and our own Manufactures, in preference to those of other Countries, has been at all times an undisputed Maxim of Policy; and for this Purpose, high duties and even Prohibitions have been laid upon foreign Commodities, while Bounties have been granted our own.[9]

In the Navigation and Trade Acts, Whately argued, Parliament exercised its "supreme" legislative power, which superintended the whole empire as to "general Provisions" for the "general Good." While the colonies enjoyed legislative power for "local purposes," this was merely "delegated" power from the imperial center, and hence local legislation "which may contradict the general Welfare" could be preempted and controlled by acts of Parliament.[10] What if, for example, the Americans found a way to start manufacturing linens for cheaper than they could import them from Britain? In such a case, Whately disavowed any suggestion of "prohibitory Laws" that would criminalize local manufacture of linens. Rather, Parliament had authority to adjust the duties accordingly to make such endeavors prohibitively expensive and incentivize American purchase of British-made linens. In this way, private profit seeking would be checked and subordinated to the national interest.

Whatever limits Whately may have been hinting at in his distinction between local and superintending authority, he maintained Parliament had the authority to impose the stamp duties. Whately's conclusion in favor of parliamentary authority rested on three arguments: a proportionality argument, an argument from precedent and analogy, and a virtual representation argument. First, the American colonies had enjoyed benefits of imperial security that they had not contributed a fair portion toward. Second, the Americans had already acquiesced for decades to the Acts of Trade and Navigation and the establishment of a post office. Admittedly, a stamp act had never been imposed, but the authority to enact the former entailed the authority to enact the latter. For, the "Constitution ... knows no distinction between Impost Duties and internal Taxation," and at any rate, the post office law functioned to impose a public tax that brought in revenues.[11] These acts were sufficiently analogous to provide precedents for the Stamp Act. Finally, the Americans could not maintain that they had a right of "actual" representation in Parliament, which "Nine Tenths of the People of *Britain*" did not enjoy.[12] Rather, like all the British subjects who lacked the franchise, the colonists were "virtually" represented in Parliament by MPs whom Whately conceived of as not mere delegates of their

---

[9] Ibid., 202–3.   [10] Ibid., 191.   [11] Ibid., 234.
[12] Ibid., 236. All emphases are in the original unless otherwise noted.

boroughs but trustees duty bound take an enlarged view of the whole imperial interest.

The reaction in the colonies to the Stamp Act was swift in opposition. The American pamphleteers tended to focus their argument on the nature of the constitution and first principles, but there was also engagement on the economic arguments. As Benjamin Franklin explained in his Examination before Parliament, the colonists thought that the right of Parliament to impose "internal" taxes was "unconstitutional, and unjust." Franklin laid out the standard arguments popularized by James Otis, John Dickinson, and others that taxation without representation "was not just, nor agreeable to the nature of the English constitution." He contended that the colonists "find in the great charters, and the petition and declaration of rights, that one of the privileges of English subjects is, that they are not to be taxed but by their common consent"[13] and accentuated this argument by outlining the burden he conceived the stamp tax would lay upon the colonists' pursuit of the various goods constitutive of happiness:

The stamp-act says, we shall have no commerce, make no exchange of property with each other, neither purchase nor grant, nor recover debts; we shall neither marry, nor make our wills, unless we pay such and such sums, and thus it is intended to extort our money from us, or ruin us by the consequences of refusing to pay it.[14]

Franklin also punched back on the economic arguments. He contended that the cost of distributing stamps through the hinterlands of North America would be prohibitive and overly burdensome, and he testified that the Americans were unhappy about the trade restrictions because this would lessen the inflows of foreign hard currency. As to Whately's proportionality argument, Franklin argued that it rested on a faulty assumption. The Americans made significant expenditures to raise and field 25,000 men, and only a small fraction of that cost was reimbursed by Parliament based on what was judged to be "beyond our proportion."[15] In other words, Franklin suggested the Americans had paid their fair share of the costs of the Seven Years War already.

In seeking to maintain British authority over trade and to establish a post office, but distinguishing these from the Stamp Act, Franklin defended the American pamphleteers' distinction between internal taxes and external duties, noting that external duties were just for maintenance of the British naval protection of shipment of goods. Regarding the postal service, Franklin pointed out that this was disanalogous to the Stamp Act, because the money paid for postage is not a tax, but a fee for a service rendered that is voluntarily chosen. Hence, Franklin maintained the American position that the stamp taxes were unprecedented. Still, when Franklin was pressed as to whether the consent-

---

[13] "The Examination of Franklin," in Wood, *Writings from the Pamphlet Debate*, 340, 342, 359.
[14] Ibid., 343.   [15] Ibid., 338.

based objections would not also render external duties (or taxes) unconstitutional, he replied wryly:

> Many arguments have been lately used here to shew them that there is no difference, and that if you have no right to tax them internally, you have not to tax them externally, or make any other law to bind them. At present they do not reason so, but in time they may possibly be convinced by these arguments.[16]

In sum, Franklin testified that only military force could compel colonial acquiescence to the Stamp Act – and that while such a force "will not find a rebellion; they may indeed make one."[17]

Across the Atlantic seaboard, Americans resisted the Stamp Act by a variety of methods from boycotts to mob violence. It is evident from the various public documents – the Resolutions of the Virginia House of Burgesses, John Adams' Instructions of the Town of Braintree to their Representative, the Declarations of the Stamp Act Congress, for example – that there was a widespread belief among the colonists that they enjoyed a basic right to property as freemen that was accompanied by a fundamental right to be taxed only by their consent or the consent of their representative. The repeal of the Stamp Act came shortly after its enactment under Rockingham but was coupled with the Declaratory Act, which reasserted parliamentary sovereignty against the colonists' dominion theory of the English constitution, asserting that Parliament "had, hath, and of right ought to have, full power and authority to make laws and statutes of sufficient force and validity to bind the colonies and people of America, subjects of the crown of Great Britain, in all cases whatsoever."[18] For the colonial pamphleteers, the imperial partisans had doubled down on a principle that implied Americans were not subjects but slaves. For imperial pamphleteers, this was simply a restatement of their constitutional authority. As Blackstone had articulated it, representing the imperial perspective, even "the whole of their constitution[s] [are] also liable to be new-modelled and reformed by the general superintending power of the legislature in the mother-country."[19] The Townshend Acts beginning in 1767 served only to stoke the controversy over parliamentary authority anew.

2.1.2 Constitutional and Natural Rights

Franklin, like many colonial pamphleteers and legislatures, comingled claims of unconstitutionality and natural injustice. Imperial pamphleteers, on the other hand, sought to dispatch this tactic. William Knox contended that British

---

[16] Ibid., 359.   [17] Ibid., 346.
[18] "Great Britain: Parliament – The Declaratory Act; March 18, 1766." Accessed March 6, 2022, from https://avalon.law.yale.edu/18th_century/declaratory_act_1766.asp
[19] William Blackstone, *Commentaries on the Laws of England in Four Books* (Philadelphia: J. B. Lippincott, 1893 [1753]), vol. 1, 107.

subjects indeed are entitled to those natural rights "in common with all man-kind, or such as we derive from the *laws of God* or *Nature* ... such rights they are certainly intitled to, as they are men, and as they are Christians."[20] Still, Knox pointed out that citizens of each particular political society enjoy rights and privileges peculiar to that polity and that entitlement to natural rights is no guarantee of entitlement to any particular political rights.

When therefore we are discussing the rights and privileges of British subjects, we must confine our enquiries to such rights as a natural-born subject of the British society or state is intitled to, and to which an *alien*, or one who is not a member of that society has no claim. The laws of God or of *Nature*, or the *common rights* of mankind, cannot therefore give the inhabitants of Massachusetts any title to the *peculiar* privileges of British subjects, if they are not also members of the British community or state.[21]

For then, natural rights claims, he concluded, could equally entitle them to political rights of "Dutchmen, Frenchmen, Italians, or any other Christian society or state ...." By cutting out the logical possibility of appeal to first principles, Knox sought to force the argument solely onto the terrain of the British constitution. His argument was simple: If you claim the privileges and rights of Englishmen, you are ipso facto subject to the authority of Parliament.

The Americans wanted it both ways in the first stage of the pamphlet debates. They wanted the rights and privileges of Englishmen without accepting the authority of Parliament to tax them "internally." Most still professed belief in and allegiance to Parliament's authority, yet their claim was that *particular exercises* of that authority were unjust. Like Whately, Charles Townshend rejected the American argument that the particular exercise of taxation in the Stamp Act was distinguishable from external duties, but he was nonetheless willing to indulge the American position in the Townshend duties. Townshend shepherded through Parliament a set of "external" duties on glass, lead, tea, paint, and paper imported to the colonies, the revenue from which would defray "the charge of the administration of justice, and the support of civil government."[22]

The pen of John Dickinson would respond for the Americans. Although Dickinson's arguments will be considered in more detail later in this chapter, it is notable here that Dickinson maintained fealty to parliamentary authority over trade regulation but protested that Parliament had a wicked intention. Prior to the Grenville acts, the Navigation and Trade Acts "never intended" to raise revenue, Dickinson claimed.[23] Such was the novelty of the Townsend Acts

---

[20] William Knox, "The Controversy Reviewed" in Wood, *Writings from the Pamphlet Debate*, 623–24.

[21] Ibid., 624.

[22] "The Townsend Act, 1767," The Avalon Project, Yale Law School. Accessed July 1, 2021, from https://avalon.law.yale.edu/18th_century/townsend_act_1767.asp

[23] John Dickinson, "Letters from a Pennsylvania Farmer (II)," in Wood, *Writings from the Pamphlet Debate*, 414.

that violated Americans' fundamental right to consent to revenue-raising measures. Dickinson's constitutional argument adverted to the ideas of consent to taxation in such documents as Magna Carta (1215) and the Petition of Right to Charles I (1628). But these documents were indecisive at best for the Americans. Magna Carta spoke of a right of "common counsel of the kingdom" regarding "scutage" (the so-called knight's fee) or "aid" – the imposition of which requires summoning "archbishops, bishops, abbots, earls, and greater barons," and other landholders. The Petition of Right repeats this language, adding "Freemen of the Comonaltie of this Realm," and claims a right not to be taxed apart from "common consent by act of parliament."[24]

The imperial interpretation of the Constitution was readily at hand. None of these documents guaranteed any particular mode of representation, imperial pamphleteers argued, much less the radically expanded franchise that the Americans' arguments at times seemed to suggest was necessary for justice. As Knox pointed out, "if it be applied, as in the instance before us, to an actual or a *distinct* representation of *all those who are taxed*, and no other will serve the purpose of the Colonies, it is not true of any government now existing, nor, I believe, of any which ever did exist."[25] Representation in England was a patchwork quilt of custom, crown patronage, and migration patterns that left some districts over- and others underrepresented. As Locke described it:

we see the bare Name of a Town, of which there remains not so much as the ruines, where scarce so much Housing as a Sheep-coat; or more Inhabitants than a Shepherd is to be found, sends *as many Representatives* to the grand Assembly of Law-makers, as a whole County numerous in People, and powerful in riches.[26]

Knox echoed Whately's virtual representation argument, contending that everyone in the realm *is represented*, inasmuch as they have delegated their individual rights and continues to live under the constitutional monarchy.

Knox chided Dickinson's reasoning about parliamentary purposes as "curious reasoning."[27] Absurdities would follow, he averred. Suppose Parliament imposed a tax meant to be prohibitory, not revenue raising – would this be acceptable, but then become unconstitutional should people begin to pay it? Or would an intended revenue-raising measure that actually operated as a prohibition still raise a constitutional issue? Knox's arguments were powerful enough to garner a direct reply from American pamphleteer Edward Bancroft. In a pamphlet published anonymously in England in 1769 and then under his name two years later in America, Bancroft maintained that Knox's argument was

---

[24] "Magna Carta, 1215," The Avalon Project, Yale Law School. Accessed July 1, 2021, from https://avalon.law.yale.edu/medieval/magframe.asp
[25] Wood, *Writings from the Pamphlet Debate*, 642.
[26] John Locke, *Two Treatises of Government*, ed. Peter Laslett (New York: Cambridge University Press, 1988), bk. II, 372.
[27] Knox, *Writings from the Pamphlet Debate*, 632.

fallacious. Echoing Dulany's argument about the heterogeneity of British and American interests, Bancroft sharpened the rhetoric. Faux virtual representation was a worse state of affairs than that of the Spartan Helots, who at least were in physical proximity to their masters; the Americans were an ocean away from their oppressors. Bancroft intimated that the English constitution could be traced back to its "*Saxon* origin, where every one, who had any Landed Property, however small, was instated to a personal Suffrage in ... Parliament."[28] But rather than reach that far back into the mists of time, Bancroft focused his historical constitutional argument on a detailed analysis of the language of the colonial charters.

Hence, Bancroft's argument focused on the constitutional theme and introduced a way out of the logical trap Knox had set. The confirmation of the colonists' rights lay in the details of their royal charters, which entitled them to the rights and privileges of Englishmen. Bancroft sought to confute Knox's imperial history of parliamentary regulation of the colonies. He recounted details of the charters for settling the various colonies, including Virginia, Massachusetts, Maryland, Connecticut, Rhode Island, and Carolina, and contended that the language therein granting them certain liberties and immunities and/or vesting them with legislative and executive powers indicated that the Crown had created distinct states. The riders in each grant that conditioned the grant on conformity of the laws with the laws and statutes of England represented a prudential general guiding principle, but did not subject the colonies to Parliament. Similar language in the other charters should be interpreted accordingly. In short, the colonies subsisted as polities "with all the Powers of distinct Legislation and Government," subject only to the king.[29]

2.1.3 The Second Stage of the Pamphlet Debates

Bancroft's argument represented the opening salvo of the patriots in the second stage of the pamphlet debates. It was not long after the publication of Bancroft's pamphlet that Parliament repealed the Townshend duties – indeed, on the same day as the Boston Massacre, which ignited patriotic feelings across the colonies. The administration under Lord North retained only the duties on tea – and this was the basis of colonial policy for the next few years, and was background for American affairs in Parliament during that time. Accordingly, the pamphlets published on the imperial constitutional debate declined significantly between 1769 and 1772.[30] In this period, the most important pamphlet published was the so-called Boston Pamphlet, collectively authored by members of the Boston committee of correspondence, which included James Otis, Samuel Adams, and Josiah Quincy. The Boston patriots articulated a Lockean account

---

[28] Edward Bancroft, "Remarks on the Review ...," in Wood, *Writings from the Pamphlet Debate*, 718.
[29] Ibid., 713.   [30] Christie and Labaree, *Empire or Independence*, 153.

of the foundations of legislative power and distilled the key American grievances up to that point, including the system of customs officers, the military
presence in the city, and the violation of the right to trial by jury. Notably, the
pamphlet did not explicitly invoke the dominion theory, suggesting that many
Americans were not yet willing to go that far publicly. Still, the Boston
Pamphlet articulated a clear rejection of parliamentary legislative authority
on the basis of Lockean principles.

The financial straits of the East India Company and the North
Administration's legislation, the Tea Act, to deal with the company set up the
next flashpoint in the pamphlet debates. Parliament granted the company
customs drawbacks on tea exported, which was seen as a way to profit from
surpluses of tea the company needed to off-load and which the administration
saw as a way to increase revenues from the Townshend duty. Meanwhile,
Americans were smuggling in most of their tea from Dutch sources. When the
patriot pamphleteers caught wind of this plan, they framed the forthcoming tea
shipment in dire terms. Writing under the pseudonym Hamden, Benjamin Rush
argued that "the baneful chests contain in them a slow poison in a political as
well as a physical sense. They contain something worse than death – the seeds
of Slavery." This was a renewed attempt of Parliament to tax the colonies that
would provide a dangerous precedent and "fix the constitution of America
forever." Resistance to it, Rush contended, was a "moral and religious duty."[31]

The Boston Tea Party of December 1773 was carried out in this spirit – the
refusal to admit the revenue-raising tea into the colonies was a matter of
constitutional and moral principle. This act of defiance and destruction of
10,000 pounds of tea provoked outrage in Parliament and the London press.
Whatever patience remaining in Parliament had run out. The North administration then sought to crack down hard to reassert parliamentary sovereignty
and colonial dependence. King George saw the contest as a stark either-or:
either the colonies were dependent and subordinate to Parliament, or they were
enemies. There was a palpable worry about the colonies falling into the hands
of the French or the Spanish. Parliament thus passed the Coercive Acts, which
included the Boston Port Bill, closing the Boston harbor; the Massachusetts
Governing Act, which altered the colonial charter to strengthen the governor
and weaken democratic checks on the executive; the Administration of Justice
Act, which sought to protect British troops from partial juries for misdeeds in
suppressing riots by allowing them to be tried outside the colony; the
Quartering Act, which empowered commanders to requisition unoccupied
buildings to quarter troops; and the Quebec Act, which added substantial
territory north of the Ohio River to Quebec and restored French civil law and
religious freedom for Roman Catholics.

---

[31] Benjamin Rush, *Letters of Benjamin Rush*, ed. Lyman Henry Butterfield (Princeton: Princeton
University Press, 1951), vol. I, 83.

American pamphleteer and convert to the patriotic cause, William Henry Drayton, spoke for many Americans when he denounced these as the "*Tragedy of five acts.*"[32] The acts were seen as a beachhead for despotic rule of all the colonies, and thus the American pamphleteers increasingly saw reconciliation with parliamentary sovereignty as quixotic. Some Americans still admitted parliamentary authority publicly, albeit one limited only to regulation of trade. For example, in their Declaration and Resolves, the First Continental Congress "cheerfully" consented to parliamentary regulation of commerce.[33] Yet many patriots were pivoting toward the dominion theory of the constitution, which would be articulated by various colonial luminaries such as Adams, Jefferson, Wilson, and Hamilton. As Hamilton would explain it, the dominion of the king spanned the empire even as each distinct political community would have a coequal legislative jurisdiction: "the power of every distinct branch will be limited to itself, and the authority of his Majesty over the whole, will, like a central force, attract them all to the same point."[34] And, as in the first phase, there continued to be a duality of argumentation in appealing to first principles and to the established legal order: "The law of nature and the British constitution both confine allegiance to the person of the King."[35] Hamilton, along with Wilson, contended that the natural justice root of allegiance to the king consisted in a protection-obedience formula.

Yet metropolitan interlocutors remained unpersuaded. The claims of local legislative authority continued to amount to a logically absurd *imperium in imperio* – or empire within an empire – and the purported solution of the dominion theory smacked of the royal prerogative associated with the seventeenth-century Stuart monarchs. As Thomas Hutchinson put it, a "supreme and uncontroulable" power was the necessary principle for every government – and such a power must be unitary or ultimately dissolve. The patriots had been "mislead" by "an anonimous Pamphlet" (Bancroft's) and the dominion theory was based on an erroneous doctrine of "absolute Monarchs," which was not true to the English Constitution.[36] By 1775, the metropolitan and colonial sides of the debate had, if anything, grown more polarized. Samuel Johnson insisted that taxation was no tyranny but merely a necessary power of authority to require from subjects in contribution toward the public safety. Ten years after the Stamp Act, metropolitan partisans remained steadfast in their

---

[32] William Henry Drayton, "A Letter from Freeman of South Carolina ...," in Wood, *Writings from the Pamphlet Debate*, vol. 2, 152.

[33] "Declaration and Resolves of the First Continental Congress, 1774," The Avalon Project, Yale Law School. Accessed July 1, 2021, from https://avalon.law.yale.edu/18th_century/resolves.asp

[34] Alexander Hamilton, *The Farmer Refuted in The Papers of Alexander Hamilton*, ed. Harold C. Syrett (New York: Columbia University Press, 1961), vol. 1, 81–165.

[35] Ibid., 91.

[36] "The Speeches of His Excellency Governor Hutchinson ...," in Gordon S. Wood, *Writings from the Pamphlet Debate* (New York: Library of America, 2015), vol. 2, 44, 79.

belief that the Americans needed to pay their portion for the expenses in the French and Indian War.

2.1.4 The Culmination of the Pamphlet Debates

The dominion theory along with the full convergence of the three principal themes of argument takes center stage in the culmination of the pamphlet debates, the Declaration of Independence. The Declaration's opening appeal to the "Laws of Nature and of Nature's God" and the trio of Creator-endowed, self-evident, and unalienable rights is followed by specific allegations of unconstitutional acts. Parliament is never even explicitly mentioned, but rather a list of allegations against the king is set forth. Parliament is alluded to only as a "jurisdiction foreign to our constitution, and unacknowledged by our laws," whose enactments were "Acts of pretended Legislation." A range of historic liberties appears. In addition to the right to consent to taxes, the Declaration claims deprivation of the right of trial by jury of one's peers (another Magna Carta guarantee that Blackstone referred to as a great bulwark of English liberty), deprivation of the right of local legislation, and deprivation of the right of free commerce and transportation.

2.2 THE CLASSICAL NATURAL-LAW PRINCIPLES OF THE AMERICAN PAMPHLETEERS

The contours of the two stages and three principal themes of the pamphlet debates provide the political and intellectual context of the American revolution. At first glance, the debates appear to be political and constitutional rather than religious or theological. One of the most influential analyses of the pamphlet debates emphasizes the influence on the American colonists of the "country" tradition associated with the English Whig politicians, publicists, and clerics including Milton, Sidney, Benjamin Hoadly, and John Trenchard and Thomas Gordon (the latter coauthors of *Cato's Letters*). As Bernard Bailyn argues, Trenchard and Gordon "dominated the colonists' miscellaneous learning and shaped it into a coherent whole."[37] This country tradition provided the ideas to harmonize the disparate strands of covenant theology, Enlightenment abstraction, English common law, and analogous classical history. When Bailyn contrasts the harmonizing power of this stream of thought with New England Puritanism and covenant theology, he contends the latter was "restricted in its appeal to those who continued to understand the world, as the original Puritans had, in theological terms."[38]

The colonial pamphleteers, Bailyn suggests, did not understand the world in theological terms. Yet the use of the term "theological" here is equivocal. If the point is to say that there was not a consensus in the revolutionary mind as to the truth of Calvinist theology in its Puritan expression, then this is almost trivially true. But, if "theological" is construed more broadly to mean theistic visions of the world, then the claim is clearly false, not the least because Trenchard and Gordon were theists for whom God was the source of natural law and natural rights.[39] Indeed, as we dig further into the pamphlet debates, a theological vision of the world is precisely what we find, marked by classical and Christian natural law. Looking backward through the prism of the Declaration of Independence, as the culmination of the pamphlet debates, we see the mutual reinforcement of the various constitutional, philosophical, and theological strands of argumentation throughout the debates of the 1760s and 1770s.

Scholars such as Jack Greene and John Phillip Reid have done much to recover the constitutional and legal dimension of the colonial argument, but they are wrong that "Natural law simply was not a significant part of the American Whig constitutional case."[40] Constitutional and legal arguments were a crucial part of the Americans' case, of course, but the principles of natural law nonetheless underpinned those very arguments. It was primarily the argument about first principles cast in the language of natural law and natural rights that provided the unifying and harmonizing ideas for the Americans. The patriots deployed a classical, theistic natural-law theory of morality, rather than the radically modern doctrine that some scholars have suggested.[41]

It is true that the Americans' arguments were replete with references to a range of modern natural-law theorists including John Locke, William Blackstone, Samuel von Pufendorf, Hugo Grotius, Emer de Vattel, and Jean-Jacques Burlamaqui whose continuity with classical and Christian natural law on various points is contested. Still, when the Americans deployed these thinkers, their philosophical-theological anthropology and axiology tended to be in substantial continuity with the older tradition either because the cited passage was *in fact* continuous with it or because they modulated the source to fit the patriot perspective. Sometimes the patriots selectively quoted from these

---

[39] From *Cato's Letters, or Essays on Liberty, Civil and Religious, and Other Important Subjects*, annot. Ronald Hamowy (Indianapolis, IN: Liberty Fund, 1995), vols. 1 and 2, God is invoked as a being worthy of being thanked. Peoples are subject to the "hand of God," and it is a sign of prudence for private persons "calmly to expect reparation from God." God is both omnipotent and just, and also exemplifies "mercy and goodness." Cato avers "That there is a providence, and a gracious providence presiding over the world, is manifest and undeniable." And God is the source of the law of nature, which is the ground of positive law. See Letters 1, 2, 33, 42, 45, 52.
[40] John Phillip Reid, *Constitutional History of the American Revolution: Abridged Edition* (Madison: University of Wisconsin Press, 1995), 14; cf. Jack P. Greene, *The Constitutional Origins of the American Revolution* (New York: Cambridge University Press, 2011), xviii.
[41] See, e.g., Thomas L. Pangle, *The Spirit of Modern Republicanism: The Moral Vision of the American Founders and the Philosophy of Locke* (Chicago: University of Chicago Press, 1990). For a recent example of this sort of interpretation, see C. Bradley Thompson, *America's Revolutionary Mind: A Moral History of the American Revolution and the Declaration That Defined It* (New York: Encounter Books, 2019).

sources, passing over in silence the things with which they disagreed. At other times, they signaled when they believed the modern natural lawyers were not consonant with their views, as when James Otis expressed dissatisfaction with Pufendorf and Grotius and likened them to impure fountains.[42]

2.2.1 Foundational Principles of Natural Law

American pamphleteers consistently affirmed the key foundational theses of classical natural law and wedded them to liberal political principles. Classical natural-law theory posited two essential theses about practical reason. First, practical reason grasps goods proper to human beings as reasons for action that are not merely instrumental, and in that sense, those goods are natural. Second, the practical necessities or norms that correspond to the pursuit of these goods are morally obligatory and in that sense constitute natural laws. The tradition posited an account of human inclinations that corresponded to the kind of being man is: a rational animal. Hence, in man is evident a range of inclinations: (1) that which we share with all other substances (real entities holding existence within themselves), (2) that which we share with the animals, and (3) that which is proper to us in light of the endowments of reason and speech. These inclinations point human beings toward the objective goods of preservation of life, marriage and child-rearing, friendship and communal life, and the pursuit of truth, including the truth about God. Corresponding to these goods is a range of practical necessities, norms, or laws that binds agents in matters of judgment about what to do or not to do regarding the preservation of life, sexual ethics, the education and rearing of children, shunning ignorance, and living peaceably with others. Broadly speaking, classical natural law is radically contrary to subjectivist theories of the good that are often tied to instrumentalist accounts of practical reason, conventionalist accounts of moral and legal obligation, and metaphysical atheism.[43]

How do these norms have the character of law in classical natural-law moral theory? The answer lies in the createdness of human nature. Natural law meets the conditions of *being* law in that it is something of reason, made by a proper authority, for the common good, and made known. God creates and orders all things to their proper good and ultimately to the common good of the whole universe. Having proper authority over the universe, God makes known the precepts of natural law to the rational creature just in the act of creating man with reason, which gives him a share of knowledge of God's providential plan governing the universe. In the order of knowledge, the goods and first precepts are right for all and at some level known by all. Proximately, it can be

[42] Wood, *Writings from the Pamphlet Debate*, vol. 1, 66–67.
[43] Thomas Aquinas, *Summa Theologica*, trans. Fathers of the English Dominican Province (Chicago: Encyclopedia Britannica, 1952), I–II.94.2; Richard Hooker, *Laws of Ecclesiastical Polity* (Cambridge: Cambridge University Press, 1989), vol. 2, 215–16.

said that a particular philosophical anthropology provides a ground for a classical natural-law account of morality. But the ultimate ground of their legal character rests in their divine pedigree.[44] These are the premises woven into the two most influential patriot pamphleteers of the first stage, James Otis and John Dickinson, as well as the most influential American voices in the second stage. Far from rhetorical vestiges of an earlier era, these references to God ground the authority of the natural law and give the argument from first principles its weight and force.

2.3 JAMES OTIS

God's existence, perfection, and providential causal relation to the world is foundational in Otis' *The Rights of the British Colonies Asserted and Proved*, one of the most widely read pamphlets in the first stage of the debates. This Massachusetts lawyer who made his name in the writs of assistance cases was, according to John Adams, "by far the most able, manly and commanding Character of his Age at the Bar," and this was the "the universal opinion of Judges, Lawyers and the public" in Boston.[45] According to Adams, Otis was not only essential reading to understand the logic of the patriotic position in the pamphlet debates, but he was also the human spark that lit the American revolution.[46] Describing Otis' argument in the writs of assistance cases (discussed further later in this section), Adams declared:

But Otis was a flame of fire! With a promptitude of Classical Allusions, a depth of research, a rapid summary of historical events & dates, a profusion of Legal Authorities, a prophetic glance of his eyes into futurity, and a rapid torrent of impetuous Eloquence he hurried away all before him. American Independence was then & there born. The seeds of Patriots & Heroes to defend the Non sine Diis Animosus Infans; to defend the Vigorous Youth were then & there sown. Every Man of an immense crouded Audience appeared to me to go away, as I did, ready to take Arms against Writs of Assistants. Then and there was the first scene of the first Act of opposition to the Arbitrary claims of Great Britain. Then and there the Child Independence was born. In fifteen years i.e. in 1776. he grew up to Manhood, & declared himself free.[47]

---

[44] Aquinas, *Summa Theologica*, I–II.90.4, ad. 1; Hooker, *Laws of Ecclesiastical Polity*, ch. 2, 200.

[45] John Adams, "Diary and Autobiography of John Adams," *The Adams Papers*, ed. L. H. Butterfield (Cambridge, MA: Harvard University Press, 1961), vol. 3, 275–76. Accessed July 12, 2021, from https://founders.archives.gov/documents/Adams/01-01-02-0002-0005

[46] John Adams, "III. To the Abbé de Mably, 15 January 1783," Founders Online, National Archives. Accessed July 12, 2021, from https://founders.archives.gov/documents/Adams/06-14-02-0111-0004

[47] John Adams, "From John Adams to William Tudor, Sr., 29 March 1817," Founders Online, National Archives. Accessed July 12, 2021, from https://founders.archives.gov/documents/Adams/99-02-02-6735

In Otis' pamphlet – advertised in 1764 England as "'universally approved' of in the colonies" – God is said to be the "supreme *ruler* of the universe."[48] As such, God is the foundational principle of all government. For Otis, the first principle is neither force, nor grace, nor property, nor mere social compact. Rather, government

> has an everlasting foundation in the *unchangeable will of* God, the author of nature, whose laws never vary. The same omniscient, omnipotent, infinitely good and gracious Creator of the universe, who has been pleased to make it necessary that what we call matter should *gravitate*, for the celestial bodies to roll round their axes, dance their orbits and perform their various revolutions in that beautiful order and concert, which we all admire, has made it *equally* necessary that from *Adam* and *Eve* to these degenerate days, the different sexes should sweetly *attract* each other, form societies of *single* families, of which *larger* bodies and communities are as naturally, mechanically, and necessarily combined, as the dew of Heaven and the soft distilling rain is collected by the all enliv'ning heat of the sun.[49]

Ellis Sandoz intriguingly suggested that Otis' theistic natural-law theory is essentially Thomistic, and, indeed, Otis' theory can be seen as within the broad classical natural-law tradition in its axiology, its account of the human good.[50] Otis professes a classical anthropology of man as a naturally social and political animal and holds that the natural law is divinely pedigreed in God's creation of man. Thus, political scientist C. Bradley Thompson is mistaken when he contends that the Americans discarded classical teleology for the Enlightenment mechanistic science launched by Copernicus, Tycho Brahe, Galileo, and Newton, the scientific method of Bacon, and the epistemology and metaphysics of Locke. While it is true that Americans such as Adams, Jefferson, and James Wilson praised Bacon, Newton, and Locke, it does not follow that the Americans rejected teleology, especially in political and moral philosophy. As John Adams wrote,

> Now every Animal that we see in this Prospect, Men and Beasts, are endued with most curiously organized Bodies. They consist of Bones, and Blood, and muscles, and nerves, and ligaments and Tendons, and Chile and a million other things, all exactly fitted for the purposes of Life and motion, and Action. Every Plant has almost as complex and curious a structure, as animals, and the minutest Twigg is supported, and supplied with Juices and Life, by organs and Filaments proper to draw this Nutrition of the Earth. It would be endless to consider minutely every Substance or Species of Substances that falls under our Eyes in this one Prospect .... God whose almighty Fiat first produced this

---

[48] James Otis, "The Rights of the British Colonies Asserted and Proved," in Wood, *Writings from the Pamphlet Debate*, vol. 1, 41, 46.

[49] Wood, *Writings from the Pamphlet Debate*, vol. 1, 49–50.

[50] Ellis Sandoz, *A Government of Laws: Political Theory, Religion, and the American Founding* (Baton Rouge: Louisiana State University Press, 1990), 88.

amazing Universe, had the whole Plan in View from all Eternity, intimately and perfectly knew the Nature and all the Properties of all these his Creatures.[51]

Moreover, the founders broadly shared the assumption that natural teleology was reflective of God's creation of nature. John Witherspoon, who became president of the College of New Jersey (Princeton) during the pamphlet debates and would emerge as a leader in the Continental Congress and sign the Declaration of Independence, pointed out that "It seems a point agreed upon, that the principles of duty and obligation must be drawn from the nature of man. That is to say, if we can discover how his Maker formed him, or for what he intended him, that certainly is what it ought to be."[52] As we argue at length in subsequent chapters, Jefferson and Wilson also explicitly affirm divinely pedigreed teleology.[53]

Otis provides us an example of how a leading patriot at times used language suggestive of the new mechanical science but that was actually teleological. Inclinations toward familial and political society are likened ("equally necessary") to mechanical "laws" regulating gravity, evaporation, and precipitation. In the context of a pamphlet, one would not expect a detailed elaboration of the analogy. But the sense in which human action and nonrational bodily attraction are "equally necessary" is apparent. Opposite-sex attraction, marriage and family life, and the formation of communities of families are not "necessary" exactly like a rock or rain that necessarily falls from the heavens. Rather, the point is one consistent with classical natural law: These goods do have something akin to a gravitational pull about them, drawing human persons in pursuit of them. They are "necessary" in the classical natural-law tradition in the sense that practical reason judges familial and political life to be genuine goods that are objectively required for human flourishing.[54] Otis' remark that nonanimal substances' motions are part of a "beautiful order and concert" reaffirms his belief in final causality. All substances have inbuilt purposes. Hence, Otis' use of the term "necessity" is an affirmation of a teleological conception of the universe. Moreover, for Otis, God clearly plays a meaningful causal role in relation to the world that is providential and moralistic, which Otis considered essential to his protest against imperial tax policy. Finally, Otis suggests the reason-dependence of the goods of human nature when he speaks of "the first principles of reason," and the "the law of universal reason."[55]

---

[51] Adams, *The Adams Papers*, 23–32.
[52] John Witherspoon, *Lectures on Moral Philosophy* (Princeton: Princeton University Press, 1912), 4.
[53] See Chapters 3 and 7 of this volume for our interpretations of Jefferson and Wilson, respectively.
[54] Sometimes Aristotle's "naturalistic" *zoon politikon* anthropology was read to imply the former, but Aristotle explicitly acknowledges the role of reflection and choice: "By nature, then, the drive for such community exists in everyone; but the first to set one up is responsible for things of very great goodness" (*Politics*, trans. Peter L. Simpson, 1253a29).
[55] Wood, *Writings from the Pamphlet Debate*, vol. 1, 51–53.

Otis concludes that, from the human inclinations toward survival, propagation of the species, and formation of community, government is "founded *on the necessities of our nature.*"[56] But this is not an autonomous order in nature; rather, it is divinely pedigreed. Hence, "Government is founded *immediately* on the necessities of human nature, and *ultimately* on the will of God, the author of nature."[57] It is thus misleading to speak of the "authority of nature" for the founders as if this were not a mediate expression of the divine will.[58] Accordingly, on Otis' classical natural-law vision of morality, the will is directed toward real goods (the necessities of our nature) and therefore is not *sovereign* in the sense of a power intrinsically indifferent to the good, which confers value through choice. Such a voluntarist and subjectivist view "overturns all morality, and leaves it to every man to do what is right in his own eyes." Otis sees this moral vision as the implication of positivist accounts of political authority, as well as "skepticism" and "atheism."[59]

The moral law is at least partly known through the conscience, Otis insists. In his argument against the Writs of Assistance, Otis expressed his willingness to undergo calumny "for conscience' sake," which called upon a man to sacrifice for the common good to defend principles "founded in truth." The bases of moral truth are the laws of nature that are "are uniform and invariable" and are expressed in the "dictates of conscience." A "good conscience" is associated with adherence to that which is honorable and is the basis of right action in public and private. A well-ordered conscience prizes the public good and takes pleasure in public service: "There is no pleasure in this life besides a good conscience, equal to that resulting from the just esteem of ones [sic] country, founded on a sincere desire of serving it, & of having strained every nerve for that purpose." On the other hand, a bad conscience involves acting against the known truth (as Otis accused his pamphlet opponent Martin Howard) and/or malformation of the conscience according to principles contrary to natural law, as in the case of the "conscience of a highwayman."[60]

Otis' teleological anthropology is seamlessly tied to an account of the fundamental political equality of human persons. The colonists "by the law of nature are free born, as indeed all men are, white or black." Hence, Otis decried the slave trade of kidnapped Africans "the most shocking violation of the law of nature."[61] But race was not the only quality of human beings that made no moral difference for political equality. In the reform of a rhetorical question, Otis clarified that the principle of political equality applies to all regardless of

---

[56] Ibid., 50.   [57] Ibid., 52.
[58] See, e.g., John Phillip Reid, *Constitutional History of the American Revolution: Abridged Edition* (Madison: University of Wisconsin Press, 1995), 13.
[59] Wood, *Writings from the Pamphlet Debate*, vol. 1, 45.
[60] James Otis, *The Collected Political Writings of James Otis*, ed. Richard Samuelson (Indianapolis, IN: Liberty Fund, 2015), 12, 185, 202, 213, 220, 235, 286.
[61] Wood, *Writings from the Pamphlet Debate*, vol. 1, 70.

sex: "Are not women born as free as men? Would it not be infamous to assert that the ladies are all slaves by nature?"[62]

2.3.1 The State of Nature

When Otis uses the locution "born free," it is suggestive of the state of nature doctrine of the modern natural-law theorists. As political theorist Thomas G. West has argued, the state of nature doctrine was a key concept for the American founders.[63] Sometimes the state of nature device is portrayed by scholars as providing a secular foundation for politics in radical rejection of the Christian Aristotelian tradition, because it imagines a condition of sovereign individuals contracting to create the state out of self-interest. It is of course true that there is a distinctively modern emergence and use of the concept as a device for reconstructing political authority out of the rubble of a fractured Christendom and widespread dissensus as to the truth about God and peoples' collective duties toward him, which generated bloody religious wars such as the Thirty Years War and the English Civil War. The state of nature device sought to uncover the true nature of man and ground of government, the law of nations, and emphasized the role of consent as a necessary condition of political authority. But there was a radical divide among the modern natural lawyers about the freedom of the individual in that condition. On the one hand, Hobbism emphasized the radical autonomy of individuals in the state of nature in a way that seemed to derive obligations from epistemologically and ontologically prior individual rights. On the other hand, Locke, Grotius, Pufendorf, Burlamaqui, Vattel, and Montesquieu, for all their individual differences, rejected Hobbist radicalism and contended that liberty in the state of nature was limited by the moral law. They also tended to suggest there were social inclinations in that condition toward community.[64] The latter usage was the one typical of the Americans and the way Otis uses the concept.

Medieval natural-law theorists did not use the "state of nature" concept, but this does not mean that the teleological anthropology of classical natural-law philosophy is necessarily incompatible with philosophical reflection on human nature and moral norms in a prepolitical state of nature. Exponents of classical

---

[62] Ibid., 46.

[63] Thomas G. West, *The Political Theory of the American Founding* (New York: Cambridge University Press, 2017), 96–101.

[64] Jean-Jacques Burlamaqui, *The Principles of Law Natural and Politic*, ed. Petter Korkman (Indianapolis, IN: Liberty Fund, 2006), 151–55; Samuel von Pufendorf, *The Whole Duty of Man According to the Law of Nature*, trans. Andrew Tooke, ed. Ian Hunter and David Saunders (Indianapolis, IN: Liberty Fund, 2003), author's preface at 24; 84; Hugo Grotius, *The Rights of War and Peace*, ed. Richard Tuck (Indianapolis, IN: Liberty Fund, 2005), II.VII.27.1, II.VI.5; Montesquieu, *Spirit of the Laws* (New York: Cambridge University Press, 1998), ed. and trans. Anne M. Cohler, Basia C. Miller, and Harold S. Stone, bk. 1, ch. 2, 6–7; Vattel, *The Law of Nations*, Preface.

natural law such as Thomas Aquinas tended to key in on focal cases of governmental authority in the exposition of law rather than massive worst-case scenarios in which governmental authority had been dissolved, or even had not yet formed. But classical natural law is compatible with affirming fundamental political equality in conditions void of political authority. The rudiments of this position are already present in Aquinas and developed in Suárez and Bellarmine. Aquinas held that political authority resided in the whole people or a vicegerent of the whole people. While scholars have debated whether this passage entails a principle of democratic legitimacy,[65] Thomistic principles are open to being taken in the direction of virtuous republicanism.[66]

The Thomistic philosopher Suárez who argued forcefully against the absolutist claims of sovereignty by James I contended that man is "by his nature free and subject to no one, save only to the Creator."[67] Again,

in the nature of things all men are born free; so that, consequently, no person has political jurisdiction over another person, even as no person has dominion over another; nor is there any reason why such power should, [simply] in the nature of things, be attributed to certain persons over certain other persons, rather than *vice versa*.[68]

Suárez located the natural ground of political authority in the inclinations of man toward family and community. Marriage and the union of parents and children over time in families are necessary for the good of children and orderly reproduction of society. But families of themselves do not suffice for the pursuit of flourishing, and so families come together to form a "perfect" society or political community. This moral union and constitution of political authority is achieved through an "express or tacit pact."[69] While the people transfer their original right to a constituted authority, they retain it in potentiality in cases of grave abuse. Thus, the Suárezian community retained a right of resistance to

---

[65] For a discussion, see John P. Hittinger, *Liberty, Wisdom, and Grace: Thomism and Democratic Political Theory* (Washington, DC: Lexington Books, 2003).

[66] Aristotle offers an argument in Book III of the *Politics* for the rule of the many on the basis of the wisdom of the multitude (1281b–1282a). Aquinas' commentary on Aristotle famously ends before this. But Peter of Auvergne picks up Thomas' commentary and makes the suggestion that Aristotle is thinking of well-ordered multitudes. See Peter of Auvergne, *Continuatio S. Thomae in Politicam*, Liber 3, Lectio 7, 9, 14. Accessed February 14, 2022, from www.corpusthomisticum.org.

[67] Francisco Suárez, *Selections from Three Works: A Treatise on Laws and God the Lawgiver; A Defence of the Catholic and Apostolic Faith; A Work on the Three Theological Virtues: Faith, Hope, and Charity*, ed. Thomas Pink (Indianapolis, IN: Liberty Fund, 2015), 417.

[68] Ibid., 430.

[69] Francisco Suárez, *De Opere sex dierum, ac tertium De Anima*, 2nd ed., (Lvgdvni, Sumpt. Gabrielis Boissat & Sociorum, 1635), vol. 7.3, 287. Also discussed in "Francisco Suárez," *Stanford Encyclopedia of Philosophy*. Accessed July 13, 2021, from https://plato.stanford.edu/entries/suarez/. See also, Suárez, *Selections from Three Works*, 438–39.

tyranny which, Suárez contended, should be "sufficiently ascertained either from ancient and authentic documents or from immemorial custom."[70]

Along these same lines, Bellarmine affirmed fundamental natural political equality, contending that "once we remove the positive law, there is no good reason why among many equals one rather than another should rule." Hence, political power by the natural law is held originally by the people to be delegated by them and reclaimable by them to alter political forms for legitimate cause, such as a sufficiently evil tyranny.[71] Against the arbitrary rule of absolutist regimes, Bellarmine extolled the virtues of the rule of law.[72] In short, as Moorhouse F. X. Millar correctly argued – and as Robert Reilly has more recently contended – there is a social compact tradition with older roots in Christian Aristotelian and neoscholastic thought that stands in essential contrast with radically individualist and voluntarist social contract theories.[73] The American arguments were in many ways more in substantial continuity with the former than the latter.

Political scientist Lee Ward makes the mistake of attributing to Otis the radical perspective associated with Hobbism. Ward advances a contestable interpretation of Locke as a subversive, radically individualist theorist of modernity who emphasizes the "primacy of individual natural rights over moral duties and the dictates of natural law."[74] Ward then mistakenly attributes this vision to Otis, who is said to have an account of natural rights that is "emphatically Lockean."[75] In Ward's telling "the starting point for any explication of the origin of government" is the natural rights of individuals that precede the law of self-preservation.[76] But as we have seen, the ultimate starting point for Otis is the unchangeable will of God who creates and orders man. Otis explicitly rejects radical individualism and the notion that an individual right of autonomy precedes duties and goods. God's providential governance and ordering of human beings toward real goods provides moral limits to the

---

[70] Francisco Suárez, *Defensio Fidei Catholicae et Apostolicae contra Errores Anglicanae Sectae*, Pars Prima (Naples: ex typis Fibrenianis, 1872), bk. 3, ch. 3, 190; also quoted by Moorhouse F. X. Millar, "Scholastic Philosophy and American Political Theory," *Thought: Fordham University Quarterly* 1(1) (June 1926), 130–31.

[71] Robert Bellarmine, *De Laicis*, in *On Temporal and Spiritual Authority: On Laymen or Secular People; On the Temporal Power of the Pope against William Barclay; On the Primary Duty of the Supreme Pontiff*, ed. and trans. Stefania Tutino (Indianapolis, IN: Liberty Fund, 2012), 22.

[72] Ibid., 36–39.

[73] Millar, "Scholastic Philosophy and American Political Theory," 112–36. For a more recent argument in this vein, see Robert Reilly, *America on Trial: A Defense of the Founding* (San Francisco: Ignatius Press, 2020), 214–17. For a critical discussion, see Gary D. Glenn, "Natural Rights and Social Contract in Burke and Bellarmine" in Bruce P. Frohnen and Kenneth L. Grasso, eds. *Rethinking Rights: Historical, Political, and Philosophical Perspectives* (Columbia: University of Missouri Press, 2008).

[74] Lee Ward, *The Politics of Liberty in England and Revolutionary America* (New York: Cambridge University Press, 2004), 226.

[75] Ibid., 334.   [76] Ibid., 333.

exercise of natural rights. Accordingly, Otis disavows belief in "some real general state of nature ... antecedent to and independent to society."[77] Hence, the imperial pamphleteer Allan Ramsay's critique that the state of nature was "unsound" as a foundation for government because human beings never existed in a such a condition but possibly a few minutes "like fishes out of the water, in great agonies, terror and convulsions" did not land a glove on Otis.[78]

Otis' teleological account of human inclination to "form societies of *single families*" indicates that human beings are members of the familial society from birth – and "most" are born into political society as well. He affirms this again in his 1765 pamphlet "A Vindication of the *British Colonies*" in which he defended himself against critiques of Martin Howard who argued that from the reciprocal duties of parent-child, husband-wife, and master-servant, obligations can be deduced. Otis replied that in a state of nature "where all are equal," there is no master-servant relation; he did not contest Howard's point about family relations because he believed that such relationships and attendant obligations were present in a state of nature, a potentially real condition of human beings devoid of political authority.[79] In short, the state of nature was a device for asserting man's fundamental political equality. It was not a claim about prehistory or about the right prior to duty and good or about the a-sociality of man.[80] Returning to the *Rights of the British Colonies Asserted and Proved*, Otis suggests it is conceivable that, from the *prior* duty of self-preservation, there could be extreme circumstances that would justify a person separating from society. But Otis makes a point to argue that, from the fact that there have existed "few *Hermits* and *Misanthropes*," it follows that "those states are *unnatural*."[81]

In his distillation of key lessons from the liberalism-republicanism debates, Alan Gibson contends that the work of political theorists such as Paul Rahe and Michael Zuckert established beyond a reasonable doubt that the founders rejected classical republicanism, which defenders of the republican thesis contended was transmitted through English opposition ideology,[82] for classical republicanism was built on the *zoon politikon* philosophical anthropology that

---

77 Wood, *Writings from the Pamphlet Debate*, vol. 1, 69.   78 Ibid., 497.

79 James Otis, "A Vindication of the *British Colonies*, against the Aspersions of the *Halifax Gentleman* in his Letter to a *Rhode-Island* Friend," *Political Writings of James Otis* (Indianapolis, IN: Liberty Fund, 2015), 188.

80 Thompson concedes that the "evidence is compelling that, at least before 1776, most revolutionary Americans saw the moral rights of nature as deriving from the moral laws of nature," even as he criticizes the revolutionaries' argument on this matter. See C. Bradley Thompson, *America's Revolutionary Mind: A Moral History of the American Revolution and the Declaration that Defined It* (New York: Encounter Books, 2019), 175.

81 Wood, *Writings from the Pamphlet Debate*, vol. 1, 53.

82 Alan Gibson, *Understanding the Founding: The Crucial Questions* (Lawrence: University Press of Kansas: 2007), ch. 4.

Aristotle articulated. On the Aristotelian view, participation in the *polis* through political rule and being ruled in turn was essential to fulfilling the human *telos*. The claim of the *polis* on citizens was well-nigh comprehensive, leaving only a small sphere of privacy in the home for procreation.

It is true that the founders rejected the notion that the political community had authority to make comprehensive claims on persons. One of the most important reasons for this was that the founders' conception of the nature and limits of political authority was informed by the classical Christian separation of the jurisdictions of state and church and the rupture of the hegemony of ancient *polis* and empire this entailed. For the founders, the principle of separation was coupled with the principles of liberty of conscience, free exercise of religion, equality, and the civic value of religion.[83] The more or less free proliferation of churches is a major feature of the development of American civil society. So, it is correct to say that the founders had a more limited conception of the political common good.[84] But it would be incorrect to infer from this that they therefore rejected the natural sociality of man, the importance of civic friendship, that there was a patriotic duty to serve one's country, and so on. Moreover, they believed that both government and civil society had roles to play in cultivating virtue. This suggests that Aristotelian and Lockean elements of the founding amalgam were in important ways modulated by the Christian component.

Otis does reference Locke frequently – but Otis' Locke is actually in substantial continuity with the metaphysic of the classical natural-law tradition. For example, Otis cites Locke to provide a philosophical and theological anthropology as the ground of political equality:

There is nothing more evident says Mr. Locke, than "that creatures of the same species and rank promiscuously born to all the same advantages of nature, and the use of the same faculties, should also be equal one among another, without subordination and subjection, unless the master of them all should by any manifest declaration of his will set one above another, and confer on him by an evident and clear appointment, an undoubted right to dominion and sovereignty."[85]

The first thing to be noticed here is that Otis' deployment of Locke emphatically rejects nominalism, the view that "man" is but a word that does not pick out a universally shared nature or natural kind (Locke's *Essay on Human Understanding* notwithstanding). Rather, human beings share an essential nature specified by a set of faculties including reason and will. Second,

---

[83] See John Witte and Joel P. Nichols, *Religion and the American Constitutional Experiment* (New York: Oxford University Press, 2016), ch. 3.

[84] The political common good does not comprehensively encompass the full human good, but that does not entail that it is merely instrumental. For a recent discussion, see Matthew D. Wright, *A Vindication of Politics: On the Common Good and Human Flourishing* (Lawrence: University Press of Kansas, 2019).

[85] Wood, *Writings from the Pamphlet Debate*, vol. 1, 70–71.

Locke's emphasis on "the use" of the same faculties suggests that there could be wide variegation in how those faculties are actualized ("used"), which suggests there could be wide differences in intelligence or manual abilities, *without* entailing subordination or subjection in natural rights. Third, Otis' Lockean philosophical anthropology of a common human nature has a divine pedigree ("the master of them all").

The state of nature is a condition devoid of political authority (including cases in which the constituted authority makes war on its people, forfeiting its own authority, as it were) in which case persons of age are in a position of political equality (unless God, the creator of human nature, manifestly imparted a superhuman or demigod status to someone in that condition). In such a condition: "The natural liberty of man is to be free from any superior power on earth, and not to be under the will or legislative authority of man, but only to have the law of nature for his rule."[86] The duties of natural law are always in effect. Political equality entails an individual liberty to pursue the goods constitutive of human happiness in all the multitudinous ways it can be; it does not entail radical autonomy. It does entail an individual right to leave a political society (a right subordinate to and conditioned by the prior duty of self-preservation, which includes preservation of one's family), as well as a right of a people or community to resist tyranny and/or alteration of their form of government.

2.3.2 Parliamentary and Divine Sovereignty

In this first stage of the pamphlet debates, Otis deploys his natural-law argumentation alongside constitutional argument to call for American representation in Parliament and an American legislature. Some scholars have emphasized the originality of Otis' constitutional thought. For example, political scientist Howard L. Lubert interprets Otis as breaking from the imperial perspective of the British constitution as a venerable set of laws and institutions that could be essentially altered by the parliamentary sovereign. In contrast with the imperial view, Otis conceived of the British constitution as a "body of fundamental law that limits governmental authority" and suggested a role for the judiciary in upholding constitutional limits to legislative power.[87] Yet, as Lubert points out, Otis did not draw the inference of a power of judicial review. He remained steadfast in his belief in the sovereignty of Parliament and his faith in constitutional measures such as the ability of loyal judges and subjects to publicly express their dissent when they believe an act is inequitable, which would lead to parliamentary self-correction.

---

[86] Ibid., 71.

[87] Howard L. Hubert, "Thomas Hutchinson and James Otis on Sovereignty, Obedience, and Rebellion," in Bryan-Paul Frost and Jeffrey Sikkenga, eds., *History of American Political Thought* (Lanham, MD: Lexington Books, 2019), 2nd ed., 44.

Still, Otis' faith in parliamentary sovereignty emphatically rejected any positivist account of Parliament's legislative power – the view that the parliamentary *source* of an edict is sufficient to make law and binds its addressees in conscience. On the contrary, "there must be in every instance, a higher authority, viz. GOD. Should an act of parliament be against any of *his* natural laws, which are *immutably* true, *their* declaration would be contrary to eternal truth, equity and justice, and consequently void ...." [88] Otis' affirmation of divinely pedigreed higher law is the cornerstone of his argument of classical natural law against parliamentary tyranny and signaled what would become a thematic argument of the patriots against the absolutist claims to sovereignty made by the imperial center.

In the natural-law tradition, civil authority and human positive law must aim at the common good, which is constituted by justice and peace. In Otis' words, "It is above all things to provide for the security, the quiet, and happy enjoyment of life, liberty, and property." Again, the just society Otis envisions is not an aggregate of monads: "the experience of ages has proved that such is the nature of man, a weak, imperfect being; that the valuable ends of life cannot be obtained, without the union and assistance of many."[89] While just law must respect the natural rights of individuals, the individual is conceived of as a social animal with duties in respect of the societies of which he is a member, not least of which is the family. The threat of parliamentary taxation without representation was understood as a threat to property rights, but this was not understood in a radically individualistic way. In tune with the classical natural-law tradition, Otis ties the rights of property to the family.

2.3.3 Otis on the Right of Property and Family

Otis' defense of the rights of property must be understood in this light. Property is the indispensable means of preservation. The natural duty and therefore right of preservation entails a natural duty and right to acquire and keep property. So far, these premises are in substantial continuity with the classical natural-law perspective on property.[90] Following Locke's formulation, Otis draws the

---

[88] Wood, *Writings from the Pamphlet Debate*, vol. 1, 87. Otis continued "and so it would be adjudged by the parliament itself, when convinced of their mistake," placing his faith in the Parliament's deliberative and corrective capacities.

[89] Ibid., 52.

[90] Aquinas differentiates moral rights to property regarding what is absolutely necessary for survival, what is relatively necessary to fulfill one's responsibilities for the support and maintenance of one's household, and what is leftover, the *superflua*. The latter is held "in common" and available to the destitute in the order of justice. Yet generally it is the right of the owner or head of household to judge what is necessary and what is superfluous, and how to dispose of the latter. This right is the ground of a liberty "to confront the state's rulers with the firm and rightful claim that their authority is limited." John Finnis, *Aquinas* (Oxford University Press, 1999), 194, 188–96.

inference that an invasion of the subjects' property by the government thus violates all of their natural rights. Government being necessary for the better securing of natural rights, subjects must provide the revenues essential to its existence and maintenance – but this must be by and through the consent of property owners. For Otis, this account is the foundation in natural law for the British Constitution's guarantee of a civil right of property: *"The supreme power cannot take from any man any part of his property*, without his consent in *person, or by representation."*[91] As we have seen, Otis' constitutional argument against the Stamp Act is rooted in principles of natural law.

Otis does not celebrate possessive individualism or the unleashing of acquisitiveness in his defense of the natural right of property. Rather, he tethers the right of property to the duty of citizens toward the common good and the right of families to a peaceful, quiet pursuit of happiness. Regarding the first, Otis believed that virtuous men subordinated their wealth to the good of their fellow man: "The only conceivable value of riches is, that they may place an honest man and a lover of his country at ease to study, and at leisure to push the best interests of the human species."[92] Hence, it should be apparent that Otis' arguments were not the forensic tactics of a member of the propertied elite seeking to mobilize the energies of the poor for the sake of his own class interests. Such a Marxist attempt to reduce all argument to the economic vector entirely misses the point of Otis' appeals to God and nature to ground an equal right of all persons and families to acquire and keep property in the pursuit of happiness. Lacking any substantive engagement with Otis' writings or any actual evidence to support it, such ideologically driven narratives have all historical truth, but none of the charm, of *Just So Stories.*[93]

Otis' connection of the right of property to the dignity of the family is apparent in his critique of the writs of assistance in the early 1760s, which John Adams saw as the beginning of the movement toward independence. Writs of assistance were one of the imperial measures to fight smuggling; they empowered customs officials to enter and search any vessel or private building on suspicion of hidden contraband goods. Otis contrasted such writs with special writs with specific places to be searched issued by a judge who has the sworn testimony of someone who suspects contraband goods. But the writs of assistance empowered customs officials to enter private residences at will with bare suspicion. Otis remonstrated that the writs cut against the fundamental principle that "A man's house is his castle; and whilst he is quiet, he is as well guarded as a prince in his castle." Otis predicted that customs officers so empowered – or any person deputized with a writ – would become petty tyrants who might harass their neighbors out of "revenge, ill humor, or wantonness."

[91] Wood, *Writings from the Pamphlet Debate*, vol. 1, 77.
[92] Otis, *Political Writings of James Otis*, 236.
[93] See Howard Zinn, *A People's History of the United States* (New York: Harper Perennial Modern Classics, 2005), 57–62; cf. Rudyard Kipling, *Just So Stories*.

This would be a power to "put a family which has a right to the kings peace, to the utmost confusion and terror." Clearly, Otis' concern with the writs of assistance was a concern not merely for the integrity of people's possessions. Neither was it a call for free trade – he condemned smuggling unequivocally. His fundamental concern was for the very sanctity of families to be secure in their homes unmolested under the rule of law.[94] Otis' arguments spurred an imperial reply. The Townshend Acts included an amendment to clarify the law to permit issuances of writs of assistance and to create the American Board of Commissioners of Customs to carry out customs enforcement – with only very limited success.[95]

In the end, Otis was a political moderate who attempted to reconcile parliamentary sovereignty with natural-law philosophy. Parliament could not "make 2 and 2, 5: Omnipotency cannot do it."[96] Yet, if it enacted arbitrary laws, Otis trusted to the mechanisms of checks and balances in the British Constitution to correct the error. In the first stage of the pamphlet debates, Otis sought to appeal to Parliament's better angels; the Americans had not yet shifted to a dominion theory in which Parliament was just another coequal legislature in the empire. Still, Otis rejected the imperial absolutist theory of sovereignty, sounding a reason that reverberates thematically throughout the debates: claims of absolute civil sovereignty are usurpations of God's authority in violation of the natural law:

Salus populi suprema lex esto, is of the law of nature, and part of that grand charter given the human race, (tho' too many of them are afraid to assert it,) by the only monarch in the universe, who has a clear and indisputable right to *absolute* power; because he is the *only* ONE who is *omniscient* as well as *omnipotent*.[97]

Otis' explicit citation of the Book of Genesis account of Adam and Eve was illustrative of how he framed his natural-law theory with the Judeo-Christian tradition of revelation. We shall see that John Dickinson's *Letters from a Farmer in Pennsylvania*, which Bailyn refers to as "most influential pamphlet published in America before 1776" developed a rich theological, and explicitly Christian, backdrop to its political arguments.[98]

2.4 JOHN DICKINSON

John Dickinson, perhaps the "most underrated of all the Founders of this nation," was a successful lawyer from Pennsylvania who played a major role

---

[94] "John Adams' Reconstruction of Otis's Speech on the *Writs of Assistance* Case"; "Essay on the *Writs of Assistance* Case, *Boston Gazette*, January 4, 1762," in Otis, *Political Writings of James Otis*, 13–16.

[95] For a discussion, see Joseph R. Frese, "James Otis and Writs of Assistance," *The New England Quarterly* 30 (4) (December 1957): 496–508.

[96] Wood, *Writings from the Pamphlet Debate*, vol. 1, 87.   [97] Ibid., 51.

[98] Bailyn, *Ideological Origins*, 100–1.

in the pamphlet debates.[99] In her groundbreaking study of Dickinson, Jane E. Calvert has argued that scholars have misunderstood Dickinson's thought insofar as their analyses "fail to take seriously … the religious climate in which Dickinson lived and worked as well as his personal religious belief."[100] The same could be said of the classical and theological components of his natural-law philosophy.

Dickinson contended that "the first principles of government are to be found in human nature" and his arguments throughout are presented as resting on dictates of reason – "reason and equity," "justice and reason" – and as aiming at genuine human happiness. In his Preface to an edition of Dickinson's *Letters from a Pennsylvania*, Benjamin Franklin pointed out that both British and Americans were "*rational creatures*" who had understanding. Reason is contrasted in the *Letters* with passion, which Dickinson identifies as a source of "wrong measures."[101] Reason is a corrective, not a slave, to the passions. Through reason, human beings know the moral law, the basis of their natural rights.

According to Calvert, the Quakers distinguished knowing by reason and Light – the former was corrupted by sin and unreliable. Meanwhile, the way of knowing by Light was a sort of direct supernatural illumination from Christ of the divine will. While she tries to locate Dickinson in this tradition, Calvert acknowledges that there were differences among Quakers on how much they distrusted reason.[102] For example, Quakers such as William Penn can be seen as broadly in continuity with the Thomistic view of conscience in defining *synderesis* as "that eternal principle of truth and sapience, more or less disseminated through mankind" that can be summarized in the maxim "To live honestly, not to hurt another, and to give every one their right" and is the foundation of reasonable and just societies. Moreover, notably, Penn emphasized property as a foundational natural right.[103] Because, as Calvert notes, Dickinson does not use the term Light, and since he does repeatedly appeal to reason, Dickinson is better seen as being in line with Penn, who transmits key doctrines of Christian natural law like the concept of *synderesis*. Thus, Dickinson speaks of duties in conjunction with "the *unbiassed* [sic] *dictates* of my *reason* and *conscience*."[104]

[99] Forrest McDonald and Ellen Shapiro, *Requiem: Variations on Eighteenth-Century Themes* (Lawrence: University of Kansas Press, 1988), 86; quoted in William Muchison, *The Cost of Liberty: The Life of John Dickinson* (Wilmington, DE: ISI Books, 2014), Introduction.

[100] Jane E. Calvert, *Quaker Constitutionalism and the Political Thought of John Dickinson* (New York: Cambridge University Press, 2009), 16.

[101] Wood, *Writings from the Pamphlet Debate*, vol. 1, 423.

[102] Calvert, *Quaker Constitutionalism*, 68–72, 283–84.

[103] William Penn, *The Political Writings of William Penn*, intro. and anno. Andrew R. Murphy (Indianapolis, IN: Liberty Fund, 2002), 26, 48.

[104] John Dickinson, *Political Writings of John Dickinson* (Philadelphia: The Historical Society of Pennsylvania, 1895), ed. Paul Leicester Ford, vol. I, 49 [Dickinson cites Galatians 5:1].

In reaction to the Townshend Acts, Dickinson argues that political freedom is a blessing ordered by Providence, and understands his duty to speak against the Stamp Act in this light:

But while Divine Providence, that gave me existence in a land of freedom, permits my head to think, my lips to speak, and my hand to move, I shall so highly and gratefully value the blessing received, as to take care, that my silence and inactivity shall not give my implied assent to any act, degrading my brethren and myself from the birthright, wherewith heaven itself "hath made us free."[105]

Dickinson underscored the point in the Address to the Committee of Correspondence in Barbados occasioned by their remonstration of Americans for their reaction to the Stamp Act:

KINGS or parliaments could not *give* the *rights essential to happiness*, as you confess those invaded by the Stamp Act to be. We claim them from a higher source – from the King of kings, and Lord of all the earth. They are not annexed to us by parchments and seals. They are created in us by the decrees of Providence, which establish the laws of our nature. They are born with us; exist with us; and cannot be taken from us by any human power, without taking our lives. In short, they are founded on the immutable maxims of reason and justice.[106]

Like Penn, Dickinson emphasizes the foundational role of property and its divine sanction. As Richard Henry Lee explained in his preface to the Williamsburg edition of Dickinson's Letters, Dickinson contended for "our just and legal possession of property and freedom ... [which] has its foundation on the clearest principle of the law of nature."[107] For Dickinson, property is foundational because the pursuit of happiness requires liberty, and liberty is founded on the security of property, which the colonists "acquired with so much pain and hazard."[108] Property was foundational in the sense that it was constitutive of the exercise of rightful freedom and the pursuit happiness. But it was also foundational in the sense of facilitating the independence of subjects and their ability to defend natural rights and insist upon limited government. At the cornerstone of this argument was divine providence. As Lee put it,

The truth is that the great Author of nature has created nothing in vain, and having with the life of man joined liberty, the virtuous enjoyment of and free possession of property honestly gained, has undoubtedly furnished all nations with the means of defending their natural rights, if they have the wisdom and fortitude to make the proper use of such means.[109]

---

[105] Wood, *Writings from the Pamphlet Debate*, vol. 1, 421.
[106] John Dickinson, *An Address to the Committee of Correspondence in Barbados. Occasioned by a Late Letter from Them to Their Agent in London* (Philadelphia: William Bradford, 1766), 4.
[107] Dickinson, *Political Writings of John Dickinson*, 49.
[108] John Dickinson, Letter V, in Forrest McDonald, ed., *Empire and Nation* (Liberty Fund, 1999), 2nd ed., 29; Dickinson, *An Address to the Committee of Correspondence in Barbados*, 5.
[109] Dickinson, *Political Writings of John Dickinson*, 290.

And divine positive law specifically sanctions the right of personal property: "that they should sit *every man* under his vine, and under his fig-tree, and NONE SHOULD MAKE THEM AFRAID."[110] Here, Dickinson deployed a biblical passage commonly used by the Americans to suggest that the right of personal property had biblical sanction. As we shall see, for Dickinson (in harmony with the suggestions of Otis and Lee), the value of property is essentially tethered to the cultivation of and living in accord with virtue.

In a later pamphlet coming in the second stage of the pamphlet debates written in response to the Coercive Acts, Dickinson lays out a classical natural-law perspective on the virtue of justice as a principle of order in the cosmos that is in principle affirmable by unaided reason. Quoting and translating from Johannes Stobaeus' anthology of classical texts, Dickinson writes:

It seems to me, that the *natural justice*, which is a duty of man, ought to be styled *parent, and nourisher, of every other virtue*: and assuredly, without this habit, a man can neither moderate his desires, nor be brave, nor wise. For it is a harmony, and peace, of the whole soul; with a full concert of words, and actions . . . . In the celestial system of the world, as it marshals out the universal rule of things, which are thus decreed of God; it is *providence*, and *harmony*, and *right*. In a *civil state*, it is justly called *peace*, and *good order*. In a *domestic state*, it is *like mindedness* of husband, and wife, towards each other; the *good will* of subordinate members. In the body, it is health, and symmetry of parts; which are principal things, and much beloved by every living creature. In the *soul*, it is wisdom; that wisdom which arises amongst men, from the *knowledge of causes*, and from *natural justice*.[111]

Not only do we see here an adumbration of goods such as life and health, marriage and family, civil peace and friendship, and knowledge of truth, but we also see reaffirmed that this teleological order of man is the product of divine providence. As already suggested, there is an order in human nature of soul and body. Rational creatures can know by reason and moderate their desires or bodily passions according to virtue. The natural rights to life, liberty, and property entail duties toward others in respect of rights. But the duties not to kill, steal, or enslave are only the guardrails of the moral life – they are not sufficient for human flourishing. There is a need to develop fundamental character traits that order the person internally in relation to himself and externally toward others.

Dickinson thus articulates the need for virtue in order for a republican government to function and for people to obtain happiness. Virtue is a quality by which the citizen aligns his desires and interests with the public good. Dickinson decries those who seek out only their private interests in "*wealth,*

---

[110] For a discussion of Micah 4:4 in founding political thought with specific attention given to Washington, see Daniel Dreisbach, *Reading the Bible with the Founders* (New York: Oxford University Press, 2017), 211–27.

[111] John Dickinson, *An Essay on the Constitutional Power of Great Britain over the Colonies in America* (Philadelphia: William and Thomas Bradford), 330–31.

power, and credit." Virtuous citizens are vigilant in defense of their country and liberties. They ought to set aside small-mindedness, pettiness, and illiberal thinking and strive for civic unity and friendship. This supposed a substantive ideational common imaginary: "Let us consider ourselves as MEN – FREEMEN – CHRISTIAN FREEMEN – *separated from the rest of the world, and firmly bound together* by the *same rights, interests* and *dangers.*"[112] Near the end of the war, as president of Pennsylvania, Dickinson issued a proclamation for the suppression of vice, profaneness, and immorality, which explicitly grounded itself in a Christian natural-law tradition. Referencing Christ's restoration of postlapsarian man through grace, the proclamation stated:

the laws of righteousness have been with such infinite wisdom adjusted, and united to the obligations of nature, that while they jointly tended to promote the felicity of men in a future state, they evidently co-operate to advance their welfare in the present, and to offend against the sanctions of revelation, or the dictates of reason and conscience, is assuredly to betray the joys of this life, as well as those of another.[113]

As in the Christian natural-law tradition, grace is not seen as violative but perfective of the strivings of nature. Accordingly, for Dickinson, the revelation of the Bible is harmonious with the principles of reason.[114] Dickinson's point here is that all the natural-law precepts associated with the pursuit of human goods such as preservation of life and health, marriage and child-rearing, and living peaceably with others (the obligations of nature) are congruent with the New Law of Christ (the laws of righteousness), such that living according to the precepts of natural law conduces to temporal and eternal happiness.

The proclamation declares "virtue will be the chief promoter of success" and exhorts parents, teachers, guardians and others charged with the care and rearing of children to be schooled in a range of virtues: "piety, filial reverence, submission to superiors in age or station, modesty, sincerity, benevolence, temperance, industry, consistency of behaviour, and a frugality regulated by an humble reliance on Providence, and a kind respect for others." They were to be taught, moreover, that "[r]eligion is the friend of their peace, health and happiness; and that to displease their Maker, or to trespass against their neighbour, is inevitably to injure themselves." All of this is indicative of Dickinson's belief in an objective moral order and set of goods and virtues that are necessary to constitute human happiness. Moreover, it indicates that Dickinson viewed the state as playing a facilitating role in the promotion of virtue. The responsibility for the habituation of children into becoming virtuous

---

[112] John Dickinson, "Letter XII," in Forrest McDonald, ed., *Empire and Nation: Letters from a Farmer in Pennsylvania (Dickinson); Letters from the Federal Farmer (Richard Henry Lee)* (Indianapolis, IN: Liberty Fund 1999), 80.

[113] "A Proclamation by the President and Supreme Executive Council of the Commonwealth of Pennsylvania" Library of Congress. Accessed July 1, 2021, from https://cdn.loc.gov/service/rbc/rbpe14/rbpe146/14601300/14601300.pdf

[114] Calvert, *Quaker Constitutionalism*, 283–84.

persons and citizens is seen as primarily the role of educational institutions, families, churches, and the like. It should also be noted that Dickinson rejected state coercion in matters of religion. In his first draft of the Articles of Confederation, Dickinson emphasized religious freedom, including freedom from compulsion to support churches by taxes. Yet he coupled this with the duty of religious worship of God, conditioning the former on regular church attendance of one's choice. Strikingly, like Otis, Dickinson affirms the fundamental political equality of the sexes and the races. Dickinson proposed that one shall not be molested "in his or her person" on account of religious belief, and Dickinson proposed an amendment to the Pennsylvania constitution for the emancipation and relief of those who were enslaved.[115]

*

James Otis and John Dickinson – two of the most influential patriot pamphleteers in the first stage of the debates – grounded their political arguments in a theistic and teleological natural-law theory of morality. The liberal principles associated with political equality – rights of individual freedom, property, consent, and so on – were not seen as contradictory to or even in tension with the classical natural-law theory of morality. Rather the latter was seen as the ground of the former in which liberty, property, and consent would be tethered to the virtuous pursuit of the human good in the context of a community constituted by intact families. Hence, it would be a mistake to understand these arguments as proceeding from a framework of "theistic rationalism" as if Americans drew from radically disparate elements of rationalist Enlightenment deism and Christianity.[116] While concepts such as the state of nature had a modern flavor associated with the Enlightenment, Otis and Dickinson were Trinitarian Christians whose rational argumentation was in substantial continuity with the Christian natural-law tradition.

2.5 THEISTIC NATURAL LAW IN THE SECOND STAGE

The classical natural-law theory of morality in its divinely pedigreed and teleological dimensions continued to be assumed in the second stage of the pamphlet debates. Recent scholarly discussion of the dominion theory has sought to show that the patriotic arguments in the second stage were not merely forensic. In this vein, Eric Nelson has argued that the Americans genuinely saw

---

[115] John Dickinson, "Draft of the Articles of Confederation, 1776." Preserving American Freedom, Historical Society of Pennsylvania. Accessed July 14, 2021, from http://digitalhistory.hsp.org/pafrm/doc/draft-articles-confederation-john-dickinson-june-1776; Calvert, *Quaker Constitutionalism*, 274.

[116] See Gregg L. Frazer, *The Religious Beliefs of America's Founders: Reason, Revelation, and Revolution* (Lawrence: University Press of Kansas, 2012).

the English constitution in the royalist spirit of the Stuart kings. Nelson challenges the standard historiography of the Revolution associated with the work of scholars such as Caroline Robbins, Bernard Bailyn, Gordon Wood, and J. G. A. Pocock, which emphasized the Whig character of revolutionary ideology, and contends that the Americans' defense of the royal prerogative as the governing principle of the colonies was not merely an instrumental and cynical ploy but amounted to a fundamental rethinking of their constitutional position.[117] Nelson helpfully highlights the importance of the constitutional dimensions of the American revolution, but, like others, does not emphasize the role of natural-law theory in structuring the Americans' arguments. In the second stage of the debates involving contests about the nature of the English constitution, the Americans continued to make a bona fide appeal to first principles in a way that was substantially continuous with the classical natural-law theory of morality. Indeed, the Americans' unwavering adherence to natural-law principles provided not only a deep consistency of argumentation across the various stages of debate but also facilitated maneuvering between parliamentary Whig and royalist understandings of the constitution in that the Americans consistently maintained that neither Parliament nor the king had unlimited sovereignty unconstrained by natural law.

When offering the initial articulation of the dominion theory, Bancroft focused his argument on the history of the colonial charters to show that they belonged to the "Crown alone," alienated from "the realm," and had been contracted away in agreements with various proprietors and companies. In support of this argument, he highlighted key historical moments when the Stuart kings asserted prerogative rights over the colonies as when James I and Charles refused to assent to a bill that would grant fishing rights to English subjects in North America, arguing that Parliament lacked jurisdiction. Yet Bancroft noted "the law of God and Nature" and the "natural rights of mankind" were the first facts that Americans had appealed to and which were unavailing to William Knox.[118] Flowing from a natural-law and natural-rights foundation, legislative authority in the empire was dispersed among the various distinct states that constituted it, including each colonial legislature. For Parliament to exercise authority over a distinct state with its own legislature would therefore be "repugnant to the Laws of Nature."[119]

The important point here is that the historical case for colonial liberty on the basis of the dominion theory was not merely a constitutional argument from

[117] Eric Nelson, *The Royalist Revolution: Monarchy and the American Revolution* (Cambridge, MA: Belknap Press, 2014); cf. Caroline Robbins, *The Eighteenth Century Commonwealthman* (Indianapolis, IN: Liberty Fund, 2004); Bernard Bailyn, *Ideological Origins;* Gordon Wood, *The Creation of the American Republic, 1776–1787* (Chapel Hill: University of North Carolina Press, 1998); J. G. A. Pocock, *The Machiavellian Moment: Florentine Political Thought and the Atlantic Republican Tradition* (Princeton: Princeton University Press, 2003).
[118] Wood, *Writings from the Pamphlet Debate*, vol. 1, 673.   [119] Ibid., 696.

custom but essentially rested on natural-law premises. Bancroft did not elaborate a theology or axiology. Given the context and aims of the pamphlet, we should not expect him to do so. Still, classical natural-law assumptions remain a core feature of the argument, such as when Bancroft appeals to basic human inclinations toward objective goods. For example, Bancroft at one point acknowledges the essential human inclination toward objective goods of family and children as a matter of course when considering the increase of population in the colonies and the implications of the colonial population for the integrity of the empire. He quotes Montesquieu to suggest that there is a propensity in human beings to marry and have many children provided they are not constrained by the "difficulties of subsistence."[120]

2.5.1 Hamilton's Invocation of Classical Natural-Law Principles

In the *Farmer Refuted*, one of the outstanding expressions of the dominion theory in the second stage of the pamphlet debates, Alexander Hamilton gave a more detailed picture of how classical natural-law axioms are wed to liberal political principles. Hamilton based his arguments on the standards of "reason and nature" or the "law of nature" as established by God and approvingly invoked Blackstone's definition of natural law: It is a dictate of God, coeval with human nature, universally binding, and the source of validity of all human law mediately or immediately. Hamilton accused the loyalist and Anglican Bishop Samuel Seabury (the "Farmer") of ignorance of these principles, and exhorted him: "Apply yourself, without delay, to the study of the law of nature." The debate began when Seabury criticized the Continental Congress in a pamphlet, which elicited a critique from Hamilton and then a reply from Seabury. In Seabury's reply, *A View of the Controversy*, he equated natural rights with possessions in a state of nature, which consisted of a freedom from "all restraints of law and government." In this condition, the weak would be dominated by the strong, a state of affairs from which it is preferable to exit into civil society and trade natural rights for the civil liberties that come packaged with governmental authority and obedience. Hamilton's reply accused Seabury of being a disciple of Thomas Hobbes. To suggest that a state of nature is free of *all* restraints of law suggested a conventionalist account of moral obligation and virtue and a nominalist account of goodness. Hamilton found the roots of this version of Hobbism to be atheism: "But the reason he run into this absurd and impious doctrine, was, that he disbelieved the existence of an intelligent superintending principle, who is the governor, and will be the final judge of the universe." This is a striking passage. The suggestion is that a foundational philosophical error about the existence of a providential and

---

[120] Ibid., 108, quoting Montesquieu, *The Spirit of the Laws*, bk. XXIII, ch. 10.

moralistic God and his causal relation to the world leads to a failure to understand the law of nature and therefore the foundations of government.[121]

Hamilton then went on to articulate a theistic natural law and natural rights account of the foundations of morality and law. The law of nature, established by God, is prior to natural rights and the basis for them. God endowed man with the power of reason "to discern and pursue such things, as were consistent with his duty and interest." This encapsulates concisely the classical, teleological natural-law theory of morality: Human beings are obligated to pursue their genuine happiness. Accordingly, the law of nature binds human beings with obligations to one another, by which they are morally bound not to harm another's "life, limbs, property, or liberty." In virtue of this law, human beings enjoy natural rights to personal safety and liberty. Being thus equal as persons under the same law and endowed with the same natural rights, no person has a right to command political obedience from another without his or her own consent. Hamilton then applied this account of natural justice to assess Parliament:

First, they are subversive of our natural liberty, because an authority is assumed over us, which we by no means assent to. And secondly, they divest us of that moral security, for our lives and properties, which we are intitled to, and which it is the primary end of society to bestow. For such security can never exist, while we have no part in making the laws, that are to bind us.[122]

In the vein of Otis' argument about God's legitimate authority forbidding arbitrary exercises of civil power, Hamilton's argument about Hobbism and atheism suggested that a proper understanding of the existence of God and his causal relation to the world was a precondition for sound thinking about politics.

2.5.2 The Patriots' Classical Theistic Natural-Law Arguments against Absolutist Authority

In their exchange in 1774 with Governor Thomas Hutchinson, the *Speeches with Answers*, the patriots on His Majesty's Council in Massachusetts elaborated on this thread of argument. Hutchinson explicitly argued for an understanding of parliamentary authority as a "supreme and uncontroulable Power, an absolute Authority to decide and determine."[123] The patriots replied:

Supreme or unlimited Authority can with Fitness belong only to the Sovereign of the Universe: And that Fitness is derived from the Perfection of his Nature – To such Authority, directed by Wisdom and infinite Goodness, is due both Active and Passive Obedience: Which as it constitutes the Happiness of rational Creatures, should with

[121] Alexander Hamilton, "The Farmer Refuted," in Harold C. Syrrett, ed. *The Papers of Alexander Hamilton, Volume I: 1768–1778* (New York: Columbia University Press, 1961), 87.
[122] Ibid.   [123] Wood, *Writings from the Pamphlet Debate*, vol. 2, 84.

Chearfulness [*sic*] and from Choice be unlimitedly paid by them – But with Truth this can be said of no other Authority whatever. If then from the Nature and End of Government, the Supreme Authority of every Government is limited, the Supreme Authority of Parliament must be limited.[124]

In his interpretation of this passage, Thomas West contends that the Americans' argument was not actually theological and did not depend on the proposition that God really exists. Rather, according to West, the point was *merely* that the claimants to rule without consent would require possession of the qualities of infinite goodness, wisdom, and power.[125] Yet the patriots contended that human beings are naturally governed by a directing Wisdom prior to their individual and collective choices and that such Wisdom orders them toward their genuine happiness. This is consistent with other examples we have considered of a classical philosophical-theological anthropology, which essentially rested on the truth of God's existence and providence, and was deployed to make a specific claim about the vertical boundaries of civil sovereignty. Hutchinson tried to dodge this argument, suggesting that his arguments did not imply unlimited passive obedience to civil power. He accepted that there was a distinction between divine and human government, but denied it was "pertinent."[126] He averred that he intended "absolute and unlimited" to entail no more than the power that subsists in the very nature of government. His explanation of absolute and unlimited to mean that "no other Power within such Government can have right to withstand or control [it]" indicated his view that sovereignty was indivisible.[127] Hence, the patriots believed their point remained unrebutted: The imperial pamphleteers' erroneous account of civil sovereignty was due to their error in judgment about the nature of divine government.

The Massachusetts House also made a claim about God's nature as both infinitely good and omnipotent that was in line with classical theism. The patriots at times explicitly made this argument against civil absolutism while framing their theology in specifically Christian terms. One example comes from the Suffolk Resolves, which were passed in response to the Coercive Acts and which subtly alluded to Acts 17:28 in decrying the imperial claim to absolute civil sovereignty: "If a boundless extent of continent, swarming with millions, will tamely submit to live, move, and have their being at the arbitrary will of a licentious minister, they basely yield to voluntary slavery; and future generations shall load their memories with incessant execrations."[128] The point would not have been lost on imperial and patriot readers: Christians believed they were radically existentially dependent on God for their continuation in being moment to moment; hence, the Book of Acts declares "in him we live,

---

[124] Ibid., 15.   [125] West, *The Political Theory of the American Founding*, 90–91.
[126] Wood, *Writings from the Pamphlet Debate*, vol. 2, 77.   [127] Ibid.
[128] "Suffolk Resolves," *Essex Gazette*, September 20, 1774.

move, and have our being." The Americans were again suggesting that the imperial administrators were arrogating authority over them that was metaphysically forbidden. The Resolves continued to declare that because the Coercive Acts were in violation of the laws of nature and natural rights, the legislation was of no legal force and could be justly disobeyed. The particularly Protestant Christian frame of their natural-law theory shined through again when the Resolves specifically condemned the Quebec Act as a threat to Protestant Christianity in America. Sometimes the local resolves passed in the aftermath of the Coercive Acts explicitly framed themselves as Protestant Christian natural-law arguments; sometimes the natural-law principles were presented independent of revelation.[129]

Some imperial pamphleteers were more willing to concede the patriotic point about the limits of civil authority under God. One example is John Gray in his *Right of the British Legislature to Tax the American Colonies Vindicated*. While he repeated the rhetoric about a "Supreme, all-controlling power," Gray concedes the classical natural-law maxim that the highest civil power is not unlimited and that if it ordained things "contrary to the laws of God," then it "has no authority to ordain," rendering void such enactments such that "individuals may disobey, not that they have any inherent right over the enacting power; but because, in fact, nothing has been enacted, when an iniquitous statute has been promulgated."[130] Gray simply denied that Parliament's taxing the colonies amounted to such an iniquity. For Gray, it is only true to say that the law of nature entitles each person to the fruits of his own labor unqualifiedly in the state of nature. Property rights are subjected to governmental authority in the condition of civil society. Gray thus takes aim at Locke's "weak" and "inconclusive" propositions regarding the necessity of consent to taking of property – these are "false conclusion[s] from false premise[s]."[131] Lockean property rights also contradicted Lockean majority rule, because a dissenting minority (or representatives thereof) could not be taken to have consented to taking of their property.

Sometimes imperial pamphleteers tried to turn the tables on the patriots' appeal to God's rule. In his *Massachusettensis*, to which John Adams' *Novanglus* was directed, Daniel Leonard maintained the imperial line about the necessity of a supreme civil power. But he invoked Almighty God as the "supreme Governor of the universe" to suggest that rebellion against the latter

---

[129] For another example of the former, see the Fincastle Resolutions, which declared the colonists "support for the Protestant religion" (see Jim Glanville, "The Fincastle Resolutions," *The Smithfield Review* (2010), app. A, vol. XIV, 102. For an example of the latter, see the Fairfax County Resolves by George Mason in *The Founders' Constitution*, ed. Philip B. Kurland and Ralph Lerner (Indianapolis, IN: Liberty Fund, 2001), vol. 1, ch. 17, doc. 14. Accessed February 14, 2022, from http://press-pubs.uchicago.edu/founders/documents/v1ch17s14.html.

[130] John Gray, *Right of the British Legislature to Tax the American Colonies Vindicated* (London: 1774), 6.

[131] Ibid., 5.

was the only thing worse than rebellion against civil authorities. Leonard warned that rebellion would break the fundamental protection-obedience bond, dissolve law and order, and introduce "fraud, violence, rapine, murder, sacrilege, and the long train of evils that riot uncontrouled in a state of nature."[132]

Hutchinson's reply to the House of Representatives (led by John Adams) focused on the dominion theory arguments they had propounded. Hutchinson maintained that he knew "of no Line that can be drawn between the Supreme Authority of Parliament and the total Independence of the Colonies: It is impossible that there should be two independent legislatures in one and the same state."[133] To this Adams replied: your logic implies we are either vassals or independent states – the former is an absurdity, so we must be independent states. Yet "what hinders but that being united in one Head and common Sovereign, they may live happily in that Connection, and mutually support and protect each other?"[134] In support of this argument that coequal legislatures coexist under one executive head, the patriots appealed to a shared premise with Hutchinson that the colonies were feudatory grants from the king, who thereby had the prerogative to "alienate and dispose of Countries acquired by the Discovery of his Subjects."

The preceding argument quickly moved from the historical-constitutional vector to first principles. Hutchinson had argued that by the law of nations the colonies were part of Great Britain. Adams responded:

> The Law of Nations is or ought to be founded on the Law of Reason .... The Opinions therefore, and Determinations of the greatest Sages and Judges of the Law in the Exchequer Chamber ought not to be considered as decisive or binding in our present Controversy with your Excellency, any further than they are consonant to *natural Reason.*[135]

The ultimate touchstone of constitutionality was therefore the law of nature. At this point, the patriots cited passages from Pufendorf and Grotius to bolster their test of reason. Pufendorf noted that some colonies in history were erected into distinct commonwealths with the same rights as the mother state. Grotius quoted King Tullius to the effect that the law of nature permitted the independence of colonies. The patriotic point of deploying these sources was to show that the Americans' test of reason was justified; it was consonant to reason and the laws of nature to reject the idea that colonies they were *necessarily* part of

---

[132] Daniel Leonard, *Massachusettensis: or a Series of Letters, Containing a Faithful State of Many Important and Striking Facts, Which Laid the Foundation of the Present Troubles in the Province of Massachusetts-Bay* (Boston: J. Matthews, 1776), letter IX, 63–64. Accessed July 1, 2021, from https://oll.libertyfund.org/titles/1332.
[133] Wood, *Writings from the Pamphlet Debate*, vol. 2, 10.   [134] Ibid., 39.   [135] Ibid., 64–65.

the mother state.[136] The patriots concluded their argument by citing Hooker to the effect that Parliament's attempts to legislate for the colonies amounted to tyranny.[137]

2.5.3 James Wilson's Classical Natural Law and Constitutionalist Contribution to the Pamphlet Debates

As the Hutchinson-Adams dialogue just described shows, when the constitutional arguments seemed to stalemate in the pamphlet debates, the patriots fell back on first principles. Self-preservation was a law of nature that entailed natural rights to life, liberty, property, and representation. James Wilson's *Considerations on the Nature and Extent of the Legislative Authority of the British Parliament* (1774), another of the most notable defenses of the dominion theory, provides an example of how the patriotic emphasis on the natural-law vector of argument seemed to converge with the constitutional vector. Wilson contended that the Americans' rights are grounded in both the "supreme and uncontrollable laws of nature" and the "fundamental principles of the British constitution."[138] He began with similar Lockean-sounding postulates of natural freedom and equality where there is no natural authority of one over another and where legitimate authority comes from consent alone. His citation of Burlamaqui, an important German political theorist in the theistic natural-law tradition, points us to his discussion of the various inconveniences of a state of nature: the tendency of the passions to weaken the force of natural law in conscience, the lack of a common judge to settle disputes, and the lack of a common executive power to enforce obedience to the law of nature.[139] In contrast with a Hobbist state of nature of sovereign individuals, this state of nature is one replete with natural moral obligations. In this condition, Burlamaqui points out, and Wilson elaborates elsewhere, that all persons are "in a state of dependence on God and his laws."[140] Individuals entering a social contract find it reasonable to trade natural liberty for civil liberty with the aim of achieving a collective happiness they could not otherwise obtain given the inconveniences of the state of nature. The creation of civil authority comes with the condition that the people have a right to insist that authority be used well, precisely because the people always retain the right to pursue happiness.

---

[136] Ibid., 65; cf. Samuel von Pufendorf, *Of the Law of Nature and Nations*, trans. Basil Kennett, 2nd ed. (Oxford: L. Lichfield for A. and J. Churchil, 1710), bk. VIII, 719; Grotius, *The Rights of War and Peace*, bk. II, chs. IX and X, 674.

[137] Wood, *Writings from the Pamphlet Debate*, vol. 2, 75.   [138] Ibid., 116.

[139] Jean-Jacques Burlamaqui, *The Principles of Natural and Politic Law*, trans. Thomas Nugent (Indianapolis, IN: Liberty Fund, 2006), 280–83.

[140] Burlamaqui, *The Principles of Natural and Politic Law*, 284.

Wilson speaks of persons in the state of nature as "independent and uncon-
nected."[141] By this Wilson means that they are politically equal – no one is
bound by any prior right of another to political rule. Hence, like Otis and
Dickinson, Wilson rejects the radical perspective on the state of nature. Instead,
Wilson's account of the foundations of law and government rested on a
teleological and morally realist understanding of human nature. It is reasonable
to leave the state of nature because civil society is more conducive to the pursuit
of happiness. Hence, the "happiness of society" is what Wilson identifies as the
"first law of every government" and is an immediate deduction from the
natural law. As he detailed nearly two decades later in his lectures on law at
the College of Philadelphia, this first law flows from the divinely pedigreed
teleological order in man:

By his wisdom, [God] knows our nature, our faculties, and our interests: he cannot be
mistaken in the designs, which he proposes, nor in the means, which he employs to
accomplish them. By his goodness, he proposes our happiness: and to that end directs the
operations of his power and wisdom . . . . The rule of his government we shall find to be
reduced to this one paternal command – Let man pursue his own perfection and
happiness.

By the faculty of reason, man can grasp his genuine interests, the goods befitting
his nature and constitutive of happiness. Reason and will are faculties, "our
intellectual and our moral powers," that distinguishes us from brutes – by them
we can deliberate and choose rather than be "carried away irresistibly by the
force of blind and impetuous appetites."[142] Duties that bind human persons in
pursuit of happiness are grasped by conscience or the moral sense. The moral
law is promulgated to man by God through "reason and conscience, the divine
monitors within us . . . . For, in this manner, they may be said to be engraven by
God on the hearts of men: in this manner, he is the promulgator as well as the
author of natural law."[143] Wilson's classically theistic and teleological moral
theory is antithetical to a godless account of philosophical anthropology in
which the passions reign and reason is a mere instrument to the strongest desire.

Wilson thus insists on substantial electoral checks on the legislative power,
because legislators are delegated by the represented to advance their interests.
He recalls the electoral checks the English have on Parliament: "The constitution is thus frequently renewed, and drawn back, as it were, to its first
principles; which is the most effectual method of perpetuating the liberties of
a state."[144] At this point, the constitutional arguments and the arguments from
first principles have almost entirely converged. Democratic elections are personal exercises of one's natural rights. The implication is that the failure of

---

[141] Wood, *Writings from the Pamphlet Debate*, vol. 2, 116.
[142] James Wilson, *Collected Works of James Wilson*, ed. Mark David Hall and Kermit L. Hall
(Indianapolis, IN: Liberty Fund, 2007), vol. 1, 464, 501, 505.
[143] Ibid., 470.   [144] Wood, *Writings from the Pamphlet Debate*, vol. 2, 122.

mechanisms to ensure regular universal participation in electoral republicanism is violative of natural rights.[145] Wilson goes on to show how the checks and arrangements in place fall short of ensuring that Parliament's acts for the colonies align with their collective happiness and therefore the natural law.

Wilson's natural-law theory does important work in this pamphlet when he turns to show that the American claims were sourced in the principles of the British constitution as well. The dominion theory posited that the various localities of the empire had a local legislative autonomy and therefore coequality with Parliament. Wilson developed this argument by trying to show that this vision of the English constitution was traditionally acknowledged by prominent sources. He drew from three cases. First, he discussed *Calvin's Case*, decided during the time of Richard III and cited as an authority that held that Ireland had its own parliament and laws and that English Parliament's statutes did not bind them because they did not send representatives to Parliament. Ireland's dependent status was as subjects to the king. From this, Wilson infers that the source of Parliament's authority is the authorization that comes with representation. The second case he mentions is *Blankard v. Galdy*, a Jamaican case in which Lord Chief Justice John Holt found that English statutes had not supplanted those in force before the English conquest because they lacked representation in Parliament. The third case he cited, also decided by Holt, was *Smith v. Browne and Cooper*, a case in which parties disputed a debt over the sale of one enslaved in Virginia who had been brought to England. Holt held that the laws of England did not extend to Virginia but that their laws were at the pleasure of the king, because America was a conquered country.

Wilson's use of these cases faced an immediate objection. The judgments had come with riders that the legislative jurisdiction was exempt "unless it be named." In other words, the jurists had sometimes suggested that the British Parliament actually did have ultimate sovereignty if it chose to so act (as in fact it would in the case of Ireland in the Declaratory Act of 1719). Wilson replied that these riders amounted to absurd dicta:

Does naming them give those, who do them that honour, a right to rule over them? Is this the source of the supreme, the absolute, the irresistible, the uncontrolled authority of parliament? These positions are too absurd to be alleged; and a thousand judicial determinations in their favour would never induce one man of sense to subscribe his assent to them.[146]

In a supporting footnote, Wilson quotes another towering figure in the theistic natural-law tradition, William Blackstone.[147] As Wilson paraphrases him, "Where a decision is manifestly absurd and unjust, such a sentence is not

---

[145] For a helpful discussion of Wilson's election theory of representation and authorization, see Nelson, *The Royalist Revolution: Monarchy and the American Revolution*, 91–93.

[146] Wood, *Writings from the Pamphlet Debate*, vol. 2, 136.

[147] For Blackstone's account of the divine pedigree of natural law, see *Commentaries on the Laws of England in Four Books*, vol. 1 (Philadelphia: J. P. Lippincott, 1893), 39–43.

law."[148] As Blackstone had put it, "no human laws are of any validity, if contrary to [the law of nature]."[149] At the crux of Wilson's argument for the dominion theory, he appeals to an axiomatic principle of classical natural-law theory. The divinely pedigreed natural moral law – which as we have seen is promulgated to man via reason and conscience, "the divine monitors within us" – provides the standard for the moral validity of law for all bodies politic, and therefore an essential limiting principle to Parliament's authority.[150]

2.5.4 Thomas Jefferson's Appeal to God, Natural Law, and Constitutional History

While his pamphlet differed in significant ways from other American proponents of the dominion theory, Thomas Jefferson also clearly articulated a divine pedigree for revolutionary natural law. Jefferson held Otis "in high estimation" and would eventually work with Dickinson in the Continental Congress on the Declaration Setting Forth the Causes and Necessity of Taking Up Arms (1775) (a document that in Jefferson's draft called upon "Almighty God" to dispose the King and Parliament to reconciliation, and the final draft of which expressed trust in the "mercies of the supreme and impartial Judge and Ruler of the Universe" and implored "his divine goodness" for assistance in the conflict). Jefferson wrote his *Summary View of the Rights of British America* late in the pamphlet debates. One year prior to working with Dickinson, Jefferson, in his words, had hastily "prepared what I thought might be given in instruction to the Delegates who should be appointed to attend the General Congress proposed."[151]

Jefferson contended that "God and the laws" provided the source for coequal legislative jurisdiction throughout the empire that had been violated by "unwarrantable encroachments and usurpations." But, for his part, Jefferson dug more deeply into the history of the British constitution to its "free and antient principles" in the "wilds and woods in the north of Europe" to its Saxon origins. On Jefferson's reading, the Saxons were possessed of the same natural right of emigration and settlement that the first Americans possessed. It was by this natural right that Americans labored at the expense of their own blood and treasure to take possession of the land: "for themselves alone they have a right to hold." The Americans freely established the system of

---

[148] Wood, *Writings from the Pamphlet Debate*, vol. 2, 136.

[149] Blackstone, *Commentaries*, 41. Blackstone turned somersaults to try to reconcile this axiom with an unlimited view of parliamentary sovereignty.

[150] Wilson, *Collected Works of James Wilson*, vol. 1, 471.

[151] "Jefferson to William Tudor, 14 February 1823. Jefferson's Fair Copy for the Committee, 26 June–6 July 1775," in Julian P. Boyd, ed., *The Papers of Thomas Jefferson* (Princeton: Princeton University Press, 1950), vol. 1, 199–204; "Thomas Jefferson: Memorandum on instructions to Virginia delegates to Congress in 1774 (1820)." Accessed February 14, 2022, from https://founders.archives.gov/documents/Jefferson/98-01-02-1736

laws they knew from England, and their ongoing political union with empire was through voluntary submission to the king. Natural right and constitutional law converge in the Saxons' absolute dominion over their property. Monarchical feudalism – in which lands were seen as possessed of the king and granted to loyal subjects on feudal tenures – was thus characterized as a Norman innovation that applied only to actual conquests, and which therefore applied only to all English subjects through legal fictions. At any rate, it did not apply to the colonists. In this respect, Jefferson's history differed from that of Bancroft, who had emphasized the king's prerogative power and the original status of the colonies as his personal dominions.[152] For Jefferson, it would not do merely to advert to the constitutional vector. The Americans' rights were "derived from the laws of nature, and not as the gift of their chief magistrate."[153]

Jefferson's argument thus called into question even the "external" regulation of trade with the colonies. For, if they possessed their property by natural right, it would follow that the colonies had a right to trade it freely with whomever they choose. Hence, Jefferson sought to undercut Parliament's claim to authority by tracing it to an encroachment by the Long Parliament later rescinded by the same but renewed after the Restoration. And he lists various onerous statutes passed previously that he suggests would not have been passed by a legislature with jurisdiction derived from representation. But it could be objected that the dominion theory was a novelty, because the various parliamentary acts Jefferson cites did not excite resistance. Anticipating this objection, Jefferson remarks that the previous violations were more minor and occasional whereas the late acts of Parliament were a "series of oppressions" through subsequent administrations. A catalog of acts that went beyond Parliament's constitutional authority thus was sufficient neither to disprove the dominion theory nor to justify Parliament's most recent acts. Jefferson ended by emphasizing the theistic natural-law frame of the argument: "The God who gave us life gave us liberty at the same time; the hand of force may destroy, but cannot disjoin them." Jefferson's theistic natural-law theory, discussed at length in the next chapter, provided the foundation for his insistence that "force cannot give right."[154]

*

By the end of the pamphlet debates, the prospects of reconciliation were quickly waning. Highly practical solutions did not find much support as the

[152] On Jefferson's "idiosyncrasy" vis à vis the Bancroftian dominion theory, see Nelson, *The Royalist Revolution*, 58–60.

[153] Thomas Jefferson, *Summary View*, in Julian P. Boyd, ed., *The Papers of Thomas Jefferson* (Princeton: Princeton University Press, 1950), vol. 1, 121–37.

[154] Ibid., 121–37.

parties to the contest increasingly polarized toward independence or loyalty. Edmund Burke's proposal for conciliatory measures and abandonment of taxation in the colonies went nowhere. Neither did American conservative Joseph Galloway's proposal for a Grand Council elected by the colonies with joint jurisdiction with Parliament over American affairs. Because the dominion theory tied the cord of loyalty directly to the king, arguments for independence turned against monarchy itself in the minds of many of the patriots. Thomas Paine's *Common Sense*, which sold 100,000 copies and was the most widely read pamphlet on the eve of the revolution, is the outstanding example of this shift. In contrast with the American pamphleteers so far examined, Paine used a much more individualistic and priority-of-rights portrayal of the state of nature. Unlike Otis' and Wilson's view, Paine portrays government as, at best, a "necessary evil." Persons are driven to society from a state of nature out of self-interest. Paine could be read to suggest that there is a moral standard in the state of nature when he suggests it would be possible for a time for people to be "perfectly just to each other" – but the thrust of his account suggests that natural rights are prior to moral duties. Thus, regarding the foundational philosophical-theological anthropology grounding of law and government, Paine's state of nature teaching was an outlier among the pamphleteers and drew criticism from discerning Christians for just this reason.[155] Still, a central argument of his pamphlet turned on a biblical interpretation that many orthodox Christians found convincing. Kingship, Paine argued, was an alien corruption of the people of God "first introduced into the world by Heathens."[156]

The Declaration of Independence, the culminating American argument in the pamphlet debates, adopted the dominion theory wholesale and focused its case for independence on crimes of the king. Its appeal to self-evident principles knowable by reason was in deep continuity with the metaphysics and epistemology of the classical natural-law tradition. The significant proximate channels of classical Christian metaphysical and epistemological realism included the Reformed tradition (as encapsulated in the Westminster Confession that influenced American Presbyterians and their institutions of learning such as Princeton) and the Scottish common sense realism of philosophers such as Francis Hutcheson and Thomas Reid (who influenced and were channeled to American audiences by founders such as John Witherspoon, one of the most influential educators in American history as president of Princeton).[157]

---

[155] For example, Paine castigated the doctrine of original sin as having an "inglorious connexion" with the doctrine of hereditary monarchy; see Thomas Paine, *Common Sense* (Mineola, NY: Dover, 1997), 14. John Witherspoon took Paine to task for his comments as asserted "without the shadow of reasoning"; John Witherspoon, "The Dominion of Providence over the Passions of Men," in Ellis Sandoz, ed., *The Political Sermons of the Founding Era*, 2nd ed. (Indianapolis, IN: Liberty Fund, 1998), vol. 1, 538.

[156] Paine, *Common Sense*, 9.

[157] See Owen Anderson, *The Declaration of Independence and God: Self-Evident Truths in American Law* (New York: Cambridge University Press, 2015), 50–85; Jeffry H. Morrison,

Moreover, as an analytical matter, the Declaration's account of self-evident principles was in deep continuity with Thomas Aquinas's analysis of self-evident principles known by all (per se *nota omnibus*) and known by the learned (per se *nota quoad nos*).[158]

Furthermore, the Declaration maintained the classical theism that had animated patriotic argumentation in the pamphlet debates. The Declaration began its case by appealing to the "Laws of Nature and of Nature's God." Nature's God is the Creator who endows persons with unalienable natural rights to life, liberty, and the pursuit of happiness. The purpose of governments is to secure these rights, and the people enjoy an original right to institute, alter, and abolish the forms of government in order to better secure rights. The colonies had suffered a long train of abuses and usurpations designed to establish despotism. The Declaration then gives evidence that the king had engaged in tyranny. The argument disavows Parliament as a "jurisdiction foreign to our constitution" and makes the case against George III by detailing his legislative, executive, and judicial malpractices.

The king's legislative abuses included his refused assent to laws and effects of delayed assent such as inefficiency and maladministration. He had dealt unjustly toward colonial assemblies: seeking to diminish their representation, irregular calling and dissolving legislatures, delaying new elections, and performing substantive legislative abuses such as preventing laws conducive to growing the American population, cutting off American trade from the rest of the world, taxing Americans without their consent, and taking away or altering their charters. His judicial malpractices included refusing assent to laws for establishing judiciary powers, making judges dependent on his will for salary and tenure, erecting new judicial offices to molest the Americans, shielding soldiers who murder colonists with mock trials, and depriving Americans in many cases of the right of trial by jury. His executive crimes included erecting and maintaining a standing army in the colonies and quartering them there, subordinating civil to military government, imposing acts of war on American towns and lives, abdicating government and protection of the laws in the colonies, impressing Americans by the British navy, stoking Indian attacks on the colonists, and sending armies of foreign mercenaries to bring death and destruction to the Americans. "A Prince, whose character is thus marked by every act which may define a Tyrant, is unfit to be the ruler of a free people."

The king is thus implicitly contrasted with the only other individual specifically referenced in the body of the Declaration: God. Given the patriotic theme throughout the pamphlet debates of arguing against the British absolutist

---

John Witherspoon and the Founding of the American Republic (Notre Dame, IN: University of Notre Dame Press, 2003), 9, 51–57; Sandoz, ed., *The Political Sermons of the Founding Era*, vol. 1, 531–32.

[158] Christopher Kaczor, "Created Equal: An Interpretation and Defense of the American Proposition" (PDF format, 2015).

theory of civil sovereignty by contrasting divine and civil government, this should not be a surprise. God as Creator and author of the laws of nature is the supremely just legislator who provides the moral standards for assessing the moral validity of the king's actions. God is also the supreme judicial power of the universe who will be the supremely just judge between the parties whose decade-long contest had ended in an appeal to heaven. Hence, the Americans appealed to the "Supreme Judge of the world for the rectitude of our intentions." Finally, God is the supreme executive power of the universe who enforces the laws of nature, and upon whom the colonists profess a "a firm reliance on the protection of Divine Providence."[159]

The American pamphleteers developed a range of arguments against Parliament and King in the 1760s and 1770s that wed the doctrines of liberty and equality to a classical Christian natural-law account of the nature of man. While there were exceptions, many of the most influential pamphleteers retained the classical and Christian ideas of the createdness of man, the inclination toward genuine interests or goods befitting his nature and constitutive of his happiness (the inclination toward civil society), and the priority of natural duties that tether and condition the natural rights to life, liberty, and the pursuit of happiness.

But does this interpretation square with the theological and political thought of the Declaration's principal draftsman, Thomas Jefferson? While the Declaration was a public document and its meaning cannot be reduced to the private views of any one individual, it would seem strange if it did not fit with Jefferson's thought. In the next chapter, we focus in to reexamine Jefferson's political theology and natural-law theory.

---

[159] For discussions of the three powers of government in the God of the Declaration, see George Anastapolo, "The Declaration of Independence," *St. Louis University Law Journal* 9 (1965): 390–416; Harry V. Jaffa, "What Is Equality? The Declaration of Independence Revisited," *Journal of Christian Jurisprudence* 6 (1987): 98–99.

3

Thomas Jefferson, Nature's God, and the Theological Foundations of Natural-Rights Republicanism

In the Declaration of Independence, the culmination of the pamphlet debates that had begun in the wake of the Seven Years War just twelve years prior, the Continental Congress invoked the "Laws of Nature and of Nature's God" to claim for the United States an independent sovereign existence. Among the truths the colonists held out to be self-evident was, to borrow Lincoln's formulation, the proposition that "all men are created equal" and "endowed by their Creator with certain unalienable Rights." After listing twenty-seven separate grievances against King George, the Declaration closed with an appeal "to the Supreme Judge of the world" and a professed "reliance on the protection of divine Providence." On the surface, at least, the Declaration's various references to God thus seem to be compatible with the Congregationalist, Episcopalian, Catholic, Quaker, and Presbyterian traditions represented by the members of the Continental Congress and thus an ecumenical expression of theistic belief. If not a Christian document, the Declaration is a theological-political document that appears compatible with the broad swath of theological beliefs held by Americans in the colonial era.

Historically, this makes sense: The aim of the Declaration was to unite the colonists, and so we should expect any theological references to transverse the differences among major religious sects. On this reading, the theological references in the Declaration are evidence of a broad public consensus among American colonists in the late eighteenth century that God is the creator of the cosmos, independent of nature, both moralistic and provident, whose existence is profoundly relevant to the theoretical foundations of rightful political rule. Yet as we have seen, some scholars argue that the natural theology invoked by the Declaration is subtly and intentionally subversive of traditional biblical and philosophical theology and that the Declaration's primary draftsman, Thomas Jefferson, gave voice to this impiety when he invoked the God of Nature. Nature's God, on this account, is *not* the God of classical theism, whose existence, goodness, justice, and providential governance of the universe was thought to be knowable and demonstrable by reason but is instead tied to the modern natural-rights philosophy developed by Hobbes, Spinoza, Locke, and others as part of a larger project to pour the new wine of secular liberal individualism into the old wineskins of the classical theistic natural-law tradition. From this vantage point, the God of Nature is a pantheistic being who radically challenges and supplants the God of classical natural law. Nature's God is instead tantamount to the rational organizing principle of the universe and is thus radically different than the providential, moralistic creator of the classical tradition.[1] Call this the subversive theology thesis.

In this chapter, we challenge the idea that Jefferson – admittedly among the most religiously skeptical of the founders – was a vehicle of subversive theology, so understood. We argue that Jefferson understood Nature's God to be a creating, particularly providential, and moralistic being whose existence and causal relation to the world was essential to the foundations of natural-rights republicanism. For Jefferson, belief in such a God was warranted on the basis of reason, and thus is akin to the propositions that Thomas Aquinas called the *preambula fidei*. Jefferson's theology was essential to natural-rights republicanism in that God's creation and ordering of man to happiness grounded the moral law, human moral equality, and the natural right of property. John Dewey noted in an essay originally published in 1940 that although Jefferson's

rejection of supernaturalism and of the authority of churches and their creeds caused him to be denounced as an atheist, he was convinced, beyond any peradventure, on *natural* and rational grounds of the existence of a divine righteous Creator who manifested his purposes in the structure of the world, especially in that of society and human conscience.[2]

Jefferson's adopted motto, "Rebellion to Tyrants Is Obedience to God," reflects his belief in a moral order established by God's will, which human will must accord with to be just.

Jefferson's theism was not orthodox. It is well known, for example, that he excised various miracles from the Gospel narratives in his private collation of excerpts. As Annette Gordon-Reed and Peter Onuf note, Jefferson saw those miracles "as distractions from the real messages that the philosopher, whom he

---

[1] See, e.g., Thomas L. Pangle, *The Spirit of Modern Republicanism* (Chicago: University of Chicago Press, 1987); Thomas L. Pangle, *Political Philosophy and the God of Abraham* (Washington, DC: Johns Hopkins University Press, 2007); Matthew Stewart, *Nature's God: The Heretical Origins of the American Republic* (New York: W. W. Norton, 2014); Leo Strauss, *Natural Right and History* (Chicago: University of Chicago Press, 1953); Leo Strauss, *Spinoza's Critique of Religion* (Chicago: University of Chicago Press, 1997); Michael Zuckert, *Launching Liberalism: On Lockean Political Philosophy* (Lawrence: University of Kansas Press, 2002).

[2] John Dewey, *John Dewey: The Later Works, 1925–1953*, ed. Joy Ann Boydston (Carbondale: Southern Illinois University Press, 2008), vol. 14, 218. Emphasis in original in all quotes unless otherwise noted.

deliberately called 'Jesus of Nazareth,' brought to the world."[3] Jefferson did not adhere to the major tenets of orthodox Christianity as presented in the religion's earliest creeds, but he nonetheless affirmed the existence of a God of Nature whose attributes included being a providential, moralistic creator. And while Jefferson can appear at times as a philosophical dilettante with scattered thoughts, at no point did he ever affirm pantheism. Indeed, a roughly consistent theistic outlook can be reconstructed from his corpus of writings.

Although he was not an orthodox religious believer, Jefferson developed a natural theology that has surprising continuities and some important discontinuities with the classical natural-law tradition. There is an ongoing scholarly interest in Jefferson's natural theology,[4] but the ample body of literature on Jefferson's theology has so emphasized its novelty that it has missed important continuities between Jefferson and the classical Christian natural-law tradition. We argue in the following sections that Jefferson followed the classical tradition in affirming the existence of a personal creator independent of nature who imbued nature with lawful properties and a rational design. In contrast to the classical tradition, however, Jefferson insisted that moral knowledge is gained primarily through conscience or the moral sense rather than reason. Each of these claims has important implications for how Jefferson understood the role of Nature's God in grounding the political claims in the Declaration of Independence.

How Jefferson understood the theological foundations of natural-rights republicanism is an important question in the history of political thought – but it is more than that. Jefferson's natural theology ventures answers to three separate but interrelated questions that have long been of interest to normative political theorists: What is the ultimate source or ground of nature? Is nature teleological? And how do we come to know the moral dictates of nature? Our argument – that Jefferson espoused a natural theology of creation – has implications for how we interpret the Declaration of Independence, and challenges the conclusion of recent scholarship that Jefferson's Declaration stands for the "emancipation of the political order from God"[5] – a conclusion shared by prominent secularist readings of the Declaration.[6]

---

[3] Annette Gordon-Reed and Peter S. Onuf, *"Most Blessed of the Patriarchs": Thomas Jefferson and the Empire of the Imagination* (New York: W. W. Norton, 2016), 274.

[4] J. Judd Owen, "The Struggle between 'Religion and Nonreligion': Jefferson, Backus, and the Dissonance of America's Founding Principles," *American Political Science Review* 101 (2007): 493–503; Jeremy Bailey, "Nature and Nature's God in Notes on the State of Virginia," in Christopher Nadon, ed., *Enlightenment and Secularism: Essays on the Mobilization of Reason* (Lanham, MD: Lexington Books, 2015); Owen Anderson, *The Declaration of Independence and God* (New York: Cambridge University Press, 2015).

[5] Stewart, *Nature's God*, 8.

[6] Danielle Allen, *Our Declaration: A Reading of the Declaration of Independence in Defense of Equality* (New York: Liveright, 2015), 138.

Although there is a large body of scholarship arguing for the compatibility between theism and Lockean natural-rights republicanism in late eighteenth-century American political thought,[7] debate on the vexed question of the relationship between theism and the modern Lockean natural-rights tradition has not subsided. Here we provide a new perspective on that important question. Taking Thomas Aquinas as a representative of the broader classical Christian natural-law tradition, we demonstrate that Jefferson's thought espouses a number of surprising and overlooked continuities with that tradition.

Jefferson's thought blends a moral and metaphysical Epicureanism with a rationalized, theistic metaphysics and a Christian ethics, a set of beliefs that does not lend itself to a fast and ready label. Indeed, Jefferson professed to be "of a sect by myself."[8] Still, we can consider the theoretical and practical vectors of Jefferson's thought as follows. First, Jefferson affirms a creational metaphysics that is bound up with his providential-moralistic theism. Second, and precisely in virtue of this creational metaphysic, Jefferson espouses a natural-law eudaimonistic theory of morality. The idea of existential dependence underpins Jefferson's interlocking ideas about property and fundamental human moral equality. Although various references to God in the Declaration were added and modified in the editorial process of drafting the Declaration, Jefferson's original rough draft does explicitly derive "inherent & inalienable" rights from humanity's "equal creation."[9] Our argument demonstrates that Jefferson also affirmed the theological concepts of divine omnipotence, providence, and justice invoked elsewhere in the final draft of the Declaration. Because our account of Jefferson's creational metaphysics, natural-law ethics, and theory of property proceeds as a dialogical critique of the subversive theology thesis, we begin with a further elaboration of that thesis.

3.1 THE SUBVERSIVE THEOLOGY THESIS

The subversive theology thesis can be traced to the interpretation of early modern political philosophy in the writings of Leo Strauss. By his own

---

[7] James T. Kloppenberg, *The Virtues of Liberalism* (New York: Oxford University Press, 1998); John Patrick Diggins, *The Lost Soul of American Politics: Virtue, Self-Interest, and the Foundations of Liberalism* (Chicago: University of Chicago Press, 1984); Barry Alan Shain, *The Myth of American Individualism: The Protestant Origins of American Political Thought* (Princeton: Princeton University Press, 1996); Steven M. Dworetz, *The Unvarnished Doctrine: Locke, Liberalism, and the American Revolution* (Durham, NC: Duke University Press, 1990).

[8] Thomas Jefferson, "Thomas Jefferson to Ezra Stiles Ely, 25 June 1819," Founder Online, National Archives. Accessed July 12, 2021, from https://founders.archives.gov/documents/Jefferson/03-14-02-0428.

[9] Justin Buckley Dyer, *American Soul: The Contested Legacy of the Declaration of Independence* (Lanham, MD: Rowman & Littlefield, 2012), 7–11; cf. Allen, *Our Declaration: A Reading of the Declaration of Independence in Defense of Equality*, 72; Pauline Maier, *American Scripture: Making the Declaration of Independence* (New York: Alfred Knopf, 1997), 148–49.

profession, from his earliest writings forward, the theologico-political problem was *the theme* of his writings.[10] Strauss's exploration of the problem began with his study of Spinoza and Maimonides and continued through his magnum opus, *Natural Right and History*, which opens by quoting the Declaration's proclamation of self-evident and divinely sanctioned truths.[11] According to Strauss, Spinoza's confrontation with Maimonides is a philosophic confrontation with divine revelation that can be boiled down to one question: "Creation of the world or eternity of the world?"[12] Spinoza presented *Deus seu Natura*, God or Nature, as the infinite, indivisible, and eternal substance of the universe[13] and argued for the eternality of matter. Belief in the doctrine of the eternity of the world, Strauss asserts, is "characteristic of the philosophers"[14] and incompatible with a doctrine of divine creation.

Although ancient philosophers had spoken of "essences" to identify regularities and order in the world, modern political philosophers spoke most often of the "laws of nature" when discussing observable patterns and causal relationships in the world. According to the subversive theology thesis, the very notion of divine creation of the universe places a Person above the "impersonal necessities" of nature, thereby radically subordinating and ultimately vitiating the possibility of rational knowledge of nature.[15] The ordering principle of a created universe would instead be a rationally inscrutable divine will. Spinoza is then one expression of the philosopher's attempt to give an account of nature that preserves the intelligibility and rationality of the world and therefore the very possibility of philosophy. On this account, the Declaration's philosophic appeal to the "Laws of Nature and of Nature's God" is a subtle way of emphasizing Nature and undercutting theological accounts of divine creation. The Spinozistic or philosophic doctrine of *Deus seu Natura*, Strauss suggested, deeply influenced John Locke.[16] This implied that the hidden intellectual source of "Nature's God" in the Declaration of Independence is Spinoza, inasmuch as the Declaration is deeply Lockean.

The subversive theology thesis has been taken up and defended in subsequent scholarship. In one of its most sophisticated defenses, Thomas Pangle identifies "Nature's God" with Locke's God and contends that Locke's key philosophical-theological doctrines were "virtually identical" with Spinoza's.[17] More recently, Matthew Stewart has argued that, inasmuch as Jefferson traded

---

[10] Leo Strauss, "Preface to Hobbes Politische Wissenschaft," *Interpretation: A Journal of Political Philosophy* 8 (1979): 1.

[11] Strauss, *Natural Right and History*, 1.   [12] Strauss, *Spinoza's Critique of Religion*, 177.

[13] Baruch Spinoza, *Ethics*, in Edwin Curley, ed. and trans., *The Collected Writings of Spinoza*, no. 1 (Princeton: Princeton University Press, 1985 [1677]), part IV, preface.

[14] Strauss, *Spinoza's Critique of Religion*, 149.

[15] Leo Strauss, "Progress or Return? The Contemporary Crisis in Western Civilization," *Modern Judaism* 1 (1981): 39–43.

[16] Strauss, *Natural Right and History*, 210–11.

[17] Pangle, *Spirit of Modern Republicanism*, 239, 304.

in Lockean metaphysical coin, it was with the dark money of Spinoza, and therefore the phrase "Nature's God" implies Spinozistic pantheism, which, Stewart tells us, is "really just a pretty word for atheism."[18]

3.2 JEFFERSON'S CREATIONAL METAPHYSICS

Contrary to the subversive theology thesis, we contend that Jefferson's natural theology represents a genuine attempt to synthesize elements of Epicurean materialism with a classical Christian metaphysics. A number of scholars have argued Jefferson was a theist.[19] Scholarship has tended to focus on the modern and rationalist Protestant influences on Jefferson's religious thought, such as Bolingbroke, Priestley, or other English deists. Others have noted the influence of the seventeenth-century French priest and philosopher Pierre Gassendi, albeit with scant discussion.[20] Because Jefferson was an eclectical thinker, it should not be surprising that we can trace various lines of influence on Jefferson's theology. Here we fill in a gap in the literature by showing important continuities between Jefferson's theology and the theism of classical Christian natural-law theory.

Jefferson constantly averred the doctrine of creation that God "called [man] into being."[21] Note that this is *not* a claim about the age of the world, or even a denial that the universe might be eternal. For his part, Jefferson thought that the empirical evidence of Virginia's landscape indicated eons of geological time and therefore the improbability of "young earth" creationism. The keystone of creational metaphysics is not about a temporal starting point but is rather about the existential dependence of the natural world on something outside the chain of material causes and effects. To be existentially dependent is to be insufficient to sustain one's own existence. The classical tradition holds that God alone stands outside finite causal chains and upholds all things in being. This implies that God is all powerful, because having complete power over nature is a feature of omnipotence. But God is not merely all powerful

---

[18] Stewart, *Nature's God*, 5.

[19] David Boorstin, *The Lost World of Thomas Jefferson* (New York: Henry & Holt, 1948); Charles B. Sanford, *The Religious Life of Thomas Jefferson* (Charlottesville: University of Virginia Press, 1984); Garrett Ward Sheldon and Daniel L. Dreisbach, *Religion and Political Culture in Jefferson's Virginia* (Lanham, MD: Rowman & Littlefield, 2000); Thomas Buckley, "The Religious Rhetoric of Thomas Jefferson," in Daniel L. Dreisbach, Mark D. Hall, and Jeffry H. Morrison, eds., *The Founders on God and Government* (Lanham, MD: Roman & Littlefield, 2004); Ellis Sandoz, *Republicanism, Religion, and the Soul of America* (Columbia: University of Missouri Press, 2006); Gregg L. Frazer, *The Religious Beliefs of America's Founders* (Lawrence: University of Kansas Press, 2012).

[20] Jean Yarbrough, *American Virtues: Thomas Jefferson and the Character of a Free People* (Lawrence: University of Kansas Press, 1998), 161–62.

[21] Merrill D. Peterson, ed., *Thomas Jefferson: Writings* (New York: Library of America, 1984), 1162.

according to the classical tradition. God is also just, and human justice is an imperfect participation in a divine order of justice.

Consistent with the attributes of the God of classical theism, Jefferson conjectures that a slave revolution would be possible in virtue of "nature and natural means only," but considering the injustice of slavery, Jefferson indicated it was *probable* by "supernatural interference" in virtue of God's omnipotence and justice.[22] Jefferson has of course been accused of atheism from the very beginnings of the republic, and many have been willing to write off theological claims such as these as mere rhetorical flourishes at odds with his deeper philosophical commitments. Accusations of atheism began with many of his contemporaries, including the famous attack by Theodore Dwight, an early leader of the Federalist Party and grandson of the prominent eighteenth-century American theologian Jonathan Edwards. Dwight's argument is of interest, because, like the subversive theology thesis, it suggests theism cannot be affirmed alongside materialism. Dwight's reasoning goes like this: Neither Jefferson nor any other person in history has ever discovered a material Supreme Being. Jefferson disclaims the existence of an immaterial Supreme Being. Therefore, Jefferson is an atheist.[23] It is Dwight's first premise that bears the weight of the syllogism, but upon closer examination, the argument buckles.

It is logically possible that one could affirm (a) the existence of a material Supreme Being while also holding that (b_1) the Supreme Being is not materially observable or (b_2) the Supreme Being has not yet been materially observed. In fact, Jefferson affirms (b_1), when he restates the classical position that we cannot have quidditative knowledge of God.[24] And yet, Jefferson affirms, deploying something like the *a posteriori* fifth way reasoning of Aquinas, that God must exist to explain the evident purposiveness in the natural world. Jefferson's partially reconstructed reasoning goes like this[25]:

1. The senses provide reliable information about the real world.
2. The presence of other bodies is apparent to the senses, which is called "matter."
3. Matter exists.
4. The senses apprehend matter changing place, an event that is called "motion."

[22] Ibid., 289.
[23] Theodore Dwight, *The Character of Thomas Jefferson, as Exhibited in His Own Writings* (Boston: Weeks, Jordan, 1839), 363.
[24] Lester J. Cappon, *The Adams-Jefferson Letters: The Complete Correspondence between Thomas Jefferson and Abigail and John Adams* (Chapel Hill: University of North Carolina Press, 1988), 592.
[25] Ibid., 458, 468, 562, and 592.

5. Motion exists.
6. Regularity in motion is observable that is "perfectly organized" to conduce to the good of the whole.
7. Therefore an intelligent and powerful Agent who orders the whole universe exists.
8. But motion is impossible without the contact of a body with another body.
9. Therefore the intelligent and powerful first cause must be material.

With the various French philosophes Diderot, D'Alembert, and D'Holbach, Jefferson affirmed materialism and mechanism, but against them he inferred the existence of a first cause. In *D'Alembert's Dream*, Diderot had laid out a materialistic and atheistic vision of the universe. Jefferson is not a Diderotian. Jefferson rather traces his creed to Locke, whom he apparently understood as a materialist theist.[26]

Modern materialistic theism can be traced from Thomas Hobbes, who labored mightily to wed materialism and theism, and from whose friend and fellow member of the Mersenne circle, Pierre Gassendi, Jefferson sought to glean genuine Epicurean doctrines to be published along the genuine or primitive doctrines of Christ. We do not dispute that Hobbes was a "subversive" theologian – and we do not pretend to resolve the ongoing scholarly dispute about whether Hobbes was really an atheist – but we maintain that it is at least plausible to read Hobbes as a theist whose "subversiveness" was not atheistic.[27] While Hobbes and Gassendi concurred as to the truth of both the new mechanistic science and the truth of theism, Hobbes differed from the latter in his thoroughgoing materialism. Alongside his atomistic physics, Gassendi had maintained that God and intellectual operation were immaterial. Yet, like Gassendi, Hobbes labored to synthesize a materialistic and mechanistic universe with a traditional conception of God as nonidentical with the universe, and the omnipotent, omnibenevolent, and omniscient creator of *all* things, including the substrate of the material world.[28]

While it has been pointed out that Locke was a successor to Hobbes and Gassendi in important ways, it has been often overlooked that Locke too affirmed existential dependence. Contemporary scholarship has demonstrated, minimally, that it is plausible to read Locke as a sincere theist.[29] For his part,

---

[26] Ibid. 562.
[27] Cf. A.P. Martinich, *The Two Gods of Leviathan: Thomas Hobbes on Religion and Politics* (New York: Cambridge University Press, 1992); Kody W. Cooper, *Thomas Hobbes and the Natural Law* (Notre Dame, IN: University of Notre Dame Press, 2018).
[28] Cf. Pierre Gassendi, *Opera Omnia* (Stuttgart: Fromman-Holzboog, 1964) [facsimile]): *Opera* I, 163, 234, 280. Still, Hobbes left the impression in the minds of many readers that "Hobbist" theology was radically voluntarist.
[29] Cf. John Dunn, *The Political Thought of John Locke: An Historical Account of the Argument of the "Two Treatises of Government"* (Cambridge: Cambridge University Press, 1969); Steve Forde, *Locke, Science and Politics* (New York: Cambridge University Press, 2013); Greg Forster,

Jefferson took Locke to be a materialist theist, and he defended this view as true to uncorrupted Christianity. Inasmuch as Jefferson's theism was framed by Lockean theology, it was framed by a creational metaphysic that expressed coyness about the age of the world, but which held that the world, whether eternal or not, was existentially dependent on God: "[T]here is nothing which He cannot make exist each moment He pleases. For the existence of all things, depending upon His good pleasure, all things exist every moment that He thinks fit to have them exist."[30]

Jefferson therefore might have cited Gassendi, Hobbes, or Locke when he suggested that an eternal universe was compatible with its createdness. Yet, Jefferson instead cites Thomas Aquinas's argument that there is no logical contradiction in an eternal and created world. Jefferson apparently had knowledge of Aquinas's teaching derivatively via the Salamanca school Jesuit, Francisco de Toledo (whose training in Thomism was under the noted Thomist Domingo de Soto, himself a student of the greatest Thomist of the sixteenth century, Francisco de Vitoria): "Some early Christians," Jefferson noted, "indeed have believed in the coeternal pre-existence of both the Creator and the world, without changing their relation of cause and effect. That this was the opinion of St. Thomas, we are informed by Cardinal Toleto …."[31]

Inspired by the new mechanical science, the early moderns rejected key doctrines of Aristotelian physics, and many sought to rehabilitate various doctrines of ancient materialism and, specifically, Epicureanism. Yet, those like Gassendi, Hobbes, and Locke sought to incorporate these doctrines within a creational metaphysic where God was the author of all being, including atoms or matter. In holding that there is no logical contradiction between creation and an eternal universe, they followed a path that had already been paved by early and medieval Christian thinkers, who sought to refute the claim that Aristotle's doctrine of an eternal universe was radically antithetical to theism. In *De Aeternitate Mundi*, Aquinas recalled the image offered by Augustine of the eternal foot in eternal dust.[32] An effect can be existentially dependent on a cause without a priority in time of cause to effect, just as a hypothetically eternal footprint could be existentially dependent on an eternal foot, even though there is no relationship of temporal priority. At some point, our categories begin to break down as we try to imagine what existed *before* time, but

John Locke's Politics of Moral Consensus (New York: Cambridge University Press, 2005); Jeremy Waldron, *God, Locke, Equality: Christian Foundations in Locke's Political Thought* (Cambridge: Cambridge University Press, 2002).

[30] John Locke, *An Essay Concerning Human Understanding*, ed. Peter H. Nidditch (Oxford: Oxford University Press 1975 [1690]), bk. II, ch. 15, par, 12.

[31] Cappon, *The Adams-Jefferson Letters*, 592–93.

[32] Augustine, *The City of God against the Pagans*, R. W. Dyson, ed. and trans. (Cambridge: Cambridge University Press, 2008), X.31, 441; Thomas Aquinas, *De Aeternitate Mundi*. Accessed June 18, 2021, from www.corpusthomisticum.org/ocm.html.

the point is that if time and the material world are both brought into being together, then there is no "past" (at least as we would understand it) when the world did not exist. Thus, Aquinas held that there was no logical contradiction in maintaining that the universe always existed *and* is existentially dependent on God. In this sense, God remains the Creator in that God caused, and continues to cause, the universe to exist, whether or not the universe is eternal.[33] The distinctive move of the moderns, which Jefferson follows, was to wed materialism with this kind of creationism. For Jefferson, then, creation by a providential, moralistic God is not antithetical to the eternal existence of matter. Some have misunderstood Jefferson on this point, presuming that materialism and creation are antithetical.[34]

So far we have suggested that Jefferson held there were theistic truths about the first cause that could be known by reason independent of faith. Jefferson draws out the implications of this point, arguing that fideist arguments that God's existence cannot be demonstrated by reason are misguided and that the profession of theistic belief of at least 1 million out of every 1 million and 1 people across human history counts in its favor. Jefferson's democratic faith is apparent here – but he explicitly denies that it is a Spinozistic democratic faith, for one of the reasons Jefferson gives for rejecting fideism's antiphilosophical-theology is precisely its effect of strengthening Spinoza and his disciples.[35]

Jefferson thus affirms the existential dependence of all finite things on a being who is not identical with the whole of finite things. Even at a key moment when Jefferson enunciates the philosophical first principle, deemed Epicurus' "dangerous idea" by Stewart – that *from nothing, nothing comes* – Jefferson presupposes the truth of creation. For Jefferson, the vanity of man denying that first principle is the equivalent of erasing "the original sentence of his maker" to labor for his food.[36] As Aquinas had explained, God could have created an eternal universe *ex nihilo*, without any logical contradiction.[37] Jefferson's inferences about God's existence and creation of the world then

---

[33] For his part, Aquinas held on the basis of revelation that the universe did in fact have a beginning in time. He denied that the universe was in fact eternal, but he did not think an eternal universe was logically incompatible with creation. G. K. Chesterton notes: "Aquinas says he sees no particular reason, in reason, why this world should not be a world without end; or even without beginning. And he is quite certain that, if it were entirely without end or beginning, there would still be exactly the same logical need of a Creator. Anybody who does not see that, he gently implies, does not really understand what is meant by a Creator." See G. K. Chesterton, *St. Thomas Aquinas: "The Dumb Ox"* (New York: Image Books, 2001 [1933]), 144.

[34] Owen, "The Struggle between 'Religion and Nonreligion,'" 499.

[35] Cappon, *The Adams-Jefferson Letters*, 592.

[36] J. Jefferson Looney, ed., *The Papers of Thomas Jefferson* (Princeton: Princeton University Press, 2011), vol. 9, 328–31.

[37] As Aquinas explains, God can create with instantaneous effect such that the cause need not precede the effect in the order of time. Moreover, an eternally created universe *ex nihilo* does not posit temporal priority of nonbeing to being, because "out of nothing" means not from any prior beings. See Aquinas, *De Aeternitate Mundi*.

inform his thought about the moral sense, natural equality, and the natural right of property, key touchstones of his natural-rights republicanism.

3.3 JEFFERSON'S MORAL SENSE

Writing to his daughter Martha, Jefferson explained the moral sense. Jefferson set up the lesson in light of a rebuke of millenarianism:

I hope you will have good sense enough to disregard those foolish predictions that the world is to be at an end soon. The almighty has never made known to any body at what time he created it, nor will he tell any body when he means to put an end to it, if ever he means to do it.[38]

Jefferson continued to instruct his daughter that the true way to be prepared for the last day is "never to do or say a bad thing." Jefferson explained that "Our maker has given us all [a] faithful internal Monitor," which, whenever one is about to say or do something wrong, will tell you that you ought not to do it. The faculty of conscience, Jefferson instructed, should always be obeyed as the only sure preparation for the end of the world.

In his classic study of Jefferson's moral sense, Garry Wills argued that Jefferson was influenced most by the Scottish moral-sense school, particularly the writings of Francis Hutcheson and Thomas Reid.[39] Still, Wills downplays the fact that Reid and Hutcheson affirmed the older Judeo-Christian and medieval structural claim that God implanted the moral sense.[40] Indeed, it is on the basis of the premise that the maker has given this monitor "to us all," in virtue of God's creation of all human beings, that Jefferson appeals to the judgments of common moral sense in his *Summary View* as having binding force. The Declaration's affirming of precepts knowable by reason cannot be understood apart from its affirmation of the existence and rule of Nature's God.

The conscience or moral sense is "as much a part of our constitution as that of feeling, seeing, or hearing; as a wise creator must have seen to be necessary in an animal destined to live in society."[41] As Jefferson goes on to explain, "The Creator would indeed have been a bungling artist, had he intended man for a social animal, without planting in him social dispositions." This is simply an observation that the directedness of man to live in society is evidence of wise

[38] Julian P. Boyd, *The Papers of Thomas Jeffersonc* (Princeton: Princeton University Press, 1951), vol. 6, 380.

[39] Gary Wills, *Inventing America: Jefferson's Declaration of Independence* (New York: Double Day, 1978), 167–206.

[40] See Francis Hutcheson, *An Inquiry into the Original of Our Ideas of Beauty and Virtue*, ed. Wolfgang Leidhold (Indianapolis, IN: Liberty Fund, 2004 [1726]), §7.2; Thomas Reid, *Essays on the Active Powers of Man*, ed. Knud Haakonssen and James A. Harris (Edinburgh: Edinburgh University Press, 2010 [1788]), essay III, pt. III, ch. 7.

[41] Cappon, *The Adams-Jefferson Letters*, 492.

workmanship, of the "care of the Creator," flowing naturally from a mind convinced of the existential dependence of all finite things.[42] As Dewey notes, Jefferson summarized his democratic faith in the following syllogism: "Man was created for social intercourse; but social intercourse cannot be maintained without a sense of justice; then man must have been created with a sense of justice."[43]

Jefferson considers two common objections to his belief that God implants a moral sense into all men. The first is the empirical fact that there exist persons without a moral sense. There are sociopaths in the world. Jefferson believed that Napoleon was a prime example of a sociopath. Napoleon was a "moral monster" who had retarded French progress toward enlightened government and whose destruction of millions of lives proved that "nature had denied him the moral sense, the first excellence of well organized man."[44] But if nature – which for Jefferson is God's art – generates sociopaths, then how can the moral sense be "natural"? In answer to this objection, Jefferson sounds like a classical natural lawyer:

It is true that [the moral sense is] not planted in every man, because there is no rule without exceptions; but it is false reasoning which converts exceptions into the general rule. Some men are born without organs of sight, or of hearing, or without hands. Yet it would be wrong to say that man is born without these faculties, and sight, hearing, and hands may with truth enter into the general definition of man. The want or imperfection of the moral sense in some men, like the want or imperfection of the sense of sight and hearing in others, is no proof that it is a general characteristic of the species.[45]

In other words, to say that conscience is "natural" does not mean that it obtains without exception in every member of the human species. It is rather that it obtains in all *properly functioning* human beings. In classical natural-law theory, the proper functioning of organisms is understood in terms of the proper functioning of each of its parts for the good of whole. Animals, including human animals, are in turn seen as parts within a larger cosmic whole that is itself imbued with purpose.

Jefferson expresses such a view when he unequivocally avows a teleological conception of the universe:

I hold (without appeal to revelation) that when we take a view of the Universe, in it's parts general or particular, it is impossible for the human mind not to perceive and feel a conviction of design, consummate skill, and indefinite power in every atom of it's composition.[46]

[42] Looney, *The Papers of Thomas Jefferson*, 412.
[43] Robert Ginsburg, *A Casebook on the Declaration of Independence* (New York: Thomas Y. Crowell, 1967), 164; John Dewey, *The Later Works of John Dewey*, ed. Jo Ann Boydston, intro. Steven M. Cahn (Carbondale, IL: Southern Illinois University Press, 1998), vol. 13, 179.
[44] Cappon, *The Adams-Jefferson Letters*, 589.
[45] Looney, *The Papers of Thomas Jefferson*, 414.
[46] Cappon, *The Adams-Jefferson Letters*, 592.

Gordon-Reed and Onuf note that according to Jefferson, God did "reveal providential purposes to enlightened observers who discerned the lawful properties and intelligent design of his creation."[47] Jefferson's teleology doubtless is closely tied to his empirical and scientific bent of mind. He cites the movements of the heavenly bodies, the geographical structure of the earth, and the configuration of vegetable and animal bodies. Regarding the latter, in a parallel passage in an earlier letter to Adams, Jefferson describes the "palpable existence of final causes" evidenced in bodily organs such as the eye and the ear. The function of the eye is to see; the function of the ears is to hear. Jefferson thought these proofs of intrinsic teleology in the universe were "obvious to the senses" and sufficient to answer deniers of teleology, just as getting up and walking across the room is sufficient to refute the denier of motion.[48]

God fashions the moral sense in man to orient him to life in society with others. As in Aristotelian-Thomistic political thought, man's telos is a kind of flourishing that cannot be achieved outside of membership in society. And in common with Thomistic political thought, God's creative act impresses this purposiveness upon man. This is the frame within which Jefferson understood the Lockean theory of natural rights. As Vincent Phillip Muñoz notes within a recent discussion of the founders' conception of the natural right to religious freedom, Jefferson's moral philosophy assumes that "God created nature (including human nature) and that this created nature establishes moral guidelines for human behavior."[49]

Because Jefferson's moral instinct grasps natural-law precepts, it can be compared to Aquinas's *synderesis*, or what might be called deep conscience. For Aquinas, synderesis is a fundamental habit of first principles, and the most basic principle of practical reason is that good is to be done and evil is to be avoided. What this means is that human persons are ordered to the good in general for the purpose of their integral flourishing. This is "habitual," because, although reason grasps human goods and appoints the precepts of morality, one may or may not reflect upon the first principles as first principles.

Aquinas draws an analogy to the theoretical order, which is governed by the first principle of noncontradiction. We have an intuitive and implicit grasp of being (and therefore the principle of noncontradiction) when we compose and divide, when we assert and deny. But we usually do not reflect on the principle of noncontradiction in mundane affirmations and negations. Similarly, we have an intuitive grasp of good as that which is fulfilling, completive, or perfective when we wish, desire, want, will, and the like. Every person has minimally a general and confused knowledge of being and goodness as governors of the

---

[47] Gordon-Reed and Onuf, *"Most Blessed of the Patriarchs,"* 281.

[48] Cappon, *The Adams-Jefferson Letters*, 468.

[49] Vincent Phillip Muñoz, "Two Concepts of Religious Liberty: The Natural Rights and Moral Autonomy Approaches to the Free Exercise of Religion," *American Political Science Review*, 110 (2016): 3.

theoretical and practical orders. Aquinas's claim is that there is an essential core of goods that is common to all human beings – goods including bodily life and health, family and child-rearing, friendship (including civic friendship), knowledge, and religion (according one's will with God's) – in that they are desirable objects of pursuit for all persons. *Synderesis* is thus a habitual rather than intellectual grasp of human goods and a virtuous way of life.

In this context, let us recall a key passage of a letter from Jefferson to Adams explaining his view of conscience:

> Man was destined for society. His morality, therefore, was to be formed to this object. He was endowed with a sense of right and wrong merely relative to this. This sense is as much as part of his nature as the sense of hearing, seeing, feeling; it is the true foundation of morality .... It is given to all human beings in a stronger or weaker degree, as force of members is given them in a greater or less degree. It may be strengthened by exercise, as may any particular limb of the body. The sense is submitted, indeed, in some degree, to the guidance of reason; but it is a small stock which is required for this; even a less one than what we call common sense. State a moral case to a ploughman and a professor. The former will decide it as well and often better than the latter because he has not been led astray by artificial rules.[50]

From these and other passages so far quoted, we can see that Jefferson's difference from Aquinas and the classical natural-law tradition is not in the divine pedigree of conscience, nor the orientation of human beings toward happiness, nor in the social character of that orientation. Insofar as Jefferson's understanding of happiness was a Gassendist notion of tranquility, it was essentially a eudaimonist conception whose contrast with the Aristotelian-Thomistic ideal of rational self-mastery is more stylized than substantive.[51]

Even so, one might object that Jefferson's conception of the moral sense is distinguished from the classical tradition in that it raises sentiment above reason. This is a fair objection. Although Jefferson is at times equivocal about the relative priority of sentiment and reason in his epistemology, many of his references do prioritize moral sentiments over intellectually derived moral principles. We also know that Jefferson read and was deeply influenced by Henry Home, Lord Kames,[52] and there are strong linkages between Jefferson's moral philosophy and the Scottish moral sense school. Even here, however, the break with the classical tradition is not as stark as one would think. Although Jefferson ascribes some degree of autonomy to the moral sense to operate independent of rational inquiry, he appears to be thinking of abstract theoretical reasoning. The "small stock" of reason would then refer to theoretical or

---

[50] Julian P. Boyd, ed., *The Papers of Thomas Jefferson* (Princeton: Princeton University Press, 1955), vol. 12, 15.

[51] Cf. Lisa T. Sarasohn, *Gassendi's Ethics* (Ithaca, NY: Cornell University Press, 1996).

[52] Allen Jayne, *Jefferson's Declaration of Independence: Origins, Philosophy and Theology* (Lexington: University Press of Kentucky, 1998), 62–86.

philosophical training. If correct, Jefferson is not denying that, as rational animals, human powers are informed by reason in its practical function. Jefferson's moral sense is the medium of natural-law precepts, implanted by God, in virtue of which the act of conscience binds or morally obligates,[53] and Jefferson's scorn for the professor and preference for the humble ploughman indicates a deeper agreement with Aquinas about connatural moral knowledge.

According to Jefferson, the God of Nature creates human beings with a moral sense. It is precisely in virtue of that divine pedigree that the principles of moral common sense entail obligation. For Jefferson, the Laws of Nature and of Nature's God are what bind kings and parliaments and men to respect natural rights. The Declaration is part of what Elizabeth Anscombe called the "law tradition of ethics," because it rests on providential, moralistic theism.[54] The classical tradition saw no contradiction between the freedom and omnipotence of God and essences or laws of nature, just as there is no contradiction between God's absolute power and God's ordained power as manifested in nature. It thus turns out to be quite significant that Jefferson cites Aquinas in favor of Gassendi, Hobbes, or Locke on existential dependence, the latter of whose accounts of God's power were voluntaristic, virtually eliminating essential forms from their ontology and subjecting the laws of nature to the divine whim.[55] These theistic foundations of Jefferson's thought have important implications for his understanding of natural equality and the natural right to property.

3.4 JEFFERSON'S LOCKEAN, THEISTIC FOUNDATION FOR EQUALITY AND LIBERTY

Although various commentators have wondered at Jefferson's exclusion of the natural right of property from the Declaration, he did adhere to a Lockean understanding of property rights.[56] Yet, we would go further and argue that Jefferson adopts Locke's theistic account of human equality and property. To show this, we will first set forth reasons for concluding that Locke's theories of equality and property are theistic. In a recent article, Adam Seagrave demonstrates that Locke's affirmation of self-ownership constitutes no difficulty for the theistic interpretation, because a human being can be the concurrent

---

[53] Julian P. Boyd, ed., *The Papers of Thomas Jefferson* (Princeton: Princeton University Press, 1958), vol. 15, 363.

[54] G. E. M. Anscombe, "Modern Moral Philosophy," *Philosophy* 33 (1958): 5.

[55] Cf. Margaret J. Osler, *Divine Will and Mechanical Philosophy: Gassendi and Descartes on Contingency and Necessity in the Created World* (Cambridge: Cambridge University Press, 1994).

[56] See, e.g., Michael P. Zuckert, "Thomas Jefferson on Nature and Natural Rights," in Robert A. Licht, ed., *The Framers and Fundamental Rights* (Washington, DC: American Enterprise Institute Press, 1991), 158–63.

property of himself and God with the latter having a higher dignity precisely in virtue of man's existential dependence on God.[57] Our argument moves beyond this initial hurdle and focuses on Locke's theory of property in light of his critique of patriarchalism and shows how nontheistic accounts of Locke's argument are subject to a devastating *reductio ad absurdum*. We will then turn to consider how Locke's theory may illuminate Jefferson's revolutionary natural-rights republicanism.

3.4.1 Locke's Theistic Theory of Property and His Critique of Robert Filmer

Locke put forward what might be called an extensional theory of property, which he developed to show "how men might come to have a property in several parts of that which God gave to mankind in common, and that without any express compact of all the commoners."[58] The coassumptions of fundamental equality (and therefore equal ownership) and liberty (and therefore the individual right of acquiring and keeping property) are manifest. In order to understand the essential role of God in Locke's interlocking theories of property and equality, it is important to read the *Second Treatise* in conjunction with Chapter VI of the *First Treatise*. To recall, Locke's critique of Filmer's patriarchalism in the *First Treatise* proceeds in two broad stages. In the first stage, Locke takes on the various arguments Filmer gives to prove Adam's regal sovereignty, and therefore natural subjection.[59] In the second stage, Locke considers the "conveyance" of Adam's sovereignty to future kings.[60] Locke's presentation in the first stage is logically divided in two chief parts that group Filmer's different arguments together based on their kind. In the first chief part, Locke takes on arguments for paternal-regal authority based on divine positive right, and hence consists primarily in biblical argumentation. In the second chief part, Locke considers arguments for paternal-regal authority by natural right and is constituted primarily by philosophical argumentation, or argumentation proceeding by premises derived from reason. It is this latter part of Locke's argument that concerns us here.

When Locke turns to consider Filmer's case for patriarchalism on the basis of natural right, he signals not only the great importance of defeating the argument but also recalls what is at stake. Filmer contended that Adam and his heirs are kings by right of fatherhood, which is to say, human beings by their very birth are fettered. Locke remarks that Filmer so frequently mentions this argument that it should be considered "the main Basis of all his Frame" and

---

[57] S. Adam Seagrave, "Self-Ownership vs. Divine Ownership: A Lockean Solution to a Liberal Democratic Dilemma," *American Journal of Political Science* 55 (2011): 710–23.

[58] John Locke, *Two Treatises of Government*, ed. Peter Laslett (Cambridge: Cambridge University Press, 1988 [1690]), II.25.

[59] Ibid., I.15–I.77.   [60] Ibid., I.78–I.169.

is the "Foundation of all [patriarchalist] Doctrine."[61] Locke's language recalls the building metaphor he used before in I.6 where he indicated that the doctrine of natural liberty and equality was staked on the refutation of Filmer. Locke then restates the mutually exclusive alternatives, and for the first time since I.6 explicitly affirms his own rival doctrine in the first person: "If all men are not, as I think they are, naturally equal, I'm sure all Slaves are."[62] Having been begotten by one's father *either makes one a slave* or *it does not*. If it can be shown that it does not, then the road is open for natural freedom and equality.

Locke's editor and proponents of the subversive theology thesis have misunderstood, downplayed, or overlooked the significance of Chapter VI of the *First Treatise*.[63] Chapter VI is important for understanding Locke's argumentative strategy, but not only for that. Locke signals that in this chapter he will advance arguments whose *content* is of critical importance to the integrity of the whole argument of the *Two Treatises*. By considering Filmer's argument for "natural right of dominion over his children," Locke is tacitly pointing us ahead toward the *Second Treatise*, where he will lay out his own doctrine of equal natural rights and largely proceed by philosophical argumentation.

What is implicit at the beginning of Chapter VI becomes explicit toward the end of the chapter when Locke summarizes his arguments against Filmer and then asserts fundamental liberty and equality in language almost identical to that used in the *Second Treatise*.[64] Locke is laying the groundwork for his theory of natural rights in this chapter – in particular, his doctrine of property as distinct from fatherhood. The arguments made here will justify his claim that property and fatherhood are as different as "lord of a manor and a father of children."[65] That Locke intends us to read Chapter VI of the *First Treatise* in conjunction with Chapter V in the *Second Treatise* he signals again at the beginning of the latter, when he begins by restating his arguments regarding divine positive right that he makes against Filmer, recalling the two-part structure of stage 1 in the *First Treatise*.[66] The groundwork Locke lays in Chapter VI of the *First Treatise* consists in showing that the relationship of parents to their children is not one of proprietor to property by virtue of the former having generated the latter.

Filmer's axiom of natural parental right is *generatione jus acquiritur parentibus in liberos* (by generation a right over children is acquired by parents). Filmer takes this axiom to imply a proprietary dominion of fathers over their

---

[61] Ibid., I.50–51.   [62] Ibid., I.51.

[63] Ibid., I.52–55; cf. Strauss, *Natural Right and History*, 218, n. 75; Michael P. Zuckert, "An Introduction to Locke's First Treatise," *Interpretation: A Journal of Political Philosophy* 8 (1979): 62; Harvey Mansfield, "On the Political Character of Property in Locke," in Alkis Kontos, ed. *Powers, Possessions, and Freedom: Essays in Honor of C.B. Macpherson* (Toronto: University of Toronto Press, 1979), 29–32; Nathan Tarcov, *Locke's Education for Liberty* (Chicago: University of Chicago Press, 1984), 57–59, 66–69; Ross J. Corbett, "Locke's Biblical Critique," *The Review of Politics* 74 (2012); Stewart, *Nature's God*, 357–58.

[64] Ibid., I.67, cf. II.6.   [65] Ibid., I.73.   [66] Ibid., II.25.

children – but does not explain why. Locke thus sets out to grapple with the argument that fathers have patriarchal dominion over their children in virtue of giving them "life and being."[67] Locke goes on to indicate that the truth of this principle or argument is really the heart of his dispute with patriarchalism, because of the weight it bears and because of what its falsity would entail.

This is the *only proof it is capable of*: since there can be no reason, why naturally one man should have any claim or pretense of right over that in another, which was never his, and which he bestowed not, but was received from the bounty of another.[68]

Locke is tacitly pointing us to his extensional theory of property. According to Locke, if something is a *part* of you, then it is *your property*. The first or most basic parts of a person are his *material parts*, which is to say, his bodily parts. While one's material parts can change over time, Locke holds that consciousness unites one's shifting material parts, as well as one's actions, over time into one person. Thus, as a conscious thinking being, one can justifiably take ownership of his material parts and his actions as constituting his person.[69] Therefore, "man has a *property* in his own *person*: this no body has any right to but himself."[70] But one can *extend* one's person by transformative acts of one's intelligence and body performed on things in nature, which Locke calls labor of the body or work of the hands. This is how commonly held things are removed from the common stock and placed under the private dominion of a person.

When Locke's extensionalist account of property is read in conjunction with the first treatise, we are faced with a puzzle. Why do parents not appropriate the product of their reproductive labor? After all, if the parties to a reproductive union own their own persons, would not any product created by the joining of their reproductive parts – which they own – be, by that very fact, their *property*? Moreover, why wouldn't the mother have an equal, "if not the greater" share by virtue of her disproportionate share of the labor, which includes a literal extension of her person, "nourishing the child a long time in her own body out of her own substance?"[71] The stakes are therefore quite high in this chapter. Locke must refute the claim that children are owned by virtue of their birth, if he is to open the path for his own thesis of natural liberty and equality. But his own doctrines of personhood, labor, and property would, at least initially, appear to entail joint parental ownership or even maternal dominion, a kind of matriarchalism.

Robert Nozick contends that there are four options by which Locke can forestall patriarchalist or matriarchalist child ownership on his own terms: by holding that (1) there is something intrinsic to persons barring them from being owned by their makers; (2) some conditions within the theory of property rights excludes reproductive labor from the forms of labor that yield ownership; (3)

---

[67] Ibid., I.51.   [68] Ibid., I.51.
[69] Locke, *An Essay Concerning Human Understanding*, II.27.9–18.
[70] Locke, *Two Treatises of Government*, II.27.   [71] Ibid., I.55.

something about parents bars them from standing in the relevant ownership relation; or (4) parents do not really make their children.[72] Nozick's suggestion is that there might be a "secular" solution to the dilemma – that is, a solution that does not rely on theological premises whether natural or revealed.

Although a mother's body immediately nourishes the product of the reproductive labor in gestation – a process and burden with which Locke was intimately familiar as when he was the primary physician for a woman with a high-risk pregnancy – Locke insists that this labor does not grant a maternal or parental title of ownership. The question is why. Notice how option (1), without further specification, is denied by Locke himself if we take his theology to play an essential role in his thought. To be an *imago Dei* does not per se shield one from being owned, because by that very fact one is owned by God. To posit a purely secular, Lockean intrinsic dignity is therefore begging the question. What about option (2)? Perhaps some condition of property acquisition excludes the products of reproductive labor from ownership, but the limiting condition cannot simply be an exclusion from property of products that issue from reproductive labor without committing the fallacy of special pleading.

The third option is also unpromising on Locke's terms. Paternity, Locke tells us in the *Essay*, is a *relation*. Relations are "mixed modes," as distinct from "simple modes," in that they are combinations of distinct ideas simple or complex. The idea of "paternity" is clear, according to Locke, in that it picks out a relationship between a father and his children, and this is easy to conceive – easier to conceive of than the father or the children themselves.[73] Yet the relation father-son is "very obvious to every one" just to the extent that it considers a specific relation between two substances, and nothing more.[74] To give *cause* the name *father* is simply to signify that he has a child. But we do not yet know what, if any, rights over that child he has just by calling him a father. So we are thrown back to considering whether patriarchalism is true.

Filmer's argument can be restated as a *modus ponens*: If there are givers of life and being, then the givers have dominion over the recipients. Locke's reply is *not* to deny the antecedent, for his theory of property implicitly accepts it, and at any rate such a reply would be logically fallacious. Locke's reply rather is a version of (4): *human beings* do not bestow life and being on their offspring. The patriarchalists are so "dazzled" by monarchy that they have forgotten that God is the maker of all things: "*the author and giver of life; it is in him alone we live, move, and have our being.*"[75]

In this biblical citation of Acts 17:28, Locke echoes the classical Judeo-Christian metaphysic of existential dependence and introduces what will

---

[72] Robert Nozick, *Anarchy, State, Utopia* (New York: Basic Books, 2013), 432–33.
[73] Locke, *An Essay Concerning Human Understanding*, bk. II, ch. 25, §.8.   [74] Ibid., II.25.2
[75] Locke, *Two Treatises*, I.52.

become an important theological ground for basic liberty and equality in the *Second Treatise*: the divine workmanship thesis.[76] Neither fathers nor mothers nor both jointly own their children because *God* made them, and, therefore, God owns them. By positing God as an extrinsic source of life and being, Locke indicates that a transcendent being is the source of and preserver of the act of existence. Hence, if prospective parents really wanted to own their offspring, they would need

to give life to that which has yet not being, [which] is to frame and make a living creature, fashion the parts, and mould and suit them to their uses, and having proportioned and fitted them together to put into them a living soul.[77]

God's fatherhood "utterly excludes all pretense of title in earthly parents."[78] Locke then issues a stinging indictment of philosophy's and medicine's failure to discover the source or principle of life in creatures.[79] If even the greatest scientists and philosophers cannot unlock the secret of – and therefore ability to manufacture – life, then no one can claim to have *made* it simply by participating in the process of generation. Because God is the sole author of being, the reproductive process *itself* is existentially dependent. While aspects of Locke's theory of property are innovative, the idea of divine ownership is in continuity with classical natural law, where God is said to be *dominus* of all persons.[80] Locke's theological premise of divine workmanship is thus essential to grounding his theory of property – for without it, his entire criticism of patriarchalism would collapse. Absent the limiting principle of divine workmanship, a radical denial of natural liberty and equality would be entailed by Locke's extensionalist theory of property, for all parents would then have absolute dominion over the products of their reproductive labor. The consequence of denying the essential role of God in Locke's theory of property is serious. If, as Locke insists, the right to use all "inferior creatures ... which were serviceable to his subsistence" was possessed *prior* to God's verbal donation and specification, then we would have to ask a troubling question: Why should children or infants be excluded from the set of inferior creatures serviceable to one's subsistence? It is not a gratuitous example for Locke. He relates Garcilaso de la Vega's report of child cannibalism in his *Commentarios Reales de Peru* in gruesome detail. This is not mere sensationalism as Laslett suggests. Such a practice would be within parental property rights without the theological limiting condition. Interpretations of Locke's theism as merely exoteric, such as those offered by proponents of the subversive theology thesis, entail the nullification of the refutation of Filmer and a logical sanctioning of child cannibalism, which would reduce the argument to absurdity.

[76] Ibid., II.6, I.53.　　[77] Ibid., I.53.　　[78] Ibid., I.53.　　[79] Ibid., I.52.
[80] Thomas Aquinas, *Summa Theologica*, trans. Fathers of the English Dominican Province (Chicago: Encyclopedia Britannica, 1952), I–II.94.5, ad. 2.

3.4.2 Jefferson's Lockean Theory of Property and Intergenerational Independence

Given the limiting principle supplied by Locke's theism, it would certainly have been plausible for Jefferson to read Locke's theory of property as theistic. How then might this account illuminate Jefferson's own understanding of "created equal"? Throughout his career, Jefferson expressed belief in the natural right of property. From his proposal of the primogeniture and education bills in the Virginia legislature, to the *Summary View*, to Jefferson's diplomatic mission, through his service under the Federalist administrations and his presidency, the right of property is supposed as a matter of course. In Lockean fashion, Jefferson held that government operated justly when "restraining no man in the pursuits of honest industry, & securing to every one the property which that acquires."[81] This is not to suggest that Jefferson did not also see grave danger for republics in conditions of massive disparity of property. But he always rejected equal distribution of property as unjust, and labored to secure property rights from the encroachments of arbitrary force, from British parliamentarians to Barbary pirates.

In a remarkable letter penned amid the fervor of revolutionary France, Jefferson declared *the earth belongs in usufruct to the living*. Influential scholarly readings of this letter have suggested it was "resolutely secular."[82] But, as we have seen, Jefferson disavowed adoption of the atheistic theses of the French philosophes, which he identified with Spinozistic pantheism.[83] It seems fitting, then, to reread Jefferson's revolutionary republican theory of liberty and equality in this letter in light of his professed theistic commitments. Because Jefferson rejected pantheism, his references to "nature" in this letter should be read as synecdoche, for nature is the order that God created and through which God acts.

Jefferson and Locke agree that human beings are born to political equality in that they are subject to the rightful rule of their parents before coming of age. Coming of age, they are equal in their rights to acquire property and incur debts. Jefferson asserts that individuals cannot contract debts for more than thirty-four years while nineteen years is the maximum beyond which a *community* can contract a debt. Otherwise, the present generation could mortgage the wealth of the next to fund their profligacy today. This would violate the rights over their soil, which come not from their predecessors but from God. Once the majority of the ruling generation dies, they cease to have authority to bind "the

---

[81] Thomas Jefferson, "Sixth Annual Message to Congress, December 2, 1806," The Avalon Project, Yale Law School. Accessed July 12, 2021, from https://avalon.law.yale.edu/19th_century/jeffmes6.asp

[82] Herbert Sloan, "The Rights of the Living Generation: Jefferson and the Public Debt," *Philosophy and Public Policy* 13 (1993): 21.

[83] Cappon, *The Adams-Jefferson Letters*, 592.

persons and property [that] make the sum of the objects of government."[84] To permit this, including attempted enforcement of any law older than nineteen years, "is an act of force and not of right," like one independent nation trying to force its will on another.[85] This would violate the law of nature that is truly *law* and is promulgated through the moral sense.

Jefferson thus extends Locke's critique of patriarchalism in the family and monarchy to intergenerational patriarchalism in democracy. God's gift of the land to the usufruct of the living entails that parents cannot collectively bind their children to pay for the parents' own greed or avarice. The concupiscent patriarchal generation stands in a state of nature relation to the "living generation" and violates the law of nature in its violent force. This is deeply theistically Lockean, for God creates every generation equally and authors the law that binds persons to respect equality. Thus, it is God's ownership of the living generation that forbids the patriarchal generation from enslaving it to pay for its debts.

Contrary to the subversive theology thesis, this natural-rights conception of republican government is antithetical to Spinozistic pantheism.[86] Because *Deus seu Nautura* has a sovereign right to all things, it follows that the parts that constitute *Deus seu Nautura* (individuals) have rights coextensive with their power. In a Spinozistic state of nature, there is no sin or wrong, and the only limit to acquisition and disposal of property is power.[87] Whereas Spinozistic pantheism would justify patriarchal power in the intergenerational state of nature as "right," Jefferson's Lockean-theistic account of equality and property condemns it as force without right. This is the logical ground upon which Jeffersonian democratic theory condemns all violations of natural human rights as unreasonable, because such justifications are always logically incompatible with God's authorship of natural rights.

3.5 CONCLUSION

Some might object that we should not take at face value Jefferson's explanation of the divine pedigree of conscience, the precepts of natural law, and his theological professions to Adams, for he may conceal his skepticism even in his private letters.[88] Indeed, it might be argued that such letters are paternal

---

[84] Merrill D. Peterson, *Thomas Jefferson: Writings* (New York: Library of America, 1984), 963.
[85] Ibid., 963.   [86] Cf. Stewart, *Nature's God*, 357–58.
[87] Baruch Spinoza, *Theologico-Political Treatise*, ed. and trans. Martin Yaffe (Cambridge, MA: Focus Philosophical Library, 2004 [1670]), ch. XVI.
[88] Cf. Christopher Hitchens, *Thomas Jefferson: Author of America* (New York: Harper-Collins, 2009), 182; Pangle, *Spirit of Modern Republicanism*, 289, n. 17; Michael P. Zuckert, *The Natural Rights Republic: Studies in the Foundation of the American Political Tradition* (Notre Dame, IN: University of Notre Dame Press, 1996), 87–89.

cajolery on par with the alleged "noble lies" advanced by Jefferson throughout his career – a sort of surface message or impression that conceals deeper atheistic beliefs and intentions. In this vein, Arthur Melzer has recently suggested Jefferson was engaged in political esotericism, a project to actualize a harmony between reason and political life through "gradual subversion of traditional society and its replacement with a philosophically grounded politics."[89]

Doubtless Jefferson had faith in the progress of reason and science – but it is doubtful that he cloaked his skepticism or atheism in his letters to Adams. In one letter from which we already quoted, Jefferson bluntly denounces belief in the Trinity as absurd tri-theism and accuses Calvin of atheism. Jefferson even goes so far as to say that the Incarnation and the Virgin Birth will be classed as a fable on par with Jupiter's generation of Minerva from his brain. The concealment thesis supposes that the *really* naughty thing is Jefferson's atheistic belief as if classing the vast majority of American Christians with polytheistic paganism were a safe exoteric teaching.

The burden of proof is on the interpreter who would reduce Jefferson's providential-moralistic theism to intentional deception, whatever its alleged purpose. Yet there is strong evidence that Jefferson shared in the general consensus of the colonists, that Nature's God symbolically expressed providential, moralistic theism as the essential foundation of natural rights precisely in virtue of God's creation of nature. Even as he seeks to transcend and improve upon what he takes to be the superstitions of a corrupted Christianity, Jefferson nevertheless retains a natural theology that is in important respects consistent with and derived from the classical tradition. For Jefferson, Nature's God is not the god of philosophical pantheism in which *Deus seu Natura* is indistinguishable from an uncreated and eternal universe. The structure of the Declaration, even in Jefferson's own initial draft, depends for its force and coherence on the notion that "all men are created equal" and "from that equal creation they derive rights inherent & inalienable."[90]

It is striking that, for all of Jefferson's private and idiosyncratic religious beliefs that constituted his "sect by himself," he still affirmed the core essentials of classical Christian natural-law theory broadly affirmed in revolutionary era public theology: There is an omnipotent and omnibenevolent first cause and creator of all things. This created order was imbued with a purpose that reason discerns. As we have seen so far, for the founders, human orientation toward

---

[89] Arthur M. Melzer, *Philosophy between the Lines: The Lost History of Esoteric Writing* (Chicago: University of Chicago Press, 2014), 235–36.

[90] Boyd, *The Papers of Thomas Jefferson*, vol. 1, 243–47. Owen Anderson helpfully underscores that the rights in the Declaration rest on a claim of the self-evidence of our equal creation, something not often emphasized in the scholarship on the political theory of the Declaration. See Anderson, *The Declaration of Independence and God*, 14.

the achievement of natural human goods entailed corresponding natural rights and duties. But even if the evidence indicates that the founders affirmed a broadly classical, theistic natural-law theory of morality, it is not immediately apparent how these principles might translate into politics, and specifically, the question of the justifiability of the American revolution, or, for that matter, any revolution – a question to which we turn in the next chapter.

4

Reason, Revelation, and Revolution

Was the American revolutionary argument justifiable on classical, Christian natural law, and just war principles? This question is not merely of quaint historical interest but has been the subject of scholarly discussion in recent years on the basis of Thomistic natural law and just war principles.[1] Moreover, there has been renewed scholarly interest in the debate between the patriots and the loyalists over whether resistance can be justified on biblical grounds. In this chapter, we argue that the American Revolution was justifiable on the grounds of Thomistic jurisprudence. We then turn to reconsider the case for revolution in light of Christian Scripture with particular attention to how Romans 13 was interpreted in the Christian tradition and in the American colonies.

According to classical Christian natural-law principles, a range of conditions must be met in order for a war to be just. Revolution can be justified on classical natural-law principles if the conditions of just war are met. First, there must be a just cause, which is triggered by a sufficiently evil tyranny. Second, there must be a right intention animating a group of actors resisting who can act authoritatively on behalf of the people and who intend to establish just authority. Third, there must be a reasonable chance of success in defeating the tyrant and establishing new authority. Fourth, the actors must exhaust peaceful measures and engage in war only as a last resort. Fifth, the war must be fought avoiding unjust violence (such as deliberately targeting innocents). And sixth, the good sought for the political whole must outweigh the evil they will suffer.[2] The first

---

[1] See John Keown, "America's War of Independence: Just or Unjust?" *Journal of Catholic Social Thought* 6(2)(2009), 277–304.

[2] For this summary of Thomistic principles of justified revolution, we are indebted to Michael P. Krom's recent discussion. See Michael Krom, *Justice and Charity: An Introduction to Aquinas's Moral, Economic, and Political Thought* (Grand Rapids, MI: Baker Academic, 2020), 144–51.

through sixth conditions deserve more discussion than we can give here. It is at least plausible that they could have been met. The actuality of success of course implies its plausibility in retrospect. While the Americans could be accused of committing unjust acts of violence during wartime, this need not necessarily have been the case and proportionality could nonetheless have been judged to weigh in favor of revolution.[3] In other words, one could reasonably judge that the good of going to war outweighed the evils that would accompany it. The first condition is perhaps the most difficult condition to consider. Was the metropolis sufficiently tyrannical to justify resistance and eventually revolution?

Paul Johnson is probably correct in his assessment during the years of the pamphlet debates that "it would be hard to think of a more dismal succession of nonentities" who led the British government.[4] Yet even stubborn persistence in imprudent policy by incompetent statesmen does not necessarily rise to the level of a sufficiently evil tyranny warranting revolution, especially if those policies were lawful. Hence, scholars such as Jack P. Greene and John Phillip Reid are correct to point our attention to the importance of argumentation over legal-constitutional matters such as representation and the distribution of power in the empire.

In classical natural-law theory, proper authority is an essential feature of law. In Aquinas' expression of this principle, authority in the human realm is proper when exercised by the whole people or a vicegerent of the whole people.[5] Some twentieth-century Thomists such as Jacques Maritain, Yves Simon, and Michael Novak have found in this passage a principle of democratic legitimacy. On the other hand, careful readers of Aquinas such as John Hittinger have argued that the passage is entirely compatible with a range of constitutional arrangements, including hereditary monarchy, and does not at all necessitate what modern democratic theory would take to be an essential mechanism of representation such as one person, one vote. Suppose for the sake of argument that the latter, more conservative reading is the correct one and that in the classical Christian natural-law tradition, the charge of proper authority to take care of the common good must include "representation" at least in the broad sense of genuine intention of the ruler to protect and foster the people's rights, interests, and well-being. The Americans' legal-constitutional case for revolution would in that case still be in deep continuity with a conservative reading of classical Christian natural-law theory.

---

[3] One example of a policy and practice that may have violated *ius in bello* principles was Thomas Sumter's promise to recruits in his guerilla southern campaign that they could kill and plunder all they could from Loyalists.

[4] Paul Johnson, *A History of the American People* (New York: Harper Perennial, 1999), 127.

[5] Thomas Aquinas, *Summa Theologica*, trans. Fathers of the English Dominican Province (Chicago: Encyclopedia Britannica, 1952), I–II, 90.3.

To see why, consider the often overlooked fact that custom plays a crucial role in a sound theory of positive law. For Aquinas, the long usage of custom "has the force of law, abolishes law, and is the interpreter of law." Hence, custom itself will be crucial in determining whether some enactment counts as unjust because it was issued by an illegitimate authority, which Aquinas identified as one way a law can be unjust and fail to bind in conscience *as law*. And indeed, when Aquinas discusses justified revolution in *De Regno*, it is with regard to the right of the multitude (*ius multitudinis*) to provide itself with a king that is *contingent*. In other words, not all multitudes necessarily enjoy this as an immediately exercisable right. Hence, it seems that, for Aquinas, the contingency of a right of the multitude turns precisely on the constitutional arrangements of that polity. Thus, Aquinas' favorable citations of the Roman overthrow of Tarquin and Domitian are favorable in part *because* they are exercises of a constitutional right held by the people and recognized by custom.[6]

Moreover, it is worth noting that a set of constitutional arrangements can obtain the force of law through widespread acceptance over a long period, even if those arrangements grew out of an unjust revolt to proper authority. For example, one might suppose with Hilaire Belloc that James II of England and Ireland (VII of Scotland), who was dethroned by conspirators distinguished in history for how "steeped in falsehood" they were, was the "last legitimate king of the three kingdoms."[7] In that case, the constitutional arrangements of 1688–1689 were conceived in an unjust revolt, but those same arrangements could come to have the force of law through long general acceptance.[8] For the purposes of assessing the justness of the colonists' claims of a right of resistance from a Christian natural-law perspective, then, the question *would* seem to significantly turn on the merits of the rival interpretations of the British constitution. The difficulty in assessing the debate is that, as we have seen, constitutional argument proceeded alongside and was often mingled with moral argument and direct appeal to first principles.

It is significant that the Americans comingled appeals to first principles with constitutional arguments to the point of fusing them. On one reading, the Americans forensically deployed any argument they thought might stick. But another reading would be that they sincerely believed it would be an insufficient justification of resistance to advert *merely* to custom or *merely* to abstract rights claims. Instead, they saw these two vectors of argument as two sides of the same coin. That abstract principles of natural justice are translated in a specific way

---

[6] Aquinas, *Summa Theologica*, I–II, 97.3; *De Regno*, ch. 7, para. 49. Accessed June 14, 2021, from www.corpusthomisticum.org.

[7] Hillaire Belloc, *James the Second* (Philadelphia: J. B. Lippincott, 1928), 13, 212.

[8] It is hard to speak with precision about when custom has sufficient acceptance to be accounted law – but at least it could be said that, in this case, Stuart claims were probably at an end after the failed Jacobite rising of 1745, two generations later.

into customary law is a standard claim of natural-law theory. Moreover, from the classical natural-law perspective, resistance and/or revolution cannot be premised on appeals solely to abstract natural rights formulated as flowing from a state of nature. This is not because natural rights do not exist – care of the common good includes respect of genuine natural-rights correlative of natural duties – but because community and authority are necessary features of embodied human existence: place, context, history, and custom matter.

The context in which the American patriots in fact appealed to natural rights was a variegated network of societies — familial, religious, political, and otherwise — each with a narrative tradition and principle of unity (authority). By the nature of the case, natural rights were not unconditioned and were not subsisting in a vacuum for any particular American. Their meaning was in part defined by the context of the genuine communities in which they were members. For the conservative Christian Aristotelian, even St. Anthony the Hermit camping out in the desert – whom Aquinas identifies in his commentary on Aristotle's *Politics* as an example of the "god" of the Aristotelian disjunctive regarding persons living outside of the polis – continues to be a member of his family and communes with the saints and angels. All of this suggests that from the perspective of the classical natural lawyer, when resistance/revolution arguments are premised on natural-rights claims, their primary force derives from their life and substance in the positive law. This is akin to William Knox's point, and one established in different ways by conservatives such as Samuel Johnson, Edmund Burke, Joseph de Maistre, and, more recently, Alasdair MacIntyre. The convergence of constitutional and natural-rights arguments in colonial pamphlets indicates that many Americans accepted this point as well.

Notably, the Americans seemed to think that the positive law could incorporate first principles as potentially actionable legal claims. One interesting Revolutionary Era example of this is in the *Quock Walker* case involving an enslaved man who sued for his freedom in Massachusetts in 1781. The counsel for Walker, Levi Lincoln, appealed to first principles: "Is it not a law of nature that all men are equal & free – Is it not the law of nature and God – Is not the law of God then against slavery..."[9] The Court's opinion recounted how first principles were incorporated into Article I of the Massachusetts Constitution of 1780:

Sentiments more favorable to the natural rights of mankind, and to that innate desire for liberty which heaven, without regard to complexion or shape, has planted in the human breast – have prevailed since the glorious struggle for our rights began. And these sentiments led the framers of our constitution of government – by which the people of this commonwealth have solemnly bound themselves to each other – to declare – that all men are born free and equal; and that every subject is entitled to liberty, and to have it

---

[9] John D. Cushing, "The Cushing Court and the Abolition of Slavery in Massachusetts: More Notes on the 'Quock Walker Case,'" *American Journal of Legal History* 5(2) (1961): 125.

guarded by the laws as well as his life and property. In short, without resorting to implication in constructing the constitution, slavery is in my judgement as effectively abolished as it can be by the granting of rights and privileges wholly incompatible and repugnant to its existence.[10]

In cases in which civil authority and/or positive law denies entire classes of persons positive protections of the most basic natural rights, the political community may be so radically defective as to warrant direct appeal to first principles. But, even here, the appeal is not made *outside* community, for natural law governs the natural commonwealth and, for the classical natural lawyer, is expressed by way of deduction in the law of nations; and, failing that, the members of the City of God are governed by a law that transcends that of any terrene city.

The grounds of the dominion theory and its corollary, the rights of local legislative control, *as a matter of custom*, had already been articulated in seminal form by Franklin in 1767. As Franklin contended:

It is a common but mistaken Notion here [Britain], that the Colonies were planted at the Expence of Parliament, and that therefore the Parliament has a Right to tax them, &c. The Truth is, they were planted at the Expence of private Adventurers, who went over there to settle with Leave of the King given by Charter. On receiving this Leave and these Charters, the Adventurers voluntarily engag'd to remain the King's Subjects, though in a foreign Country, a Country which had not been conquer'd by either King or Parliament, but was possess'd by a free People. When our Planters arriv'd, they purchas'd the Lands of the Natives without putting King or Parliament to any Expence. Parliament had no hand in their Settlement, was never so much as consulted about their Constitution, and took no kind of Notice of them till many Years after they were established; never attempted to meddle with the Government of them, till that Period when it destroy'd the Constitution of all Parts of the Empire, and usurp'd a Power over Scotland, Ireland, Lords and King . . .. Thus all the Colonies acknowledge the King as their Sovereign: His Governors there represent his Person. Laws are made by their Assemblies or little Parliaments, with the Governor's Assent, subject still to the King's Pleasure to confirm or annul them.[11]

The laws made by American assemblies, Franklin pointed out in another place, was a constitutional enjoyment "as to their internal government."[12] Bancroft added the meat to the bones of this argument from the customary arrangements of the British constitution. He argued that various charters – Elizabeth's charter

---

[10] Ibid., 133. The unwritten constitution matters for how one interprets the abstract provisions. Compare *Goodridge v. Department of Public Health* in which the same passage is cited favorably (440 Mass. 309, 2003).

[11] "From Benjamin Franklin to Lord Kames, 25 February 1767," Founders Online, National Archives. Accessed February 20, 2022, from https://founders.archives.gov/documents/Franklin/01-14-02-0032.

[12] "Arguments Pro and Con: I, 18–20 October 1768," Founders Online, National Archives. Accessed July 14, 2021, from http://founders.archives.gov/documents/Franklin/01-15-02-0132.

to Sir Walter Raleigh; the Virginia Company charter from James I; the Plymouth, Massachusetts, and Maryland Charters from Charles I; the Connecticut, Carolina, and Rhode Island Charters from Charles II; and so on – granted local legislative control. For Bancroft, the delimiting language of legislative power that is standard throughout these charters, for example, that ordinances be "not repugnant or contrary, but (so far as conveniently may be) agreeable to the Laws, Statutes, Customs, and Rights of this Our Kingdom of England" is intended to accord local legislation with the British constitution, not to subordinate the colonies to the legislative jurisdiction of Parliament, generally, and specifically, not in the point of taxation.[13]

John Keown argues that the American revolution fails the just cause desideratum of classical just war theory.[14] Keown channels the imperial argument of Samuel Johnson, one of the most eloquent of the imperial pamphleteers. Keown contends that taxation was not so burdensome as it was sometimes made out to be. Rather, free Americans had a relatively light tax burden and were doing quite well relative to the rest of the world in living standards. And the massive debt incurred by the empire in the French and Indian War left the government in need of revenues. As Johnson put it, "they who thus flourish under the protection of our government, should contribute something toward its expense."[15]

It is true that the tax burden was not so onerous as to fail basic principles of *ex forma*, for example, placing a disproportionate burden on specific sectors of the populace.[16] We can suppose that the average yearly income of an urban free person in the Middle Colonies was 27 pounds.[17] If such an average Virginian wanted to get married, he would have had to pay 2 shillings and 6 pence under the Stamp Act to get a marriage license. This would amount to about 0.4 percent of his annual salary. If one compared the amount it cost to get a marriage license in, say, the state of Tennessee to the median income in Tennessee in the 2010s, the amount would have been about 0.2 percent of one's salary. It would have been a bit more expensive for the average Virginian to get married in 1765, but not much.[18] The percentages of average income on the range of other things taxed, from liquor licenses to attorney licenses, are not extremely

[13] See the Charter of Maryland (1632). Accessed February 20, 2022, from https://avalon.law.yale .edu/17th_century/ma01.asp.
[14] Our thanks to Michael Moreland for alerting us to Keown's argument.
[15] Samuel Johnson, "Taxation No Tyranny: An Answer to the Resolutions and Address of the American Congress" in Gordon S. Wood, ed., *Writings from the Pamphlet Debate* (New York: Library of America, 2015), vol. 2, 465.
[16] See Aquinas, *Summa Theologica*, I–II, 96.4.
[17] Data and estimates regarding American incomes ca. 1650–1870 are from a research project by Peter H. Lindert and Jeffrey G. Williamson. Accessed July 28, 2021, from https://gpih.ucdavis .edu/tables.htm
[18] Still, the average freeman in Boston would have felt a greater burden. With an average income between 11 and 12 pounds, the tax would have been around 1 percent of his income.

dissimilar to what one would find today. Moreover, as Keown recounts, the relative tax burden on the residents of Britain was significantly higher than that on the colonists. In short, the tax burden does not seem to per se violate natural-law precepts that would forbid disproportionate imposition of tax burdens.

But this does not resolve the question of authority, for a tax imposed by an unjust authority, however great or small, fails to be just law. Again, Johnson's conservative argument for basic governmental authority to tax is forceful and true as far as it goes. But his working first premise, which Keown fails to mention, is simply false from a classical natural-law perspective. Johnson traces colonial government historically back to European imperialism, but then he remarks, "All government is ultimately and essentially absolute, but subordinate societies may have more immunities, or individuals greater liberty, as the operations of government are differently conducted." In other words, Johnson's vision of sovereignty was essentially Hobbist. The state is at root absolute, according to Johnson, and whatever liberties subjects enjoy are at root merely concessions of the absolute sovereign. Hence, Johnson bluntly contends that "there can be no limited government."[19] Johnson emphasizes that there must be some power from which there is no appeal – the same logic Hobbes deployed in his argument for absolutism. A concomitant of this view of sovereignty is that the sovereign is the sole source of law and therefore exists above or outside the confines of the rule of law. The rest of Johnson's arguments hinges on this claim about the nature of the British constitution, because on this view, the constitutional order itself is subject to be unmade and remade by the king and Parliament.

This position fails to make distinctions that were essential in classical natural-law accounts of authority in two respects: (1) the source of all constitutional authority in natural law and (2) the distinction between the directive and the coercive force of law. First, as the influential classical natural lawyer, jurist, and English constitutional theorist Sir John Fortescue articulated it, the law of nature is the only source of regal authority, and it is the ultimate test and judge of all claims of regal power. The same goes for other constitutional forms. Because the natural law is the "mother and mistress of all human laws," deviations from the natural law fail to *be* law.[20] In other words, sovereign edicts can fail to meet the existence conditions of law by failing to be morally valid. The class of such edicts would include edicts made outside legislative authority. Such edicts fail to bind in conscience. Second, while it is true that the sovereign in regal systems is not subject to the coercive force of law because no man can coerce himself, the just sovereign in the framing of general rules

[19] Samuel Johnson, "Taxation No Tyranny: An Answer to the Resolutions and Address of the American Congress" in Gordon S. Wood, ed., *Writings from the Pamphlet Debate* (New York: Library of America, 2015), vol. 2, 471.
[20] John Fortescue, *De Natura Legis Naturae* in *The Works of John Fortescue* (London: Printed for Private Distribution, 1869), vol. 1, 221.

subjects himself to the law's directive force. This distinction has roots in Aquinas' thought and was made in classical English jurisprudence from Henry de Bracton to Matthew Hale.[21] And, as John Finnis points out, while this distinction permits the sole monarch acting *qua* sovereign a power of dispensation in emergencies for the common good, it does not follow that such a sovereign is not genuinely bound by the rule of law.[22] On this view, the king and Parliament are bound by the directive force of law. If correct, then the question remains what sort of legal-constitutional order grew out of the proprietary colonies (originally Maine, Maryland, South Carolina, North Carolina, East Jersey, West Jersey, New York, Pennsylvania, and Delaware – of which all except Maryland, Pennsylvania, and Delaware became royal colonies by 1730), the largely autonomous charter governments of Connecticut and Rhode Island, and the remaining royal charters? Keown does not address the American arguments on this point and so fails to provide a convincing case.

Another recent critic of the American argument deploying classical just war principles, Gregg Frazer, has contended that the Americans failed to establish a just cause for resistance and war.[23] He specifically takes on James Wilson's arguments already discussed. Frazer takes issue with each of the cases Wilson cites by focusing on the inapplicability of the cases cited to the American context. Ireland was a conquered territory, which is what placed it directly under the king. Similarly, in the Jamaica case, Frazer highlights how the case rested on its status as a conquered territory. But, as Wilson himself insists, America was not a conquered territory. Frazer also points out that in *Smith vs. Browne and Cooper*, Holt refers to Virginia as a conquered country, thus undercutting Wilson's use of it as an example. Frazer dismisses Wilson's arguments from natural law as a "theoretical concept" that had no part in the British constitution and was not falsifiable.[24]

It is true that the examples that the patriots drew from the history of the British constitution were not exact likenesses to the American case, but Wilson did not suggest that they were. As John Adams and others also pointed out, these cases were merely analogous. Adams explained:

[T]he case of America differs totally from the case of Wales, Ireland, Man, or any other case which is known at common law or in English history. There is no one precedent in point in any English records, and, therefore, it can be determined only by eternal reason and the law of nature. But yet that the analogy of all these cases of Ireland, Wales, Man, Chester, Durham, Lancaster, &c. clearly concur with the dictates of reason and nature, that Americans are entitled to all the liberties of Englishmen, and that they are not bound

---

[21] See John Finnis, *Natural Law and Natural Rights* (Oxford: Clarendon Press, 1980), 239.

[22] Ibid., 275.

[23] Gregg L. Frazer, "The American Revolution: Not a Just War," *Journal of Military Ethics* 14(1) (2015): 35–56. See also Gregg L. Frazer, *God against the Revolution: The Loyalist Clergy's Case against the American Revolution* (Lawrence: University of Kansas Press, 2020).

[24] Frazer, *God against the Revolution*, 42.

by any acts of parliament whatever, by any law known in English records or history, excepting those for the regulation of trade, which they have consented to and acquiesced in.[25]

The American case was analogous to cases such as Ireland and Wales to the extent that they had, at various points in British constitutional history, shared the features of local legislative authority under the executive power of the king and nonsubjection to Parliament for lack of representation. As both Adams and Wilson contended, the American argument was ultimately rooted in the law of nature, which, far from being a mere "theoretical concept," was appealed to directly in the history of common law and considered by the greatest exponents of that tradition from Fortescue to Coke to Blackstone as a limiting condition on the legal validity of human enactments. Wilson's contention that absurd and unjust rules are not binding as law thus cannot be dismissed merely as his arbitrary preference.[26] The patriotic argument ultimately turns on whether electoral representation is indeed a proximate deduction from the first principles of natural law, and whether something approximating it had grown into a customary right in the American colonies.

Although the previous chapter provided only a broad outline of the pamphlet debates, the discussion did suggest that there was a rational warrant among the revolutionary pamphleteers for believing that the metropolis had become tyrannical. From the classical natural-law perspective, a strong case can be made for American resistance on the grounds that that local control over local communities (where natural rights ultimately are expressed and protected) had obtained the force of law by custom. And, indeed, the most convincing historical work on the legal-constitutional basis of revolution has concluded that the imperial constitution in effect in the 1760s and 70s

remained a customary constitution in which, according to the colonial point of view, sovereignty resided not in an all-powerful Parliament but in the Crown, the power of which had been considerably reduced over the previous century by the specific "gains made over the years in the direction of self-determination" by each representative body within the empire.[27]

The perspectival language should not be read through a postmodern lens, but rather as a frank inference from the historical evidence to the existence of polycentric authority. Hence, Greene concludes that by the time of the Revolution "the antiquity of the notion of a customary imperial constitution of principled limitation, the strength of local institutions, the comparative

---

[25] John Adams, "Novanglus No. IX," *The Works of John Adams* (Boston: Charles C. Little and James Brown, 1851), vol. 4, 149.

[26] As Frazer suggests in "The American Revolution," 42.

[27] Jack P. Greene, *The Constitutional Origins of the American Revolution* (New York: Cambridge University Press, 2011), 173. Internal quotation is to Peter S. Onuf, *Maryland and Empire, 1773: The Antilon: First Citizen Letters* (Baltimore: Johns Hopkins University Press, 1974), 29.

recency of the doctrine of parliamentary supremacy, and the weakness of metropolitan authority in the colonies combined to make the perspective of the center a 'tory perspective.'"[28]

Neither was the colonial point of view a mere prejudice confined to one side of the Atlantic. Edmund Burke contended that Americans were jealously attached to the principle of liberty – but not to an abstraction: "Abstract liberty, like other mere abstractions, is not to be found." In Burke's view, Americans were attached to liberty as it inhered "in some sensible object," as was evident in their concrete protests over taxation. Closely connected to this – and, indeed, logically prior – was their attachment to their provincial legislative assemblies and a concomitant "strong aversion from whatever tends to deprive them of their chief importance." And thus, Burke proposed a plan of reconciliation that "guarded the privileges of local legislature," which Burke saw as the outgrowth of decades of "salutary neglect."[29]

If, indeed, this was a plausible interpretation of what had actually come to be accepted by custom, then the legislative encroachments on local authority could justifiably be seen as meeting the first condition, because they are tyrannical in the mode of *ultra vires*, something that goes beyond the scope of the government's legitimate authority.

4.1 THE JUSTIFIABILITY OF REVOLUTION IN LIGHT OF SCRIPTURE

Many of the patriots formulated public appeals to God in an ecumenical way, and they treated theistic natural-law arguments as compatible with a range of rival religious traditions. And yet, as Donald Lutz has shown, the founders frequently cited the Bible in their political writings, accounting for one-third of all citations in his sample.[30] As Daniel Dreisbach has demonstrated, the Bible was a powerful influence on the thinking of the founders in several ways, including as an enrichment of their common language and political rhetoric, as a source for normative standards, and as a window into God's character and providential plan.[31]

It was the patriotic clergy who sought to demonstrate that, properly interpreted, the Bible concurred with reason regarding the revolutionary cause. Under the light of revelation, liberty was seen as man's birthright and an

[28] Greene, *Constitutional Origins*, 185.
[29] Edmund Burke, "Speech on Conciliation," *The Works of Edmund Burke* (Boston, C. C. Little & J. Brown, 1839), vol. 2, 30, 69. It should be noted, however, that Burke is careful not to affirm the dominion theory.
[30] Donald S. Lutz, *The Origins of American Constitutionalism* (Baton Rouge: Louisiana University Press, 1988), 140.
[31] Daniel L. Dreisbach, *Reading the Bible with the Founding Fathers* (New York: Oxford University Press, 2017), 71–96.

essential limitation on rightful authority. For the patriotic clergy, faith and reason concurred as to the justness and ultimately necessity of resistance. Before elaborating on the patriotic arguments, it is helpful to provide a brief survey of traditional Christian exposition of the idea of passive obedience in Romans 13, a critical concept in the debates among the American clergy. There Paul wrote that whoever resists temporal power resists the ordinance of God and "shall receive to themselves damnation."

The Patristics had tended to emphasize civil obedience in their expositions of this passage and never articulated a Christian theory of civil disobedience, resistance, or revolution. This is true of both the pre- and post-Constantinian eras. Before the legalization of Christianity, Origen sounded a theme that echoed Peter's response to the Sanhedrin and that would be common to all the most influential theologians: God must be obeyed rather than men.[32] Still, Origen maintained that a civil power that persecuted the faith was like the power of sight made use for evil things. Both could be considered ordained of God.[33] In the face of Roman persecution of Christianity for Christian refusal to sacrifice to the pagan gods, Tertullian defended Christian religious liberty and sought to refute the accusation of treason by showing that the pagans worshipped false gods that did not really exist. But he also emphasized that Christians owed "reverence and sacred respect" to the emperor and that even in the face of persecution, they were bound by Christ to pray for the authorities.[34]

The post-Constantinian Fathers continued to articulate the duty of obedience. John Chrysostom took the passage to be aimed at quashing the rumor that the Apostles were revolutionaries.[35] Gregory of Nazianzus emphasized obedience to constituted authorities.[36] Ambrosiaster gave a straightforward exegesis about the duty of Christian people to obey civil authority.[37] Augustine averred that civil authority cannot bind Christians in conscience to act against their faith. He continued to argue that Christian pilgrims should accept the need to obey worldly authorities in their charge to provide for the temporal common good, and he insisted that they should accept punishment

---

[32] Acts 5:29.

[33] Origen, *Commentary on the Epistle to the Romans Books 6–10*, trans. Thomas P. Scheck (Washington, DC: Catholic University Press of America, 2002), bk. 9, ch. 25, p. 222–25.

[34] Tertullian, *Apology*, in Alexander Roberts, James Donaldson, and A. Cleveland Coxe, eds., *Ante-Nicene Fathers*, trans. S. Thelwall (Buffalo, NY: Christian Literature Publishing, 1885), vol. 3, 42–43.

[35] St. John Chrysostom, "Homilies on Romans, Homily 23," in Philip Schaff, ed., *Nicene and Post-Nicene Fathers*, trans. J. Walker, J. Sheppard, and H. Browne, rev. George B. Stevens (New York: Cosimo Classics, 2007), 1st series, vol. 11.

[36] Oration 17.6, *St. Gregory of Nazianzus: Select Orations*, trans. Martha Vinson (Washington, DC: Catholic University Press of America, 2003), 89.

[37] Ambrosiaster, *Commentaries on Romans and 1–2 Corinthians*, trans. and ed. Gerald L. Bray (Downer's Grove, IL: Intervarsity Press, 2009), 100–1.

even to the point of persecution. Either the Christian will win over his persecutors by his witness, or he will receive the crown of martyrdom, according to Augustine.[38]

Aquinas, representative of the high point of medieval scholasticism, offered a nuanced account of the passage. He echoed the point about clarifying the meaning of Christian liberty as a liberty of spirit from sin. While we continue in the flesh, we are subject to temporal authorities. Regarding wicked rulers, the apostles and martyrs were justified in resisting authorities when they commanded contrary to God's command. Still, Aquinas appealed to biblical passages to suggest that tyrants ought to be patiently endured rather than violently resisted. Unjust persecution will end in the glory of the persecuted. Tyrants are still an instrument of punishment under the wings of God's providence.[39] And yet, in other places, Aquinas suggested there were circumstances in which tyranny could legitimately be resisted – we return to this point later.

The Magisterial Reformers continued to sound the themes of passive obedience in their interpretations of Romans 13. Luther emphasized that secular authority was instituted by God to restrain the wicked. In their spiritual liberty through obedience to the Holy Spirit, Christians are radically free from the law, Luther argued, but they submit to it for the sake of their neighbors and the common good that cannot be secured in a sin-ridden world without civil authority. Magistrates became tyrannical when they violated the liberty of conscience. A Christian could not obey a command to profess belief in heresy, for example, but such injustice does not warrant violent resistance: "If he then takes away your goods and punishes you for your disobedience, then blessed are you, and you should thank God for counting you worthy to suffer for the sake of his Word. Let the fool rage; he shall surely find his judge."[40]

Calvin emphasized that Romans 13 taught the goodness of authority and the benefits of civil obedience. On the other hand, he held that God-ordained magistrates were not endowed with unbridled power. Tyrannies were not ordained of God because they are full of disorder.[41] While this might signal an openness to resistance arguments, Calvin did not go on to make an argument for resistance, instead asserting that tyrants were to be obeyed as a service acceptable to God and suggesting that in God's providence they are instruments

[38] Augustine, *Augustine on Romans: Propositions from the Epistle to the Romans, Unfinished Commentary on the Epistle to the Romans*, trans. Paula Frederiksen Landes (Chico, CA: Scholars Press, 1982), 43.

[39] Ibid.

[40] Martin Luther, "On Secular Authority," in Harro Höpfl, ed. and trans., *Luther and Calvin on Secular Authority* (Cambridge: Cambridge University Press, 1991), 29.

[41] John Calvin, *Commentaries on the Epistle of Paul the Apostle to the Romans*, ed. and trans. Rev. John Owen (Edinburgh: Calvin Translation Society, 1749).

of punishment for the iniquities of the people.[42] During the Reformation era, the legacy of nonresistance and defense of temporal civil autonomy from ecclesiastical meddling by Rome combined with historical circumstances to provide the theological ground for a system of nationally independent churches in which princes would have authority over clergy and church property. The Lutheran principles can thus be seen as sowing the germ of absolutism that would grow up in early modern Europe to the point where these principles would also inform Catholic defenses of absolutism.[43]

Yet, as Glenn Moots and Valerie Ona Morkevičius have argued, Luther and his followers permitted "self-defense against unlawful or immoral force," and a robust resistance theory nonetheless developed in the Reformed tradition.[44] Luther and other leading Lutheran theologians would thus eventually endorse resistance to Charles V. Calvin began to warm more to a doctrine of resistance while his followers such as Theodore Beza, John Knox, and Peter Martyr Vermigli developed a doctrine of resistance and accompanying exposition of Romans 13. By the time of the Saint Bartholomew's Day massacre of the Huguenots in 1752, there had developed within the Calvinist tradition a full-blown theory of a right to resistance. Meanwhile, there were strands in the Catholic tradition that also pointed toward a theory of resistance to tyranny. Skinner traces this line of thinking among the conciliarists, from Jean Gerson to Jacques Almain and John Mair, and the conciliarist influence can be traced directly to the American founding via the Catholic founding fathers Charles and John Carroll.[45]

Representative of the developing resistance theory in the Calvinist tradition is the exposition of Romans 13 developed in the *Vindiciae Contra Tyrranos* (1579) written under the pseudonym Junius Brutus. Brutus contended that nothing in Romans 13 supported unlimited obedience. This made room for him to develop his covenantal theory of political obligation in which the people and the king covenant to obey God and the people covenant with the ruler to obey provided he rules justly. The argument drew extensively from the examples of God's covenant with Israel to conclude that a right of resistance "must be allowed to the whole people of any Christian Kingdom or Country whatsoever."[46] Brutus specified that the authority of the people was manifested

---

[42] John Calvin, "On Civil Government," in *Luther and Calvin on Secular Authority*, 76–77; Quentin Skinner, *The Foundations of Modern Thought* (New York: Cambridge University Press, 1978), vol. 2, 192.

[43] Skinner, *The Foundations of Modern Thought*, 15, 113.

[44] Glenn A. Moots and Valerie Ona Morkevičius, "Just Revolution: Protestant Precedents for Rebellion,"in *Justifying Revolution: Law, Virtue, and Violence* (Norman: University of Oklahoma Press, 2018), 37.

[45] Skinner, *Foundations*, 65; Michael D. Breidenbach, "Conciliarism and the American Founding," *William and Mary Quarterly* 73(3)(July 2016): 467–500.

[46] Stephen Junius Brutus [pseudonym], *Vindiciae contra Tyrannos: A Defence of Liberty against Tyrants, Or, of the Lawful Power of the Prince over the People and of the People over the Prince*

through magistrates whom the people have established, who mediate between the people and the king.

Francisco Suárez, the Spanish Jesuit Thomist of the Salamancan school, provides a roughly contemporary example of how the right of resistance was being developed in Catholic thought. Whereas, Brutus' arguments were forged in the crucible of Catholic persecution of the Huguenots, Suárez's argument was forged in the crucible of Anglican persecution of Catholics, in particular James I's Oath of Allegiance. Suárez criticizes James for misunderstanding Romans 13. Following Thomas Aquinas, Suárez holds that laws bind in conscience when they maintain the essential nexus of natural law and eternal law. Such laws will be ordered to the common weal – this is what it means for authorities to be ministers of God. This is the sort of authority to which Paul says we must be subject. Hence, he distinguishes between just authorities and tyrants. There are two sorts of tyrants: outside aggressors who seize the throne by mere force and those with a just title to rule who commit gross injustices. With regard to the latter, Suárez maintains that it would be unjust for a private individual to assassinate him. He maintains this because the right to resist a tyrant resides rather in the whole community, acting through "the general deliberations of its communities and leading men."[47]

4.1.1 Jonathan Mayhew on Romans 13

Jonathan Mayhew's sermon "A Discourse Concerning Unlimited Submission and Nonresistance to the Higher Powers" (1750) is the quintessential expression of the patriotic interpretation of Romans 13. As J. Patrick Mullins has pointed out, "More than any other clergyman, Mayhew helped prepare the New England conscience for disobedience to British authority in the 1760s."[48] In this sermon, which John Adams suggested was an essential document to study for anyone who really wished "to investigate the principles and Feelings which produced the Revolution," Mayhew sought to build the biblical case for resistance to unjust government. Mayhew engaged in an extended exegesis of Romans 13:1–7, where Paul enjoined obedience to temporal authorities.

(London: Richard Baldwin, 1689), 23. For a discussion, see Mark David Hall, "Vindiciae, Contra Tyrannos: The Influence of the Reformed Tradition in the American Founding," in Daniel L. Dreisbach and Mark David Hall, eds., *Faith and the Founders of the American Republic* (New York: Oxford University Press, 2014). See also generally David P. Henreckson, *The Immortal Commonwealth: Covenant, Community, and Political Resistance in Early Reformed Thought* (New York: Cambridge University Press, 2019).

[47] Francisco Suárez, *Selections from Three Works: A Treatise on Laws and God the Lawgiver; A Defence of the Catholic and Apostolic Faith; A Work on the Three Theological Virtues: Faith, Hope, and Charity*, ed. Thomas Pink (Indianapolis, IN: Liberty Fund, 2015), 12, 51, 106, 191, and 820.

[48] J. Patrick Mullins, *Father of Liberty: Jonathan Mayhew and the Principles of the American Revolution* (Lawrence: University of Kansas Press, 2017), 4.

1   Let every soul be subject unto the higher powers. For there is no power but of God: the powers that be are ordained of God.
2   Whosoever therefore resisteth the power, resisteth the ordinance of God: and they that resist shall receive to themselves damnation.
3   For rulers are not a terror to good works, but to the evil. Wilt thou then not be afraid of the power? do that which is good, and thou shalt have praise of the same:
4   For he is the minister of God to thee for good. But if thou do that which is evil, be afraid; for he beareth not the sword in vain: for he is the minister of God, a revenger to execute wrath upon him that doeth evil.
5   Wherefore ye must needs be subject, not only for wrath, but also for conscience sake.
6   For this cause pay ye tribute also: for they are God's ministers, attending continually upon this very thing.
7   Render therefore to all their dues: tribute to whom tribute is due; custom to whom custom; fear to whom fear; honour to whom honour.

The importance of this passage for considering the American revolutionary argument under the light of Christian revelation is apparent. As Mayhew points out, it is the "most full and express of any in the New Testament relating to rulers and subjects."[49] The thrust of Mayhew's exposition was to reject a doctrine of passive obedience and nonresistance. Authority was intrinsically limited to essential purposes of securing justice and the common good, and when governments failed to do this, they no longer counted as authorities to which obedience is due. For Mayhew, the claim that authority is a terror to evil works rather than good ones logically entailed that powers that are a terror to good works do not deserve our obedience and may legitimately be resisted.

Mayhew's argument can thus be understood as taking place within the larger Christian conversation that had been going on for centuries about the nature and limits of obedience to civil power. Mayhew makes a number of important interpretive moves in expositing the Romans verses. While the expressions such as *"be subject to the higher powers"* are indefinite expressions that may be taken to imply an unqualified duty of passive obedience, Mayhew shows that this would not be consistent with how other Christian precepts were typically understood. Precepts such as "Lay not up for yourselves treasures upon the earth," "Take therefore no thought for the morrow; children, obey your parents in the Lord, for this is right," and "Wives submit yourselves unto your own husbands as unto the Lord," Mayhew argued, allow restriction and qualification because "common sense" shows that they are not to be

---

[49] Jonathan Mayhew, "A Discourse Concerning Unlimited Submission and Nonresistance to the Higher Powers ...," in Bernard Bailyn, ed., *Pamphlets of the American Revolution 1750–1776* (Boston: Belknap Press, 1965), vol. 1, 216.

understood literally and absolutely. For example, children would not be bound to obey parents who ordered them to break one of God's commandments.

Mayhew leans on specific language in the passage to build the case that Paul sees a civil magistrate teleologically, ordained to certain legitimate ends, and Mayhew uses civil authority as a functional concept. On Mayhew's reading, Paul is commanding obedience to nondefective, that is, "*just*" civil authority in the passage. The higher powers spoken of are not "a terror to good works but to the evil and they are God's ministers for good, revengers to execute wrath upon him that doth evil." It follows that St. Paul provides no obligation to obey a power that is a terror to virtue and a boon to knavery. The argument shows that it is no more a sin to resist such a power than it is to "resist the devil, that he may *flee* from us. For one is as truly the minister of God as the other."[50] It would follow that the specific duty to pay taxes mentioned in verse 6 would, like other biblical precepts, admit of qualifications and exceptions.

In Mayhew's interpretation, the duty of submission to just authority is essentially coupled to a duty of resistance to tyranny. Mayhew again analogizes to the family. Suppose the case of a parent gone mad who tried to cut the throats of his children. The very reason for his authority, their common good, is the ground they are justified in standing upon to disobey and resist. Mayhew admits that this teaching is subject to a slippery slope counterargument: where do we draw the line regarding obedience to authority? The principle of resistance could lead to anarchy and confusion. Mayhew returns to the family: just because a principle might be misused to disobey just parental authority does not mean we are incapable of drawing lines somewhere or that all qualifications of authority are somehow arbitrary. Before resistance is legitimate, tyranny must be both *severe* and *habitual* – but the people retain the right of judgment of when these lines have been crossed.[51] All of this was rooted in Mayhew's conception of God as a supreme being of goodness and wisdom, a conception that was in fundamental continuity with the philosophical theology of the natural-law tradition. "The power of this Almighty King is *limited by law* ... the eternal *laws* of truth, wisdom, and equity, and the everlasting *tables* of right reason," Mayhew affirmed.[52]

Mullins has traced the influence of the latitudinarian Anglican Bishop Benjamin Hoadly on Mayhew's sermon, concluding that he owes more to Hoadly and Locke than to the Apostle Paul.[53] While these influences are apparent, Mullins' conclusion about the relative weight of influence is not so apparent. Mullins declines to articulate and defend from rival interpretations *the* authentically Pauline position. Meanwhile, we have traced more than one recognizably Pauline tradition within Christian theology. There is a distinctive line emphasizing passive obedience and nonresistance. But there are other lines of Pauline thinking in the Catholic and Protestant traditions that sanction

---

[50] Ibid., 230.   [51] Ibid., 237–38.   [52] Ibid., 242.   [53] Mullins, *Father of Liberty*, 56.

resistance. Moreover, Mullins does not show that Mayhew's analogy from political to parental authority is Hoadlyan and Lockean rather than Pauline.

Consider Paul's instructions in Ephesians 6. As quoted earlier, Paul exhorts children to "obey their parents, for this is right." He continues to quote the commandment to honor one's father and mother approvingly. He then immediately exhorts fathers not to provoke their children to anger, but to "bring them up in the discipline and instruction of the Lord." In other words, Paul insists that there is a mutuality of obligation in the parent–child relationship, precisely the point that Mayhew leveraged to build his case against passive obedience. The most that could be said about this passage, Romans 13, and others where Mayhew talks about filial, spousal, and civic obedience is that Paul does not specifically address situations in which authorities become terrors to good works. But then that would permit a legitimate plurality of interpretations of Paul on this point. In short, it is simply incorrect to suggest that Mayhew turned the teaching of Romans 13 "on its head" or that there was no precedent in the Christian tradition for interpreting Romans 13 in ways compatible with resistance to tyranny.[54]

Mayhew entered directly into the pamphlet debates in 1766 shortly after the repeal of the Stamp Act. His *The Snare Broken* offered thanksgiving to God for confounding the "execrable design" to enslave the colonies and gave effusive praises to William Pitt for his advocacy of the American cause. The sermon waxes almost obsequious to the Parliament and King George III for their moderation and apparent wisdom for changing course. The readiness of the king to listen to his subjects and change course is a reason that the people should reinvigorate their loyalty and obedience. Mayhew returned to his favored analogy:

Natural parents, thro' human frailty, and mistakes about facts and circumstances, sometimes *provoke their children to* wrath, tho' they tenderly love them, and sincerely desire their good. But what affectionate and dutiful child ever harboured resentment on any such account if the grievance was removed, on a dutiful representation of it?[55]

The king is a political father to his people, and he had replied like a good father to his children. Mayhew's general prayer and hope for reconciliation is the probable reason for his silence regarding the claims of the Declaratory Act. Mayhew would die shortly after this sermon and thus would not live to see the failure of reconciliation. Still, he continued his appeal to the first principles that patriot pamphleteers would later deploy to revolutionary effect. The Americans were born free and endowed with a natural right to property, which they cannot part with except by their own consent or that of their representative.

---

[54] Gregg L. Frazer, "The American Revolution: Not a Just War," *Journal of Military Ethics* 14(1) (2015), 50.

[55] Ellis Sandoz, foreword to *Political Sermons of the American Founding Era: 1730–1805*, 2nd ed. (Indianapolis, IN: Liberty Fund, 1998), vol. 1, 252. Emphasis in original.

This natural and constitutional right was guaranteed by Magna Carta. In the end, self-preservation remained "a great and primary law of nature" that could justify resistance.[56] In grounding a right of resistance on the primacy and urgency of the natural-law precept of self-preservation, Mayhew channeled a theme that was common to both Junius Brutus and Francisco Suárez.

While the New England clergy would continue to lead the way for the patriotic argument and channel natural-law principles in their expositions of Scripture, the defenders of passive obedience replied in kind. North Carolina Anglican minister George Micklejohn argued that Romans 13:1–2 meant that all de facto authorities were ordained of God:

WE are commanded, therefore, *to be subject to the higher powers*, because the authority they are invested with is from HEAVEN: *The powers that be, are ordained of God!* – They are God's vicegerents upon earth, and instruments in the hand of his providence, for carrying on the grand purposes of protection and government, and for securing the peace and happiness of mankind.[57]

Micklejohn emphasized Christ's exchange with Pontius Pilate in John 19 and his payment of the Temple tax in Matthew 17, insisting that these stories confirmed the Christian doctrine that all civil authority is ordained by God. In defense of Mickeljohn's approach, Gregg Frazer takes issue with the patriots' teleological reading of the office of the magistrate. Frazer argues that patriot clergy like the earlier John Joachim Zubly misleadingly glossed Romans 13:4 to say that God gives authority to civil magistrates *to be* "ministers of God, for the good of the subject," rather than the text's statement that magistrates *are*, essentially, ordained of God. In Frazer's words, "It is akin to the difference between saying that someone is a human being and saying that someone must prove to be a human being by meeting certain qualifications." Frazer continues:

The subtle textual change allows for the idea that the people are the proper judges. The actual text makes God the judge. If the people are the proper judges, then rebellion may be an option. If God is the proper judge, then only he may remove a magistrate by legal or extralegal means.[58]

The text is not as clearly defactoist as Frazer suggests. It is not unreasonable to read the sentence "he is the minister of God to thee for good" teleologically, that is, as tethering the office of the civil magistrate essentially to the function or purpose of promoting justice and securing the common good. Similarly, the concept of a "human being" or a human person in classical natural-law theory is functional. There is a distinction between defective and nondefective human persons in virtue of whether they have chosen to live in accord with right reason

---

[56] Ibid., 263. Emphasis in original.

[57] George Micklejohn, "On the Important Duty of Subjection to the Civil Powers: A Sermon Preached on Sunday September 25, 1768" (Newbern, NC: James Davis, 1768), 4.

[58] Frazer, *God against the Revolution*, 50.

or not. The share that human beings have in the eternal law, by the power of reason, is the source of their capacity to judge between nondefective and defective, good and evil. This was affirmed in practice by the early Christians as when Peter had to judge whether the Jewish authorities had overstepped their bounds when they forbade him and the apostles to preach the name of Christ.[59]

Thomas Aquinas outlined several ways in which a person in a position of authority might establish laws or directives that are unjust and fail to impose moral obligation. A law might be unjust by virtue of being contrary to the human good when (1) it is oriented toward the private and unjust ends of the ruler, (2) it exceeds the legitimate authority of the one who makes it, (3) or it imposes burdens inequitably on some part of the community. A final way in which a law might be unjust is if (4) it commands something contrary to the divine good, as when a law commands acts of idolatry.[60] Laws contrary to the human good, in those first three modes of injustice, do not bind in conscience, although obedience to them may be prudent to avoid scandal or some greater evil. Christ's submission to the Roman and Jewish authorities can reasonably be seen in this light. Laws contrary to the divine good, however, must never be obeyed. There is, instead, a duty to disobey.

Aquinas' discussion of legal injustice suggests that Christians enjoy a basic dignity and authority to exercise their faith-informed reason to judge of the magistrate's laws and the correlative obligations those laws impose upon them. It is not correct, therefore, from the perspective of classical Christian natural-law theory to say that God alone is the proper judge of the goodness and justice of the acts of the civil magistrate, if that entails a denial that human persons may participate in that judgment through the exercise of right reason. Moreover, it seems strange to suggest that only God, apart from human secondary causes, can authoritatively remove tyrants legally or extralegally. For God to remove a tyrant "legally," God apparently acts through secondary causes who conform their removal power to the rule of recognition of a polity. For God to remove a tyrant "extralegally," God apparently acts through secondary causes which exercise a removal power that is not, in terms of analytical jurisprudence, authorized by the rule of recognition. In either case, rightly judging persons would be cooperating with God's judgment and will. Hence, the dichotomy Frazer sets up between God's judgment and the legal/extralegal judgment of persons makes little metaphysical sense from the perspective of the classical Christian natural-law tradition. If it were the case that there are no secondary causes, then either human persons would be mere tools of the divine master or God would never deign to remove tyrants except by preternatural or miraculous means. Such a suggestion is far from the obviously correct or orthodox reading of the Bible, including Romans 13, and a

---

[59] See Acts 4.   [60] Aquinas, *Summa Theologica*, I–II, 96.4.

distinctively Christian theology of resistance had already been developing around interpretations of Romans 13 for centuries. "Rather than deviating from their inherited modes of thought on this matter," Gary Steward notes, "the clergy who supported resistance did so in ways that were consistent with their own theological tradition."[61]

What is contested in the Christian tradition is not whether it is ever morally legitimate to refuse to comply with an unjust law – the apostles affirmed as much – but whether or not armed resistance or revolution is ever justified in the face of tyranny or legal injustice. By the end of the pamphlet debates, there was little doubt that the patriotic clergy were winning the argument among the colonists that armed resistance may be justified in certain conditions and that those conditions had been met in Britain's North American colonies. Because the dominion theory tied the cord of loyalty directly to the king, arguments for independence turned against monarchy itself in the minds of many of the patriots. Thomas Paine's *Common Sense*, which sold 100,000 copies and was the most widely read pamphlet on the eve of the revolution, is the outstanding example of this shift. Of course, the English-born pamphleteer was not a clergyman. Indeed, he held various heterodox opinions about Christianity for which orthodox Christian clergy such as John Witherspoon criticized him.[62] Still, the central argument of his pamphlet turned on biblical interpretation. Kingship, Paine argued, was an alien corruption of the people of God "first introduced into the world by Heathens."[63] Paine speculated that the devil himself was the extrinsic cause of its coming to be, and he focused his argument on two passages from the Hebrew Scriptures: Judges 8:22–23 and 1 Samuel 8.

In the former, following Gideon's miraculous routing of the Midianites narrated in Judges 6–8, the Israelites call upon Gideon to be their king: "Rule over us – you, your son and your grandson – because you have saved us from the hand of Midian." For Paine, this was temptation "to the fullest extent" because Gideon was offered a *hereditary* monarchy.[64] Gideon's refusal and proclamation that the Lord will rule over Israel was for Paine both a denial of the people's authority to confer a hereditary monarchy and a confirmation of God's sole kingship over Israel. Paine continued to quote from 1 Samuel at length, highlighting the sinfulness of Israel's demand for a king from the prophet Samuel. Paine's key inference is that, rather than these passages showing merely that Israel had sinned by rejecting God's direct rule (as classical

---

[61] Gary L. Steward, *Justifying Revolution: The American Clergy's Argument for Political Resistance, 1750–1776* (New York: Oxford University Press, 2021), 2.

[62] For example, Paine castigated the doctrine of original sin as having an "inglorious connexion" with the doctrine of hereditary monarchy; see Thomas Paine, *Common Sense* (Mineola, NY: Dover Publications, 1997), 14. John Witherspoon took Paine to task for his comments as asserted "without the shadow of reasoning" ("The Dominion of Providence over the Passions of Men," 538).

[63] Paine, *Common Sense*, 9.   [64] Ibid., 10.

natural lawyers in the English tradition such as Sir John Fortescue had argued), God had actually shown his disapproval for monarchy per se, as a *kind* of government.[65] Paine's suggestion that Israel was a republic prior to this fed into the belief of many of his Christian readers that, in throwing off monarchy, the revolutionaries would be carrying forward God's plan in creating a new Israel by establishing a civilly and religiously free republic in America.

Whatever his personal views, Paine's biblical arguments were thought to be sufficiently theologically serious to merit a reply by the loyalist clergy. In one of the more prominent replies to Paine, Anglican Bishop Charles Inglis argued that the Bible only proved that God disapproves of monarchies at specific times and places, not per se. Inglis charged Paine with overlooking the promonarchy parts of Scripture: "The Jewish polity, in which the Almighty himself condescended to be King (and thence called a Theocracy) is rather in favour of monarchy than against it."[66] Inglis then gave a sophisticated exposition of 1 Samuel in which he contended God was condemning specifically "eastern despotic monarchs," before citing Romans 13 and other passages exhorting civil obedience, concluding that "I must therefore renounce my bible, if I believe this republican."[67]

Jonathan Boucher's "On Liberty, Passive Obedience, and Non-resistance" provides another example of how loyalists argued against the patriots. Doubtless with Romans 13 in mind, Boucher insisted that the Bible is "particularly solicitous" to inculcate "obedience to lawful governors."[68] Of interest here is how Boucher attacked the patriotic argument by focusing on scriptural passages that spoke of Christian freedom, such as Galatians 5:1: "Stand fast, therefore, in the liberty wherewith Christ hath made us free." Boucher contended that this is a freedom from the bondage of sin and cannot be weaponized to mean *civil* liberty with any specific implication for the duty of political obedience. Boucher argued that the word *liberty* never refers to civil liberty. Indeed, on Boucher's view, the Bible is simply unconcerned with civil liberty. Boucher made a case for a teleological understanding of liberty as a moral capacity to do right and avoid wrong (making clear that liberty is essentially distinct from license), and he maintained that there is a general Christian duty to obey constituted authorities.

Boucher's citation of 1 Maccabees, however, seems actually to subvert his argument that the Bible values only spiritual liberty to the exclusion of civil liberty, including local and customary freedom. The colonists would have been familiar with Maccabees because, as Daniel Dreisbach points out, "Most English Bibles of the eighteenth century, including the Protestant Bibles, also

---

[65] Cf. Fortescue, *De natura legis naturae*, 201–5.

[66] Charles Inglis, *The True Interest of America Impartially Stated, in Certain Stictures [sic] on a Pamphlet Intitled Common sense. By an American* (Philadelphia: James Humphries, 1776), 25.

[67] Ibid., 31–33.

[68] Jonathan Boucher, "On Liberty, Passive Obedience, and Non-resistance," in Bruce Frohnen, ed., *The American Republic: Primary Sources* (Indianapolis, IN: Liberty Fund, 2002), 162.

contained the books commonly called Apocrypha."[69] The fourteenth chapter of Maccabees narrates the outcome of the Maccabean revolt (167–160 BC) led by the Maccabee family – the priest Mattathias and his five sons John, Simon, Judas, Eleazar, and Jonathan – against Antiochus IV and his successor rulers of the Seleucid Empire, whose policies of Hellenization sought to coerce the Jews into accepting Greek paganism. The high priesthood began to be bought and sold to the highest bidder who promised to push Hellenization, and Antiochus' agents outlawed Jewish worship on the pain of death and desecrated the temple with pagan sacrifices and orgies. The Maccabees then led an amazingly successful multiyear guerrilla campaign against Seleucid rule.

The author of 1 Maccabees offered the following encomium to Simon Maccabeus (1 Maccabees 14:4–12):

As for the land of Judea, that was quiet all the days of Simon; for he sought the good of his nation in such wise, as that evermore his authority and honour pleased them well . . . .

And enlarged the bounds of his nation, and recovered the country . . . .

Then did they till their ground in peace, and the earth gave her increase, and the trees of the field their fruit.

The ancient men sat all in the streets, communing together of good things, and the young men put on glorious and warlike apparel.

He provided victuals for the cities, and set in them all manner of munition, so that his honourable name was renowned unto the end of the world.

He made peace in the land, and Israel rejoiced with great joy:

For every man sat under his vine and his fig tree, and there was none to fray them . . . .

This passage provides the backdrop to the verse in question: "For he and his brethren and the house of his father have established Israel, and chased away in fight their enemies from them, and confirmed their liberty" (1 Maccabees 14:26). Rather than supporting the imperial perspective, as Boucher suggests, the story of the Maccabees may actually be the strongest scriptural support of the patriotic cause in the annals of the ancient Jews. What had been introduced (aggressive Hellenization, violation of Jewish liberty) was not only contrary to the divine law, but was in violation of the customary right the Jews had enjoyed after the Alexandrian conquests. The civil liberty that the Bible confirms as valuable consisted of the capacity to pursue in tranquility the goods of family, friendship, religion, and commerce in the bonds of justice and peace.

Similarly, the Americans saw the acts of Parliament in the 1760s and 1770s as comprising an unlawful innovation that upended their customary liberty. The patriots argued that resistance was warranted both under the light of reason and the authority of revelation, an argument that was consistent in

---

[69] Dreisbach, *Reading the Bible with the Founding Fathers*, 11.

principle with the classical Christian natural-law tradition. That tradition, including in its reception in American moral philosophy and jurisprudence, held that natural law is a participation in the eternal law of God, which is a rational plan by which the created world is ordered to its perfection or end. To act according to reason was to participate in God's providential rule. So held Richard Hooker and William Blackstone, and so held the most reflective American writers on jurisprudence, such as James Wilson (to whom we return at length in Chapter 7), and so held those participants in the American War of Independence who appealed repeatedly in their writings and essays to the providence of God. "Almost all agreed," as Daniel Dreisbach notes of the American founders, "that there was a Supreme Being who intervened in the affairs of men and nations. They believed God was the author of the rights of men; and the rights God had granted to humankind, no man should take away."[70] When those rights were taken away, the colonists then cataloged "a long train of abuses and usurpations" before declaring their independence and affirming their "reliance on the protection of divine Providence." The theme of God's providence then carried forward into the war, and, as we explore in detail in the next chapter, structured the way key participants understood and interpreted the course of human events.

[70] Ibid., 12.

5

Providence and Natural Law in the War for Independence

From the founding on, a dominant stream of American political thought and statesmanship has understood the polity in providentialist terms. Although a multifaceted and historically complex concept, providentialism was in eighteenth-century American political thought a form of human participation in the divine reason and plan for the governance of the universe. In the classical Christian natural-law tradition influential in the North American colonies, God is a providential governor, and through his wisdom and foreknowledge, God orders all things under his care toward their well-being. There is an analogy between God's providence and human providence. Just as a father and mother are provident over their household in governing their children and directing them toward fulfillment, a political ruler is provident in directing the affairs of the community toward the common good. In human events, such are the acts of prudence.[1]

Prudential deliberation and action are ways for human beings to participate in God's providence. With God, however, there is no memory of past, understanding of present, or plan for the future. Rather, God is eternally simple, self-identical, and outside of time. Hence, the design plans of all things are eternally and simply in the mind of God. Providence is this *ratio*, or reason, in God's intellect that is the archetype ordering all of creation in their respective kinds toward their proper ends. This ordering extends to all species, and it includes (even though is not limited to) a general providence of created matter through the scientific laws that govern material cause and effect. In the classical Christian tradition, God is the *causa causarum*, the cause of all causes. God works both in and through material cause and effect, and through secondary

---

[1] Cf. Thomas Aquinas, *Summa Theologica*, trans. Fathers of the English Dominican Province (Chicago: Encyclopedia Britannica, 1952), I.22.1.

causes to achieve his own purposes. The metaphysic of participated existence, in which human acts participate in divine providence, offers an account of this classical Christian conception of providence that Christian philosophers and theologians have long argued can be understood and affirmed by reason.[2]

The Americans affirmed God's providence, and the influence of Christian revelation was apparent in their affirmation. As John Witherspoon put it:

> The doctrine of divine providence is very full and complete in the sacred oracles. It extends not only to things which we may think of great moment, and therefore worthy of notice, but to things the most indifferent and inconsiderable; "Are not two sparrows sold for a farthing," says our Lord, "and one of them falleth not to the ground without your heavenly Father"; nay, "the very hairs of your head are all numbered.["] It extends not only to things beneficial and salutary, or to the direction and assistance of those who are the servants of the living God; but to things seemingly most hurtful and destructive, and to persons the most refractory and disobedient. He overrules all his creatures, and all their actions. Thus we are told, that "fire, hail, snow, vapour, and stormy wind, fulfil his word," in the course of nature; and even so the most impetuous and disorderly passions of men, that are under no restraint from themselves, are yet perfectly subject to the dominion of Jehovah. They carry his commission, they obey his orders, they are limited and restrained by his authority, and they conspire with every thing else in promoting his glory.[3]

One of the political implications of providentialism is that when "human beings reason correctly about basic matters of policy and right, we advance God's purposes, in ways we may not fully comprehend because of unforeseen consequences."[4] Moreover, because God is both omnipotent and omnibenevolent, God is not the direct cause of evil. Hence, free will is posited by classical Christian theology as one explanation of the existence of evil. Human beings, in the exercise of free will, are secondary causes in their own right. God's permissive will allows secondary causes to break the moral law. This is compatible with God's intrinsic goodness because he can, in his wisdom and foreknowledge, somehow bring good out of evil. In this way, even evil political actors – or political actors who commit evil acts – can advance God's purposes, as it were, in spite of themselves. "The Almighty has His own purposes," Lincoln concluded in his Second Inaugural Address.

Major players in American history have understood the epochal moments in the American drama in just these terms. From the Declaration's appeal to divine providence and the Continental Congress's providential framing of the

---

[2] We shall return to and elucidate this point in our discussion of Orestes Brownson in the next chapter.

[3] John Witherspoon, "The Dominion of Providence over the Passions of Men," *Political Sermons of the American Founding Era: 1730–1805*, 2nd ed. (Indianapolis, IN: Liberty Fund, 1998), vol. 1, 533.

[4] Michael Pakaluk, "Religion in Liberal Democracy," *The Naked Public Square Reconsidered* (Wilmington, DE: Intercollegiate Studies Institute, 2009), 91.

revolution, to Benjamin Franklin's appeal for divine aid at the Constitutional Convention, to Abraham Lincoln's conceptualization of the Civil War as divine retribution for the sin of slavery, the polity's major constitutional moments have been framed by principal leaders in those moments in providentialist terms, that is, moments in which God brought good out of evil.

In this chapter, we contend that the revolutionary leaders believed in a *particularly* providential God, which is what we would expect if they also held to a classical Christian conception of natural law rather than the pantheistic naturalism alleged by modern scholars. We take our investigative cues from the providentialist proclamation by the Continental Congress that bookended the Revolutionary War, and we then engage in historical case studies of key players and events in American counterintelligence and French diplomacy. These case studies show that prominent actors in the war affirmed core tenets of classical theism: the existence of a creator God who providentially governs the cosmos and the destiny of men. According to these key participants engaged in espionage and diplomacy, the providential creator was also a moralistic God of justice who favored the side of liberty such that the revolutionary actors saw themselves carrying out the divine will on the world-historic stage in obedience to the dictates of right reason.

5.1 NATURAL LAW AND PROVIDENCE

According to the classical natural-law tradition, there is a divine lawgiver whose promulgation of the moral law aims at the flourishing of every individual. For natural law to be law in its fullest sense, it must be a dictate of practical reason, directed toward the common good, and promulgated by a proper authority. Metaphysically, such a view requires a particularly providential governor of the universe, an authority to promulgate the natural law. It is not sufficient that the divine government be merely general in the conventionally deist or pantheistic sense of general, observable patterns of cause and effect. Such an understanding collapses providence and natural law into merely hypothetical imperatives, or what Hobbes called "theorems of prudence."[5] Such laws of nature would not be prescriptive in any meaningful sense. One of the proper effects of law, however, is to punish its breach, and the framer of the law retains the authority to determine the appropriate punishment.[6] Natural law would thus not be truly law if it lacked a framer with a (necessarily particular) judicial and executive power. As Robert Bellah correctly points out, the Providential God of the revolutionary leaders may not necessarily have been the Christian God, but neither were the characteristics of the God the revolutionaries appealed to metaphysically incompatible with the God of the classical

---

[5] Thomas Hobbes, *Leviathan*, ed. Edwin Curley (Indianapolis, IN: Hackett, 1994), ch. 15.41, 100.
[6] Aquinas, *Summa Theologica*, I–II.92.2, ad. 3.

Christian tradition.[7] The particular providentialism of the patriots was a unifying public theology that could be, and was, affirmed from a wide range of perspectives.

5.2 PROVIDENTIALISM IN THE CONTINENTAL CONGRESS

As Nicholas Guyatt has argued, revolutionary providentialism was not limited to the pulpit, nor even to those who affirmed Judeo-Christian revelation. Rather, "it shaped political addresses, orations, newspaper articles, and numerous other forms of Patriot propaganda," and contemporaries of the founders such as Robert Smith could say that "the rankest deist can scarcely deny the hand of Providence in our successes."[8] This consensus regarding God's particular providence is apparent in the actions of the Continental Congress. In the same letter in which Adams says that the revolutionary mind was formed between 1760 and 1775, he speaks specifically about the Continental Congress of 1774.[9] This gathering of statesmen, he remarked, was like the Council of Nicaea in ecclesiastical history. It was a forum for the political sages of the day to engage in enlightened discussion and debate and to project a common American mind to the world. The likeness Adams observed between the two gatherings was that small voting margins sometimes carried important questions. He might have drawn another analogy about the role of prayer. Both the Council of Nicaea and the First Continental Congress believed it fitting to open their deliberations with prayer premised on belief in a providential and moralistic God.

As Adams recounts, when the Congress opened, it was moved that it should begin with prayer. John Jay and Edward Rutledge opposed the motion because the delegates were too religiously diverse to join in a common act of worship: "some Episcopalians, some Quakers, some Anabaptists, some Presbyterians, and some Congregationalists."[10] Yet Sam Adams suggested that it would be bigoted not to hear a prayer from a "gentleman of piety and virtue," and this ecumenical sentiment carried the day. On the morning of Wednesday, September 7, 1774, the Anglican clergyman Jacob Duché gave the invocation from the Book of Common Prayer.[11] The 1662 edition divided the Psalms into thirty days to cover each month. On the seventh day of each month, the morning prayer was Psalm 35. Consider just some of the verses from this Psalm:

---

[7] Robert Bellah, "Civil Religion in America," *Daedalus* (Winter 1967) 96(1): 7.

[8] Nicholas Guyatt, *Providence and the Invention of the United States* (New York: Cambridge University Press, 2007), 105.

[9] "John Adams to Thomas Jefferson, 24 August 1815," *The Papers of Thomas Jefferson*, ed. J. Jefferson Looney (Princeton: Princeton University Press, 2011), vol. 8, 682–84.

[10] "Letter from John Adams to Abigail Adams (September 16, 1774)," *Adams Family Papers: An Electronic Archive.* Accessed February 23, 2022, from www.masshist.org/digitaladams/.

[11] Worthington C. Ford et al., eds., *Journals of the Continental Congress 1774–1789* (Washington, DC: Government Printing Office, 1908), vol. I, 27.

Plead thou my cause, O Lord, with them that strive with me: and fight thou against them that fight against me.

Lay hand upon the shield and buckler: and stand up to help me.

Bring forth the spear, and stop the way against them that persecute me: say unto my soul, I am thy salvation ....

Awake and stand up to judge my quarrel: avenge thou my cause, my God, and my Lord.

Judge me, O Lord my God, according to thy righteousness: and let them not triumph over me.

Let them not say in their hearts, There, there, so would we have it: neither let them say, We have devoured him.

Let them be put to confusion and shame together, that rejoice at my trouble; let them be clothed with rebuke and dishonour, that boast themselves against me.

Let them be glad and rejoice, that favour my righteous dealing: yea, let them say always, Blessed be the Lord, who hath pleasure in the prosperity of this servant.

And as for my tongue, it shall be talking of thy righteousness: and of thy praise all the day long.[12]

It is easy to imagine how, on that occasion, the attendees would have heard this Psalm and seen themselves as the persecuted, the British Parliament and Crown as their persecutors, and God as the righteous judge who would deliver them. Congress had been informed the previous day of a rumor about a possible cannon bombardment of Boston, which, even though ultimately unfounded, gave them a heightened sense of the contest that was upon them. Adams observed in a letter to Abigail that Congress's reaction to the prayer was profound: "I never saw a greater effect upon an audience. It seemed to those in attendance that Heaven had ordained that Psalm to be read on that morning."[13]

For Adams, the Continental Congress reflected the revolutionary mind – and from its outset that mind had a decidedly providentialist frame.[14] For all the religious diversity among the attendees, there appeared to be consensus as to the attributes ascribed to God in Psalm 35, including the quality of being a providential and just judge. Shortly after the first shots of the Revolutionary War rang out from Lexington and Concord, the Second Continental Congress called for public fasting and prayer in penance and supplication to God for

[12] *The Book of Common Prayer* (Cambridge: John Baskerville, 1662).

[13] "Letter from John Adams to Abigail Adams (September 16, 1774)."

[14] This point is paid little attention to by some scholars. See, e.g., Jack N. Rakove, *The Beginnings of National Politics: An Interpretive History of the Continental Congress* (Baltimore, MD: Johns Hopkins University Press, 2019).

forgiveness and aid in their struggle. In the call to prayer, Congress referred to God as the "great Governor of the World," "all wise," "omnipotent," the "merciful Disposer of events," the providential conductor of the "course of nature," and providential influencer of the "minds of men."[15] Of this proclamation, Adams wrote, "We have appointed a continental Fast. Millions will be upon their Knees at once before their great Creator, imploring his Forgiveness and Blessing, his Smiles on American Councils and Arms."[16] The public pronouncements of Adams and his fellow congressmen affirmed a particularly providential God who governs, disposes events, and influences men's minds. (In the classical Christian natural-law tradition, God's foreknowledge and providence were seen as compatible with free will because, as the free first cause of free secondary causes, God is uniquely capable of operating in and through persons without violating their freedom.)[17] Congress can thus be seen as affirming a version of what Guyatt has called "judicial providentialism," which holds that God's providential favor or disfavor of a nation is tethered to the virtue or lack thereof in its inhabitants.[18]

Six years later, following Cornwallis' surrender at Yorktown, Congress issued a proclamation of Thanksgiving to God for his providential interpositions on behalf of the United States, stating that "Through the whole of the contest, from its first rise to this time, the influence of divine Providence may be clearly perceived in many signal instances, of which we mention but a few." Those few mentioned instances included "revealing the councils of our enemies," "raising up for us a powerful and generous ally," and "making the extreme cruelty of [Britain's] officers and soldiers to the inhabitants of these states ... the very means of cementing our union."[19]

The Continental Congress thus bookended the war with invocations of a God who was considered to be particularly providential. To the Congress, the proof of divine superintendence was to be found in the details of the revolution, and they mentioned three pieces of evidence from the war: counterintelligence, the alliance with France, and the good of colonial union resulting from the evil of British cruelty. The same members who signed the Declaration of Independence drafted and issued these proclamations and others like them throughout the war.

---

[15] Worthington C. Ford et al., eds., *Journals of the Continental Congress 1774–1789* (Washington, DC: Washington Government Printing Office, 1908), vol. II, 87–88.
[16] *The Adams Papers, December 1761 – May 1776*, ed. Lyman H. Butterfield (Cambridge, MA: Harvard University Press, 1963), vol. 1, 215–17.
[17] Aquinas, *Summa Theologica*, I.83.1, ad. 3.
[18] Guyatt, *Providence and the Invention of the United States*; Guyatt helpfully traces the transatlantic intellectual roots of this belief.
[19] Worthington C. Ford et al., eds., *Journals of the Continental Congress 1774–1789* (Washington, DC: Government Printing Office, 1904–1937), vol. XXI, 1074–75.

5.3 PROVIDENCE, DIPLOMACY, AND COUNTERINTELLIGENCE

It had been essential to the success of the revolution that the revolutionaries discover the councils of their enemies. At key moments throughout the revolution, various founders prosecuted the revolution by means of counterintelligence, and it is widely acknowledged that the Franco-American alliance proved essential to American victory. The revolutionary moment did not mark the emancipation of politics from God, as Stewart contends.[20] Far from it. The Americans engaged in counterintelligence, diplomacy to France, and fighting the battles against British soldiers engaged in cruelty understood the historical moment in providentialist terms that dovetailed with Congress' own outlook. They took themselves to be playing their part within a grand plan of a providential and moralistic deity, who willed the success of the American cause of liberty. Specific histories of these events too often have ranged from downplaying the significance of providentialist self-understandings to rejecting them outright for the historian's preferred secular framing of the events, failing to give an accurate picture of how the key players in these events made sense of the world.[21] And yet, the providential framing of the revolution is evident in the careers of key players engaged in intelligence and secret diplomacy between America and France: John Jay, George Washington, and Washington's secret agents operating in New York, Silas Deane, Pierre Beaumarchais, and Benjamin Franklin.

5.3.1 John Jay

John Jay was a member of the New York delegation to the Continental Congress, was elected president of the Second Continental Congress, served as a diplomat and negotiated landmark treaties, helped write the Federalist Papers in defense of the new Constitution, and served as the first chief justice of the Supreme Court. During the Revolutionary War, he played a significant role in counterintelligence. Jay was a member of the Continental Congress' Committee of Secret Correspondence, which provided instructions to his friend Silas Deane as a secret agent and diplomat to France in the spring of 1776.[22] Jay did not sign the Declaration, because he was in attendance at New York's Provincial Congress, which convened July 9, 1776. Still, Jay's reputation was

---

[20] Matthew Stewart, *Nature's God: The Heretical Origins of the American Republic* (New York: W. W. Norton, 2014), 7.

[21] Alexander Rose, *Washington's Spies: The Story of America's First Spy Ring* (New York: Bantam, 2007) is an example of the former; Joel Richard Paul, *Unlikely Allies: How a Merchant, a Playwright, and a Spy Saved the American Revolution* (New York: Riverhead Books, 2009) is an example of the latter.

[22] *The Papers of Benjamin Franklin*, ed. William B. Willcox (New Haven and London: Yale University Press, 1982), vol. 22, 369–74.

such that his services were ardently sought by Congress.[23] Additionally, Jay headed the committee that drafted New York's response to the Declaration, which proclaimed the Declaration's reasons for separation were "cogent and conclusive" and pledged to "risk of our lives and fortunes" in support of it.[24] Later, Jay would commend the timing of the Declaration: "in the Face of so powerful a Fleet and Army, will impress them with an Opinion of our Strength and Spirit."[25]

In September 1776, Jay was appointed as head of New York's counterintelligence committee that was empowered to gather information about conspiracies against the state, to arrest suspects, to call the militia to the committee's aid, to imprison or deport the guilty, "and in general to do every act and thing whatsoever, which may be necessary to enable them to execute the trust hereby reposed in them."[26] Jay had experience in this area in a previous iteration of the committee when earlier that summer he had helped to suppress a plot by New York Tories to assassinate George Washington through his personal bodyguard. The British had defeated Washington at Long Island in August, and General Howe's army of 25,000 men occupied New York City by September. In this situation, there were strong grounds to suspect Tory conspiracies of disaffected New Yorkers, and the sense among the revolutionaries was that the success of the revolution may very well have depended on holding New York.

From its inception, Jay's Committee for Detecting and Defeating Conspiracies organized an intelligence network, heard hundreds of cases, and issued edicts to arrest and imprison scores of persons suspected of disaffection. The committee framed its proclamations in existential terms. The very survival of the state of New York was at stake, and its survival was deemed essential to the American cause of liberty, for its fall was feared to be the first domino that would lead to British victory. Hence, the committee proclaimed it was the civic duty of all persons, especially those who had claimed "neutrality" in the contest, to defend the state through the provision of useful information:

Therefore Resolved that it is the duty of every virtuous citizen when a mortal blow is aimed at the liberties of his country to stand forth in an open & spirited manner & to assist by his example by his council or by his arms in vindicating and defending her cause.[27]

---

[23] See, e.g., "Edward Rutledge to John Jay, 29 June 1776," *The Papers of John Jay*. Accessed July 19, 2021, from https://dlc.library.columbia.edu/jay/ldpd:9616

[24] John Jay, *The Correspondence and Public Papers of John Jay*, ed. Henry P. Johnston (New York: G.P. Putnam's Sons, 1890–93), vol. 1, 72; *Journals of the Provincial Congress* (Albany: Printed by Thurlow Weed), vol. 1, 894; George Pellew, *John Jay* (Boston and New York: Houghton, Mifflin, 1890), 53.

[25] "John Jay to Robert Morris, 6 October 1776." Accessed July 21, 2021, from https://dlc.library.columbia.edu/jay.

[26] *Journals of the Provincial Congress*, 638.

[27] *Minutes of the Committee and of the First Commission for Detecting and Defeating Conspiracies in the State of New York* (New York: Printed for the New York Historical Society, 1924), vol. 1, 13.

One of the members of the committee, Nathaniel Sackett, ran the network of virtuous informers and reported its findings. Jay would head the committee's efforts at intelligence gathering over the next several months and arrest dozens of disaffected conspirators. For Jay, utmost secrecy was paramount for the committee's success. Hence, Jay maintained that in its reports to the Continental Congress, no intelligence should be communicated "than what may be necessary to promote the Common Weal" rather than what might merely gratify "the curiosity of Individuals."[28]

Throughout the ordeal, Jay held firm to his belief that "Providence has been kind to us" and that gratitude to God should be expressed by "acquiescing to all of [God's] dispensations."[29] Jay's self-understanding of his counterintelligence exertions were deeply theological as he articulated in his *Address of the Convention of the Representatives of the State of New York to Their Constituents*, which he wrote while still on the committee to detect and defeat conspiracy. Jay penned this address in December 1776 on the heels of a string of defeats in New York and before Washington's crossing of the Delaware. Amid peace feelers from the British, Jay thought it important to rouse the people to stay the course. Jay's draft of the address, with some minor alterations, was published with the unanimous order of the New York convention.

From the beginning of the address, it was apparent in its framing that God's creation of man and providential care of America were essential grounds of the rightness of the patriotic defense of liberty. The people faced an either/or of "freedom and happiness" versus "slavery and misery," the outcome of which would be determined "by solemn appeal to the Supreme Ruler of all events." Jay began with the same first principles announced in the Declaration:

You and all men were created free, and authorized to establish civil government, for the preservation of your rights against oppression, and the security of that freedom which God hath given you, against the rapacious hand of tyranny and lawless power.[30]

Jay then continued to supplement these philosophical-theological first principles with a familiar historical narrative of American settlement, exercise, and enjoyment of liberty. Americans had settled and tilled the land "under the auspices of and direction of Divine Providence" and reaped the blessings of peace and plenty. Alluding to Micah 4, a biblical passage frequently referenced in founding era political writing, Jay pointed out that "during the space of between one and two hundred years, every man sat under his own vine and his own fig-tree, and there was none to make us afraid."[31] That freedom was now under threat. During King George III's reign (beginning in 1760), British

---

[28] "John Jay to Robert Morris, 6 October 1776." Accessed July 19, 2021, from https://dlc.library.columbia.edu/jay/ldpd:72080.

[29] "John Jay to Sarah Jay, 17 July 1776." Accessed July 19, 2021, from https://dlc.library.columbia.edu/jay/ldpd:32416.

[30] Jay, *Correspondence and Public Papers of John Jay*, 103.　　　[31] Ibid., 104.

imperial policy had swerved from what Burke had called "salutary neglect" to aggressive hostility. Jay alluded to the string of measures from the Stamp Act to the Coercive Acts, which were underpinned by an "abominable claim" to arbitrary rule over the colonies without their consent, which the British now sought to enforce by military invasion. Jay also recalled how the colonies had sent numerous petitions to King George, most recently the Olive Branch Petition, which the King refused to even read before issuing the Proclamation for Suppressing Rebellion and Sedition, which effectively ended any chance of a peaceful resolution.

To persuade his readers to stay the course, Jay developed a theme, common from the Old Testament prophets to Augustine, to explain the sufferings Americans were experiencing from an invading army intending "to plunder your houses; ravish your wives and daughters; strip your infant children; expose whole families naked, miserable, and forlorn, to want, to hunger, to inclement skies, and wretched deaths." Like the Prophetic and Augustinian tradition, Jay placed affliction of good and evil under the wings of divine providence with a focus on its punitive dimension. Affliction at the hands of the British was providentially ordained by God "as instruments to punish the guilt of this country, and bring us back to a sense of duty to our Creator," Jay insisted.[32]

Jay sought to place the punitive dispensation of providence within a sacred and secular history. The Jews, "those favourites of Heaven" had repeatedly been chastised "by tyrants of Egypt, of Babylon, of Syria, and of Rome," who themselves were destroyed for their own crimes after they had served their providential punitive purpose. It was a feature of the Old Law that the Jewish nation would be blessed or cursed according to their righteousness.[33] This was framed as a covenant between God and the people.[34] Jay implicitly accepts something like a covenantal relationship between America and God, for Americans "were born equally free with the Jews, and have as good a right to be exempted from the arbitrary domination of Britain, as they had from the invasions of Egypt, Babylon, Syria, or Rome."[35] Yet Jay distinguished the two cases in that Americans and the English shared ties of history, language, culture, and religion while the Hebrews and their Gentile rulers did not.

Jay's address did not advocate for an apocalyptic providentialism in which Americans were the "favourites of Heaven" *qua* patrons of protestant evangelization that ultimately ushers in Christ's return and millennial reign. Such a view had a place in American colonial history and was central to the Puritan's self-understanding, as is apparent in Winthrop's Atlantic crossing sermon, "A Model of Christian Charity." Winthrop transposed God's covenantal promise

---

[32] Ibid., 104.   [33] Deuteronomy 23:14; 30:1–30.   [34] See also Joshua 24:14–28.
[35] Jay, *Correspondence and Public Papers of John Jay*, 103.

to the Hebrews in Deuteronomy to be the premise of the Massachusetts Bay Colony in which obedience to God promised that

> Wee shall finde that the God of Israell is among us, when ten of us shall be able to resist a thousand of our enemies; when hee shall make us a prayse and glory that men shall say of succeeding plantations, "the Lord make it likely that of *New England*."[36]

Jay's judicial providentialism is not reducible to Puritan covenant theology. For Jay, it is a maxim that "*no* virtuous people were ever oppressed," and all men are created free.[37] The biblical illustrations may have had a special power to capture the imaginations of a Christian audience – but freedom was not the birthright only of Jews or Christians. It was the birthright of all people, and virtue was necessary for its preservation. When Jay invoked Roman people of the republican era as an example of virtue, he was offering an example of the connection between virtue and self-government. While the Romans were not "favorites of heaven," they could nonetheless be confident in heaven's protection on account of their virtues and invocation of "the protection of the Supreme Being." In the face of repeated defeats at the hands of Hannibal, the Romans "bravely defended their city with undaunted resolution; they repelled the enemy and recovered their country."[38]

Jay's judicial providentialism thus affirmed the rationality of belief in an omnipotent and moralistic God, who rewards virtuous, publicly spirited behavior in defense of the liberty of one's country. Because God gave everyone liberty, "our cause is the cause of God, of human nature and posterity," Jay maintained, and Americans "[are] responsible to [God] for that." Jay then issued the practical upshot of his analysis in a flourish: "Rouse, therefore, brave Citizens! Do your duty like men! and be persuaded that Divine Providence will not permit this Western World to be involved in the horrours of slavery."[39] As already mentioned in the edict of the committee to detect conspiracy, the duty of virtuous citizens – "to oppose and repel all those … who prostitute the powers of Government to destroy the happiness and freedom of the people over whom they may be appointed to rule" – included cooperation with its counterintelligence operations.[40]

Within a few weeks of its publication of Jay's address, the Continental Congress "earnestly recommended" that all Americans give it "serious perusal and attention" and directed that it be translated into German at the expense of Congress.[41] In this act, Congress again appealed to a particularly providential

---

[36] John Winthrop, "A Modell of Christian Charity" (1630). Accessed February 23, 2022, from https://history.hanover.edu/texts/winthmod.html.

[37] *Correspondence and Public Papers of John Jay*, 103. Emphasis ours.   [38] Ibid., 112.

[39] In light of Jay's rhetorical appeal to slavery, see also Frank Monaghan, "The Anti-Slavery Papers of John Jay," *Journal of Negro History* 17(4) (1932): 481–96.

[40] Jay, *Correspondence and Public Papers of John Jay*, 103, 116, 118.

[41] *Journals of the Continental Congress*, vol. 7, 42.

and moralistic God who favored the American cause of liberty. Patriotic clergy then took up the task of arguing that the God of Abraham specifically favored the Americans. As tensions spilled over into armed hostilities in 1775, the clergy more and more contended that providence favored America in the coming contest. In his contemporaneous account of the events following Lexington and Concord, Peter Oxenbridge Thacher wrote of the American patriots that "trusting to the divine protection, from that hour we determined never to sheathe the sword" while attributing the early successes of the Americans to the "favor of heaven." God, the "Being of all beings" who by his providence held "the fate of empires in his hands," Thacher maintained, had intervened on behalf of the Americans such that he could be referred to as "the guardian God of America."[42]

As Glenn Moots has shown, many of the American clergy's arguments channeled the themes and symbols of covenant theology, a principal legacy of the reformed tradition in American public life.[43] Interpretations of God's interposition on America's behalf ranged from the apocalyptic to more measured. Preachers such as Samuel Sherwood and Abraham Keteltas offered apocalyptic interpretations of events. Sherwood's "The Church's Flight into the Wilderness" purported that God's will for the contest between Britain and America had been prophesied in Revelation 12's imagery of the woman, her seed, and the dragon. Abraham Keteltas, a Presbyterian minister who claimed that Americans were God's elect, went so far as to identify America's revolutionary cause with the Incarnation and Crucifixion: "Our cause ... [is that] for which the Son of God came down from his celestial throne, and expired on a cross."[44] Leaders of the revolution in Congress, however, offered more sober analyses. In his "The Dominion of Providence over the Passions of Men," John Witherspoon offered a broadly Augustinian theodicy in his reflection on God's sovereignty over good and evil and suggested that when Americans found success in arms, they should "content ourselves with a modest ascription of it to the power of the Highest" – a view consistent with Jay's as he lead the American counterintelligence efforts.[45]

5.3.2 George Washington and the Culper Spy Ring

George Washington had already learned of the importance of counterintelligence during the French and Indian War. As he wrote early in his career,

---

[42] Peter Oxenbridge Thacher, "Oration Delivered at Watertown, March 5, 1776," *Principles and Acts of the Revolution*, collected by Hezekiah Niles (Baltimore, MD: William Ogden Niles, 1822), 23–26.
[43] Glenn A. Moots, *Politics Reformed: The Anglo-American Legacy of Covenant Theology* (Columbia: University of Missouri Press, 2010), 99–116.
[44] Abraham Keteltas, "God Arising and Pleading His People's Cause," *Political Sermons of the American Founding Era* (Indianapolis, IN: Liberty Fund, 1998), vol. 1, 582–606, especially 603.
[45] Witherspoon, "The Dominion of Providence over the Passions of Men," 547. Sherwood's sermon can be found in the same volume.

"There is nothing more necessary than good intelligence to frustrate a designing Enemy: and nothing that requires greater pains to obtain."[46] For Washington, there was an analogy between the knowledge that is possible of the hidden plans of man and the hidden plans of God: "the ways of Men in power, like the ways of Providence are not Inscrutable."[47] Hence, during his service in the French and Indian War, Washington had engaged in intelligence gathering about French activities. Later, as commander in chief of the Continental Army, Washington added that secrecy in intelligence gathering is essential: "For upon Secrecy, Success depends in most Enterprizes of the kind, and for want of it, they are generally defeated, however well planned & promising a favourable issue."[48] Throughout Washington's Revolutionary War correspondence, one can see the importance and difficulty of obtaining good intelligence.

From the first flickers of war and Washington's commission as general of the Continental Army, he consistently described the contest within a larger frame of divine causation. Washington was commissioned as commander in chief by the Continental Congress in June 1775.[49] After receiving his commission, he wrote to Martha with "inexpressable [*sic*] concern" to inform her of his appointment leading the Continental Army. He believed he would reap more happiness at home with Martha in one month than adventuring abroad in "Seven times Seven years." But he expressed hope that his commission was "designd to answer some good purpose." He would "rely therefore, confidently, on that Providence which has heretofore preservd, & been bountiful to me."[50] Shortly thereafter, he wrote Jonathan Trumbull, governor of Connecticut, that as "the Cause of our Common Country calls us both to an Active & dangerous Duty, I trust that Divine Providence which wisely orders the Affairs of Men will enable us to discharge it with Fidelity & Success."[51]

In a dustup the next month over prisoner of war conditions with then Commander in Chief Thomas Gage of the British forces, Washington framed the contest in terms of God's just judgment. After Lexington and Concord,

---

[46] "George Washington to Robert Hunter Morris, 1 January 1756," *The Papers of George Washington*, ed. W. W. Abbot (Charlottesville: University Press of Virginia, 1983), vol. 2, 249–50.

[47] "George Washington to John Robinson, 1 September 1758," *The Papers of George Washington*, ed. W. W. Abbot (Charlottesville: University Press of Virginia, 1988), vol. 5, 432–34.

[48] "George Washington to Colonel Elias Dayton, 26 July 1777," *The Papers of George Washington*, ed. Frank E. Grizzard, Jr. (Charlottesville: University Press of Virginia, 2000), vol. 10, 425–26.

[49] *Journals of the Continental Congress*, vol. II, 96.

[50] "George Washington to Martha Washington, 18 June 1775," *The Papers of George Washington, 16 June 1775–15 September 1775*, ed. Philander D. Chase (Charlottesville: University Press of Virginia, 1985), vol. 1, 3–6.

[51] "Washington to Trumbull, 18 July 1775," *The Papers of George Washington*, ed. Philander D. Chase (Charlottesville: University Press of Virginia, 1985), vol. 1, 131.

there were reports of squalid conditions of prisoners held in Boston. Washington wrote to Gage to implore him to respect the rank and dignity of the prisoners who were held in undifferentiated conditions, and threatened retribution: he also would ignore the ranks of his own British prisoners. Gage replied that he acknowledged "no Rank that is not derived from the King," and retorted that his intelligence indicated that "the King's faithfull Subjects" were "labouring like Negro Slaves, to gain their daily Subsistence." For the Americans to justify this "severity" under the guise of "retaliation" is to subject themselves to the "dreadful consequences" of God's judgment.[52] Washington's counterreply skillfully suggested the causes of taking up arms: citizens were merely defending their lives, properties, and families against tyranny and the authority of Congress was founded upon the genuine principles of liberty. These principles warranted acknowledgment of American rank, for it reflected "the uncorrupted Choice of a brave and free People – The purest Source & original Fountain of all Power." Washington then took up Gage's theological challenge in judicial-providentialist terms: "May that God to whom you then appealed, judge between America & you!"

Washington continued to aver that it was under the direction of God's judicial providence that common citizens and the revolutionary leaders were resolved to risk their lives to "hand down to Posterity those just & invaluable Privileges which they received from their Ancestors."[53] Washington's confidence that the cause of liberty was divinely sanctioned was evident after military successes as when the Americans took Fort Saint-Jean in the Canadian campaign in the fall of 1775. "The Commander in Chief is confident," he wrote in an order, "the Army under his immediate direction, will shew their Gratitude to providence, for thus favouring the Cause of Freedom and America; and by their thankfulness to God, their zeal and perseverance in this righteous Cause, continue to dese[r]ve his future blessings."[54] Still, the Canadian invasion, building on the success at Ticonderoga, foundered at the Battle of Quebec when the Americans failed to take Quebec City in the final days of December 1775. One year later, the fledgling revolution was like a delicate ember at risk at any moment of being stomped out. While Congress had declared independence midway through 1776, that year had also seen Washington's army suffer successive defeats with desertion waxing and morale waning. The United States needed a victory. In one of the most memorable events of the revolution, Washington delivered a Christmastide victory against a group of Hessian soldiers after the iconic crossing of the Delaware. Essential

[52] "Thomas Gage to George Washington, 13 August 1775," *The Papers of George Washington*, vol. 1, 301–2.

[53] "George Washington to Thomas Gage, 19 August 1775," *The Papers of George Washington*, vol. 1, 326–28.

[54] "General Orders, 14 November 1775," *The Papers of George Washington*, ed. Philander D. Chase (Charlottesville: University Press of Virginia, 1987), vol. 2, 369–70.

to this operation was intelligence provided by a double agent named John Honeyman.[55] Honeyman posed as a loyalist to British troops in New Jersey and reported about the state of the Hessian troops to Washington. He then returned to the British playing the escapee, and fed them false information about Washington's army, setting the stage for Washington's raid. In her reply to her husband's report of the battles of Trenton and Princeton, Abigail Adams rejoiced in the successes of the Continental army, and prayed, "Heaven grant us a continuation of them."[56]

Washington sought to stoke the ember further by expanding his counter-intelligence operations, which included employing Nathaniel Sackett as a salar-ied agent in New York.[57] Washington eventually replaced the ineffective Sackett, making Major Benjamin Tallmadge the head of spy operations in New York by August 1778.[58] Washington's move was in part motivated by the need to provide intelligence to Vice Admiral Charles Hector, Comte d'Estaing, who was arriving with a French fleet of twelve ships of the line and five frigates, including ships that would eventually assist the American victory at Yorktown. Comte d'Estaing arrived at Delaware Bay on July 8 carrying home Silas Deane, who played an essential role in securing the French alliance but had since been recalled by Congress. Upon his arrival, d'Estaing quickly notified Washington of his desire to be informed of Washington's movements and to act in concert with his army.[59] Admiral d'Estaing concurred with Washington about the importance of intelligence:

In order to counteract the enemy's projects, it is essential to penetrate them without loss of time – it is impossible to employ money more usefully than on this object – and I would readily engage for the Kings Share of the expence of Spies – in order to act is [sic] essential to have intelligence.[60]

[55] See "In Defense of John Honeyman (and George Washington)," *Studies in Intelligence* 53 (December 2009), 87–90.

[56] "Abigail Adams to John Adams, 26 January 1777," *The Adams Papers, June 1776 – March 1778*, ed. L. H. Butterfield (Cambridge, MA: Harvard University Press, 1963), vol. 2, 149–50. Accessed February 21, 2022, from https://founders.archives.gov/documents/Adams/04-02-02-0107.

[57] "George Washington Orders to Nathaniel Sackett, 4 February 1777," *The Papers of George Washington, 6 January 1777–27 March 1777*, ed. Frank E. Grizzard, Jr. (Charlottesville: University Press of Virginia, 1998), vol. 8, 242–43. For an account of Sackett's exploits, see Rose, *Washington's Spies*, 48–50.

[58] "George Washington to Benjamin Tallmadge, 25 August 1778," *The Papers of George Washington*, ed. David R. Hoth (Charlottesville: University of Virginia Press, 2006), vol. 16, 376–77; Kenneth A. Daigler, *Spies, Patriots, and Traitors: American Intelligence in the Revolutionary War* (Washington, DC: Georgetown University Press, 2015), 174.

[59] "d'Estaing to George Washington, 13 July 1778," *The Papers of George Washington*, vol. 16, 63.

[60] "d'Estaing to George Washington, 5 September 1778," *The Papers of George Washington*, vol. 16, 522–25.

Tallmadge would organize and direct the Culper spy ring, which employed various agents under assumed identities. Abraham Woodhull, Tallmadge's chief agent, played the eponymous Samuel Culper, posing as a loyalist farmer from Setauket. Unlike Tallmadge, who was a graduate of Yale college, Woodhull was not highly educated. As a farmer from Long Island, Woodhull's outlook was representative of that of a common patriot rather than the revolution's highly educated leaders.

Woodhull's mission was to travel back and forth to New York City, gather information, pen his findings, and hide the letters intended for Tallmadge where they could be retrieved by a courier. Eventually, Woodhull's efforts would be assisted by a supply of invisible ink (which John Jay's older brother, James, had manufactured).[61] Washington had come to understand with more urgency the need for sound spy tactics after the British execution of patriot spy Nathan Hale. Woodhull's anxiety about being detected is understandable given Hale's precedent. Woodhull not only faced suspicious British officers but also highway robbers, who would be all too willing to sell information to the British. On one occasion, he reported that "It is two [*sic*] great a resque to write with ink in this Country of Robbers" after he narrowly escaped with his life, but not after the thieves searched every pocket and lining on his person. Woodhull reported that his secret correspondence was in his saddle, "but thank kind Providence they did not find it."[62]

Woodhull may not have understood the full import of his remark. Had he been discovered, the Culper ring might have been compromised and unable to keep the revolutionary ember burning in the summer of 1780 when it did so by reporting to Washington about troop movements preparing a surprise attack on the French fleet arriving at Rhode Island. By then, Woodhull had a partner working from inside New York City. Amid his anxiety, Woodhull had reported that he found a "faithful friend and one of the first characters in the City to make it his business and keep his eyes upon every movement and assist me in all respects and meet and consult weekly in or near the city." This friend was Robert Townsend, who would issue reports as Culper Jr. Woodhull attributed the success of finding Townsend to divine providence, saying "blessed be God" that he had "been prospered and particularly successful" in engaging Townsend.[63]

As Comte de Rochambeau and his 5,000 French soldiers were landing in Newport, Rhode Island, in July 1780, Washington wrote to Tallmadge seeking

---

[61] Rose, *Washington's Spies*, 107, 132.

[62] "Samuel Culper Jr. to John Bolton, 10 October 1779." Accessed February 21, 2022, from www .loc.gov/collections/george-washington-papers/about-this-collection/.

[63] "Samuel Culper to Charles Scott, October 31, 1778." Accessed February 21, 2022, from www .loc.gov/collections/george-washington-papers/about-this-collection/. Letter also quoted in Morton Pennypacker, *General Washington's Spies on Long Island and in New York* (Brooklyn: Long Island Historical Society, 1939), 32.

any available intelligence: "As we may every moment expect the arrival of the French Feet a revival of the correspondence will be of very great importance."[64] Townsend was engaged in the city to collect information and sent urgent information to Woodhull to be relayed. Woodhull wrote a forward to Townsend's intelligence that the information would require the utmost speed in delivery: "by all means let not an hour pass: for this day must not be lost." The enclosed provided "news of the greatest consequence perhaps that ever happened to your country."[65] Townsend's note informed the revolutionaries that British Admiral Graves had arrived with six ships of the line destined for Newport along with 8,000 troops. Alexander Hamilton received this vital news about the impending British attack on Rochambeau and immediately forwarded it to Rochambeau; meanwhile, Tallmadge forwarded the intelligence to Washington. With this information, Washington feigned an attack on New York, which successfully deterred the British offensive on Rhode Island and secured the passage of the arriving French.

The strategic importance of securing Rochambeau's troops was immense. He would eventually combine with Washington's force and march for Yorktown in 1781. The French navy would be essential to victory in the Battle of the Chesapeake in which Comte de Grasse (who had succeeded d'Estaing) defeated the British, setting the stage for the Franco-American land and naval forces to surround Cornwallis and force his surrender.

We should not expect deep philosophical or theological reflections in the Culper letters. These letters were not a medium for metaphysical disquisition but for communicating concise information about germane British activities with economical use of paper and expensive ink. For just this reason, they reflect common understandings, and the providentialist frame of mind of the participants in the Culper ring shines through at times, as we have already seen. The spies describe God as being providentially involved in the revolutionary struggle as when God protected Woodhull from detection. They operate as though God is the author of a moral law that imposes obligations. Regarding the great risks he took as a spy, Woodhull remarked that it had been done as principle "of duty rather than any mercenary end," and he indicated in one letter that this duty to spy on the enemy in defense of American liberty was compatible with his fear of the God of the Christian Gospel.[66] Regarding the presence of the French fleet in aid of the Americans, Woodhull remarked on the

[64] "George Washington to Benjamin Tallmadge, 11 July 1780." Accessed February 23, 2022, from http://memory.loc.gov/ammem/gwhtml/gwhome.html.

[65] "Samuel Culper to Caleb Brewster, 20 July 1780." Accessed February 23, 2022, from http://memory.loc.gov/ammem/gwhtml/gwhome.html. Letter also quoted in Pennypacker, *George Washington's Spies*, 82.

[66] "Samuel Culper to John Bolton, 12 December 1779," *George Washington Papers, Series 4, General Correspondence: Samuel Culper to John Bolton, Intelligence*. Accessed February 22, 2022, from www.loc.gov/item/mgw456376/. Accessed July 13, 2021, from http://memory.loc.gov/ammem/gwhtml/gwhome.html. Also see Rose, *Washington's Spies*, 72.

interpositions of providence: "This Glorious assistance together with the dejection of our Enemies, bids fair for our delivery," praying "may God grant us Success."[67]

Following the arrival of the French fleet, the patriotic cause experienced high-level treachery. In September 1780, General Benedict Arnold made a secret pact with the British through British Major John André to deliver West Point. Before André could return to British command with the detailed plans of how to take the fort, however, American militiamen captured him using a false name with forged papers from Arnold. When his capture came to the attention of Tallmadge, he took measures to secure André in consultation with the commanding officer and smoke out the plot. He tried to stop a letter from being sent to Arnold about the capture that ended up forewarning him and enabling him to escape.[68] While Arnold escaped, his plans to deliver the intelligence that would enable a surprise attack on West Point failed.

Recounting this episode, American General Nathanael Greene wrote that it was "by the most providential train of accidents" that André had been captured. In another letter reflecting on the episode, Greene commented: "We have seen many instances in the course of this revolution the favourable interposition of Providence in our behalf; but none that I recollect have been more conspicuous than this. It is sufficient to command the belief of an infidel."[69] The providential interposition, in this instance, was particular, not general. As Washington explained:

A combination of extraordinary circumstances – an unaccountable deprivation of presence of Mind in a Man of the first abilities – and the virtuous conduct of three Militia Men – threw the Adjutant General of the British forces in America (with full proofs of Arnolds treachery) into our hands . . . .[70]

The providentialist interpretation of this episode was widespread among Americans, but it was not limited to them. The Comte de Rochambeau spoke for the French, commenting: "this plainly shews that the Divine Providence is favorable to Us and to our Cause, which I have more than once experienced since the opening of this Campaign."[71]

---

[67] "Culper to Bolton, 26 October 1779." Accessed November 3, 2015, at http://memory.loc.gov/ammem/gwhtml/gwhome.html. Also see Rose, *Washington's Spies*, 257–58.

[68] For Tallmadge's account, see *Memoir of Colonel Benjamin Tallmadge*, ed. Henry Phelps Johnston (New York: Gillis Press, 1904), 51–57.

[69] *The Papers of General Nathanael Greene*, ed. Dennis M. Conrad (Chapel Hill: University of North Carolina Press, 1991), vol. 6, 345.

[70] "From George Washington to John Laurens, 13 October 1780," Founders Online, National Archives. Accessed February 22, 2022, from https://founders.archives.gov/documents/Washington/99-01-02-03563.

[71] "To George Washington from Jean-Baptiste Donatien de Vimeur, comte de Rochambeau, 30 September 1780," Founders Online, National Archives. Accessed February 22, 2022, from https://founders.archives.gov/documents/Washington/99-01-02-03445.

Tallmadge highlighted his own providentialist beliefs that God had been involved in the war from the beginning. Tallmadge recalled in his memoirs when the Declaration of Independence was read to the army, and how it "filled every one with enthusiastic zeal." There was no reason for Tallmadge to think that the God of the Declaration of Independence was somehow incompatible with the providential moralistic God he believed in. Shortly thereafter, Tallmadge was among Washington's troops who fought the Battle of Long Island. His memoir recalled the horrors of this early battle and went on to describe the perilous position that Washington's army was in: no entrenchment, massively outnumbered to their front, and their retreat over the East River subject to being cut off at any moment by the British fleet. Tallmadge recounted the all-night evacuations that took place over two days: August 29 to 30, 1776. But, by daybreak, several regiments were left, including Tallmadge's, leaving them anxious for their safety. According to Tallmadge: "At this time a very dense fog began to rise, and it seemed to settle in a peculiar manner over both encampments." Tallmadge's regiment was ordered to depart, but then that order was countermanded and they had to remain in their positions as the sun rose. And yet "the fog remained as dense as ever." Finally, they were called to depart, and the fog covered their retreat. Tallmadge remarks that "I recollect this peculiar providential occurrence perfectly well," and voices his belief that "the providential appearance of the fog saved a part of our army from being captured, and certainly myself, among others who formed the rear guard."[72]

After the war, Tallmadge wrote to Washington in order to seek settlement and pay of monies promised to Culper and his coworkers. For his part, Tallmadge's letters to Washington were usually matter of fact, but in this letter Tallmadge expressed gratitude for serving under Washington and for Washington's approbation for the part Tallmadge played in the general's plans. Tallmadge concluded by wishing Washington good health and satisfaction from knowing that he had been "the Instrument, under God, in obtaining the freedom & Independence of this Country."[73] It was thus that Tallmadge reflected a belief held in common by those key participants that the members of the Culper spy ring had been instruments of the inscrutable God in discovering the hidden plans of the enemy.

5.4 THE FRANCO-AMERICAN ALLIANCE AND THE PROVIDENTIAL DIPLOMATIC MISSION TO FRANCE

The French alliance was essential to the achievement of independence, and Silas Deane played an essential role in securing it. Deane was a Yale graduate, a

[72] Benjamin Tallmadge, *Memoir of Colonel Benjamin Tallmadge*, ed. Henry Phelps Johnston (New York: Gillis Press, 1904), 11–14.
[73] "Benjamin Tallmadge to George Washington, 16 August 1783," Founders Online, National Archives. Accessed February 22, 2022, from http://founders.archives.gov/documents/Washington/99-01-02-11698.

lawyer-turned-successful merchant in Connecticut, and a delegate to the First and Second Continental Congresses. In March 1776, the Committee of Secret Correspondence commissioned Deane to be an agent and ambassador to France. Deane was sent with the purpose of acquiring clothing and arms for 25,000 troops. He was also charged with seeking to secure treaties of commercial and military alliance.[74] Deane was selected for this difficult task after distinguishing himself in the early days of the revolution. A successful merchant, he had been elected to Connecticut's general assembly before being elected to represent Connecticut in the Continental Congress. Shortly after the battles at Lexington and Concord, Deane saw an opportunity for the revolutionaries to seize the desperately needed weapons cache at Fort Ticonderoga. It was then garrisoned with only a token force, but haste would be necessary to take it before British reinforcements arrived. In his capacity on the Connecticut Committee of Correspondence, Deane authorized Connecticut treasury funds to bankroll an assault on Fort Ticonderoga. While Deane formally lacked authority to do this without the assent of the assembly, the need for secrecy and dispatch was manifest.[75] With this financial backing, Fort Ticonderoga would be taken by Benedict Arnold and Ethan Allen commanding his Vermont Green Mountain Boys, providing not only needed materiel but also a significant psychological boost to the revolutionaries, given that the fort was a symbol of British imperial power in the Americas. Following Fort Ticonderoga, Deane's stature rose in Congress as he worked on numerous committees, including Ways and Means, the Committee on Trade, and the Committee of Secrecy.

Yet Deane's membership in Congress was not without controversy. At the opening of Congress, Deane had expressed his desire that "the God of wisdom" would preside over their deliberations.[76] But he quickly found out that wisdom would clash with faction and interest in the legislative body. Deane had a falling out with his fellow representative from Connecticut and eventual member of the drafting committee of the Declaration of Independence, Roger Sherman. While differences between Deane and Sherman arose partly from personality clashes and regional rivalries, the divide between them became a chasm due to a clash over who should be the Connecticut appointee to a major generalship under Washington.[77] After losing this nomination battle to Deane, Sherman likely used his influence in Connecticut to scuttle Deane's reelection to Congress. After this ordeal, Deane wrote to his wife that he was unfit for the "trimming, courting, and intrigues with the populace" that were necessary in

[74] "The Committee of Secret Correspondence: Instructions to Silas Deane, 2 March 1776," *The Papers of Benjamin Franklin, March 23, 1775–October 27, 1776*, ed. William B. Willcox (New Haven and London: Yale University Press, 1982), vol. 22, 369–74.

[75] Paul, *Unlikely Allies*, 79.

[76] *The Silas Deane Papers* (New York: New York Historical Society, 1886–1890), vol. 1, 48.

[77] Paul, *Unlikely Allies*, 99–101.

political life. He wondered "how I ever became popular at all," and took solace in his education: "I have too much philosophy to be in distress at losing."[78]

And yet it was mere months after being replaced in Congress that the Committee of Secret Correspondence tapped Deane for the mission to France. As he prepared to leave behind his wife and son, he wrote to Mrs. Deane acknowledging the pain it must be giving her that public life continued to call him away from his family. She was already aware that Deane's fundamental moral principle – which the "Eye of God" knew, and the envious eye of man could not contradict – was "to sacrifice all lesser considerations to the service of the whole, and in this tempestuous season to throw cheerfully overboard, private fortune, private emoluments, and all partial or interested views, even my Life, – if the Ship with the jewel Liberty on board may be saved."[79] Deane then explained that he was acting upon his moral principles in accepting the commission to France:

I wish as much as any man for the enjoyments of domestic ease, peace, and society, but am forbid expecting them soon; indeed, must be criminal in my own eyes, did I balance them one moment in opposition to the Public Good and the Calls of my Country.

While acting on his principles would risk his life and fortune, Deane considered himself "Safe in the hand of that protecting Power, Who rul'd my natal, and must fix my mortal hour." Deane closed this letter with a striking affirmation of God's providence:

And now, my Dear, are not the ways of Providence dark and inscrutable to us, short-sighted mortals? Surely they are. My enemies tho't to triumph over me and bring me down, yet all they did has been turned to the opening a door for the greatest and most extensive usefulness, if I succeed . . . .[80]

Deane here suggested that God used the malice of his political enemies and his failed reelection to bring about his appointment as ambassador to France. This is a far cry from a worldview in which events are driven by "materialistically self-interested individuals," as Deane's biographer suggests.[81]

After months of delays and setbacks, Deane finally arrived in France in June 1776. Shortly after his arrival, he was directed by the French foreign minister Charles Gravier, Comte de Vergennes, to make contact with the famous watch-maker, playwright, and sometime royal secret agent, the Caron de Beaumarchais. Beaumarchais had recently returned to England after a secret mission to retrieve incriminating correspondence between King Louis XV and Chevalier d'Eon, who was something of a rogue French agent and one of the most mysterious and fascinating characters in all of European history. The story of how Beaumarchais came to be both the principal champion of

[78] *Deane Papers*, 93.   [79] Ibid., 74–75.   [80] Ibid, 121–22.
[81] See Milton C. Vlack, *Silas Deane: Revolutionary War Diplomat and Politician* (Jefferson, NC: Macfarland Incorporated, 2013), 69.

American interests to the French monarchy and the chief French purveyor of arms to the Americans is, in a word, incredible. It is almost an understatement to say that Beaumarchais and Deane were "unlikely allies."[82]

Beaumarchais was a French aristocrat with a penchant for extravagant living and an inclination to flout authority. A few of the memorable events that eventually led to his aid to America illustrate this. Beaumarchais burned through piles of money that he had acquired through marriage to two rich widows in the 1750s and 1760s. His Figaro plays satirized the French aristocracy and government. He got into legal trouble for insulting a duke (with whose mistress Beaumarchais was having an affair). When he lost a court battle over an inheritance settlement following the death of his benefactor (his opponent had bribed the judge), Beaumarchais was ordered to pay thousands of livres he did not have. He excoriated the corrupt French courts in his "Memorials," which deeply influenced Voltaire. This led Beaumarchais to fall out of favor with Versailles and to be exiled. Seeking to restore his place at court, he accepted King Louis XVI's secret commission to recover damning letters carried by one Chevalier d'Eon, the cross-dressing French soldier-spy, also an exile seeking to restore honor and return to France. D'eon had secret correspondence with Louis XV about plans to invade England, which if published would be damning to France and ignite war. It was during this mission of several months that Beaumarchais happened to meet the American Arthur Lee at one of London Mayor Wilkes' dinner parties. Lee asked Beaumarchais about assistance in buying arms to be shipped to the American troops. From the providentialist patriotic perspective, God used the events and secondary causes that led to this conversation, thereby providentially allowing the successful development of a plot to smuggle French materiel to America without implicating the French government.[83]

Beaumarchais was able to negotiate a deal with d'Eon who would give over the incriminating documents, agree to live publicly as a woman, and then be received back at Versailles. This, it was thought, would undermine d'Eon's credibility in any future attempt to blackmail the king. Beaumarchais returned in late 1775 successful, carrying most of the incriminating correspondence, although negotiations continued. He also came home with an idea to smuggle arms to the Americans, which he sought to present to the king. The king would secretly bankroll the endeavor, and Beaumarchais would set up a dummy corporation to conduct the operation, giving Versailles plausible deniability. The initial investment would be comparatively modest and would be repaid in Virginian tobacco.[84] The French diplomat Charles Gravier, Comte de Vergennes, initially spurned this idea, because the king was wary of taking

---

[82] The following discussion is indebted to Paul, *Unlikely Allies.*   [83] Ibid., 139–41.

[84] *For the Good of Mankind: Pierre-Augustin Caron de Beaumarchais Political Correspondence Relative to the American Revolution,* compiled, ed. and trans. Antoine Shewmake (Lanham, MD: University Press of America, 1987), 75–81; *Deane Papers,* 110.

any course of action that would violate the 1763 treaty with Britain. Even so, Beaumarchais' success with the d'Eon issue earned him an ear with the king, and he was able to convince the king that it was in France's national interest to covertly arm the Americans.

Beaumarchais developed a number of arguments under the guiding principle of French national interest. The common theme through his entreaties to the king was that relatively small French expenditures would keep the Americans afloat long enough to drastically weaken the British. The longer the Americans could hold on, the more money the British would have to spend to keep their armies in the field, which could not continue indefinitely. In his Peace or War Memo, sent in late February 1777, Beaumarchais argued that the security of the French sugar islands was at stake if the British either won or were reconciled to the Americans or the Americans won.[85] In the first case, the British would be powerful enough to seize the islands; in the second, the Americans would assist the British out of spite for France's refusal to aid their cause; in the last case, the British would need new sources of revenue and raw goods to keep up their living standards.

For some time, the king remained cool toward arguments from national interest because of his sense of justice and the apparently just demands to adhere to the 1763 treaty with Britain. In response to this, Beaumarchais developed a realist argument. The only law binding international relations was the "natural law," by which Beaumarchais meant the principles of "self-preservation, well-being and prosperity of each state ... to do your own good as the first law; with the least possible harm to other States as the second."[86] Beaumarchais thus advanced a concept of natural law with recognizably Hobbesian (but *not* Hobbist) overtones. For Hobbes, self-preservation is the paramount rational necessity, and the social virtues are derived from this good. Upon this understanding of natural law was built a notion of international relations where the good of the realm is paramount, even as relationships with other states are to be conducted honorably.[87] On this conception, the spark of cupidity as manifest in glory and dominion seeking, generative of the state of nature, is condemned as unreasonable and evil. Cupidity and therefore competition in the state of nature is not, however, altogether quashed when persons incorporate through the social covenant. Rather, cupidity is sublimated into the competition of the marketplace and the political sphere. This "realist" approach is broadly compatible with classical, Christian natural-law anthropology, which has a realistic account of the role of self-interest in human behavior.

---

[85] Shewmake, *For the Good of Mankind*, 95–98.   [86] Ibid., 85.

[87] See Kody W. Cooper, "Thomas Hobbes," in *The Edinburgh Companion to Political Realism*, ed. Robert Schuett and Miles Hollingsworth (Edinburgh: Edinburgh University Press, 2018), 189–201.

By Beaumarchais' time, this vision of English society was manifest: "England offers a microcosmic picture of the universe, where general harmony is founded on the continual warring of all beings against one another. No other country in Europe can compare."[88] In other words, the good of the realm ought to be paramount on a stage in which actors act in their self-interest.[89] Men are not angels, Beaumarchais reminded the king.[90] The king ought to be willing to break the treaty and secretly aid the Americans, Beaumarchais urged, because the tranquility of France would rest on the division of its enemies. Beaumarchais' arguments won the day, in part through the medium of Vergennes, whose arguments to the king were influenced by Beaumarchais' Peace or War Memo.[91] By March 1776, Versailles had committed 1 million livres of seed money to Beaumarchais' secret arms-smuggling operation.

This was the state of things when Silas Deane arrived a few months later and immediately began cooperating with Beaumarchais. That the mission would be carried off with some success seems shocking in light of their obstacles. The obstacles were not merely financial (Beaumarchais sank millions into the operation on the promise of remuneration that he never received) but also diplomatic (avoiding alerting the British) and logistic (avoiding detection and seizure by the British navy). Some of their most significant obstacles arose from supposed allies, such as the jealous and conniving Arthur Lee (who would defame Deane in letters to Congress, inciting his recall) and the Janus-faced Edward Bancroft (Deane's personal secretary and contact at Franklin's recommendation, who was actually a double agent feeding the British intelligence about every detail of the Franco-American meetings and plans with almost digital speed). Nevertheless, over a year after Beaumarchais' plan had been approved, massive arms deliveries of much needed cannon, powder, balls, and clothing arrived on American shores aboard the ships *Mercure* and the *Amphirite*. The materiel made its way into the colonists' hands in New York, who were under General Horatio Gates' command by late summer of 1777.

These supplies outfitted the troops who fought in the momentous turning point at the Battle of Saratoga – an American victory that probably would not have happened without this French materiel. As Mercy Otis Warren recounted, it was a "reverse of fortune . . . that had not fallen under the calculation of either party . . . undoubtedly the most fortunate circumstance for the United States,

---

[88] Shewmake, *For the Good of Mankind*, 123.

[89] Beaumarchais cites Montesquieu to support the maxim that a nation ought to do its own good first, and the least amount of harm to others as a second. See Montesquieu, *Spirit of the Laws*, ed. and trans. Anne M. Cohler, Basia C. Miller, and Harold S. Stone (New York: Cambridge University Press, 1998), I.3.

[90] Shewmake, *For the Good of Mankind*, 85.

[91] *Unlikely Allies*, 162–64; John J. Meng, "A Footnote to Secret Aid in the American Revolution," *The American Historical Review* 43(4) (1938): 791–95.

that had yet taken place."⁹² This was not only because of the American gains in arms and the British loss of troops. The symbolic and expressive effect was massive:

So many thousands of brave men and distinguished officers, led captive through the wilderness, the plains, and the cities of the United States, was a spectacle never before beheld by the inhabitants; and the impression it made on their minds, was in proportion to the novelty of the scene, and the magnitude of its consequences ... British *battalions* were no longer deemed invulnerable, even by the most timid and uninformed sons of America.⁹³

General Washington immediately interpreted the outcome of the battle as a sign of divine favor:

This singular favour of Providence is to be received with thankfulness and the happy moment which Heaven has pointed out for the firm establishment of American Liberty ought to be embraced with becoming spirit.⁹⁴

Roughly simultaneous with the arrival of the *Amphirite* and the *Mercure* and the much needed supplies, Franklin (who had recently arrived in France) and Deane were framing their diplomatic mission in these providentialist terms:

All Europe is for us ... it is a very general Opinion that if we succeed in establishing our Liberties, we shall as soon as Peace is restored receive an immense Addition of Numbers and Wealth from Europe, by the Families who will come over to participate our Privileges and bring their Estates with them. Tyranny is so generally established in the rest of the World that the Prospect of an Asylum in America for those who love Liberty gives general Joy, and our Cause is esteem'd the Cause of all Mankind. Slaves naturally become base as well as wretched. We are fighting for the Dignity and Happiness of Human Nature. Glorious is it for the Americans to be call'd by Providence to this Post of Honour.⁹⁵

Writing to Franklin to first tell him of the victory at Saratoga, Reverend Dr. Samuel Cooper reported the "glorious success" of the Americans in that battle. Cooper then suggested that the setbacks leading up to Saratoga were providentially ordained toward ultimate American victory: "divine Providence has

⁹² Mercy Otis Warren, *History of The Rise, Progress and Termination of The American Revolution*, ed. Lester H. Cohen (Indianapolis, IN: Liberty Fund, 1989), vol. 2, 241, 246.

⁹³ Ibid., 247. Emphasis in original.

⁹⁴ "George Washington to Brigadier General James Potter, 18 October 1777," *The Papers of George Washington, 19 August 1777–25 October 1777*, ed. Philander D. Chase and Edward G. Lengel (Charlottesville: University Press of Virginia, 2001), vol. 11, 547–48.

⁹⁵ "The American Commissioners to the Committee of Secret Correspondence, 12 March–9 April 1777," *The Papers of Benjamin Franklin, October 27, 1776, through April 30, 1777*, ed. William B. Willcox (New Haven and London: Yale University Press, 1983), vol. 23, 466–76.

supported and sav'd us in Ways we little thought of."[96] When news of the victory at Saratoga arrived in France, the American diplomats understood the significance of the moment. They seized the opportunity to urge the king toward entering a formal alliance.[97]

The diplomats built on the legwork already done by Deane several months before in a memo to Vergennes and the king. Deane briefly narrated the history of the conflict between Britain and the united colonies up through the Declaration of Independence. He framed it as a widespread resistance of the colonists who appealed to the "rights and immunities of the British Constitution," to absolutist claims of the British administration, which sought to "bind the Colonies in all cases whatsoever."[98] Now that America had finally declared independence, Deane pressed Vergennes about whether France would acknowledge the colonies' independence and whether it would be willing to enter into a formal commercial and military alliance. Deane made various appeals to French national interest, but, significantly, he also framed his argument in theological and providentialist terms.

Britain had entered the late Seven Years' War "ostensibly" to settle frontier boundaries and protect the colonies. But "the real ground of that bloody and expensive war," Dean asserted, was that France had gained ascendancy in the fur trade and Indian relations.[99] Deane hinted that France's West Indies possessions might be just as enticing a prize to the British this time around. He pointed out that Britain was forced to quit the last war "by the Enormity of her National Debt," but now, after one campaign, the revenues of twelve peaceful years were squandered, and the British national debt was higher than before. That France was now in a unique position to tip the scales in favor of the Americans and ruin her rival was an eventuality that "no human Eye could have foreseen." Neither could anyone have predicted that France had the opportunity to pull the economic rug out from under Britain and reap the commercial benefits for itself. But French aid, Deane intimated, was urgently needed. He declared that reconciliation with Britain was improbable – but he suggested that without French aid the Americans would be forced to settle a separate peace to the potential prejudice of French interests and West Indies possessions.[100]

---

[96] "To Benjamin Franklin from Samuel Cooper: Two Letters, 25 October 1777," *Founders Online*, National Archives. Accessed February 23, 2022, from https://founders.archives.gov/documents/Franklin/01-25-02-0065.

[97] "The American Commissioners to Vergennes," *The Papers of Benjamin Franklin, October 1, 1777, through February 28, 1778*, ed. William B. Willcox (New Haven and London: Yale University Press, 1986), vol. 25, 260.

[98] *Deane Papers*, 254.   [99] Ibid, 272.

[100] It is one of the great ironies of history that the British fate described by Deane actually befell France. French aid to the Americans tallied several billion dollars in today's currency, for which it received little valuable return, sinking it into such debt that it was in desperate need of tax revenues on the eve of the French Revolution.

We should not miss the providentialist frame of Deane's argument. Just as he believed his fall from political grace and subsequent appointment as agent to France were humanly unforeseeable, but divinely ordained, so with the opportunity for a Franco-American alliance:

It has been so ordered by the Power which invisibly governs & directs human Events, that the command & direction of these probable as well as possible Events should be committed to France.[101]

In Deane's view, God had so arranged the course of events as to place the fate of American liberty in the hands of the French. The abstract unlikelihood of a Catholic monarchy coming to the aid of largely protestant republicans revolting against their protestant monarch, only a few generations removed from the ouster of the legitimate Catholic king, doubtless sharpened the sense, in the minds of the players, that these events were indeed remarkable.

Returning to December 1777, it is notable that even Beaumarchais offered a striking providential interpretation of the events. He tended to sketch politics in humanistic terms – his *realpolitik* is evident throughout his letters, and when he does speak of events outside of human control, he sometimes speaks of luck and fortune. Still, even Beaumarchais ultimately set this conception within a providentialist frame, supposing throughout his letters that a superintending providence would protect the covert shipments to America.[102] God is moralistic, meting out deserved punishments, and Beaumarchais believed that God willed the Franco-American alliance.[103] Following Saratoga, Beaumarchais wrote to Vergennes that "some God whispers in my ear that the King will not let such auspicious events be marred by a total desertion from the true friends of America." Beaumarchais did not in this instance specify which God spoke to him, but this nameless God was nonetheless particularly providential.

Beaumarchais then cleverly adopted Psalm 130 in his plea to France. Where the Psalmist had cried out to the God of Abraham, Beaumarchais cried to the king for a Franco-American alliance: *De profundis clamavi ad te, Domine, Domine, exaudi vocem mea* (From the depths, I have cried out to you, O Lord; Lord, hear my voice).[104] In the coming weeks, Beaumarchais would continue to press Versailles to act quickly to forestall the possibility of American reconciliation with the British.[105] Deane saw Saratoga in providential terms, as did Washington, and Deane joined his pleas to France with those of Beaumarchais. For his part, from his pamphleteering days in London, Arthur Lee thought events were unfolding "under Divine Providence" and believed that the colonists' fight was a last-resort "appeal to the God of battles."[106]

[101] *Deane Papers*, 273.   [102] Shewmake, *For the Good of Mankind*, 173, 205.
[103] Ibid., 253.   [104] Ibid., 254.   [105] Ibid. 280–81.
[106] Arthur Lee, *A Second Appeal to Justice and Interests of the People on the Measures Respecting America* (London: Printed for J. Almon, 1775), 6–8.

The three diplomats' voices were heard by the King, and the Americans and French signed treaties of alliance and commerce in secret on February 6, 1778, pending ratification by Congress. They promised mutual aid in war against Britain, renunciation of any right to conclude a separate peace with Britain, a most favored status trade relationship, a mutual pledge of naval protection of commercial ships, and a resolution of a number of particular issues of concern, such as a moratorium on molasses duties shipped from French possessions and mutual recognition of specific fishing rights.[107] The ambassadors wrote Congress summarizing the achievement:

This is an Event that will give our States such an Appearance of Stability, as must strengthen our Credit, encourage other Powers in Europe to ally themselves with us, weaken the Hopes of our internal, as well as external Enemies, fortify our Friends, and be in many other Respects so advantageous to us, that we congratulate you upon it most heartily.[108]

A few days later, Franklin wrote to John Langdon, fellow delegate to the Continental Congress and eventual signer of the Constitution, that the new Franco-American alliance "will probably bring on a War" between France and Britain. And indeed, hardly a month had gone by when, having discovered the treaty, Britain declared war on France on March 17, 1778. The Spanish, Dutch, and colonial possessions around the globe would soon be drawn into a world war that would decide the fate of America's independence movement.

Weeks later, Deane boarded d'Estaing's fleet to answer Congress's recall, which had been instigated by Arthur Lee who had lied to his allies in Congress that the materiel sent by Beaumarchais was a gift and misrepresented Deane as unfaithful to the public trust. Before Deane left, he wrote to Beaumarchais, pledging to help him retrieve the debts owed to him, "which by the envy of some and the wickedness of others, have been most strangely misrepresented." Deane went on to congratulate Beaumarchais on the Franco-American alliance, a "great and glorious event, to which you have contributed more than any other person."[109] Beaumarchais reciprocated the praise, arming Deane with a letter lauding Deane's efforts to bring off the smuggling operation.

The so-called Deane-Lee controversy would play out over the next several months in Congress and the public, in which Thomas Paine would join the Lee faction in an attempt to discredit Deane. Still, Deane was able to enter into the public record his own account of his achievement for the American cause:

I procured thirty thousand stand of arms, thirty thousand suits of clothes, more than two hundred and fifty pieces of brass artillery, tents, and other stores to a large amount, provided the ships to transport them, and shipped a great part of them for America. Many of these supplies fortunately arrived at the commencement of the last year's

---

[107] *The Papers of Benjamin Franklin, October 1, 1777, through February 28, 1778*, ed. William B. Willcox (New Haven and London: Yale University Press, 1986), vol. 25, 583–626.

[108] Ibid., 675–78.   [109] Shewmake, *For the Good of Mankind*, 300–1.

operations, and enabled my brave countrymen in some parts of America to make a good stand against the enemy, and in the north to acquire immortal renown by the defeat and surrender of General Burgoyne and his whole army, an event peculiarly fortunate in its consequences, as it accelerated the completion of that alliance, to which the honorable Congress, with every true friend to the United States, have given their approbation.[110]

Beaumarchais would struggle for years to retrieve his payment. Yet John Jay did thank him for his help on behalf of Congress and told him that he had "gained the esteem of this infant republic, and will receive the merited applause of a new world."[111] As the Lee-Deane controversy was playing out, Congress then expressed its belief that God's purposes in the previous year had played out in these events. Congress resolved to set December 30 as a national day of public thanksgiving and praise to God, specifically enjoining Americans to thank God that

it hath pleased him, by his overruling providence, to support us in a just and necessary war, for the defence of our rights and liberties, by affording us seasonable supplies for our armies, by disposing the heart of a powerful monarch to enter into alliance with us, and aid our cause.[112]

Congress left no room to doubt its reliance on particular providence, a public affirmation that remained consistent from the Olive Branch Petition to the Declaration of Independence and to the end of the war. God was understood to be superintending the players in the drama that brought materiel to the continental army and the choice of King Louis XVI to ally his kingdom with America. God's particular providence was manifest, moreover, in "defeating the councils and evil designs of our enemies, and giving us victory over their troops." Finally, Congress thanked God for the union, which would be the source of America's "future strength and glory."[113] The essentials of this proclamation would be reaffirmed after the war had been won.

5.4.1 Benjamin Franklin's Providentialism

After hearing the news of this proclamation in France, Franklin concurred that God's favor of America was evident. Looking back on the diplomats' work in the past year, Franklin declared that "with great Sincerity" he joined in "acknowledging and admiring the Dispensations of Providence in our Favour." He continued to predict that "God will finish his Work, and establish their Freedom," and that America would be a beacon of liberty that would

---

[110] *Deane Papers*, vol. 3, 6.
[111] "John Jay to Pierre Beaumarchais, 15 January 1779," *The Selected Papers of John Jay, 1760–1779*, ed. Elizabeth M. Nuxoll (Charlottesville: University of Virginia Press, 2010), vol. 1, 572–73.
[112] *Journals of the Continental Congress*, vol. 12, 1139.   [113] Ibid.

attract peoples from all over Europe to her shores.[114] We have already seen how Franklin suggested his diplomatic post was a call of Providence – a sentiment he suggested more than once.[115]

But, it could be objected, was Franklin sincere when he insisted that he operated "with great Sincerity"? When he was just nineteen years old, Franklin published *A Dissertation on Liberty and Necessity* in which he purported to deduce from God's wisdom, goodness, and omnipotence the lack of free will in man, a reductionist account of human psychology and action, and other propositions heterodox in the classical Christian tradition. Some readers of Franklin have found in this pamphlet the metaphysical cornerstone of a secular and materialist humanism that he adhered to throughout his life.[116] Yet Franklin wrote in his *Autobiography* that this pamphlet was an *erratum*, and he later wrote that from God's ordinance of prayer it could be deduced that necessitarianism was false, because prayer would then be useless.[117] Moreover, he affirmed in his *Autobiography* that "I never doubted, for instance, the existence of the Deity; that he made the world, and govern'd it by his Providence …."[118] Of course, these words could be driven by exoteric concerns. But such a thesis seems weakened by the fact that, at eighty-one years old in the context of secret deliberations, he would reaffirm this belief. At the Constitutional Convention, he argued that all the attendees were witnesses to God's assistance in the revolution, that America could not rise without divine aid, and called on the delegates to pray to the Father of Lights for guidance. In his words:

In the beginning of the Contest with G. Britain, when we were sensible of danger we had daily prayer in this room for the divine protection. – Our prayers, Sir, were heard, & they were graciously answered. All of us who were engaged in the struggle must have observed frequent instances of a superintending providence in our favor. I have lived, Sir, a long time, and the longer I live, the more convincing proofs I see of this truth – that God Governs in the affairs of men …. I firmly believe this; and I also believe that without his concurring aid we shall succeed in this political building no better, than the Builders

---

[114] *The Papers of Benjamin Franklin, March 1 through June 30, 1779*, ed. Barbara B. Oberg (New Haven and London: Yale University Press, 1992), vol. 29, 358–60.

[115] See "Franklin to Samuel Cooper, May 1, 1777," *The Papers of Benjamin Franklin, May 1 through September 30, 1777*, ed. William B. Willcox (New Haven and London: Yale University Press, 1984), vol. 24, 6–7.

[116] For an example of this sort of interpretation, see Benjamin E. Park, "Benjamin Franklin, Richard Price, and the Division of the Sacred and Secular in the Age of Revolutions" in Paul E. Kerry and Matthew S. Holland, eds., *Benjamin Franklin's Intellectual World* (Madison and Teaneck: Farleigh Dickinson University Press, 2012), 119–35.

[117] "Franklin to Benjamin Vaughan, November 9, 1779," *The Papers of Benjamin Franklin November 1, 1779, through February 29, 1780*, ed. Barbara B. Oberg (New Haven and London: Yale University Press, 1995), vol. 31, 57–60.

[118] Benjamin Franklin, *The Works of Benjamin Franklin, including the Private as well as the Official and Scientific Correspondence, together with the Unmutilated and Correct Version of the Autobiography*, ed. John Bigelow (New York: G. P. Putnam, 1904), 186.

of Babel: We shall be divided by our little partial local interests; our projects will be confounded, and we ourselves shall become a reproach and bye word down to future ages.[119]

Clearly, Franklin had a utilitarian view of religion as providing an essential support for morality and republicanism. And this passage can plausibly be read as invoking God for useful ends: an appeal to a transcendent principle designed to draw the delegates from their factious interests toward the national common good. Still, it also can be plausibly read as "the most remarkable religious episode of Franklin's life" precisely because Franklin explicitly proclaims providential theism is not merely useful but also *true*.[120] This episode suggests that he genuinely did come to a deeper or more genuine belief in providence as he lived through the revolution. This belief, we have seen, was one shared by the other key players in the drama of Franco-American diplomacy.

5.5 BRINGING GOOD OUT OF EVIL

The Continental Congress did not list the specific events it had in mind when it cited discovery of British councils as evidence of God's superintending providence. Yet in our case study of America's first spy ring, it has been seen that Washington's agents understood themselves to be acting under God's providential direction and protection. We do know to whom Congress was referring to when it thanked God for raising up a powerful and generous ally. The key players in the drama of forging the Franco-American alliance understood themselves to be instruments of a *particular* divine providence.

Congress also identified the unitive effects of British cruelty as a blessing of Providence, which, by way of conclusion, we briefly discuss along with the theoretical implications for founding political thought. The Southern Campaign of the Revolutionary War — which followed after the British failure at Saratoga, was inaugurated by the sack of Savannah in late 1778 and aimed at subduing the South — was a bloody affair. General Nathanael Greene described the struggle between patriots and Tories as characterized by "savage fury," and patriot leader Francis Marion described in his letters the "distress of poor Women & Children" brought about by the burning and destruction of homes.[121] Following the fall of Charleston in May 1780, General Cornwallis dispatched Colonel Banastre Tarleton to attack a group of American troops under the command of Colonel Abraham Buford. The subsequent Battle of

[119] *The Records of the Federal Convention of 1787*, ed. Max Farrand (New Haven: Yale University Press, 1911), vol. 1, 450–51.
[120] Thomas S. Kidd, *Benjamin Franklin: The Religious Life of a Founding Father* (New Haven and London: Yale University Press, 2017), 229.
[121] "Letter from Francis Marion to Horatio Gates, 4 October, 1780," *State Records of North Carolina* (1896), vol. 14 (1896), 665–66. Accessed February 22, 2022, from https://docsouth.unc.edu/csr/index.php/document/csr14-0564.

Waxhaws was a disastrous defeat for the Americans in which Buford's forces were routed; 113 Americans were killed and 150 wounded while the British suffered only 19 casualties. Buford reported to the Virginia assembly that his men surrendered and asked for quarter to no avail before being ruthlessly cut to pieces. The story of "Tarleton's quarter" spread through countryside, igniting anti-British sentiment, a will to resist, and bloody reprisals. Having just lost Charleston and with Gates' disastrous loss at Camden in August, the American cause in the South was hanging by a thread. Hence, historians have noted the importance of how the Americans turned this defeat into a propaganda victory.

While this is correct so far as it goes, it would be false to characterize it as *mere* propaganda from the American perspective. Americans deeply believed in the notion that God would and eventually did bring good out of evil. As Washington put it, military withdrawals and defeats "may appear to us as real misfortunes," but both affliction and victory are "under the direction of a wise providence, who, no doubt, directs them for the best of purposes, and to bring round the greatest degree of happiness to the greatest number of his people."[122]

Spurred by British cruelty and the looming specter of British domination, the overmountain men from settlements in and near modern-day East Tennessee assembled and appeared out of the Appalachian mists to join other patriot militia. Constituted by rugged frontiersmen with no formal military training, this "Ghost Legion" smashed a detachment of 1,000 loyalist Tories at the Battle of Kings Mountain. Spurred by the southern rallying cry of "Remember Buford and His Quarter," the overmountain men won a victory that was a turning point in the war. This victory effectively ended British attempts to organize loyalist militia and breathed new life into the patriot cause in the South. Remarking upon the victory at Kings Mountain, Benjamin Rush wrote to John Adams, underscoring how God brought good out of evil: "We had forgotten former deliverances under our late losses and mortifications. But we now find that providence is on our Side, and that our independence [*sic*] is as secure as the everlasting mountains."[123]

The tide of the war in the South continued to turn for the Americans with Daniel Morgan's daring victory at Cowpens a few months later. Reporting his victory, Morgan contrasted his humane treatment of prisoners with the "most cruel warfare" that the British had engaged in.[124] French officers reacted with bewilderment, unable to "'conceive how regular troops, and they superior to in

[122] From "George Washington to Jonathan Trumbull, Sr., 6 September 1778," *The Papers of George Washington, 1 July–14 September 1778*, ed. David R. Hoth (Charlottesville: University of Virginia Press, 2006), vol. 16, 533–34.

[123] "To John Adams from Benjamin Rush, 23 October 1780," *The Adams Papers, July 1780–December 1780*, ed. Gregg L. Lint and Richard Alan Ryerson (Cambridge, MA: Harvard University Press, 1996), vol. 10, 302–4.

[124] *The Papers of General Nathanael Greene*, ed. Dennis M. Conrad (Chapel Hill: University of North Carolina Press, 1994), vol. 7, 153.

numbers allowed themselves to be beaten by peasants.'"[125] The Americans reacted by framing the victory in providentialist terms. Charles Lee remarked: "Providence has blessed the American arms with signal success in the defeat of Tarleton."[126] Recently made the new commander of the Southern forces, General Nathanael Greene echoed this sentiment.[127] Reporting to Continental Congress, Greene remarked that, in spite of the Americans' under-manned, outgunned, and destitute situation (that behooved Greene to con-stantly plea for more aid) – "Providence has blessed the American arms in this department with more success than we had reason to expect in our miserable situation."[128] Cornwallis would surrender less than a year later in Yorktown.

Evidence surrounding the counterintelligence, the diplomatic efforts to secure the Franco-American alliance, and the Southern Campaign point to a shared American worldview that included a particularly providential and mor-alistic God. In their interpretations of the events of the war, key actors empha-sized that they were both agents and instruments of providence. Scholars have noted and emphasized the utility of religion in classical American civil religion, but, whatever its utility, participants put forward providential interpretations of events as ultimate accounts of the course of human events. It was doubtless useful for leaders of the Revolution to call upon God's favor to engender and stoke courage and a willingness to sacrifice in the minds of the patriots. In the democratic republic that was being forged, where all men were said to be free and equal, there were no aristocratic cords of hierarchical fealty to call men to great deeds. There was a need to draw men out of their private pursuits for wealth and domestic happiness to sacrifice for the common good, and classical civil religion provided a common imaginary that was useful for this end. God would reward virtuous acts performed in the defense of liberty on both an individual and communal level. The existence of such a God and the promise of such a reward provide a powerful incentive to behavior for humans who cannot help but to act *sub ratione boni*, for the sake of some good.

Protestant Christians of various denominations, Catholic Christians, Jews, and those influenced by certain providential strands of Enlightenment deism could affirm such a particularly providential God. The political utility of providential belief did not negate, but rather dovetailed, with its truth – value in the minds of the patriots. Plato taught that myths were essential to provide the social glue of polity – and sometimes these myths point to deeper truths. Plato's insight was into the nature of human beings as storytelling animals, and his insight remains relevant. Even as the secular age was coming into being during the Enlightenment, human beings had what Wilfrid Sellars called a

[125] Ibid., 161.
[126] Banastre Tarleton, *A History of the Southern Campaigns of 1780 and 1781 in the Southern Provinces of North America* (Dublin: Printed for Coles, Exshaw, et al., 1787), 259.
[127] *The Papers of General Nathanael Greene*, 226.   [128] Ibid.

manifest image of themselves as beings of intrinsic dignity, value, and worth. From the classical natural-law perspective, this manifest image does not ultimately make any sense if human beings are simply parts in a materialistic and mechanistic whole, for mere matter in motion is without purpose, and therefore, without meaning. Our manifest image is only reasonable in light of a foundational story that provides a rational warrant for our unavoidable beliefs about the meaningfulness of our lives. With its set of claims about a Creator God who made the universe and man, American civil religion provided the foundation of this story. To be endowed by a Creator with certain unalienable rights is to be something more than mere matter in motion in a godless universe. It is to be a person capable of participating in an existence of meaning and purpose. To see one's fight for the recognition and securing of these rights as just, because acting under the auspices of a just God, is to see one's struggle as more than merely a game of power. The North American colonists, like all human beings, had an implacable drive to see their actions as meaningful in light of nature and history. They also sought a justification, a reason, for their settled conviction about the essentially limited nature and purposes of government as the protector rather than the source of rights. Whether one was of a protestant sect, a Jew, a Catholic, or a deist, the classical elements of American civil religion functioned as the "true myth" that helped key participants see purpose and meaning in the events of the war.

*

With the Revolutionary War raging, citizens of individual states began drafting and ratifying written constitutions of government, beginning with the Pennsylvania Constitution of 1776. The subjects turned citizens were forced to confront a theoretical and practical question: What would it mean to create political institutions based on the principle of popular sovereignty? And did such a notion of popular sovereignty, of rule under the authority the people, represent, in its own way, the same turn toward the unlimited power and unbounded sovereignty of the modern state that the colonists had resisted with the force of arms?

After the crucible of the war, the early experience of state constitution writing and the experiment of national government under the Articles of Confederation, delegates to the Philadelphia Convention of 1787 then drafted a Constitution of the United States of America, written in the name and under the authority of "We the People." Debate over the theoretical foundations of popular sovereignty in the United States remains relevant in contemporary constitutional theory. Drawing on insights from the nineteenth-century constitutional theorist Orestes Brownson, we pick up this thread in the next chapter with an analysis of the theoretical foundations of popular sovereignty in the U.S. Constitution of 1787.

6

Reason, Will, and Popular Sovereignty

James Madison reported in his notes on the federal convention that his friend and fellow delegate James Wilson "was never really fond of oaths, considering them as left handed security only." Good governments, Wilson argued during one of the debates that summer, did not need oaths to impose obligation or compel obedience, and bad governments "ought not to be supported."[1] Despite Wilson's objections, the convention delegates adopted language that became Article VI of the U.S. Constitution, requiring members of Congress, all executive and judicial officers – state and federal – and all elected members of state legislatures to take an oath or state an affirmation of fidelity to the U.S. Constitution. By congressional statute, the specific language of the oath is to "support and defend the Constitution of the United States against all enemies, foreign and domestic" and to "bear true faith and allegiance" to it. This oath or affirmation has become a highly visible public ceremony that signals how the Constitution functions as "higher law" in the American polity.

But, to pick up on Wilson's objection, why should the Constitution be considered authoritative and demand our loyalty? The answer to this question is tightly bound up with how we think about popular sovereignty, and it is necessarily connected to the question of the proper approach to constitutional interpretation. What does it mean for political actors and judges to exercise authority under the Constitution? And what, if any, authority does a judge have under the Constitution to appeal to principles of natural law when deciding cases and controversies? These are questions of ongoing concern that

---

[1] *The Records of the Federal Convention of 1787*, ed. Max Farrand (New Haven: Yale University Press, 1911), vol. 2, 87.

are illuminated by a return to those founding era debates over the locus of sovereignty in the United States and the constitution-making authority of the people. Crucially, the American colonists reaffirmed the rule of law over the rule of will, whether as it had been theorized both by partisans of absolutist monarchy (e.g., Filmer) or partisans of absolutist democracy (e.g., Rousseau). To understand the founders' perspective on popular sovereignty under the rule of law, it is fruitful to contrast their conception with Rousseau's democratic sovereign; but to understand Rousseau, it is necessary briefly to trace the development of the modern idea of sovereignty, which is rooted in the Christian theological concepts of the absolute and ordained power of God and the parallel concepts of the antecedent and consequent will of God.

6.1 FROM GOD'S SOVEREIGNTY TO THE ROUSSEAUEAN GENERAL WILL

As Jean Bethke Elshtain has pointed out in her study of the concept of sovereignty in Western culture and thought, the notion of sovereignty was historically a deeply theological concept bound up with how God's causal relation to the world was conceived.[2] As Elshtain recounts, there was a distinctive shift from how the Augustinian and Thomistic tradition thought about God's sovereignty as bound up with God as *Summa Ratio* or God-as-reason. The classical, Christian Aristotelian natural-law perspective held that there were structures embedded in nature that ordered things toward their proper good. Natural kinds exist in virtue of their substantial forms, which are themselves imprints of the exemplary forms in God's own mind. As such, natural kinds have a certain integrity and dignity in the order of nature that God binds himself to respect. Human persons in particular were conceived as dignified agents – genuine secondary causes with the power of reason and will.

In the Augustinian tradition of theology, Christian theologians distinguished between God's absolute and ordained power. As Thomas Aquinas articulated it, classical orthodoxy avoided two shoals: radical necessitarianism and radical libertarianism. God's creative action and the order of nature are not naturally necessary. God is free to create or not create. In creating, God necessarily wills his own goodness, and thus the creatures in which he makes manifest his goodness. Because his goodness is infinite, however, the world he chooses to create and the creatures in it are not proportionate to that goodness. Hence, it is within God's capacity or absolute power to act otherwise than he in fact did. This is a strong form of divine libertarianism. But it does not entail radical libertarianism, because God's absolute power extends only to logical possibilities, not actual unmaking and remaking of the created order. God binds

---

[2] Jean Bethke Elshtain, *Sovereignty: God, State, and Self* (New York: Basic Books, 2008).

himself to an order willed. God's ordained power is manifest in the order of nature and providential governance of things toward their proper ends.[3]

Still, the Thomistic synthesis was thought by some to unduly constrict God's freedom. We need not recount the details of this story here, but the main outline is that medieval theologians such as John Duns Scotus and William of Ockham at least upset and perhaps radically broke from Aquinas's delicate synthesis. Scotus operationalized absolute power as an always active capacity of God. In many passages, Ockham too seemed to conceive of God-as-will, apparently radically sourcing the moral order in God's absolute power. Whereas the classical view held that God's will was essentially tethered to his reason and goodness, the voluntarist view emphasized God's power as necessary to secure obligation. On the voluntarist view, it is the will, the capacity for choosing, that suffices to confer value on the objects chosen. God's will is the radical determinant of what is good and evil. Both divine and human freedom were by nature indifferent as to its object. This leads Ockham to suggest that God could command people to hate him, and that would have made it good, which at least suggested that God's absolute power is operationalized.[4]

Along the historical vector, the initial fracturing of Christendom during the Reformation led to the codification of the principle *cuius regio, eius religio* (whose realm, his religion) in the Peace of Augsburg (1555). This fracturing continued as protestant sects proliferated, contributing to the Thirty Years War that ended in the Peace of Westphalia. Westphalia confirmed the *cuius regio, eius religio* principle and set the legal basis for the modern international system of the sovereign nation–state in which national governments have control of their internal affairs and states are understood to enjoy equal rights of sovereignty. Hence, Jean Bodin, the French political theorist of modern sovereignty par excellence who lived through the first decades of the Reformation and wrote his *Six Books of the Commonwealth* not long after the Peace of Augsburg, defined sovereignty as "the absolute and perpetual power of a commonwealth," that is, the highest power to command subjects.[5]

Meanwhile, in England, beginning with Henry VIII and proceeding to the Stuart kings, the monarchy moved to consolidate its sovereignty in this sense.

---

[3] Thomas Aquinas, *De Potentia Dei*, Question 1, art. 5. Accessed February 27, 2022, from www .corpusthomisticum.org/qdp1.html; *Summa Theologica*, trans. Fathers of the English Dominican Province (Chicago: Encyclopedia Britannica, 1952), I.25.5.

[4] For a more detailed analysis of the absolute-ordained dialectic and references to Ockham and Scotus see Kody W. Cooper, *Thomas Hobbes and the Natural Law* (Notre Dame, IN: Notre Dame University Press, 2018), ch. 5. Presented there is an analytical argument how Ockham himself might be understood in a more nuanced way. The account here does not assert an interpretation as proven, and nothing here pretends to settle the debate over how to interpret Ockham. The point here is only that modern voluntarism can be traced to theological voluntarism, the rudiments at least of which can be found in Ockham.

[5] Jean Bodin, *On Sovereignty: Four Chapters from the Six Books of Commonwealth*, ed. and trans. Julian H. Franklin (Cambridge: Cambridge University Press, 1992), 1.

Henry VIII had established the Oath of Supremacy in 1535, requiring public officers to swear an oath that the king was supreme over church and state. James I, reigning over Great Britain from 1603 to 1625, carried forward this tradition when he articulated the regal sovereignty as a power over the lands of the realm and the lives of the persons in the realm. While he admitted that this power was to be exercised accordingly to law, James maintained that the king was above Parliament and was the fount of all the laws.[6] The Oath of Supremacy was essential to the maintenance of the king's sovereignty: "in that Oath onely is contained the Kings absolute power, to be Iudge ouer all persons, aswell Ciuill as Ecclesiastical, excluding al forraigne powers and Potentates to be Iudges within his dominions." The constitution and the laws are subject to alteration at the sovereign's convenience, "by the absolute power of a King."[7]

For James I, this power remained "under" God, but the king was accountable for the exercise of this power only to God. Moreover, as God's lieutenant on earth, the king reflected and exercised divine power:

The State of MONARCHIE is the supremest thing vpon earth: For Kings are not onely GODS Lieutenants vpon earth, and sit vpon GODS throne, but euen by GOD himselfe they are called Gods . . .. Kings are iustly called Gods, for that they exercise a manner or resemblance of Diuine power vpon earth: For if you wil consider the Attributes to God, you shall see how they agree in the person of a King. God hath power to create, or destroy, make, or vnmake at his pleasure, to giue life, or send death, to iudge all, and to bee iudged nor accomptable to none: To raise low things, and to make high things low at his pleasure, and to God are both soule and body due. And the like power haue Kings: they make and vnmake their subiects: they haue power of raising, and casting downe: of life, and of death: Iudges ouer all their subiects and in all causes, and yet accomptable to none but God onely.[8]

The king as God's lieutenant on earth, James argued, had an absolute power that was operationalized to make and unmake the realm. The Stuartian claim did admit that the king was bound by natural and divine law, but, as God's lieutenant, the king ultimately was the interpreter of that law and was answerable to God alone for any breach. Here then is a full-blown political application of the theological absolute/ordained power distinction. In this light, it is plausible to read Thomas Hobbes as a philosophical radical with politically "conservative" purposes, to construct a theory of an absolutist sovereign that supported the Jacobean claim. Thus, Hobbes famously called the sovereign a "mortal God," echoing James' claim that kings are justly called Gods.[9] Without seeking to resolve analytical disputes over Hobbes' teachings or intentions, it is important to note that the North American colonists in the late eighteenth

---

[6] *King James VI and I: Political Writings*, ed. Johann P. Somerville (Cambridge: Cambridge University Press, 2006), 74–75.

[7] Ibid., 180.   [8] Ibid., 181.

[9] Thomas Hobbes, *Leviathan with Selected Variants from the Latin Edition of 1668*, ed. Edwin Curley (Indianapolis, IN: Hackett Publishing Co., 1994), ch. 17, 109.

century did commonly read Hobbes to have constructed an absolutist theory of civil sovereignty, which had historically been at times referred to in shorthand as a Hobbist doctrine.[10]

The absolute-ordained power distinction in theology and politics runs parallel to a related distinction between God's antecedent will and God's consequent will. The theological dispute over how to think about antecedent/consequent will was at root a contest over how to interpret 1 Timothy 2:4, where Paul says that "God wills that all men be saved." As Patrick Riley has shown, the antecedent-consequent distinction was a precursor to the distinction between God's general will and his particular will, a distinction that informed the debate over the meaning of the will of God in 1 Timothy 2:4.[11] The classical solution was to posit that it was the antecedent will of God to save all mankind but the consequent will of God to save only some and damn others. Aquinas captured this solution when he wrote that "by His antecedent will God wants a certain man to be saved by reason of his human nature, which He made for salvation; but by His consequent will He wishes him to be damned because of the sins which are found in him."[12]

These concepts of general and particular will further developed in the context of politics in seventeenth-century France with the thought of Antoine Arnauld, Blaise Pascal, Pierre Bayle, Nicolas Malebranche, and Montesquieu all serving as precursors to Rousseau. Riley shows how Pascal first transferred the concept from soteriology to ecclesiology to political theory. Pascal took up Paul's body analogy for the church in 1 Corinthians 12. Just as the body has variegated parts that operate for the good of the whole (hands, feet, eyes, for example), Pascal observed, so the church is constituted by various offices and persons with various gifts. Pascal applied the analogy to political bodies, suggesting that, just as a foot with a particular will would lead to confusion, so a self-interested individual will in the body politic is the source of all manner of political disorder. Whereas Pascal insisted on the need for divine grace to achieve social unity, Rousseau took Pascal's insight in a different direction by insisting on the necessity of a particular kind of civic education and a particular

---

[10] From the seventeenth century forward, many readers of Hobbes identified as "Hobbism" or "Hobbist" a range of doctrines that included theological voluntarism and an absolutist theory of civil sovereignty. For just a few of many examples, see, for example, Thomas Tenison, *The Creed of Mr. Hobbes Examined in a Feigned Conference between Him and a Student in Divinity* (London: Printed for Francis Tyton, 1670), 8–9; Richard Baxter, *Catholick Theologie ...* (London: Printed by Robert White, for Nevill Simmons at Princes Arms in St. Paul's Churchyard, 1675); James Durham, "To the readers ...," *Heaven upon Earth* (Edinburgh: Printed by Heir of Andrew, 1685); James Parkinson, *An Examination of Dr. Sherlock's Book Entituled, The Case of Allegiance Due to Sovereign Powers* (London: Printed for David Hay, 1691), 27.

[11] Patrick Riley, *The General Will before Rousseau: The Transformation of the Divine into the Civic* (Princeton: Princeton University Press, 1986), ch. 1.

[12] Aquinas, *De Veritate*, 23.2, ad. 2.

kind of civil religion that would replace Christianity. Riley nonetheless concludes that the absorption of individual will into a general will manifests "a lineal descent of Rousseau from St. Paul read *á la* Pascal."[13] Deploying Christian concepts, Rousseau effected a radical break with classical Christian natural law.

In his political writings, Rousseau traced the origins of sovereignty back to a state of nature. In *The Social Contract*, Rousseau envisioned prepolitical human beings in a state of nature as autonomous and driven principally by a desire for self-preservation. Because persons in such a condition find that the obstacles to their preservation outweigh their capacities and resources to survive as individuals, the problem Rousseau must address is how individual persons can form a unity committed to the common good while also maintaining their individuality and individual freedom, which, for Rousseau, meant obeying oneself alone. Rousseau purported to find a solution in a social compact constituted by "the total alienation of each associate, together with all his rights, to the whole community."[14] Only through the complete alienation of all rights one might claim in the state of nature can the requisite social unity be achieved. As Rousseau explained:

> if the individuals retained certain rights, as there would be no common superior to decide between them and the public, each, being on one point his own judge, would ask to be so on all; the state of nature would thus continue, and the association would necessarily become inoperative or tyrannical.[15]

When a particular social compact allows individuals to retain some powers, goods, or liberties, these are merely concessions of the sovereign, who has the absolutely final right of judgment about what is necessary for the common good. In other words, there are no inviolable claims of natural right or natural rights that can be made against the sovereign – that which is retained is permitted purely on the grounds of expediency.

Through the social compact, individual persons are incorporated into a public person, the sovereign, and the members that constitute it taken collectively are called "the people." The people's exercise of sovereignty is "nothing less than the exercise of the general will."[16] When the general will acts according to the proper formal procedures, it "is an act of Sovereignty and constitutes law." Sometimes Rousseau speaks of the general will as something transcendent, always aiming at justice and the common good: "the general will is always right and tends to the public advantage."[17] Practically speaking, however, Rousseau provides little guidance for distinguishing the general will from what the democratic sovereign wills in fact, such that the two concepts

---

[13] Riley, *The General Will before Rousseau*, 22.

[14] Jean-Jacques Rousseau, *The Social Contract and Discourses by Jean-Jacques Rousseau*, trans. G. D. H. Cole (London and Toronto: J.M. Dent and Sons, 1923), bk. I, ch. 6, 15.

[15] Ibid.   [16] Ibid., bk. II, ch. 1, 22.   [17] Ibid., ch. 1, 22; ch. 2, 23; ch. 3, 25.

ultimately collapse into one.[18] The absolute power of the general will is the essential vivifying principle of the state:

> If the State is a moral person whose life is in the union of its members, and if the most important of its cares is the care for its own preservation, it must have a universal and compelling force, in order to move and dispose each part as may be most advantageous to the whole. As nature gives each man absolute power over all his members, the social compact gives the body politic absolute power over all its members also; and it is this power which, under the direction of the general will, bears, as I have said, the name of Sovereignty.[19]

Following in the steps of Pascal, Rousseau saw a high degree of corporate unity in the church that he coveted for the state. To achieve that unity, all particular wills were to be subsumed into one general will. Such a sovereign people could brook no rival. Hence, Rousseau's democratic sovereign could not abide orthodox Christianity, which broke the hegemony of ancient polis/empire when Christ inaugurated a spiritual kingdom "not of this world" but that was embodied on earth in the Church Militant.[20] Paul's analogy of the unity of the body in 1 Corinthians 12 bespoke a social unity that could only be achieved in the church, through grace. Moreover, the Christian separation of church and state entailed that the state's claims on persons were limited from above. In the place of Christianity, Rousseau advocated a new civil religion that the democratic sovereign would be empowered to enforce against dissenters with banishment and against apostates with the penalty of death. The God that Rousseau posits as necessary to believe in is one who sanctifies the social contract by rewarding those who keep it and sanctioning those who break it. Sects with more specific beliefs who sign onto these central dogmas would be rendered toothless vis-à-vis civic unity, and hence would be tolerated.[21]

Let us retrace the steps of our discussion. The language of absolute power had been reserved in traditional Christian theology for the unique capacity of God to create *ex nihilo* and sustain all created things in being. In the Medieval Christian-Aristotelian synthesis, this capacity was not thought to be an immediately exercisable power to unmake the natural order. Some later medieval theologians such as Scotus and Ockham did, however, push the notion of operationalization of God's absolute power in an attempt to vindicate the divine liberty. Theologians and philosophers downstream then radicalized this distinction into a full-blown theological and political voluntarism, which

---

[18] But, for an intriguing, nonvoluntarist account, which contends that Rousseau's general will "must conform to an eternal idea of justice," see David Lay Williams, "The Substantive Elements of Rousseau's General Will," in James Farr and David Lay Williams, eds., *The General Will: The Evolution of a Concept* (New York: Cambridge University Press, 2015), 219–47.

[19] Rousseau, *The Social Contract and Discourses*, ch. 4, 26–27.

[20] See John 18:36. The Church Militant is constituted by those members of Christ's Church who are alive on earth.

[21] Rousseau, *The Social Contract and Discourses*, bk. IV, ch. 8, 113–22.

animated the political theology of the absolutist kings. The Stuart kings saw themselves as lieutenants of God on earth, endowed with authority that reflected the divine nature – and, therefore, an absolute power over civil polity to unmake or remake that which was constitutionally established. Hobbes's work can be read in this light as an effort to provide a philosophical edifice to support the Stuartian claims of absolute sovereignty. Rousseau's achievement was to transfer this godlike absolute power from kings to the *demos* to theorize absolutist sovereignty in democratic terms: The general will was a secularized and democratized version of Jacobean absolutist sovereignty. Whatever remained left of God's power in Rousseau's thought was merely a prop for the absolute power of the democratic sovereign. In short, Rousseauean popular sovereignty was the Hobbist mortal god, baptized with the waters of democracy.[22]

6.2 POPULAR SOVEREIGNTY IN THE CONSTITUTIONAL CONVENTION AND CONSTITUTIONAL DEBATES

The American founders' rejection of the Rousseauean idea of popular sovereignty is evident in the constitutional convention and subsequent constitutional debates. Following Shays' Rebellion and other ominous signs of the failure of the Articles of Confederation, the Constitutional Convention was called in Philadelphia in May 1787. James Madison, Edmund Randolph, and their allies seized the initiative by immediately proposing the Virginia Plan. It provided for a significant expansion of the power of the national government with a bicameral legislature with the lower house based on representation proportional to population and an upper house elected by the former, a national executive, a national judiciary, and a Council of Revision formed by the latter two with the power to review the constitutionality of national and state legislative acts. This plan alarmed the delegates from the small states. They argued that the Virginia Plan's proposal for ratification by assemblies chosen by the people was extralegal. As Roger Sherman put it, "the articles of Confederation [provided] for changes and alterations with the assent of Congress and ratification of State Legislatures."[23] Indeed, Article XIII provided:

And the Articles of this Confederation shall be inviolably observed by every State, and the Union shall be perpetual; nor shall any alteration at any time hereafter be made in any of them; unless such alteration be agreed to in a Congress of the United States, and be afterwards confirmed by the legislatures of every State.[24]

---

[22] Here our conclusion is close to that of Jacques Maritain, *Man and the State* (Washington, DC: Catholic University Press of America, 1998), 46.

[23] James Madison, *Notes of Debates in the Federal Convention of 1787 Reported by James Madison* (Athens: Ohio University Press, 1987), 70.

[24] *The Articles of Confederation.* Accessed February 27, 2022, from https://avalon.law.yale.edu/18th_century/artconf.asp.

By circumventing and diminishing the power of the sovereign states who had sent delegates with the charge to amend the Articles, the Virginia Plan seemed unlawful. William Patterson contended that Article XIII entailed that unanimous consent of the state legislatures was necessary to dissolve the Articles. Hence, as John Lansing put it, there was a "want of power in the Convention to discuss and propose" the Virginia Plan.[25]

Defenders of the Virginia Plan replied by appeal to popular sovereignty. Madison argued that the popular mode of ratification was "essential" because the Articles' amendment process was flawed. Confusion and/or decisions in favor of state authority would ensue if Congress' alterations were agreed to and submitted to state legislatures. And, inasmuch as the Articles were a treaty among sovereign states, adoption of amendments by some states might be seen by other states as breaches that would absolve all parties from the treaty. More fundamentally, Madison contended that the new Constitution must derive its authority from "the supreme authority of the people themselves."[26] James Wilson gave the answer to Lansing that ultimately persuaded the delegates. The Convention had the power to *conclude* nothing, but it did have the power to *propose* anything to the people. Charles Pinckney, Edmund Randolph, and Alexander Hamilton concurred that the Convention was duty bound to propose whatever they deemed necessary to save the Union – failure to do so would be "treason to our trust."[27] The question of the mode of ratification was postponed, but the divisions over the ultimate source of sovereignty resurfaced again over how representation was to be apportioned in the national legislature.

The divide was not over whether "the people" were the root of sovereignty, but *how* they were. Wilson expressed a notion that nobody objected to, namely, that "personal sovereignty" is enjoyed in a "state of nature," which is given up for civil liberty. In that condition, every person is "naturally a sovereign over himself, and all men are therefore naturally equal."[28] As Madison put it in the preface to his *Notes*:

[T]he weakness and wants of man naturally lead to an association of individuals, under a common authority whereby each may have the protection of the whole against danger from without, and enjoy in safety within, the advantages of social intercourse, and an exchange of the necessaries & comforts of life ....[29]

As we saw in Chapter 2, the founders rejected the radical picture of the state of nature associated with Hobbist and Rousseauean thought. Rather, they believed it was a condition devoid of civil government but governed by God, in which the moral law was binding in conscience. The laws of nature imposed other-directed duties that formed the basis of natural-rights claims against others, which governments are established to secure. In short, for the delegates,

[25] Madison, *Notes*, 122.   [26] Madison, *Notes*, 70.   [27] Ibid., 125, 127, and 130.
[28] Ibid., 97–98.   [29] Ibid., 3.

"personal sovereignty" was bounded by the moral law and did not entail radical autonomy.

Where the delegates disagreed was whether and to what extent there was an analogy between a state of nature of natural persons and a state of nature of corporate persons in the American context. Luther Martin contended that after the Declaration of Independence, the states were thrown into a state of nature. As the Declaration stated, the former colonies were now "free and independent states." On this view, the Articles' one-state, one-vote system bespoke the prior equal sovereignty of the states. This equal sovereignty in a post-Westphalian world meant that they stood as equals toward one another and toward non-American states, but they were emphatically not the sovereigns dreamed up by Rousseau. The people's will was bound by natural law and natural rights. Wilson and Hamilton agreed with Luther Martin and the representatives of the small states that the people's sovereignty was intrinsically limited and that sovereigns were equals in international politics. Yet they denied that the American states had ever in fact been in such a condition, because they maintained that the American people enjoyed a prior unity that subsisted through the revolution. Hence, they countered that in the same final paragraph of the Declaration, the signers spoke of "the united States of America" and "these United Colonies." On this view, the Union preceded and persisted through the separation from Great Britain.[30]

Hence, the delegates of the small states contended that the general government should be the creation of and operate through the sovereign states, rather than being the creation of sovereign individuals of the nation as a whole forming one whole sovereign people. They worried that the unequal population of the states combined with pure proportional representation would threaten the distinct dignity of each state as a distinct social whole with its own peculiar place, borders, institutions, culture, and history. Strikingly, Madison and his allies recognized that the states had a distinct status that the Constitution would have to acknowledge. Hence, after David Brearley suggested that the only way that the Virginia Plan could be carried off equitably would be to abolish all existing boundaries and redraw the map into 13 equal parts, Madison replied that the idea amounted to an absurd nonstarter. The differences in "rules of property, as well as the manners, habits, and prejudices of the different States, amounted to a prohibition of the attempt."[31] Yet the federalists did want to circumvent the "local interests & local prejudices" insofar as they constituted obstacles to a sufficiently powerful national government, which needed to rest on a direct bond between the government and the people.[32] Hamilton contended that, while States could be seen distributively, as individual persons composing it, and collectively, as a political whole, "nothing could be more preposterous or absurd than to sacrifice the former to the latter."[33]

---

[30] Ibid., 153. [31] Ibid., 147. [32] Ibid., 189. [33] Ibid., 215.

William Samuel Johnson summed up the debate and previewed how the delegates would ultimately compromise between their rival views of the locus of sovereignty:

Those on one side considering the States as districts of people composing one Political Society; those on the other considering them as so many political societies. The fact is that the States do exist as political Societies, and a Government is to be formed for them in their political capacity, as well as for the individuals composing them ... in some respects the States are to be considered in their political capacity, and in others as districts of individual citizens, the two ideas embraced on different sides, instead of being opposed to each other, ought to be combined; that in *one* branch the *people*, ought to be represented; in the *other* the *States*.[34]

This vision formed the framework for Oliver Ellsworth's proposal for representation by proportion of population in the House and equal state suffrage in the Senate, which he hoped "would become a ground of compromise."[35] While debate continued for weeks, the delegates ultimately adopted Ellsworth's proposed compromise. The dual character of the American constitution of government that this institutional structure reflected – national and federal – was evident also in the adoption of Madison's proposal for ratification. Ratification would bypass state legislatures for special assemblies elected by the people *in their respective states*.

We saw in the previous chapter that Franklin understood this particular constitutional moment – when the convention risked breaking up over the failure to brook a compromise between small states and large states – in providentialist terms. The "longer I live, the more convincing proofs I see of this Truth – that God governs in the affairs of men," Franklin told the delegates. And "I also believe that without his concurring Aid, we shall succeed in this political Building no better than the Builders of Babel."[36] While Franklin's call for regular prayer was supported by some, others objected to it as potentially becoming a new source of division and because the convention had no funds to pay a chaplain, and the motion for regular prayer did not receive a vote. But, as Herbert Storing recounts, his call for divine aid "was not altogether fruitless." When a motion to allow each state an equal vote in the second branch of the legislature was taken up for a vote:

The Maryland delegation was divided on [the question of representation], Daniel Jenifer being opposed to equal representation and Luther Martin in favor of it. Providentially, Jenifer was late in taking his seat that morning and Martin was thus able to cast the vote of Maryland in favor of the motion. The consequence of this was that when Georgia, the last state to be polled, was reached, instead of the question having been decided in the negative, five states had voted in favor of the motion and five against. Ordinarily the whole of the four-man Georgia delegation would have voted against equal representation, but it happened that two of the members were absent. One of the remaining

---

[34] Ibid., 211. Emphasis in original.   [35] Ibid., 218.   [36] Madison, *Notes*, 209–10.

Georgians was Abraham Baldwin ... By chance or providence, the absence of two of his colleagues put in his hands the power perhaps to determine whether there was to be a Union or not. Voting, contrary to his convictions, in favor of equal representation in the second branch, Baldwin divided Georgia's vote, maintained the tie, and kept open the way for compromise.[37]

The providentialist interpretation of events was not lost on the Americans who were called upon to ratify the document. In *Federalist* no. 37, Madison connected the thread of God's superintending providence in the Revolution to the Constitutional Convention:

Would it be wonderful if, under the pressure of all these difficulties, the convention should have been forced into some deviations from that artificial structure and regular symmetry, which an abstract view of the subject might lead an ingenious theorist to bestow on a constitution planned in his closet, or in his imagination? The real wonder is, that so many difficulties should have been surmounted; and surmounted with an unanimity almost as unprecedented, as it must have been unexpected. It is impossible for any man of candour to reflect on this circumstance, without partaking of the astonishment. It is impossible, for the man of pious reflection, not to perceive in it a finger of that Almighty Hand, which has been so frequently and signally extended to our relief in the critical stages of the revolution.[38]

The animating American arguments of the pamphlet debates and the revolution that God governs in the affairs of men continued to ground the notion that sovereignty would be under the vertical limits of God's providence. Still, the opening appeal of the Constitution to popular sovereignty in the phrase "We the People" was controversial in some state ratifying conventions for what it implied about the locus of sovereignty in the United States. In North Carolina, one delegate complained that the expression was "improper" because the delegates were sent by state legislatures, not by the people of the states (let alone the people of the whole nation). The reply was that the framers did not pretend otherwise, which is why the Constitution was submitted to the people of the states in special ratifying conventions. Meanwhile, in Virginia, opponents of ratification echoed a theme from the convention debates. Patrick Henry remonstrated:

Who authorized them to speak the language of, *We, the people*, instead of, *We, the states?* States are the characteristics and the soul of a confederation. If the states be not the agents of this compact, it must be one great, consolidated, national government, of the people of all the states.[39]

---

[37] Herbert J. Storing, *Toward a More Perfect Union* (Washington, DC: AEI Press, 1995), 34.

[38] *The Federalist*, ed. George W. Carey and James McClellan (Indianapolis, IN: Liberty Fund, 2001), 184–85.

[39] Patrick Henry, "Preamble." Accessed March 2, 2022, from http://press-pubs.uchicago.edu/founders/documents/preambles14.html. Emphasis in original.

The proponents of the Constitution denied that this was so. The states were "constituent parts of the national sovereignty" and they are left with "certain exclusive, and very important, portions of the sovereign power," Hamilton wrote in *Federalist* no. 9.[40] The national sovereign was a limited sovereign over "few and defined" objects. On the other hand, the states, as "political and co-equal societies," would retain powers that are "numerous and indefinite" and include "all the objects, which, in the ordinary course of affairs, concern the lives, liberties, and properties of the people; and the internal order, improvement, and prosperity of the state."[41]

In the Pennsylvania ratifying convention, Wilson explained the meaning of "We the People":

It has not been, nor, I presume, will be denied, that somewhere there is, and of necessity must be, a supreme, absolute and uncontrollable authority. This, I believe, may justly be termed the sovereign power ... I stated further, that if the question was asked, some politician, who had not considered the subject with sufficient accuracy, where the supreme power resided in our governments, would answer, that it was vested in the State constitutions. This opinion approaches near the truth, but does not reach it; for the truth is, that the supreme, absolute and uncontrollable authority, *remains* with the people.[42]

In contrast with the British constitution, Wilson maintained, the U.S. Constitution expressed a limit to governmental authority:

The idea of a constitution, limiting and superintending the operations of legislative authority, seems not to have been accurately understood in Britain ... The British constitution is just what the British parliament pleases ... To control the power and conduct of the legislature by an overruling constitution, was an improvement in the science and practice of government reserved to the American States.[43]

Although popular sovereignty was expressed through the ratification of the Constitution in a collective act of will, Wilson's idea of sovereignty as "uncontroullable" authority was *not* a voluntaristic account of political authority.

One example that illustrates this point is Publius' discussion of the objection to the Constitution regarding debts due to the United States. The absence of an explicit provision on this point was taken to be a "tacit relinquishment of those debts and as a wicked contrivance to screen public defaulters." In reply to this charge, Hamilton drew from Thomas Rutherford's *Institutes of Natural Law*, which in continuity with classical natural law had rejected absolutist and voluntarist accounts of sovereignty. It was a "plain dictate of common sense" that "*States neither lose any of their rights, nor are discharged from any of their*

---

[40] *The Federalist*, ed. Carey and McClellan (Indianapolis, IN: Liberty Fund, 2001), no. 9, 41.
[41] Ibid., no. 45, 241.
[42] *The Works of James Wilson* (Indianapolis, IN: Liberty Fund, 2007), vol. 1, 213. Emphasis in original.
[43] *The Works of James Wilson*, vol. 1, 191.

obligations by a change in the form of their civil government."[44] We argued in Chapter 3 that Jefferson's generational-revolutionary constitutionalism was not voluntaristic in the sense that it was still bound by divinely pedigreed inalienable natural rights. But the view Jefferson expressed in that letter was an outlier and had radical implications for debts and obligations contracted by previous generations. For Hamilton and most other founders, popular sovereignty was not only tied vertically by God in the present, but also horizontally or diachronically by the ties of the dead, living, and unborn. In short, popular sovereignty meant primarily that there was no other human institution that could be normatively appealed to in the act of fundamental law making outside of the people of that polity (understood to have diachronic existence), even as the people themselves remain bound by the rule of law in the classical sense of will being subject to reason.

Moreover, popular sovereignty under the Constitution's legal structure was distinctive in that there were what Madison called "two distinct governments" within the polity.[45] The division of powers between the federal and state governments reflected a dualist understanding of popular sovereignty, in which sovereignty was divided according to the scope of objects pertaining to the common good that federal and state governments were authorized to legislate for. The former was "few and defined" while the latter was "numerous and indefinite."[46]

To further illuminate the founders' vision of popular sovereignty and its moral constraints, it will be helpful to consider the insights and shortcomings of various contemporary accounts of the founders' understanding of sovereignty.

6.3 VOLUNTARISTIC ORIGINALISM IN CONTEMPORARY CONSTITUTIONAL THEORY

Bruce Ackerman has notably described the Constitution as establishing a "dualist" democracy in a sense distinctive from the sense used in the previous section. For Ackerman, dualism means a "two-track" conception of lawmaking: a track of "higher lawmaking" consisting of various moments when *the People* speak so as to effectively change the basic structure of the Constitution, and the lower "normal" track of day-to-day lawmaking regulated by the former. The constitutional moments of modification, in turn, set new frameworks and recharacterized the ambit of political power in subsequent normal lawmaking. For Ackerman, the key for citizens and judges is to make a distinction between two different sorts of decisions that can be made in the democracy: "the first is a decision by the American People, the second by their government."[47] The "very

---

[44] *The Federalist*, ed. Carey and McClellan, no. 84, 449. Emphasis in original.
[45] Ibid., no. 51, 270.   [46] Ibid., no. 45, 241.
[47] Bruce Ackerman, *We the People: Foundations* (Cambridge, MA: The Belknap Press, 1991), 6.

point" of distinguishing between these two tracks of lawmaking is to "identify principles that represent something more than the opinions that happen to be dominant in the halls of power in Washington."[48]

Why should the dualist framework be normative in the first place? Ackerman's voluntaristic account of popular sovereignty grounds dualism historically as an attractive concept present within the American tradition. On this view, nothing more than historical accident limits the democratic sovereign and the judge is ultimately merely an agent of the popular sovereign's will. Hence, Ackerman imagines a hypothetical amendment that would be offensive to his secular liberal conception of fundamental justice, but that he believes if he were a Supreme Court Justice he would be duty bound to apply. By relying on the mere historical fact of a framework being willed as sufficient to bind political actors in conscience, Ackerman effectively attributes to We the People the absolutism of the Rousseauean sovereign and fails to explain the moral obligation to obey the law.[49]

Ackerman tried to soften the implication for progressive living constitutionalists with his framework of major constitutional moments in which the people have spoken: that is, the Founding, Reconstruction, and the New Deal. As his inclusion of the New Deal indicates, Ackerman holds that formal amendment of the Constitution by one of the modes prescribed in the constitutional text is not a necessary condition for some event to count as a "constitutional moment" that alters our fundamental law. In Ackerman's scheme, the Supreme Court functions as a *preservationist* institution – as a speaker for the people against the government after constitutional moments of higher lawmaking. The Court becomes a representative of the people in their absence, and the Court's task is to coherently synthesize the three constitutional moments as cases require.

This narrative departs from the founders' conception of popular sovereignty for a number of reasons, some of which Keith Whittington has well articulated: It unduly transfers the popular sovereign's fundamental lawmaking power to government officials and judges. This problem comes to the fore at various points, including Ackerman's description of the process of modern higher lawmaking and the judiciary's preservative power. Because the popular sovereign in its fullest expression is empowered to scrap the Constitution entirely, the popular sovereign's amendment power is a subordinate expression of democratic sovereignty, because it is *amending* rather than creating anew. If the sovereign is amending rather than creating, then on dualism's own terms, that

---

[48] Ibid., 277.

[49] Here Ackerman arguably runs into the same philosophical problem of rooting moral obligation in sovereign will helpfully discussed in Paul DeHart, "Fractured Foundations: The Contradiction between Locke's Ontology and His Moral Philosophy," *Locke Studies* (2012): 12: 111–48. In short, Ackerman contends that a judge would be duty bound to apply a certain amendment by virtue of the popular sovereign's will, but he does not offer a philosophically coherent account of how duty or obligation relates to sovereign will.

amendment process itself is still governed by the will of the popular sovereign; hence, the amendment process is bound by the terms of the Constitution. Still, Ackerman's permissive criteria for constitutional moments effectively empower national legislators to pass transformative laws that the founders' Constitution has not authorized them to pass. In short, Ackerman's scheme consolidates "the amendment power with the hands of the same government agents who will administer policy under it."[50] While Ackerman's object was to separate the will of the people from the transient will of politicians, Whittington is correct that, in the end, Ackerman is "too accommodating of governmental sovereignty."[51]

The upshot is that, outside times of active popular sovereignty, the popular sovereign is not present in ordinary politics. All that remains in those periods of constitutional time that are not transformative is the expression of the sovereign will embodied in a previously ratified constitution. Ackerman's conception of the judiciary as a representative of the people, when it synthesizes transformative constitutional moments, cannot be sustained. The judiciary is empowered only to interpret and apply the sovereign's will, because the sovereign's will is not otherwise present or active. Ackerman unduly grants the judiciary powers reserved to the popular sovereign alone. And, yet, even if the New Deal "moment" actually amended the Constitution, the judiciary's grafting onto the tree of New Deal jurisprudence of rights of individual autonomy, beginning especially with *Griswold* v. *Connecticut*, cannot fairly be said to "preserve" the sovereign's allegedly transformative New Deal-will.[52]

Whittington wants to avoid Ackerman's historicism, arguing instead that "the grounding of the theory is in the normative value of consensual government, not in its traditionalist roots in Madison."[53] So, Whittington contends, further development of the tradition of normative theorizing about popular sovereignty "can provide the justification for our continued adherence to the Constitution and the normative value of an originalist jurisprudence."[54] In his case for popular sovereignty, Whittington first reviews the modern origins of the concept of sovereignty in political philosophy. He traces the concept from the absolutism of Bodin and Hobbes to the constitutionalist reaction of Locke and Montesquieu and then to Rousseau's democratic sovereign.[55] Ultimately, this discussion culminates in Whitttington's own view: The popular sovereign's will is authoritative, and this authority does not ultimately depend on the truth or goodness of what the popular sovereign wills.[56] Whittington tempers this

---

[50] Keith E. Whittington, *Constitutional Interpretation: Textual Meaning, Original Intent, and Judicial Review* (Lawrence: University Press of Kansas, 1999), 275, n. 98.

[51] Ibid., 274, n. 92.

[52] Ackerman contends that Justices Black and Stewart offer a "statist" interpretation of the national constitutional moment and hence the nature of federal power. But *Griswold* concerns a state statute that was passed in 1879 – it has nothing to do with the nature of federal power to legislate on traditional sexual moral norms.

[53] Whittington, *Constitutional Interpretation*, 270, n. 59.   [54] Ibid., 124.   [55] Ibid., 114–23.

[56] Ibid., 140.

Rousseauean position with contention that "reason has much to say about the correct form of constitution"; that "there is reason to think [the sovereign's will] will be reasonable"; and that "popular will is not antagonistic to reason." Ultimately, however, Whittington springs for a weaker form of voluntarism and positivism. Reason is not the criterion of legitimacy, he argues, because constitutional design "is ultimately a matter of choice and will."[57] Reason "is not conclusive in and of itself" because "rights due to individuals, the goods to be achieved for them through government, and the instruments of government necessary to do both are matters of controversy."[58] Thus, in forming the Constitution, "the popular sovereign did not rule for the good of the people but governed in accord with the will of the people. The people were to determine for themselves their own good."[59] As a result, "the judgment of the people cannot be measured against some external standard of truth, found wanting, and then *laid aside as not legally binding.*"[60]

There is not a transcendent standard known to reason that grounds and limits democratic sovereignty in Whittington's scheme. The heart of its normative value consists in the proposition that, because the power to decide constitutional forms must reside somewhere, "the power of decision should reside with the people who must live under those constitutional forms."[61] That you have to lie down in this bed implies that you should be able to make or remake it, too. The Constitution's normative value essentially lies in securing the people's potential sovereignty to alter or abolish its constitutional forms. In the end, Whittington does not escape the basic problem with Ackerman's scheme from the classical natural-law perspective. If no standard of justice external to the people's will conditions and limits that will, then historical accident and collective will become the only political standards of the just and the good. If that were the case, it is not clear why the whole people should retain potential sovereignty over constitutional forms if they came to believe that the one or the few ought to have that power.

Some argue that such historicism and voluntarism provided the foundation of the American founders' vision of sovereignty. In one recent study of the original meaning of popular sovereignty in the United States, Andrew G. I. Kilberg relies on Bernard Bailyn's readings of Samuel Johnson and James Otis to contend that the Americans understood sovereignty to be absolute and arbitrary.[62] But, as we have seen, the Americans explicitly rejected the Hobbist theory of sovereignty advanced by Johnson, and although Otis initially retained hope that Parliament would correct its error, he unequivocally rejected absolutist sovereignty.[63] The founders both understood, articulated, and rejected the idea that sovereignty is absolute and arbitrary.

---

[57] Ibid., 139–41.   [58] Ibid., 139.   [59] Ibid., 151.
[60] Ibid., 275–76, n. 106. Emphasis in original.   [61] Ibid., 138.
[62] Andrew G. I. Kilberg, "We The People: The Original Meaning of Popular Sovereignty," *Virginia Law Review* 100(5) (2014): 1061–109.
[63] See Chapter 2 in this volume.

What about the possibility that the original meaning of popular sovereignty was that the people were sovereign *individually* rather than collectively? In his defense of this view, Randy Barnett contends that the key to understanding the sovereignty of "We the People" rests in the Ninth and Tenth Amendments. The Ninth Amendment reads: "The enumeration in the Constitution, of certain rights, shall not be construed to deny or disparage others retained by the people." Reading the Ninth Amendment in light of the foregoing amendments' guarantees of various rights such as speech, assembly, press, and free exercise of religion, and evidence from proposed drafts of the bill of rights that used the language of natural rights, and similar language in various state constitutions, Barnett contends that the rights retained are individual natural rights. Barnett thus reads the Ninth in conjunction with the Tenth Amendment – "The powers not delegated to the United States by the Constitution, nor prohibited by it to the states, are reserved to the states respectively, or to the people" – to conclude that the "ultimate sovereign" is the "people themselves," which means "sovereignty resides jointly in the people as individuals, each and every one."[64]

To bolster this case, Barnett draws from James Wilson's opinion in *Chisholm* v. *Georgia*, a landmark case in which the state of Georgia asserted sovereign immunity from being sued without its consent. Wilson wrote that there was only one place in the Constitution that with propriety the term "sovereign" could have been used: *We the sovereign people*. "But serenely conscious of the fact," Wilson insisted, "they avoided the ostentatious declaration."[65] Barnett then quotes Wilson to suggest that the sovereign "must be found in *the man*" and is ultimately rooted in the consent of sovereign individuals.[66]

Barnett's account of We the People is correct insofar as it suggests that the legitimate exercise of the people's sovereignty is limited by natural rights. Yet Barnett's account is misleading inasmuch as it suggests that the founders understood the sovereign people to be an aggregate of autonomous individuals. In his *Chisholm* opinion, Wilson began his discussion of sovereignty on theological grounds: "Man, fearfully and wonderfully made, is the workmanship of his all perfect Creator. A state, useful and valuable as the contrivance is, is the inferior contrivance of man, and from his native dignity derives all its acquired importance." Wilson then immediately pointed out that his object was not to attack the dignity of a state; rather, it was to affirm the higher dignity of the people whom the state is meant to serve: "A state I cheerfully fully admit, is the noblest work of Man. Man himself, free and honest, is, I speak as to this world, the noblest work of God." Wilson's emphasis on the native dignity of the individual was tempered by his acknowledgment that the states constituted real

---

[64] Randy Barnett, *Our Republican Constitution* (New York: Broadside Books, 2019), 64–65.
[65] *Chisholm* v. *Georgia*, 2 U.S. 419 (1793). Accessed July 28, 2021, from https://supreme.justia.com/cases/federal/us/2/419/.
[66] Barnett, *Our Republican Constitution*, 71. Emphasis in original.

unities that could not be reduced merely to an aggregate of individuals: "By a 'state,' I mean a complete body of free persons united together for their common benefit to enjoy peaceably what is their own and to do justice to others."[67]

Barnett's insight is that the sovereignty of the people is qualified by the prior and continual existence of natural rights. As Wilson's discussion shows, however, those natural rights depended on a theological-philosophical anthropology of divine workmanship. Even with this emphasis on the importance of the individual, popular sovereignty cannot be reduced to *merely* an aggregate of individual sovereigns for at least two reasons that Chief Justice John Jay captured in his separate *Chisolm* opinion. First, attributing to the sovereign people a merely aggregative unity would amount to something less than the union that existed prior to the revolution and the more perfect union that the people aspired to in the Constitution. As Jay put it:

The Revolution, or rather the Declaration of Independence, found the people already united for general purposes, and at the same time providing for their more domestic concerns by State conventions and other temporary arrangements ... then the people, in their collective and national capacity, established the present Constitution.[68]

Second, the "artificial person" of the state is a genuine unity that the Tenth Amendment explicitly acknowledges retains exclusive powers to pursue the common good of the citizens of each state. Again, in Jay's words, "the sovereignty of the nation is in the people of the nation, and the residuary sovereignty of each State in the people of each State."[69]

6.4 THE PEOPLE IN THE FOUNDING ERA

The social ontology that "We the People" supposes, reflected in early state constitutions, is richer and more nuanced than a mere aggregate of individual sovereigns. Consider the language of some founding era state constitutions. The constitutions of Vermont and Pennsylvania referenced "the community as such." In Virginia, power was vested in "the people," New York's constitution invoked the "authority of the good people of this State," and in New Jersey, constitutional authority was said to be "derived from the people, and held of them, for the common interest of the whole society." Massachusetts recognized the corporate rights of the "several towns, parishes, precincts, and other bodies-politic, or religious societies" in the polity, and similar language was used by New Hampshire for the sake of supporting public piety, religion and morality. South Carolina recognized "religious societies" as corporate bodies that were

---

[67] Ibid.
[68] *Chisholm* v. *Georgia*, 2 U.S. 419 (1793). Accessed July 28, 2021, from https://supreme.justia .com/cases/federal/us/2/419/.
[69] Ibid.

not reducible to its individual members.[70] The use of collective nouns – the people, community, religious associations, denominations, bodies-corporate, and the like – reflects the founders' operating assumption that social reality was constituted not only by rights-bearing individuals but also rights-bearing social wholes. In continuity with the natural-law tradition, the state constitutions recognized polity and other social forms as genuine societies animated by real common goods and the common good.

In short, neither Ackerman's voluntaristic, living constitutionalist account, nor Whittington's voluntaristic originalist account, nor Barnett's libertarian individualist account captures the founders' understanding of popular sovereignty as limited and conditioned by a preexisting natural law.

John O. McGinnis and Michael B. Rappaport offer another possibility. They accept Ackerman's and Whittington's grounding of the authority of the Constitution in the sovereign will of the people. Still, they maintain that acts of a whole people are neither necessary nor sufficient to produce *good* constitutions (goodness, i.e., orderedness to the common good of justice and peace, is a necessary condition of a constitution's normatively binding force in conscience in the classical natural-law tradition). That is, they contend that supermajoritarian procedure is *likely* to lead to a genuinely good constitution (e.g., a constitution without major institution and sociological defects). A supermajoritarian procedure is likely to produce desirable institutional features of constitutional republics such as representative institutions, separation of powers, federalism, and the like. It is also likely to produce a constitution that is the product of wide deliberation and consensus, and which is actively supported by the people for just this reason.[71]

We agree that the Rousseauean, voluntarist idea that the democratic sovereign will, generated by supermajoritarian procedures, is *sufficient* to make a good constitution is both false and not in accord with the founders' understanding of sovereignty. Rappaport and McGinnis go further and maintain that neither is a supermajoritarian procedure a necessary condition, because a "good" constitution could be created through "some other method."[72] Yet the founders themselves affirmed that popular sovereignty, a position that entails a sovereign act of the whole people (identified through a supermajoritarian procedure such as the requirement of ratification of three-fourths of the states and the Article VI amendment procedures), *is* a necessary condition for a

---

[70] For the constitutions of Vermont (1777), Pennsylvania (1776), Virginia (1776), New York (1777) New Jersey (1776), and South Carolina (1776), see The Avalon Project, Yale University. Accessed March 1, 2022, from https://avalon.law.yale.edu/subject_menus/constpap .asp; Constitution of New Hampshire (1784). Accessed March 1, 2022, from https://en .wikisource.org/wiki/Constitution_of_New_Hampshire_(1784); Constitution of Massachusetts (1780). Accessed March 1, 2022, from www.nhinet.org/ccs/docs/ma-1780.htm.

[71] John O. McGinnis and Michael B. Rappaport, *Originalism and the Good Constitution* (Cambridge, MA: Harvard University Press, 2013).

[72] Ibid., 21.

good constitution. To be more precise, drawing on the helpful framework of Rappaport and McGinnis, the founders did suggest that popular consent was a necessary condition of a "genuinely good" constitution. Rappaport and McGinnis themselves maintain that it is necessary for a genuinely good constitution to be "desired by the nation."[73] For the founders, the most fitting truth maker for this condition is that the Constitution represents the will of the popular sovereign and protects its potential sovereignty, that is, their collective capacity for higher lawmaking.

Rappaport and McGinnis worry that a "thick" moral-metaphysical theory is an inappropriate "basis for a constitution in a pluralistic society in which the people hold differing views about the good (or justice)," because "a thick theory will be open to attack by those who do not hold that particular view of the good."[74] Instead, Rappaport and McGinnis posit a form of preference utilitarianism as a framework for assessing the desirability of consequences for people under a constitution. The capacity to maintain social peace and order by accommodating rival visions of the good is, of course, a constitutional virtue. (On our reading of the founders' Constitution, this is a primary virtue of federalism.) The problem with Rappaport and McGinnis' argument is that preference utilitarianism is not actually neutral between rival visions of the good, nor is it free from controversial metaphysical assumptions. If, for example, that which is "good" is entirely reducible to subjective preference, then it follows that there are no objective goods as posited by classical natural-law theory.

A "thin" subjective and consequentialist conception of the good is still a conception of the good, and it remains "open to attack by those who do not hold that particular view of the good."[75] If there is in reality an objective good for human beings, then it also follows that there is a common human nature in virtue of which objects fulfilling or perfective of that nature are good. The affirmation of a subjectivist form of preference utilitarianism, however, entails a rejection of an existing/knowable common human nature and affirmation of a form of nominalism, itself a controversial and contested metaphysical position. If, on the other hand, as Rappaport and McGinnis suggest might be the case, there are objectively desirable goods to which subjective preferences ought to conform, then it can be validly inferred that there *is* a common human nature, a form of realism opposed to nominalism, which also is a controversial and contested metaphysical position. Either way, preference utilitarianism cannot do the work of generating the sort of noncontroversial overlapping consensus that Rappaport and McGinnis suggest it can. Controversial questions of metaphysics and metaethics cannot be bracketed *qua* political and constitutional questions.

[73] Ibid., 22.   [74] Ibid., 5.   [75] Ibid.

Although Rappaport and McGinnis make a persuasive case that supermajoritarian procedures will likely succeed in generating the features of a good constitution (nonpartisan consensus, durability, protection of minority rights, etc.), they leave open and unanswered an urgent question: *Why are such features good?* Such a question implicates foundational metaphysical assumptions that cannot be bracketed from constitutional theory. The founders' understanding of the virtue of popular sovereignty, illuminated by classical, Christian natural-law theory, offers an alternative to the various forms of voluntarism and utilitarianism that buttress some of the most sophisticated theoretical defenses of originalist constitutional theory in contemporary scholarship. The nineteenth-century social theorist and Catholic convert Orestes Brownson advanced a similar thesis, and his analysis remains insightful today.[76]

While we agree with originalist scholars that the only morally valid ground of judicial authority to decide cases and controversies is the Constitution, we maintain that the most compelling case for the Constitution's authority is a natural-law-based theory of popular sovereignty and the people's constitution-making power as an exercise of reason rather than will.

6.5 BROWNSON AND EXISTENTIAL DEPENDENCE

Orestes Brownson was born a generation after the Revolution and had a strict Calvinist upbringing in Vermont, but he came to reject Calvinism because he could not intellectually reconcile the doctrine of predestination with his understanding of God's justice. Brownson then went through a period of religious unease, first becoming a Universalist and denying Christian revelation, eventually becoming a Unitarian pastor and engaging with the transcendentalist movement, and writing trenchant social criticism while editing the *Boston Quarterly Review*. By 1844, however, he had converted to Catholicism and embraced the perennial philosophy of the classical and Thomistic natural-law tradition, a tradition from which Brownson later drew upon when offering an analysis of sovereignty under the U.S. Constitution in his 1865 book *The American Republic*. The keys to Brownson's mature account of sovereignty lie in his notions of existential dependence, secondary causality, and what he calls the providential constitution.

Brownson came to advance a classical Christian metaphysic and philosophical-theological anthropology: "man is a dependent being and neither does nor can suffice for himself."[77] This metaphysical claim was about God's

---

[76] For a Brownson-inspired interpretation of American constitutionalism, see Peter Augustine Lawler and Richard M. Reinsch II, *A Constitution in Full: Recovering the Unwritten Foundation of American Liberty* (Lawrence: University Press of Kansas, 2019).

[77] Orestes A. Brownson, *The American Republic*, ed. Peter Augustine Lawler (Wilmington, DE: ISI Books, 2003), 11. Of this work, Brownson says that it "must be taken as the authentic, and only

causal relation to man: "He [man] lives not in himself, but lives and moves and has his being in God."[78] This is, of course, a Pauline point – but it is also a metaphysical claim that is, in principle, knowable and demonstrable by reason unaided by revelation in Scripture. Brownson's Christian existentialist metaphysics can be traced to Thomas Aquinas.[79] The Thomistic argument in bare outline is as follows, which we restate as one way of proving God's existence in classical Christian philosophical theology. There are causes and effects. Causes ontologically precede effects. The nonsubsistent cannot cause. But essence and existence are nonidentical principles of being. From these premises, it is a valid inference that there must be an *Ipsum Esse Subsistens* – a Self-Subsisting Existence – that is the unique and immediate cause of all real things.

The key premise is the distinction between essence and existence. In the case of human beings, man's manifest insufficiency to cause himself to be or maintain himself in existence indicates that his act of existence does not flow from his essence. To be a *man* is apparently nonidentical with *being* a man. Being or existence (*esse*) transcends and englobes all real things of our experience and so cannot be identified with any of them. Essence is the principle of specification, to make things be this or that kind of thing: to be a *tree*, a *dog*, a *man*, and so on. If existence were identical with (say), man, then *human* would be baked into being, such that whenever an existing thing were encountered, a human would be encountered; but, the world of our experience is in fact variegated. Humans and other contingent things do exist, whose essences are also nonidentical with existence.

Moreover, no nature or essence can be the cause of its own existence, because if it were, it would exist before it existed. The nonsubsistent cannot cause. Neither can the act of existence (*esse*) of a thing produce the thing. The act of existence is not itself a thing but the very "is" – or being or *esse* – of a thing. Therefore, the act of existence of a thing cannot itself cause the nature of the thing of which it is the determined principle. The *esse* of a thing is itself dependent. Now, whatever is dependent must rely on something that is independent, that has existence in itself. We experience this when the fire heats up the pot of water, when the arm moves the pool cue, when a father carries his child upon his shoulders. The cause of the *esse* of the thing cannot be another

---

authentic statement of my political views and convictions, and whatever in any of my previous writings conflicts with the principles defended in its pages, must be regarded as retracted and rejected," CX.

[78] Ibid., 11.

[79] Aquinas understood the five ways (which had been made by previous thinkers, including non-Christians) and his argument for God's existence in *On Being and Essence* from his distinctively Judeo-Christian existentialist metaphysics, in which the act of existence is accidental and nonidentical to essence or nature. For a discussion, see Joseph Owens, "Aquinas and the Five Ways," *The Monist* (January 1974) 58(1): 16–35; cf. Thomas Aquinas, *De Ente et Essentia §80*, in *Aquinas on Being and Essence*, trans. Joseph Bobik (South Bend: University of Notre Dame Press: 1965), 160–61.

dependent *esse*, because no dependent *esse* can produce anything, just as a pool cue that is infinitely long cannot of itself strike the cue ball. We are led to the conclusion that there must be in the order of causation some noncontingent being that suffices for its own existence – a self-subsisting existence that provides the explanation for the existence of all contingent things, because they are dependent upon it for their being. There must be a first cause or that which we call God. To deny this, says Brownson, is tantamount to denying "all distinction between creator and creature, God and universe, which all the world knows is either pantheism or pure atheism – the supreme sophism."[80] Neither, Brownson points out, is a particular form of deism rationally defensible if metaphysical dependence is true, because the universe is insufficient to maintain itself in existence: "It cannot go of itself, because it does not exist of itself."[81] God's conserving causality is needed to maintain things in existence.

Brownson lamented that "For nearly two centuries the most popular and influential writers on government have rejected the divine origin and ground of civil authority" and that they have "refused to look beyond second causes, and have labored to derive authority from man alone."[82] Contemporary liberal political and constitutional theory is often characterized by refusal to look beyond secondary causes precisely because it explicitly or implicitly rejects man's existential dependence and the economy of God's sovereignty over men. Hence, justice is theorized as "political, not metaphysical."[83] But, in Brownson's view, "it is idle to attempt to separate the political question from the ethical, the metaphysical, or the theological; such a separation is possible only to the acute intellects that frame lyceum constitutions, and ordain that religion and politics shall not be introduced as topics of discussion."[84]

For Brownson, the political implications of metaphysical dependency cannot be ruled out of public discussion over constitutional fundamentals, because the thesis that man is a dependent being, if true, is of great significance for sovereignty and the foundations of constitutionalism.

First, it would follow that state-of-nature theories in the Hobbist and Rousseauean mold – in which persons are conceived as atomized, sovereign individuals – are false because the theories deny man's essential and existential dependence.[85] It also implies the falsity of theories that hold absolute sovereignty rests in the people collectively, "in their own independent might and right, as some zealous democrats explain it," for the same reason.[86] Both the radical individualist and the radical socialist make the same fundamental error:

---

[80] Brownson, *The American Republic*, 14.   [81] Ibid., 82.   [82] Ibid., 80.

[83] John Rawls, "Justice as Fairness: Political not Metaphysical," *Philosophy and Public Affairs* 14 (3)(Summer 1985): 223–51. See also John Rawls, *Justice as Fairness: A Restatement* (Cambridge, MA: Belknap Press, 2001).

[84] Brownson, *The Works of Orestes Brownson*, Collected and Arranged by Henry F. Brownson (New York: AMS, 1966), vol. XV, 355.

[85] Brownson, *The American Republic*, 32–33.   [86] Ibid., 57.

They conflate the creature with the Creator because they both reject any transcendent source of meaning and existence.

Brownson's rejection of a Rousseauean, immanentist account of democratic sovereignty is grounded in his conception of God as a vertical limiting principle on sovereignty: "No creature is creator, or has the rights of creator, and consequently no one in his own right is or can be sovereign."[87] Moreover, because all human begins are of the same kind and because all are equal in their existential dependency, they are fundamentally political equals. No one person in the multitude of a community has an antecedent claim to rule.

6.6 THE PEOPLE'S SECONDARY SOVEREIGNTY

Brownson's dependency thesis is thus the ground on which a theory of popular sovereignty more consonant with the classical Christian natural-law tradition can be built – what we call, in the spirit of Brownson, a theory of *secondary sovereignty*. To *be* a creature is to be dependent on God for one's being. But to be a *man* is to be, essentially, a particular kind of thing distinct from the rest of nature, namely, a *moral* creature "endowed with reason and free-will."[88] Whereas human nature as finite and contingent indicates dependency on God, human nature as reasonable and free indicates that God is not a despot. As Aristotle pointed out, despotic rule is like the will's power of bodily motion; the governor moves the governed without resistance as a hand moves a tool. But man's nature indicates that God's governance over man is not like this. God's governance over man is that kind of rule Aristotle referred to as royal and politic, like the will's governance of the passions. The governed have something of their own, and they can freely resist the governor's rule. Similarly, beings endowed with reason and free will can choose to resist or cooperate with God.

Brownson considered this point under the rubric of secondary causation: "God creates second causes, or substantial existences, capable themselves of acting and producing effects in a secondary sense, and hence he is said to be *causa causarum*, cause of causes."[89] Human beings, in particular, are secondary causes capable of performing acts of reason and free will. Because "God creates and governs all, each *after its kind*," it follows that God governs man in accord with this freedom.[90] This means that man is granted a share in God's governance of the universe by caring for himself and others. This is what it means to assert – as Aquinas, Hooker, Blackstone, and James Wilson all did –

---

[87] Ibid., 30.   [88] Ibid., 59.   [89] Ibid., 67.

[90] Brownson, *The Works of Orestes Brownson*, XV, 356, 359; cf. Aquinas, *Summa Contra Gentiles*, 113.4; 148.2. Accessed March 1, 2022, from www.corpusthomisticum.org/iopera .html. As Stanley Parry points out, this means that Brownson equates secondary causation with human freedom. Stanley J. Parry, "The Premises of Brownson's Political Theory," *The Review of Politics* 16(2) (1954): 200.

that natural law is a form of participation in the eternal law. This provides the theoretical ground supporting the idea of secondary sovereignty. Human beings acting individually or collectively cannot be absolute sovereigns, because "they are as dependent collectively as individually, and therefore can exist and act only as second cause, never as first cause," Brownson argued.[91] But human beings *are* second causes. It follows that "they can, then, even in the limited sphere of their sovereignty, be sovereign only in a secondary sense."[92] Because secondary sovereignty is a participation in God's governance, and because God governs every part of the universe for the common good of the whole, it follows that secondary sovereignty is teleologically oriented toward the care of the community or its common good.[93]

An objection could be raised here to the Brownson-inspired classical natural-law theory of secondary sovereignty that we are sketching. Jacques Maritain, one of the most influential natural-law theorists of the twentieth century and an outstanding defender of democracy, argued that the concept of sovereignty ought to be jettisoned altogether. Maritain contended that sovereignty, considered in its modern meaning, is "intrinsically wrong and bound to mislead us if we keep using it."[94] Maritain identified "the original error" in Bodin's characterization of the highest authority as *transcending* and *separate from* the whole. Instead of merely an existential status of the exercise of government, separation and transcendence of the sovereign from the whole were, for Bodin, "required as an *essential* quality, one with the very possession of that right, which the people have supposedly given up entirely, so that all the essence of power – henceforth monadic, as indivisible as the very person of the Sovereign – resides in the Sovereign alone."[95] Modern sovereignty, according to Maritain, logically begets the concentration of power unmoored from any external limits on that power.

Maritain saw the fundamental problem with the Hobbist and Rousseauean constructions of sovereign power as effectively annulling the people's original right of self-governance by conceiving the social compact in terms of the physical transfer of material power. But material good or power evokes the concept of ownership, and "if a material good is owned by the one, it cannot be owned by the other, and there can only be a question of transfer of ownership or donation."[96] Maritain feared that this formulation vitiated the people's right to self-government, because this right subsists as long as the rulers are understood as deputies or vicars of the people who possess the right to command but *only insofar as they participate in the people's right.* On this formulation, the highest authority is not separate and transcendent, but vicariously possesses authority by participation in the natural right of the people – a formulation inconceivable on the crude terms of physical transfer of material power.

---

[91] Brownson, *The American Republic*, 56.   [92] Ibid., 56.
[93] Cf., Aquinas, *Summa Theologica*, I, 103.1–8.   [94] Maritain, *Man and the State*, 29.
[95] Ibid., 35.   [96] Ibid., 35.

Because the topmost authority governs authoritatively only by participation, referring to it as *sovereign* is problematic, according to Maritain, because that denotes the possession of an independent and supreme power by natural right.

If the concept of sovereignty consists essentially in a separated, transcendent, unified, and absolute power, then, Maritain insisted, it is also nonsensical to speak of the *people* as sovereign, for it would imply the people govern themselves *"separately from themselves and from above themselves."*[97] Maritain interpreted Rousseau's "General Will," which mystically bears the name of sovereignty in *The Social Contract*, as falling into this trap.[98] But, beyond the absurdity of "sovereignty" implying the people govern separate and above themselves, it should be rejected inasmuch as it means "whatever would please the people would have the force of law."[99] In other words, "sovereignty" must be jettisoned because it entails the adjective "unconstrained" in its very *ratio*.

In place of popular sovereignty, Maritain argued for the internal and external "autonomy" of the people. On this conception, the people have a natural right of authority, which flows from and is embanked by the natural law. For Maritain, this meant that, while the people might legitimate a range of possible regimes, "democratic *philosophy* appears as the only true political philosophy."[100] Democratic philosophy, on Maritain's account, requires that those who exercise legitimate authority are periodically designated and managed by the people.

Maritain was quick to jettison the language of sovereignty, seeing it as bound up in the modern world with philosophical errors. Those errors, however, were not essential to the theoretical foundations of American constitutionalism as the founders understood them. It has been accurately said that Brownson "described and defended the same reality championed by Christian philosophers such as Jacques Maritain and Etienne Gilson."[101] Indeed, Brownson shows that a sound account of popular sovereignty in the United States is available on the grounds of classical natural law. One can accurately describe a people as sovereign, Brownson argued, while maintaining that God's providential reign over the universe is the focal case of sovereignty, because the people are sovereign only in a secondary sense. "Sovereignty, or the right to govern, is in [God], and he may at his will delegate it to men either mediately or immediately, by a direct and express appointment, or mediately through nature."[102] The classical doctrine of human participation in the eternal law through the natural law would seem to countenance this move.

---

[97] Ibid., 44.   [98] Cf. Rousseau, *The Social Contract*, bk. II, ch. 4.
[99] Maritain, *Man and the State*, 48.   [100] Ibid., 129.
[101] Armand Mauer, "The Christian Philosophy of Orestes Brownson," *The Monist* 75(3) (1992): 350.
[102] Brownson, *The American Republic*, 68.

Such a theory of secondary sovereignty can retain the communal right of self-rule and self-direction to the common good that properly belongs to the people, while also fending off the peculiarly modern individualist and collectivist theories of sovereignty. It can also forestall sacral notions of kingship that were pervasive in the ancient and even medieval world, divine right theories of rule, ecclesiocracy, and all forms of religious totalitarianism, because it is to be presumed that authority is mediate through secondary causes. In this way, secondary sovereignty resists both radically transcendentalist (e.g., theocracy) and radically immanentist accounts of authority. We return to discuss immanentism and transcendentalism in Chapter 8. Neither is it persuasive, on Maritain's own terms, to hold that the word "sovereignty" should be jettisoned simply because it became corrupted in the modern era. Maritain is, after all, willing to use the language of autonomy despite its corrupt usages.[103]

6.7 THE PROVIDENTIAL CONSTITUTION

Secondary sovereignty is further illuminated by Brownson's idea of the providential constitution, what Peter Augustine Lawler and Richard Reinsch describe as the unwritten constitution "that couldn't have emerged out of nothing, but is formed out of the political, cultural, philosophical, and religious elements that are given to statesmen and guide what they can do."[104] To be constituted as one nation or one sovereign political people is to be providentially ordained by God as such. God generates the organic or providential constitution of a people and orders a multitude antecedently to the people's formation of a written constitution. This comes about by God's providential governance in at least two ways: first, through the natural law, which itself requires the establishment of authority for the common good and is known in part through the law common to all nations, the *ius gentium* and, second, through "historical events or natural causes."[105] For Brownson, the challenge of constitutional moments is to discern the nature of the providential constitution and to arrange the prudential form of the written constitution in light of the preexisting providential constitution. Accordingly, the providential constitution puts particular parameters around the right exercise of human freedom.

---

[103] Maritain argues that the Aristotle's κύριος and Thomas's *principe* are mistranslated as "sovereign" – and Maritain implies that the modern English etymology of the word flows from Bodin and Hobbes. However, the term was employed by earlier writers influenced by the Thomistic tradition to signify a ruler or a person of authority without an absolutist connotation, including Chaucer, who makes the point in the context of the domestic sphere ("The Parson's Tale" in the *Canterbury Tales*, ed. Jill Mann [London: Penguin Books, 2005]) and later by Fortescue (who refers to the ruler as a "sovereign lord" [souerayn lorde] in the same breath that he is said to rule under the law of God and the natural law (*On the Laws and Governance of England*, ed. Shelly Lockwood [Cambridge: Cambridge University Press, 1997, 91–92]).

[104] Lawler and Reinsch, *A Constitution in Full*, 125.

[105] Brownson, *The American Republic*, 91.

On Brownson's reading, the U.S. Constitution does capture the spirit of the U.S. providential constitution – and the key to understanding it lies in the notion of the *United* States. The Constitution expresses the will of one people, united, from whom flows powers distributed to the government of the states united and the states individually in one integral whole. The Constitution provides the American people with its constitution of government, which

is the constitution by the sovereign authority of the nation of an agency or ministry for the management of its affairs, and the letter of instructions according to which the agent or minister is to act and conduct the matters intrusted to him.[106]

Brownson's notion of the providential constitution dovetails with the self-understanding of the founders, encapsulated in the passage already quoted from *Federalist* no. 37. In their capacity as second causes, the people cooperated with God inasmuch as they formulated a written constitution that expressed the essential features of the providential or unwritten constitution. Thus, Brownson's first substantial piece of evidence in his case for the unionist providential constitution is an appeal to the preamble of the Constitution: "We the people of the United States." The peculiarly American providential Constitution is evident when considering that the word *united* is an adjective modifying *states*. We are not the people of the States severally, nor are we a vast undifferentiated aggregate; we are one people, but one people organized into States that retain a residuum of sovereignty. Sovereignty thus rests not in the states severally, but in the Union – and yet, "there could be no sovereign union without the States, for there is no union where there is nothing united."[107] The underlying suggestion is that the providential constitution is not simply an analytic concept but also has legal force in that it is expressed in and assumed by the constitutional text.

Brownson's theories of dependence, secondary sovereignty, and the providential constitution thus provide a natural-law foundation for the sort of dualist and federalist constitutional republic enacted by "We the People." The broader argument of this book suggests that this is superior to voluntarist readings of the popular sovereignty that animated the revolution and later undergirded the founders' Constitution. Such then is the value of fidelity to the Constitution from a Brownsonian perspective: By confining constitutional actors to the parameters of the constitution, we respect the normative value of secondary sovereignty. The written text itself is the expression of the people acting in their sovereign capacity as second causes to set the boundaries of authority for constitutional actors and set the bounds for legitimate constitutional change. Our Brownsonian account can be seen as providing a thick metaphysical-theological grounding that corroborates a conclusion that Lee Strang has argued for, that the written text of the Constitution represents an

---

[106] Ibid., 114.   [107] Ibid., 143.

authoritative determination of the people to resolve the coordination problems which are inherent to polity and which are necessary to overcome to secure the common good and create the background conditions for the flourishing of the American people.[108]

Brownson's insight would seem to support Whittington's contention that the constitutional text sets, or at least should set, the terms on which the constitution is to be amended.[109] Whereas Whittington grounds the people's ultimate sovereignty in sheer will – as if the act of choice itself were sufficient to confer value – a Brownsonian notion of secondary sovereignty grounds the value of the people's will in the natural law and the providential constitution. On Brownson's account, the mere act of sovereign will cannot suffice to make a good constitution. One can, from the perspective of right reason, judge even a democratically enacted constitutional order to be more or less defective, that is, more or less conducive to justice and peace. Such a theory of secondary sovereignty thus provides a metaphysical ground more in tune with the higher law outlook of the founders that is metaphysically defensible. It therefore may be able to better support Rappaport's and McGinnis' sound conclusions about the necessity of the Constitution being genuinely good.

*

That the founders thought of the Constitution as embodying the people's will as a secondary sovereign rather than an unlimited Rousseauean sovereign is evident in the text itself. The national legislature was empowered over a specific and defined range of objects. The eighteen specific powers enumerated in Article I, Section 8 of the Constitution, placed within the reach of Congress objects primarily associated with security from external threats and commercial prosperity. Other "numerous and indefinite" powers of polity associated with the internal police of the people were then reserved to the states, which were governed by state constitutions that also reflected a vision of secondary sovereignty of the people of the state. Russell Hittinger correctly points out that "considered very generally, there is no delegated power [to pursue an object] that is, in itself, contrary to natural law."[110] On the contrary, the distribution

---

[108] Lee Strang, *Originalism's Promise: A Natural Law Account of the American Constitution* (New York: Cambridge University Press, 2019).

[109] See Brownson, *The Works of Orestes Brownson*, vol. XVIII, 582.

[110] Russell Hittinger, "The Limits of Constitutional Law," in *Common Truths: New Perspectives on Natural Law*, ed. Edward B. McLean (Wilmington, DE: ISI Books, 2000), 176. A possible counterexample here would be Article IV, Section 2 language that persons held to service or labor in another state "shall be delivered up on Claim of the Party to whom such Service or Labour may be due." While the passage is ambiguous as to who is responsible to deliver up the persons in question, if this passage essentially specifies a legal duty with regard to escaped persons unjustly held in servitude, it implies a positive legal duty to act contrary to natural-law precepts. But the language is sufficiently abstract that Frederick Douglass argued it need not be

of powers was intended to authorize the various departments and levels of government to pursue aspects of the common good proper to its sphere.

From the perspective of classical natural-law theory, positive law flows from the natural law by deduction and determination. For example, from the natural-law principle forbidding murder, positive laws criminalizing murder are deduced. But how should murderers be punished? This is a matter of determination that admits of a wide range of policies and is left to the prudence of lawmakers. Constitution making is a matter of determination, because there is more than one good way of arranging a constitutional order. Therefore, it is a matter to be determined through governing structures which objects fall under which levels and spheres of government, including the federal judiciary's scope of authority.[111] The will of the people expressed in the Constitution is to delegate the authority to make laws for the common good to *legislators*; indeed, by the vesting clause of Article I, *all* national legislative powers granted by the Constitution are vested in the bicameral legislative body. In other words, the constitution makers and the democratic sovereign charged the legislature with prudentially translating the basic requirements of natural law into positive law.

A theory of secondary sovereignty, grounded in natural law, thus does not empower or authorize judges to make freewheeling appeals to first principles in contradiction to the sovereign people's constitutional determinations. As Robert P. George correctly points out, the idea of a judiciary restrained by the prior lawmaking of the people's representatives is fully compatible with classical natural-law principles.[112] Grounding sovereignty in classical natural law need not import into a Herculean judge's arsenal a body of principles that he can wield at will to strike down the determinations of legislators when those determinations are within their jurisdictional competence.[113] Rather, the theory

---

interpreted as a positive constitutional endorsement of slavery, but merely the institution of indentured servitude. The indentured servant owes service as a matter of contract, but the slave, Douglass contends, is not countenanced because he or she is merely an article of property. See Frederick Douglass, *The Constitution of the United States: Is It Pro-Slavery or Anti-Slavery?* (Halifax, Nova Scotia: T. and W. Birtwhistle, 1860). For a detailed exploration of the moral issues faced by judges tasked with interpreting the Fugitive Slave Clause, see also Robert M. Cover, *Justice Accused: Antislavery and the Judicial Process* (New Haven: Yale University Press, 1984).

[111]   Cf. Aquinas, *Summa Theologica*, I–II, 95.2.

[112]   Robert P. George, "Natural Law and Positive Law," in Edward B. McLean, ed., *Common Truths: New Perspectives on Natural Law* (Wilmington, DE: ISI Books, 2000), 165.

[113]   But see Stuart Banner, *The Decline of Natural Law: How American Lawyers Once Used Natural Law and Why They Stopped* (New York: Oxford University Press, 2021), demonstrating the widespread phenomenon of lawyers and judges appealing to natural-law principles in 19thnineteenth- century America. For a discussion, including of instances in which direct judicial appeal to natural law may be justified, see Kody Cooper, "What Happened to Natural Law in American Jurisprudence?" *Federalist Society Review*, Vol. 22 (2021): 316––24. A corollary to the limited authority of judges is the falsity of judicial *supremacy*, in the form it has been claimed by the Supreme Court since *Cooper v. Aaron* 358 U.S. 1 (1958) inasmuch as

of secondary sovereignty better grounds the people's determination to allocate authority as the Constitution does, because that act of determination was itself an authoritative act of the sovereign. From a natural-law perspective, a theory of secondary sovereignty provides a much firmer pillar for dualist democracy and a nonpositivist theory of constitutional interpretation that gives the original determination of the sovereign pride of place. What Brownson called the providential constitution, in tandem with the idea of secondary sovereignty, therefore helps illuminate the value of fidelity to the Constitution.

Brownson believed that Providence orders every nation for some special purpose or destiny, and he thought America's destiny is best understood in light of two of her civilizational forefathers. Politically, she was destined to continue the Greco-Roman republican order of civilization – indeed, to accomplish a "greater work than was assigned to either."[114] As Virgil had recounted in verse, the Greeks and Romans had been assigned tasks of arts and sciences and government, respectively.[115] America would rival Greece in art and philosophy, but in law it would surpass Rome. For Brownson, what distinguished a civilized order of law from barbarism was that power is not held as a personal estate, but "as a trust to be exercised for the public good."[116] Brownson thus channels the founders' own providentialist understanding of their purpose, to embrace their metaphysical dignity as genuine (secondary) causes, reject arbitrary rule, and establish constitutional forms in which power is a trust from the people. As Publius put it:

It has been frequently remarked that it seems to have been reserved to the people of this country, by their conduct and example, to decide the important question, whether societies of men are really capable or not of establishing good government from reflection and choice, or whether they are forever destined to depend for their political constitutions on accident and force.[117]

The great pagan error, in Brownson's view, was theological-political: the denial of the unity of God and (hence) the unity of the human race. At root, this is a denial of creation, which, stated metaphysically, is a denial of the thesis that God alone is *Ipsum Esse Subsistens* and that all human beings are *equal* in their

---

it departs from the original meaning. As Whittington has successfully argued, judicial supremacy is not an intrinsic feature of the Constitution but was politically constructed over the life of the republic. See Keith E. Whittington, *The Political Foundations of Judicial Supremacy: The Presidency, the Supreme Court, and Constitutional Leadership in U.S. History* (Princeton: Princeton University Press, 2009).

[114] Brownson, *The American Republic*, 3.

[115] *Others, I doubt not, shall with softer mould beat out the breathing bronze, coax from marble features to the life, plead cases with greater eloquence and with a pointer trace heaven's motions and predict the risings of the stars: you Roman, be sure to rule the world (be these your arts), to crown peace with justice, to spare the vanquished and to crush the proud.* Virgil, *Eclogues. Georgics. Aeneid: Books 1–6*, trans. H. Rushton Fairclough, rev. G. P. Goold, Loeb Classical Library 63 (Cambridge, MA: Harvard University Press, 1999), bk. VI, vol. 1, 593.

[116] Brownson, *The American Republic*, 103.

[117] Carey and McClellan, eds., *The Federalist*, no. 1, 1.

essential and existential dependence on Him for their being. Again, this makes a difference politically, because "theological principles are the basis of political principles."[118] Where God is understood to be the source of persons being "created equal," it is a theological nonstarter to think about politics in terms of the personal estate of the one or the few. Hence, "the political destiny of the United States is to conform the state to the order of reality, or, so to speak, to the Divine Idea in creation."[119] For Brownson, that conformity of public order to what is real consists in a "dialectic union of authority and liberty, of the natural rights of man and those of society."[120] Where the Greek and Roman republics failed, asserting the authority of the state to the detriment of individual freedom, and where some modern republics fail in the opposite manner, by asserting individual freedom to the detriment of public authority, the United States had, according to Brownson, been charged by Providence to achieve the balance of ordered liberty.

The principles of metaphysical dependency constitute the deepest fount of the providential constitution and, consequently, of the U.S. Constitution in full. Metaphysical dependence is the essential presupposition of ordered liberty, of the dialectal unity of authority and liberty, because the divinely grounded order of justice and the common good at once authorize and limit the state while grounding natural rights and natural duties. This was indeed the theory that undergirded the colonists' case for political resistance and that later provided the foundation of James Wilson's celebrated and influential lectures on law, which he envisioned as a foundational text that laid out the fundamental principles of American sovereignty and American jurisprudence. It is to those lectures, and their contested legacy, to which we now turn.

---

[118] Brownson, *The American Republic*, 257.   [119] Ibid., 254.   [120] Ibid., 3.

The Law of Nature in James Wilson's Lectures on Law

Scholars of the US founding have come to "recognize religiosity as central to any plausible account of the intellectual origins of the American Revolution."[1] The precise character of that religiosity is contested, however, and there is an ongoing interpretive debate about whether the intellectual frame of the US founding was one that privileged Christianity or deism, or perhaps even some hybrid between the two.[2] Looming large over this scholarly dispute, as we have seen, is the question of eighteenth-century Christianity's relationship to natural theology, a rational investigation of God's existence and attributes apart from divine revelation. Natural theology's distinction between truths known by reason independent of revelation, and truths known only by revelation, was common enough in the founding era that the Presbyterian clergyman John Witherspoon, president of the College of New Jersey and signer of the Declaration of Independence, began his lectures on moral philosophy by defining the subject as "an inquiry into the nature and grounds of moral obligation by reason, as distinct from revelation."[3]

Thomas West rightly notes that the founding era distinction between reason and revelation "does not necessarily imply a conflict."[4] Yet many scholars

---

[1] J. Patrick Mullins, *Father of Liberty: Jonathan Mayhew and the Principles of the American Revolution* (Lawrence: University Press of Kansas, 2017), 14.

[2] Barry Alan Shain, *The Myth of American Individualism: The Protestant Origins of American Political Thought* (Princeton, NJ: Princeton University Press, 1994); Matthew Stewart, *Nature's God: The Heretical Origins of the American Republic* (New York: W. W. Norton, 2014); Gregg Frazer, *The Religious Beliefs of America's Founders: Reason, Revelation, and Revolution* (Lawrence: University Press of Kansas, 2012).

[3] John Witherspoon, *Lectures on Moral Philosophy* (Princeton, NJ: Princeton University Press, 1912), 1.

[4] Thomas G. West, *The Political Theory of the American Founding: Natural Rights, Public Policy, and the Moral Conditions of Freedom* (New York: Cambridge University Press, 2017), 83;

disagree and see the two traditions of biblical and natural theology as contradictory and mutually exclusive. To the extent that the Revolutionary Era clergy and statesmen were appealing to truths known by reason, they were, according to some prominent interpretations of the US founding, abandoning the theological tenets of Christianity.[5] Michael Zuckert goes so far as to suggest that the Bible and the Declaration offer discordant and mutually exclusive "narratives of the nature and destiny of humanity."[6] By eschewing reliance on biblical revelation, Zuckert contends, the Declaration and the liberal tradition it represents raise reason to a place of primacy over revelation and assert reason's self-sufficiency in moral and political philosophy.[7]

Following the twentieth-century Swiss Reformed theologian Karl Barth's wholesale rejection of natural theology, some Reformed theologians in the twentieth century also viewed natural theology and its cognate concepts of natural law and natural rights as inconsistent with Christianity's commitment to divine revelation in Scripture.[8] Beginning with the premise that Christianity is incompatible with claims rooted in natural theology and natural law, scholars and theologians from various camps have thus concluded that the prevalent idiomatic appeals to nature (e.g., law of nature, natural rights, nature's God, moral sense, and related concepts) among the US founders marks a significant shift away from Christianity and toward an Enlightenment Era natural theology that is hostile to Christianity's historic theological commitments.

The prominence of the Christian natural-law tradition in founding era political thought cuts against these interpretations. Natural-law theorists have historically held that there is a purposeful, created order in nature, including human nature, and that God providentially directs human beings to their proper ends through the faculty of reason.[9] The common emphasis in

Donald S. Lutz, *The Origins of American Constitutionalism* (Baton Rouge: Louisiana State University Press, 1997), 165.

[5] Michael P. Zuckert, "Natural Rights and Protestant Politics," in Thomas S. Engeman and Michael P. Zuckert, eds., *Protestantism and the American Founding* (Notre Dame, IN: University of Notre Dame Press, 2004), 21–78; Thomas L. Pangle, *The Spirit of Modern Republicanism: The Moral Vision of the American Founders and the Philosophy of Locke* (Chicago: University of Chicago Press, 1988); Thomas L. Pangle, *Political Philosophy and the God of Abraham* (Baltimore, MD: Johns Hopkins University Press, 2004); Harvey C. Mansfield, "Thomas Jefferson," in Morton J. Frisch and Richard G. Stevens, eds., *American Political Thought: The Philosophic Dimensions of American Statesmanship*, 3rd ed. (New Brunswick, NJ: Transaction Publishers, 2011), 49–76; Frazer, *Religious Beliefs of America's Founders.*

[6] Zuckert, "Natural Rights and Protestant Politics," 26.   [7] Ibid., 46.

[8] Stephen J. Grabill, *Rediscovering the Natural Law in Reformed Theological Ethics* (Grand Rapids, MI: Wm. B. Eerdmans, 2006), 3; John Witte, Jr., *The Reformation of Rights: Law, Religion, and Human Rights in Early Modern Calvinism* (New York: Cambridge University Press, 2007), 23.

[9] Robert P. George, "Natural Law," in Keith E. Whittington, R. Daniel Kelemen, and Gregory A. Caldeira, eds. *The Oxford Handbook of Law and Politics* (New York: Oxford University Press, 2008), 412.

natural-law theory on God both as the creator of a purposeful order in nature and as the providential author of a natural moral law known to reason predates Christianity, but Christians have nonetheless historically affirmed the rational intelligibility of a created moral order that is epistemically independent of revelation. To speak of the Christian natural-law tradition, then, is to speak of the long Christian engagement with a philosophic tradition that understands human goods and moral norms to be based on a distinctive order of nature created by God and intelligible to human reason.

Although some twentieth-century Protestant theologians did reject the claims of the natural-law tradition on epistemological grounds – fallen human reason being seen as radically defective and unreliable – we should not mistakenly equate the modern epistemological rejection of natural law and natural rights with the broader Protestant Christian tradition stretching back to the sixteenth century. As John T. McNeil noted in an article published during the period of Barth's ascendency,

> There is no real discontinuity between the teaching of the Reformers and that of their predecessors with respect to natural law …. The Assumption of some contemporary theologians that natural law has no place in the company of Reformation theology cannot be allowed to govern historical inquiry or to lead us to ignore, minimize, or evacuate of reality, the positive utterances on natural law scattered through the works of the Reformers.[10]

A growing body of revisionist scholarship has built on McNeil's work to demonstrate that the natural-law tradition, associated primarily with Roman Catholicism today, remained unbroken in the theology of the early Reformers and their successors.[11]

Political theorists have not fully integrated recent insights about the historical continuity of the natural-law tradition in Protestant, and particularly Reformed, theological ethics into interpretations of American political thought. There is a need for subtle reinterpretations of the theological ideas of those who made significant contributions to the movement for independence and the creation of new political institutions in the young republic. Pennsylvania

---

[10] John T. McNeill, "Natural Law in the Teaching of the Reformers," *The Journal of Religion* 26 (3) (1946): 168.

[11] Ibid., 168–82; Grabill, *Rediscovering the Natural Law*; Witte, *The Reformation of Rights*; David VanDrunnen, *Natural Law and the Two Kingdoms: A Study in the Development of Reformed Social Thought* (Grand Rapids, MI: Wm. B. Eerdmans, 2010); Glenn Moots, *Politics Reformed: The Anglo-American Legacy of Covenant Theology* (Columbia: University of Missouri Press, 2010); Jennifer A. Herdt, "Calvin's Legacy for Contemporary Reformed Natural Law," *Scottish Journal of Theology* 67(4) (2014): 414–35; Matthew J. Tuininga, *Calvin's Political Theology and the Public Engagement of the Church: Christ's Two Kingdoms* (New York: Cambridge University Press, 2017); Stephen Wolfe, "The American Founding and the Harmony of Reason and Revelation: A Rediscovery of Calvinist Sources," *History of Political Thought* 39(3) (2018): 491–518.

delegate to the Constitutional Convention and early Supreme Court Justice James Wilson is a case in point. Prevailing scholarly interpretations cast his Lectures on Law (1790–1791) at the College of Philadelphia as paradigmatic of the founding era's allegedly rationalist, heterodox natural theology. Yet Wilson's Lectures point in quite the opposite direction: to a vision of the founding era jurisprudence that was self-consciously rooted in a divinely created and rationally intelligible moral order that was both complemented and presupposed by Christian revelation. So understood, Wilson's Lectures bring into focus the limitations of the common scholarly conventions and categories that contrast enlightenment and religion, reason and revelation, or Nature's God and the God of Abraham. In Wilson's Lectures, these are not "either/or" categories but are rather presented together in a synthesis that emerged from the long Christian engagement with the natural-law tradition.

7.1 THE CONTESTED LEGACY OF JAMES WILSON'S LECTURES ON LAW

By any measure, James Wilson had an outsized influence on the American founding. A Scottish émigré who was one of only six men to sign both the Declaration of Independence and the US Constitution, Wilson went on to play a major role in the ratification debates in Pennsylvania and to serve on the United States Supreme Court as an associate justice from 1789 until his death in 1798. As a sitting member of the first Supreme Court, Wilson was invited by the College of Philadelphia to present a series of lectures on the foundations of US law. According to a contemporaneous article published in a Pennsylvania newspaper, the audience for the first lecture, delivered December 15, 1790, included "the President of the United States, with his lady – also the Vice-President, and both houses of Congress, the President and both houses of the Legislature of Pennsylvania, together with a great number of ladies and gentlemen ...."[12] After the initial lecture, Wilson taught fifteen students for whom he delivered a total of fifty-eight lectures, which were edited and published posthumously by his son, Bird Wilson, in 1804.[13]

Wilson aspired to be the American Blackstone, and he hoped his lectures would occupy a central place in US legal education as had Blackstone's *Commentaries on the Laws of England* during the Colonial Era.[14] The lectures

---

[12] Mark David Hall, "Notes and Documents: James Wilson's Law Lectures," *The Pennsylvania Magazine of History and Biography* 128(1) (2004): 64; Stephen Conrad, "Polite Foundation: Citizenship and Common Sense in James Wilson's Republican Theory," in Philip B. Kurland, ed., *Supreme Court Review, 1984* (Chicago: University of Chicago Press, 1985), 374.

[13] Bird Wilson, *The Works of the Honourable James Wilson* (Philadelphia: Lorenzo Press, 1804), vols. 1–3.

[14] Mark David Hall, "Bibliographical Essay History of James Wilson's Law Lectures," in Kermit L. Hall and Mark David Hall, eds., *Collected Works of James Wilson* (Indianapolis, IN: Liberty Fund, 2007), vol. 1, 401; Hall, "Notes and Documents," 65.

are quite consciously studying the foundations of law and address broad questions of moral, political, and legal philosophy. Because of his influence in the founding era and his systematic approach to philosophy, Wilson's Lectures on Law are a valuable window into early American jurisprudence.[15] Significantly, the lectures deal with first principles rather than legal precedent, and they present a vision of law that "is not the secularized natural law of some eighteenth century rationalists."[16] Indeed, "throughout his works, and particularly in his law lectures, Wilson clearly, consistently, and systematically appealed to the Christian natural law tradition."[17]

Some revisionist scholarship, however, contests this interpretation of Wilson as a representative of the Christian natural-law tradition.[18] In *The Spirit of Modern Republicanism*, political theorist Thomas Pangle discards the conventional view that "the thought of the Founders must be viewed as a *continuation* of Christian and especially Calvinist thinking" and provocatively suggests through a series of leading questions that some of the most influential founders – "Franklin, Madison, Jefferson, Wilson, and Hamilton" – were engaged in a project "to exploit and transform Christianity in the direction of a liberal rationalism[.]"[19] Other prominent scholars have brought similar philosophic assumptions to their study of the American founding. In perhaps the starkest juxtaposition, the natural philosophy of the Enlightenment – including not only its natural theology but its theory of natural justice and natural rights – is portrayed as necessarily subversive of orthodox Christianity's commitment to divine revelation, which is a great impediment to Lockean liberalism.[20] Read in this light, then, Wilson's teachings in his lectures become subtly subversive of Christianity.

---

[15] For a bibliographic essay history of the Wilson's lectures, see Hall, "Bibliographical Essay History of James Wilson's Law Lectures," 400–14.

[16] Robert Green McCloskey, ed., Introduction to *The Works of James Wilson* (Cambridge, MA: Harvard University Press, 1967), vol. 1, 38.

[17] Mark David Hall, "James Wilson: Presbyterian, Anglican, Thomist, or Deist? Does It Matter?" in Daniel L. Dreisbach, Mark D. Hall, and Jeffrey H. Morrison, eds., *The Founders on God and Government* (Lanham, MD: Rowman & Littlefield Press, 2004), 183, 189.

[18] Eduardo A. Velásquez, "Rethinking America's Modernity: Natural Law, Natural Rights and the Character of James Wilson's Liberal Republicanism," *Polity* 29(2) (1996): 193–220; cf. James R. Zink, "The Language of Liberty and Law: James Wilson on America's Written Constitution," *American Political Science Review* 103(3) (2009): 443–44; James R. Zink, "James Wilson versus the Bill of Rights: Progress, Popular Sovereignty, and the Idea of the US Constitution," *Political Research Quarterly* 67(2) (2014): 254.

[19] Pangle here directs his readers to Manent, who, in Rebecca Balinski's English translation, states bluntly that "it was in service of a political project, the radical discrediting of the Church's political claims, that numerous men who nurtured this project used Machiavelli to guide their thought and action." See Pierre Manent, *An Intellectual History of Liberalism*, trans. Rebecca Balinski (Princeton: Princeton University Press, 1994), 12.

[20] Mansfield, "Thomas Jefferson," 54–55; Walter Berns, *The First Amendment and the Future of Democracy* (New York: Basic Books, 1976), 22.

"The various efforts to categorize James Wilson's religion," Greg Frazer contends along these same lines, "epitomize the need for the label theistic rationalist."[21] The theistic rationalist, according to Frazer, is one who elevates reason, first, to make it equal to revelation, and then, next, to make it the judge of revelation. As Thomas Aquinas thought philosophy was the handmaiden of theology, so the theistic rationalist reverses that priority and makes theology the handmaiden of philosophy. Wilson, as Frazer notes, taught that "Reason and conscience can do much; but still they stand in need of support and assistance [from revelation]."[22] This is significant, according to Frazer, because "Scripture was called upon by Wilson to support and assist reason – not the reverse. For him, 'the Scriptures support, confirm, and corroborate, but do not supersede the operations of reason and the moral sense.' That is the theistic rationalist position."[23]

Wilson's assertion that the Scriptures do not supersede the operations of reason and the moral sense is not tantamount to an assertion that reason and the moral sense are ever in conflict with revelation, however. Wilson is explicit that the "law of nature and the law of revelation are both divine: they flow, though in different channels, from the same adorable source. It is indeed preposterous to separate them from each other."[24] According to Wilson, Scripture presupposes knowledge of the moral law of nature, which consists of intuitive truths known to the moral sense and reason's deductions from those intuitive truths. Based on his framing assumption, Frazer mistakenly attributes to Wilson a subversive elevation of reason over revelation. Pangle errs in a different direction, homing in on Wilson's emphasis on conscience as a moral sense and attributing to Wilson a kind of Hobbist elevation of passion over reason. Although reason has a role in correcting the moral sense and judging matters of fact, Pangle maintains in his interpretation of Wilson, the "ultimate ends or first principles are 'self-evident' – but to 'sentiment,' to 'feeling,' rather than to reason."[25]

A closer look at Wilson's Lectures on Law tells a different story and demonstrates Wilson's continuity with those traditions that he allegedly subverted. Wilson insisted that reason, revelation, and the moral sense are in harmony. As early scholarship on Wilson noted, his understanding of reason and revelation had more in common with classical Christian sources than it did with the teachings of modern rationalists,[26] and Wilson's discussion of law "displayed

---

[21] Frazer, *Religious Beliefs of America's Founders*, 166.

[22] James Wilson, *Collected Works of James Wilson*, ed. Kermit L. Hall and Mark David Hall (Indianapolis, IN: Liberty Fund, Inc, 2007), vol. 1, 520.

[23] Frazer, *Religious Beliefs of America's Founders*, 187.   [24] Wilson, *Collected Works*, 509.

[25] Pangle, *The Spirit of Modern Republicanism*, 122; Velásquez, "Rethinking America's Modernity," 195–96.

[26] William Oberling, *The Philosophy of Law of James Wilson* (Washington, DC: Catholic University of America, 1938); Geoffrey Seed, *James Wilson: Scottish Intellectual and American Statesman* (Millwood, NY: KTO Press, 1978).

his indebtedness to the Scholastic-Anglican tradition of Aquinas and Hooker" even as he wedded the classical tradition to the epistemological insights of the Common-Sense School of Thomas Reid.[27]

7.2 WILSON ON THE LAW OF NATURE

Wilson's lectures exhibit a deep engagement with the sixteenth-century English theologian and priest Richard Hooker, who was for Wilson a direct mediation of the theological and philosophical ideas of the Christian natural-law tradition. Hooker – in whose writings C. S. Lewis claimed to have found that tradition's "fullest and most beautiful expression"[28] – offered a classical exposition of natural law in the first book of his *Laws of Ecclesiastical Polity*. Wilson followed Hooker's broad classification of law nearly verbatim. Indeed, it was from Hooker that Wilson took his very conception of law as a rule of action that implies a principle of moral obligation,[29] which he deployed to criticize William Blackstone's definition of law that includes superiority as both the necessary and sufficient attribute of legal authority.[30]

Wilson drew his students' attention to Blackstone's definition of law as a "rule of action, which is prescribed by some superiour and which some inferiour is bound to obey."[31] According to Wilson, the danger with this definition – if it were to be admitted "without due caution and scrutiny"[32] – is that it collapses law into power and obligation into physical compulsion. Law becomes merely the rule of one who is superior in force. In response, Wilson turned to Hooker for a concept of lawful authority rooted both in consent among human equals,[33] on the one hand, and in a divine superiority marked by the unity of power and goodness, on the other.[34]

One authority who rivals Hooker in influence on Wilson's lectures is Thomas Reid, an eighteenth-century Scottish parish minister and successor to Adam Smith's chair at Glasgow. Wilson cited Reid nearly twenty times in his lectures, included a whole passage verbatim from Reid's *Essay on Intellectual Power*, and turned to him in particular for questions of moral epistemology.[35] "If, in his consideration of the nature of law," Wilson's mid-century biographer Charles Page Smith observed, "Wilson went back to Richard Hooker and a tradition that was both Anglican and Scholastic, he turned, in his examination of individual psychology, to the thoroughly contemporary doctrines of Thomas Reid, the father of the Common Sense School."[36] Wilson, of course, put these

---

[27] Charles Page Smith, *James Wilson: Founding Father, 1742–1798* (Chapel Hill: University of North Carolina Press, 1956), 330.

[28] C. S. Lewis, *English Literature in the Sixteenth Century, Excluding Drama* (Oxford: Clarendon Press, 1954), 49.

[29] Wilson, *Collected Works*, 468. [30] Ibid., 471; cf. 1041. [31] Ibid., 471. [32] Ibid., 492.

[33] Ibid., 483, 496. [34] Ibid., 503. [35] Hall, "Notes and Documents," 68.

[36] Smith, *James Wilson: Founding Father*, 333.

authors, and many others, to his own use while writing his lectures. He did not blindly follow any one authority but rather worked to synthesize various traditions into a coherent jurisprudence for the young United States. In doing so, he operated within the frame of the broad Christian natural-law tradition.

In his first lecture, Wilson proclaimed that the "science of law should, in some measure, and in some degree, be the study of every free citizen, and of every free man."[37] The promise of his lectures was to treat comprehensively the science of law, and he began the course, with only his fifteen pupils assembled, by describing the built-in design of the world as it is experienced. "Order, proportion, and fitness pervade the universe," Wilson declared. "Around us, we see; within us, we feel; above us, we admire a rule, from which a deviation cannot, or should not, or will not be made."[38] This order, Wilson insisted, applies to God Himself, the "great and incomprehensible Author, and Preserver, and Ruler of all things," the one who "himself works not without an eternal decree."[39]

In his first substantive treatment of the science of law, then, Wilson broached an important philosophical debate about God and ethics. Medieval scholastics, as well as some of Wilson's contemporaries, debated whether moral obligation originates in the reason of God or the will of God or some combination of the two. The stakes for this abstract question are high. On the one hand, if moral obligation originates in God's reason alone, then we seem to allow a disunity in God's nature that submits God to a law he did not create. If, on the other hand, moral obligation originates in God's will, then the content of ethics seems to be both arbitrary (i.e., lacking a reason) and rooted in power as the sufficient cause of God's authority. A middle way is to recognize the unity of power and goodness in the divine nature such that God is subject to a law that he voluntarily imposes on himself. In the formulation of Richard Hooker, "[t]hey err therefore who think that of the will of God to do this or that there is no reason besides his will."[40] Yet even so, he concludes, "the freedom of the will of God [is not in any way] abated, let or hindered, by means of this; because the imposition of this law upon himself is his own free and voluntary act."[41] This is the path Wilson took when he insisted that "from almighty power infinite goodness can never be disjoined."[42]

Leveled partly as a critique of Blackstone's definition of law as a "rule of action, which is prescribed by some superiour, and which the inferiour is bound to obey," Wilson's insistence on the unity of divine power and goodness was a claim that goodness and reason are part of the very definition of law. Power might be necessary, but it is not sufficient, to establish and promulgate

[37] Wilson, *Collected Works*, 435.   [38] Ibid., 464.   [39] Ibid.; cf. 1041.
[40] Richard Hooker, *The Works of That Learned and Judicious Divine Mr. Hooker with an Account of His Life and Death by Isaac Walton*, rev. R. W. Church and F. Paget, 7th ed. (Oxford: Clarendon Press, 1888), vol. 1, 203.
[41] Ibid., 204.   [42] Wilson, *Collected Works*, 503.

authoritative law. By analogy, this applies to human law as well, which finds its moral limits in the eternal law that emanates from the divine nature. Irresistible power does not impart a right of imposing laws, and force "exerted for the purposes of malevolence" has no right to command and imposes no obligation to obey.[43]

Where Wilson did follow Blackstone was in his account of God's one paternal precept. Blackstone had written that the deity's one precept to man is that he "should pursue his own true and substantial happiness."[44] Wilson similarly described God's one paternal precept as: "Let man pursue his happiness and perfection."[45] For both Blackstone and Wilson, the natural law is the way human beings learn how to pursue their happiness and perfection. In contrast to the "brute creation, [who] act not from design," Wilson observed, human beings deliberate rationally about various courses of action and then "propose an end," that is, a reason for action in light of a desired good.[46] Animals are still moved to their natural end or purpose, but they are not moved through rational deliberation. The law that governs the animal world is subrational and operates at the level of appetite, passion, and instinct. The faculty psychology prominent in the founding era, which understands human flourishing in terms of the proper ordering of the rational and subrational human faculties, is evident in Wilson's discussion.[47] According to Wilson, human beings are rational animals, hybrids between beasts and gods. In being subject to the laws of physics and involuntary biological processes, human beings share much in common with the beasts. What separates humanity from the animal world, however, is knowing and being subject to the natural moral law.

The moral law is a law we can choose to obey or disobey. It is indeed only in the domain of freedom that rational moral judgments are intelligible. This framework, and the faculty psychology that undergirds it, helps make sense of the taxonomy of law that Wilson took, unmodified in its fundamentals, from Hooker. Mirroring Hooker, Wilson asserted that there is a twofold eternal law that governs God himself and governs each of his creatures according to their natures. The law that governs creation may be subdivided into three main categories, the first of which concerns the laws governing "angels and the spirits of the just made perfect."[48] About this law, Wilson had little to say except that it pertains to an eschatological state of perfection and beatitude that is nonetheless governed by law and known, even if through a glass darkly, by dint of revelation. The second category concerns laws "by which the inanimate and

[43] Ibid., 502.
[44] William Blackstone, *Commentaries on the Laws of England*, ed. George Sharswood (Philadelphia: J. B. Lippincott Company, 1893 [1753]), vol. 1, 41.
[45] Wilson, *Collected Works*, 523.   [46] Ibid., 468.
[47] Daniel Walker Howe, *Making the American Self: Jonathan Edwards to Abraham Lincoln* (New York: Oxford University Press, 2009), 48–77.
[48] Wilson, *Collected Works*, 497–98.

irrational parts of the creation are governed."[49] Although these are sometimes called the laws of nature, they are not moral laws but rather are "general and fixed rules, according to which all the phenomena of the material universe are produced and regulated."[50] Finally, there is the moral law for humanity, a law we may choose to obey or disobey. This law is known to us as the law of nature (as applied to individuals) or the law of nations (as applied to societies of men), when it is promulgated by reason and the moral sense; when it is promulgated through Scripture, it is known as the revealed law.[51] The moral law, finding a twofold witness in nature and revelation, provides the foundational truths of human law or positive law, the body of specific laws and regulations posited in any particular community. The positive law, Wilson told his students, can be further divided into domestic, municipal law and international positive law, or what he called the voluntary law of nations.

The analytic reconstruction of law in Figure 7.1 demonstrates the close parallel of Wilson's conception of law with that of Hooker's.

As Wilson understood it, natural law is *law*. It is that part of the law of God for mankind known by reason and the moral sense. Its first principles are "engraven by God on the hearts of men" and "in this manner, [God] is the promulgator as well as the author of the natural law."[52] Robert McCloskey noted in his introduction to Wilson's collected works that Wilson's conception of natural law was not "merely a morally indifferent rule of necessity like the 'laws' of motion. It is God's ordainment, and it imposes duties on men and states."[53] Consistent with his prior discussion of the defining characteristics of law, Wilson insisted that the authority of the natural law to impose moral obligations does not come from God's superior physical strength alone, however. God's power and goodness are connected in the "incomprehensible Archetype," according to Wilson.[54] God's one paternal precept is that we pursue our own happiness or flourishing, and law directs us to this proper end for our own good.

7.3 FEELING AND THE MORAL SENSE

Do we have to obey the natural moral law? In one sense, of course, we do not. The natural law, known by the moral sense and reason, discloses our duty in the domain of freedom where we have a choice to obey or disobey. Unavoidable necessity is not a moral category. Alternatively, however, we might ask whether we have good reasons to obey God's one paternal precept. Should we pursue our own happiness? Why? To avoid an infinite regress, Wilson replied simply, "I can only say, I *feel* that such is my duty. Here

---

[49] Ibid., 497.   [50] Ibid.   [51] Ibid., 498.   [52] Ibid., 470.

[53] McCloskey, Introduction to *The Works of James Wilson*, 38; cf. Oberling, *The Philosophy of Law of James Wilson*, 50.

[54] Wilson, *Collected Works*, 503.

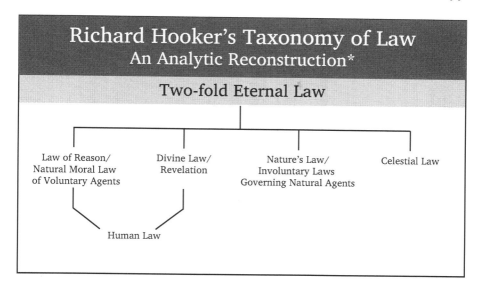

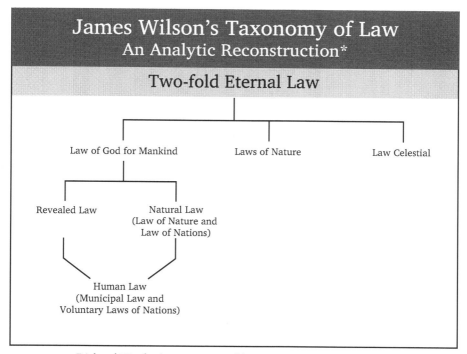

FIGURE 7.1. Richard Hooker's taxonomy of law.

Source: Richard Hooker, "Laws of Ecclesiastical Polity (1594–97)," in *The Works of That Learned and Judicious Divine Mr. Richard Hooker with an Account of His Life and Death by Isaac Walton*, 7th ed., rev. R. W. Church and W. Paget (Oxford: Clarendon Press, 1888), vol. 1, 205; James Wilson, *The Collected Works of James Wilson*, eds. Mark David Hall and Kermit L. Hall (Indianapolis, IN: Liberty Fund, 2007), vol. I, 497–98.

investigation must stop; reasoning can go no farther."[55] This is one of the places Pangle and others detect a crucial departure from the classical natural-law tradition, seeing in Wilson's emotive language an upending of the classical relationship between reason and the passions.[56] However, when Wilson used the term *feel* in connection with the moral sense, he did so in reference to undemonstrable first principles intuitively known to the intellect, whether or not that intuitive knowledge is accompanied by an emotion. This is clear from what he says elsewhere.

In a section of his lecture "Of Man, as an Individual," Wilson took to task "those philosophers, who have attempted to fan the flames of war between common sense and reason" and insisted instead that "between them, there never can be ground for real opposition: that, as they are commonly joined together in speech and in writing, they are inseparable also in their nature."[57] Common sense, he had just told his students, was "that degree of judgment, which is to be expected in men of common education and common understanding" and the term *judgment*, he maintained, meant a "determination of the mind concerning what is true or what is false," a determination that can be made "intuitively" or "discursively." That is to say, it is a determination that can be "founded on truths that are selfevident, as well as on those that are deduced from demonstration."[58] Some of the examples of self-evident truths that Wilson offered his students were the existence of the conscious self, the reality of the external world, and the freedom of the will.[59] In each of these examples, he used the word *feel* to describe a truth known intuitively, and he used *feel* and *know* interchangeably. About thinking or consciousness, for example, he said simply, "I know – I feel – it to be true; but I know it not from proof: I know it from what is greatly superiour to proof: I *see* it by the shining light of intuition."[60]

When Wilson used the ocular metaphor of sight to describe the way he knew something by intuition, he was not of course saying that he saw an object with his eye. Indeed, philosophers have long used the metaphor of seeing to describe the faculty by which human beings rationally apprehend "immediate and self-evident truth."[61] Similarly, when Wilson used the metaphor of feeling, he was not saying that he felt something as with an emotion or the sensation of touch. He *felt* that he had a moral obligation in the same way that he *felt* that the objects of consciousness, including his thoughts, exist in reality.[62] In these

[55] Ibid., 508.
[56] Pangle, *The Spirit of Modern Republicanism*, 122; Velásquez, "Rethinking America's Modernity," 199; Aaron T. Knapp, "Law's Revolutionary: James Wilson and the Birth of American Jurisprudence," *Journal of Law and Politics* 29(2) (2014): 268.
[57] Wilson, *Collected Works*, 604.   [58] Ibid., 599.   [59] Ibid., 594, 602, 801.   [60] Ibid., 617.
[61] Morton White, *The Philosophy of the American Revolution* (New York: Oxford University Press, 1978), 105.
[62] Wilson, *Collected Works*, 594.

examples, he was saying something altogether different than that moral obligation is conveyed by emotion or sentiment. What he was saying is that reason depends on undemonstrable and underived first principles that are known intuitively rather than by deduction, and are, metaphorically, simply seen or felt to be true. Only after taking these intuitive truths as a starting point can deductive reasoning proceed. "We cannot, therefore, begin to reason," he insisted, "till we are furnished, otherwise than by reason, with truths, on which we can found our arguments."[63] This is equally true of mathematics as it is of morality: "Morality, like mathematicks, has its intuitive truths, without which we cannot make a single step in our reasonings upon the subject."[64]

Wilson thus distinguished the faculty by which we perceive or intuit first principles from the faculty by which we make deductions from those first principles. The former he often called sense or perception or feeling; the latter he called reason. But he also acknowledged that the power to make intuitive judgments and the power to reason from those judgments "are frequently included under the general appellation of reason" even as he often used *reason* to refer specifically to "the process, by which we pass from one judgment to another, which is the consequence of it."[65] Nonetheless, he attributed these foundational intuitive judgments to the faculty of reason as well. "We assign to reason two offices," he observed,

or two degrees. The first is, to judge of things selfevident. The second is, from selfevident principles, to draw conclusions which are not selfevident. The first of these is the province, and the sole province, of common sense, and therefore, in its whole extent, it coincides with reason; and is only another name for one branch or degree of reason.[66]

Common sense, as we have seen, is that body of judgments we would expect from men of common education and common understanding, and some of these judgments are intuitive – that is, they do not rest on any antecedent truth.

Wilson's contemporaries associated with the Scottish Enlightenment such as David Hume, Adam Smith, Francis Hutcheson, and Thomas Reid debated whether we become aware of moral obligations through sentiment or through reason. As he did with Reid, so Wilson also included in his lecture verbatim or near verbatim passages from other theorists of the Scottish Enlightenment such as Hume and Hutcheson.[67] Yet as Hall observes, on this crucial point, Wilson followed Reid's argument that reason rather than sentiment apprehends the first principles of the natural law.[68] Indeed, Reid "contended that the first principles of morality are known through common sense, which is a degree of reason."[69] Although the word *feel* has an emotive connotation in its usage

---

[63] Ibid., 508.   [64] Ibid.   [65] Ibid., 600.   [66] Ibid., 604.

[67] White, *Philosophy of the American Revolution*, 133–34.

[68] Mark David Hall, *The Political and Legal Philosophy of James Wilson, 1742–1798* (Columbia: University of Missouri Press, 1997), 68–72.

[69] Ibid., 71; Howe, *Making the American Self*, 66.

today, the *Oxford English Dictionary* helpfully offers as one definition, "mental perception or apprehension; understanding, comprehension; knowledge."[70] Noting that this is a chiefly Scottish and now obsolete meaning, the *OED* entry captures a common eighteenth-century employment of the word *feel* to indicate the way in which foundational truths are known by intuition.

There is nothing about this particular way of framing the issue that stands in tension with the Christian natural-law tradition, even as that tradition was incorporated into the Calvinist theology of Scotland and the northern American colonies. As Grabill notes when introducing the section of Calvin's *Institutes* devoted to conscience, "Calvin teaches that natural law is discovered by the use of reason and conscience working in tandem."[71] When Calvin discussed the biblical concept of conscience, he clearly associated the faculty of conscience with moral knowledge known to the intellect. "The definition [of conscience] must be sought in the etymology of the word," Calvin insisted, alluding to the Latin *conscientia*, meaning *with knowledge*.

For as men, when they apprehend the knowledge of things by the mind and intellect, are said to know, and hence arises the term knowledge or *science*, so when they have a sense of the divine justice added as a witness which allows them not to conceal their sins, but drags them forward as culprits to the bar of God, that sense is called *conscience*. For it stands as it were between God and man, not suffering man to suppress what he knows in himself; but following him on even to conviction.[72]

Note that while Calvin clearly associated moral knowledge with the intellect, he described conscience as a partner of reason, an internal monitor that makes it difficult to suppress moral knowledge out of self-interest.

In his *Commentary on Romans*, Calvin offered further thoughts on conscience and concluded that we have certain knowledge of at least one foundational moral truth: "that one action is good and worthy of being followed, while another is to be shunned with horror."[73] Similarly, Thomas Aquinas offered as the first precept of the natural law that "good is to be done and pursued, and evil is to be avoided."[74] Following in this vein, Wilson insisted that the "science of morals, as well as other sciences, is founded on truths, that cannot be discovered or proved by reasoning,"[75] and that for a man ignorant of

---

[70] "feel, n." OED Online. Accessed July 13, 2021, from www.oed.com/view/Entry/68976?rskey=DmcYOa&result=1

[71] Grabill, *Rediscovering the Natural Law*, 93.

[72] John Calvin, *Institutes of the Christian Religion*, trans. Henry Beveridge (Edinburgh: Calvin Translation Society, 1846), vol. 1, bk. 3, ch. 19, sec. 15. Emphasis in original.

[73] John Calvin, *Commentary on the Epistles of Paul the Apostle to the Romans and to the Thessalonians*, ed. David W. Torrance and T. F. Torrance, trans. Ross Mackenzie (Grand Rapids, MI: Wm. B. Eerdmans, 1961), 49; cf. Grabill, *Rediscovering the Natural Law*, 94.

[74] Thomas Aquinas, *Summa Theologica*, trans. Fathers of the English Dominican Province (Chicago: Encyclopedia Britannica, 1952): I–II, 94.2.

[75] Wilson, *Collected Works*, 508.

the categories of right and wrong, the "terms would be to him equally unintelli-gible, as the term *colour* to one who was born and has continued blind."[76] It was important for Wilson to emphasize such a seemingly banal point – that we have intuitive knowledge of the concept of moral obligation and the distinction between right and wrong – to guard foundational moral knowledge against the skeptical philosophy of some of his contemporaries such as David Hume.[77] Before the enterprise of moral reasoning can get off the ground, he insisted, we must first recognize as an "intuitive truth" the principle of obligation founded on the distinction between right and wrong.[78] Determining the "specified action, or series of specified actions" that it is our duty to perform is then the task of moral reasoning, informed by the natural moral law (watered by the two streams of the moral sense/conscience and reason) and the law revealed in the Bible – "by our conscience, by our reason, and by the Holy Scriptures."[79]

Wilson's arguments about the moral sense emerged from a theological tradition that emphasized the need to align one's rational will with the laws of God and nature rather than being enslaved to one's passions.[80] The laws of God and nature are compatible, according to Wilson. Revelation refines and exalts, but does not contradict, moral knowledge known and discovered through conscience and reason. The Bible, he observed, presupposes "a know-ledge of the principles of morality" and is "addressed to rational and moral agents, capable of previously knowing the rights of man, and the tendencies of actions; of approving what is good, and disapproving what is evil."[81] For some commentators, there is something untoward in Wilson's formulation. As we have seen, Frazer attributes the role Wilson gave to reason, as a source of knowledge standing alongside revelation, as a departure from Protestant Christianity, something he labels "theistic rationalism."[82] In Pangle's analysis, Wilson was less a rationalist than a sentimentalist who rooted knowledge ultimately in sentiment or feeling rather than reason.[83] If we read Wilson in light of his intellectual influences and place him within the larger Christian natural-law tradition, however, we see that his arguments were not subversive of, but rather developed in concert with, that very tradition.

7.4 GOD AND THE SOURCE OF MORAL OBLIGATION

Thomas West correctly notes that many in the founding era saw no contradic-tion either between reason and revelation or between the God of Nature and the God of Revelation.[84] He does, however, suggest that reason alone cannot disclose moral obligations and that as a result, many in the founding era

[76] Ibid., 509.   [77] Ibid., 607–9.   [78] Ibid., 508–9.   [79] Ibid., 507, 509.
[80] Shain, *The Myth of American Individualism*, 301–19.   [81] Wilson, *Collected Works*, 522.
[82] Frazer, *Religious Beliefs of America's Founders*, 186–87.
[83] Pangle, *The Spirit of Modern Republicanism*, 122.
[84] West, *Political Theory of the American Founding*, 82–83.

connected natural law to the will of God rhetorically to impute to the natural law a morally obligatory force. Nonetheless, he insists, the "idea that natural law comes as a commandment from God is not so much an argument as an unsupported assertion."[85]

West, however, maintains a very limited conception of what reason can disclose, narrowing it to hypothetical imperatives and the existence of a God of Nature tantamount to the first principle that animates the world and is discoverable through reason's observations and inferences from nature.[86] "The laws of nature," West writes, "founded in reason's judgment of what is useful for human life and happiness, become morally obligatory only when they take on a juridical or legal character" – which they do not as disclosed by reason unaided by revelation, according to West – and "[t]hus the founders presented rational arguments regarding the usefulness of natural rights while supporting teachings like divine will and the moral sense to give their arguments moral weight."[87] Yet as we have seen, Wilson's teaching was that the truths intuited by the moral sense – including God's one paternal precept that man ought to pursue his own happiness and perfection – is foundational to practical reason and rests on no antecedent truths. Further, these undemonstrable first principles are presupposed by Scripture.

Wilson's framing of the issue is consistent with the historic teachings of Protestant Christianity, including the Calvinist theology that exhibited a disproportionate influence on the theological currents of eighteenth-century America. Crucial to the Reformed engagement with the natural-law tradition is the doctrine of *duplex cognitio dei*, or the twofold knowledge of God.[88] Calvin opened his *Institutes of the Christian Religion* with just this distinction. Human beings know God through reason as the Creator, the French theologian and reformer wrote, whereas they know God through revelation as the Redeemer. Although Calvin did not set about to write a systematic treatise on natural law, he did adopt the basic categories of the natural-law tradition as he described this twofold knowledge of God. On the basis of reason, according to Calvin, prior to God's revelatory self-disclosure, human beings have access to knowledge of God as Creator, and on the basis of their knowledge of God the Creator, they also have knowledge of basic moral obligations. One practical effect of this knowledge, after the fall of man described in the first chapters of Genesis, is to leave mankind without excuse for moral failure and to bring before man's mind a recognition of his alienation from God, but natural law also played a positive role in Calvin's thought by structuring and ordering our common life together and providing the "moral standard for civil government."[89]

---

[85] Ibid., 87.   [86] Ibid., 82.   [87] Ibid., 95.
[88] Grabill, *Rediscovering the Natural Law*, 71–73.
[89] Tuininga, *Calvin's Political Theology*, 369.

"The key to making sense of Calvin's variously positive and negative statements regarding the usefulness of natural law," Matthew Tuininga observes, is interpreting these statements in light of "the difference between the law's *temporal* purpose and its *spiritual* purpose, between *earthly* things and *heavenly* things."[90] Even though he thought natural philosophy and theology are neither efficacious for salvation nor fully epistemically reliable, Calvin nonetheless emphasized the sufficiency of reason in "earthly things" including "matters of policy and economy, all mechanical arts and liberal studies."[91] Civic life is one of those spheres for which the knowledge we have by reason can guide us reliably even if not infallibly. As Calvin insisted,

the view to be taken is this: Since man is by nature a social animal, he is disposed, from natural instinct, to cherish and preserve society; and accordingly we see that the minds of all men have impressions of civil order and honesty. Hence it is that every individual understands how human societies must be regulated by laws, and also is able to comprehend the principles of those laws.[92]

Calvin maintained in his discussion of civil government that there can be a legitimate diversity of constitutional forms based on circumstances, "provided they all alike aim at equity as their end."[93] The content of equity or justice, "as it is natural" according to Calvin, is "nothing else than a testimony of natural law, and of that conscience which God has engraved upon the minds of men," and the "whole of this equity of which we now speak is prescribed in it. Hence it alone ought to be the aim, the rule, and the end of all laws."[94] In other words, knowledge of the natural moral law – unable as it is to bring one to salvation and determine the manner in which one must render worship to God – can offer guidance for public affairs, and natural equity is in fact the goal, rule, and limit of civil laws, which aim at natural justice.

As John Witte has chronicled, Calvin "developed a detailed theory of moral laws and duties that foreshadowed a whole range of later Calvinist natural law and natural rights theories."[95] The Reformed Protestant engagement with the larger Christian natural-law tradition left an imprint on the intellectual world of the founders, many of whom "were schooled by Scottish Presbyterian tutors or at the Presbyterian College of New Jersey, which graduated 'ten cabinet officers, thirty-nine congressmen, twenty-one senators, twelve governors, thirty judges (including three Supreme Court justices), and fifty state legislators' under the leadership of President John Witherspoon."[96] The point of highlighting the positive role of natural law in Calvin's *Institutes* is not to suggest Wilson was

[90] Ibid., 107. Emphasis in original.
[91] Calvin, *Institutes of the Christian Religion*, bk. 2, ch. 2, sec. 13.   [92] Ibid., bk. 2, ch. 2, sec. 13.
[93] Ibid., bk. 4, ch. 20, sec. 16.   [94] Ibid., 4.20.16; cf. Grabill, *Rediscovering the Natural Law*, 91.
[95] Witte, *The Reformation of Rights*, 3.
[96] Carli N. Conklin, *The Pursuit of Happiness in the Founding Era: An Intellectual History* (Columbia: University of Missouri Press, 2019), 75; internal quotation from Carl J. Richard, *The Founders and the Classics* (Cambridge: Harvard University Press, 1994), 20.

following Calvin directly on these points but rather that Wilson's appeal to natural law did not represent a break from or subtle subversion of eighteenth-century Christianity or an affront to Reformed theology. The natural-law tradition was a point of convergence for the Presbyterian, Anglican, and Catholic traditions during the founding era.

Although Wilson was the son of a "strict Calvinist, who destined his son for a ministry in the Church of Scotland,"[97] in his law lectures he appealed primarily to the authority of the Anglican priest and theologian Richard Hooker for matters theological.[98] For Calvin as well as Hooker and Wilson, the existence of God the Creator (who stands outside his creation and thus is not tantamount to the animating first principle of nature) is among those truths understood or perceived prior to revelation, and it is God the Creator (known prior to revelation) who provides the basis of moral obligation. As Wilson noted, revelation is itself addressed to "moral and rational agents" who already have knowledge of the principles of morality. Moral knowledge may be refined by revelation, but it does not originate with revelation.

Even so, what exactly gives moral norms their binding or obligatory force? The "precise state of the question," Wilson told his students, is "what is the efficient cause of moral obligation – of the eminent distinction between right and wrong?"[99] Wilson clearly answered that the efficient cause of moral obligation – that is, the cause that brings moral obligation into being – is "the will of God. This is the supreme law. His just and full right of imposing laws, and our duty in obeying them, are the sources of our moral obligations."[100] Our duty to obey the will of God, Wilson further contended, is itself enjoined by conscience and felt or intuited as a first principle, one of those truths "that cannot be discovered or proved by reasoning."[101] Further, our intuited sense of obligation to obey the will of God derives at least in part from God's goodness, not merely his superior physical strength.

When considering the frequent contention in the founding era that moral obligation is rooted in the will of God, West comments that it is "striking how little evidence is provided for these assertions in the official documents."[102] Yet prominent founding era writers on moral philosophy such as John Witherspoon did spend time considering a priori and a posteriori "proof of

[97] William Ewald, "James Wilson and the Drafting of the Constitution." *University of Pennsylvania Journal of Constitutional Law* 10(5) (2008): 902.
[98] According to Hall, several years after his law lectures, in 1794, Wilson became an active Episcopalian, although he continued to rent a pew at the First Presbyterian Church in Philadelphia until his death in 1798. "Denominational commitments are not unimportant," Hall notes in an observation equally applicable here, "but more significant for our purpose is the extent to which Wilson's Christian beliefs influenced his political philosophy and, hence, his contributions to the creation of the American republic." See Hall, "James Wilson: Presbyterian, Anglican, Thomist, or Deist?" 181, 188.
[99] Wilson, *Collected Works*, 507.   [100] Ibid., 508.   [101] Ibid.
[102] West, *Political Theory of the American Founding*, 86.

the being of God, the great foundation of all natural religion; without which the moral sense would be weak and insufficient."[103] As Witherspoon noted, however, there also was another contemporaneous view – which he attributed to unnamed "authors of Scotland" who were responding to Humean skepticism – that knowledge of God's existence is one of those "first principles or dictates of common sense, which are either simple perceptions, or seen with intuitive evidence."[104] Wilson implicitly followed this path of treating God's existence as one of those first principles or dictates of common sense in his lectures, because he did not offer a proof of God's existence even as he located the efficient cause of moral obligation in the will of God. For Wilson, reason and revelation work together with conscience and experience to establish the goodness and will of God as the efficient cause of moral obligation and the proximate ground of all law, including the recent edifice of the US Constitution.

7.5 CONCLUSION

The jurisprudence of Wilson's Lectures emphasized a prominent place for reason in civic affairs and appealed in public life primarily to God as Creator rather than God as Redeemer. What commentators have sometimes called our "civil religion" – the set of propositions about the deity that infuses our civic realm and undergirds our founding creed – has historically been framed in terms of a shared theology. In Robert Bellah's classic formulation, these beliefs include affirmation of the existence of a divine source of sovereignty beyond the Constitution, a divinely sanctioned moral law that is the ultimate criterion of right and wrong, and the outworking of divine providence in the world.[105] Although "not antithetical to and indeed sharing much in common with Christianity," Bellah notes, American civil religion from the founding on has been "neither sectarian nor in any specific sense Christian."[106] The doctrine of the twofold knowledge of God in Christian theology has, however, given theological warrant for a civil religion that makes it possible to include as fellow citizens and full participants in public life those who have different conceptions (or no conception at all) about God's revealed plan for redemption. It is God the Creator, known by reason, whom Wilson invoked in his Lectures on Law and in whose will he grounded the moral obligation to conform to the natural law.

In Wilson's lectures, the very concept of law is embedded in a natural theology that imparts to us knowledge of moral obligation, something that is consistent with, and grows out of, the broader Christian natural-law tradition. Scholars who argue that James Wilson's Lectures on Law represent a departure from Christianity rest their case on a particular view of Christian theology that

---

[103] Witherspoon, *Lectures on Moral Philosophy*, 37.   [104] Ibid., 39.
[105] Robert N. Bellah, "Civil Religion in America," *Daedalus* 134(4) (2005 [1967]): 42–43.
[106] Ibid., 46.

sees it as theoretically incompatible with natural theology. In these accounts, the Reformed tradition in particular emphasizes the total depravity of man and the resultant inability of fallen human reason to ascertain moral truth or truth about God apart from biblical revelation. There is thus no place in Reformed Christianity for natural theology, and consequently, no place for the perennial natural-law tradition. To the extent that the pastors who delivered fiery political sermons in defense of the Revolution and the statesmen who wrote public documents to steer the ship of state did so by affirming natural-law principles and appealing to natural knowledge of God, then they were betraying their own Christian traditions.

Recent works by Stephen Grabill, John Witte, Glenn Moots, and Stephen Wolfe, among others, have demonstrated, however, that the recurrent scholarly theme about the incompatibility of Christian (and especially Reformed) theology and the natural-law tradition is no longer tenable. Whether or not they have engaged the work of the twentieth-century Swiss Reformed theologian Karl Barth, many modern scholars nonetheless read into their analyses of eighteenth-century Christianity something like Barth's rejection of natural theology and natural law as epistemologically incompatible with divine revelation.[107] Very few of Barth's Reformed predecessors held these views, however. As Grabill notes, "the older magisterial Protestant tradition (Lutheran and Reformed) not only inherited but passed on the doctrines of *lex naturalis* and *cognitio Dei naturalis*, especially the idea of an implanted knowledge of morality, as noncontroversial legacies of patristic and scholastic thought."[108]

The role of the Christian natural-law tradition in structuring founding era political thought and jurisprudence remains deeply contested today. In one prominent interpretive framework, the ideas that buttress the American founding represent a radical departure from ancient and medieval political philosophy and an inauguration of a distinctly modern turn toward voluntarism. Sometimes the alleged modernity of the founding is celebrated and other times it is condemned. One recent study in the latter genre is Patrick Deneen's best-selling and widely discussed book *Why Liberalism Failed*. For Deneen, the liberalism of the American founding entailed the grafting onto Western political thought of an anticlassical and anti-Christian anthropology. The features of this anthropology entailed a rejection of virtue politics, the overturning of social structures that inculcate virtue in "political, social, religious, economic, and familial life," and a conquering and overcoming of the moral limits imposed by nature.[109] Wilson's *Lectures on Law* challenge this

---

[107] Emil Brunner and Karl Barth, *Natural Theology*, trans. Peter Fraenkel (Eugene, OR: Wipf & Stock, 2002 [1934]).

[108] Grabill, *Rediscovering the Natural*, 3. Emphasis in original.

[109] Deneen, *Why Liberalism Failed*, 25.

common interpretative framework of the founding as anti-Christian by high-lighting the essential continuity between the Christian natural-law tradition and the first and most prominent lectures on American jurisprudence. Those lectures drew forward the classical and Christian themes that structured the American case for independence and later underwrote the idea of a sovereign people acting under God to prudentially constitute new governments for themselves and their posterity.

8

Conclusion

Classical Christian Natural Law and the American Political Order

Imprisoned in Birmingham, Alabama, just after Easter Sunday in 1963, Martin Luther King Jr. penned a letter to a group of white religious leaders who had criticized the movement of nonviolent civil disobedience as unwise and untimely. In his celebrated apology, King wove together strands from the classical and biblical traditions, drawing on Socrates, the Hebrew prophets, Paul, Jesus, Augustine, Aquinas, Martin Buber, and Paul Tillich, among others, to support his argument that nonviolent civil disobedience was morally justified, because the law of segregation was itself unjust, defective, and in a crucial Augustinian sense, "no law at all." Coming to the crux of the argument, King asked rhetorically, "How does one determine whether a law is just or unjust?" He then offered this answer:

A just law is a man made code that squares with the moral law or the law of God. An unjust law is a code that is out of harmony with the moral law. To put it in the terms of St. Thomas Aquinas: An unjust law is a human law that is not rooted in eternal and natural law.[1]

King was in that moment drawing on the classical Christian natural-law tradition as it had been represented, in its highwater mark, by Thomas Aquinas.[2] As we have argued, that tradition remained in its various permutations a dominant influence in the American founding period, and it was not, as

---

[1] Martin Luther King Jr., "Letter from Birmingham City Jail," April 16, 1963. Accessed March 3, 2022, from www.christiancentury.org/article/first-person/letter-birmingham-jail
[2] For an analysis of the role of the classical Christian natural-law tradition in structuring King's argument, see Justin Buckley Dyer and Kevin E. Stuart, "Public Reason and the Theological Framework of Martin Luther King's 'Letter from Birmingham Jail," *Politics and Religion* 6(1) (2013): 145–63.

it is sometimes suggested, displaced in the founding era by theologically subversive modern and secular theories of natural law.

In public life, that classical tradition emphasized what could be known by reason rather than by revelation. The former included natural knowledge of God as Creator even if it did not include revealed knowledge of God as redeemer, and Lincoln provides a typical and illustrative example of this dynamic at work in American public life. The sixteenth president rarely appealed to the Christian Savior's authority in his letters, orations, and public documents. A search of Lincoln's collected works, however, uncovers over 300 invocations of God (and hundreds more if we include terms like "Almighty" or "Creator"), but few even indirect references to Jesus.

In his debates with Stephen Douglas, Lincoln did quote Matthew 5:48 – "As your Father in heaven is perfect, be ye also perfect" – but only as a metaphor to argue that the Declaration of Independence should operate as Scripture for the American political order, as a standard to approximate in public life even if it cannot be fully realized this side of heaven. "So I say in relation to the principle that all men are created equal, let it be as nearly reached as we can," Lincoln insisted.[3] The other famous quote from Jesus that appeared repeatedly in Lincoln's speeches and debates is that a "house divided against itself cannot stand," a Gospel reference Lincoln used to underscore the impossibility of maintaining republican government that is half slave and half free.[4]

Why so many references to God but so few to Jesus? Lincoln gave a clue in his 1860 speech at Hartford, where he said that the wrongness of slavery could be "clearly proved by natural theology, apart from revelation."[5] In invoking the God of natural theology in public life, Lincoln was well within the mainstream of American political tradition, which begins in its foundational document by appealing to the authority of the "Laws of Nature and of Nature's God" before affirming the self-evident truth that "all men are created equal" and "endowed by their Creator with certain unalienable rights." If anything can be proved by natural theology, Lincoln said, it is that "every man, black, white or yellow, has a mouth to be fed and two hands to feed it – and that bread should be allowed to go to that mouth without controversy."[6] The premises that complete Lincoln's syllogism were supplied by the Declaration – God created us equal in natural rights, including the right to eat the bread we earn with our own hands – and in this way the Declaration had become in Lincoln's

---

[3] Roy P. Basler, ed., *The Collected Works of Abraham Lincoln* (New Brunswick, NJ: Rutgers University Press, 1953), vol. 2, 501.

[4] See, e.g., ibid., 461.

[5] Roy P. Basler, ed., *The Collected Works of Abraham Lincoln* (New Brunswick, NJ: Rutgers University Press, 1953), vol. 4, 9.

[6] Ibid.

hands a kind of American Scripture, as the title of Pauline Maier's book proclaimed.[7]

As Lincoln knew well, America's civil or political religion has long taken its bearings from God the Creator, knowable by reason. At the same time, the American civil religion as Lincoln articulated it drew powerfully from the Hebrew Bible to reflect and frame the common American imaginary in a way that could be affirmed by Christian and non-Christian monotheists alike.

> If we shall suppose that American Slavery is one of those offences which, in the providence of God, must needs come, but which, having continued through His appointed time, He now wills to remove, and that He gives to both North and South, this terrible war, as the woe due to those by whom the offence came, shall we discern therein any departure from those divine attributes which the believers in a Living God always ascribe to Him? Fondly do we hope – fervently do we pray – that this mighty scourge of war may speedily pass away. Yet, if God wills that it continue, until all the wealth piled by the bond-man's two hundred and fifty years of unrequited toil shall be sunk, and until every drop of blood drawn with the lash, shall be paid by another drawn with the sword, as was said three thousand years ago, so still it must be said "The judgments of the Lord, are true and righteous altogether."[8]

The classical American civil religion expressed by Lincoln was in essential continuity with the classical Christian natural-law philosophy and theology articulated by the founders. Nearly all of the founders affirmed a Creator God who was above and beyond nature, particularly providential in the governance of human affairs, legislator of the natural moral law and its derivative natural rights, just judge nations and persons, and benevolent enforcer of the moral order. Such a public theology was part of America's providential constitution in the sense contended for by Orestes Brownson and elaborated by Lawler and Reinsch, that is, as a set of "civilizational accomplishments that make the written Constitution and constitutional order possible."[9] As part of America's providential constitution, these theological underpinnings provided a metaphysical and moral ground for American institutions as well as a regulative ideal that could provide a standard for measuring progress and judging the justice of law and legal authority.

In offering his interpretation of God's justice in his second inaugural address, Lincoln was drawing upon the wellsprings of the American political tradition. George Mason, toward the close of the Constitutional Convention, had warned that the institution of slavery "brings the judgment of heaven on a Country" and that by "an inevitable chain of causes & effects providence punishes

[7] Pauline Maier, *American Scripture: The Making of the Declaration of Independence* (New York: Knopf, 1997).

[8] Roy P. Basler, ed., *The Collected Works of Abraham Lincoln* (New Bunswick: Rutgers University Press, 1953), vol. 8, 333.

[9] Peter Augustine Lawler and Richard M. Reinsch II, *A Constitution in Full: Recovering the Unwritten Foundation of American Liberty* (Lawrence: University Press of Kansas, 2019), 5.

national sins with national calamities."[10] Mason argued that it was essential then for the national government to have the power to prohibit the importation of enslaved persons into the United States, a legislative power the Constitution ultimately granted to Congress provided it was not exercised prior to the year 1808.[11]

Luther Martin, whose biographer has dubbed him America's drunken prophet, later recalled of the convention debates about the Constitution's twenty-year moratorium on the exercise of the national legislative power to ban the international slave trade:

It was said, that we had but just assumed a place among independent nations, in consequence of our opposition to the attempts of Great-Britain to *enslave us;* that this opposition was grounded upon the *preservation* of *those rights,* to which God and Nature had entitled *us,* not in *particular,* but in *common* with *all the rest of mankind –* That we had *appealed* to the *Supreme being* for his *assistance,* as the *God of freedom,* who could not but *approve* our efforts to preserve the *rights* which he had thus *imparted to his creatures;* that now, when we scarcely had risen from our *knees,* from *supplicating* his *aid* and *protection –* in *forming our government* over a *free people,* a government formed pretendedly on the *principles* of *liberty* and for *its preservation, –* in *that* government to have a provision, not only putting it out *of its power* to *restrain* and *prevent* the *slave trade,* but *even encouraging that most infamous traffic,* by giving the *States power* and *influence* in the *union, in proportion* as they *cruelly and wantonly sport with the rights of their fellow creatures,* ought to be considered as a *solemn mockery of,* and *insult to, that* God whose protection we had then implored, and could not fail to hold us up in *detestation,* and render us *contemptible* to every *true friend* of liberty in the world. It was said, it ought to be considered that *national* crimes can *only be,* and *frequently are, punished* in this world by *national punishments,* and that the *continuance* of the slave trade, and thus giving it a *national sanction* and *encouragement,* ought to be considered as *justly exposing* us to the *displeasure* and *vengeance* of *Him,* who is equal Lord of all, and who views with equal eye, the poor *African slave* and his *American master!*[12]

The principles of the Declaration of Independence – emphasizing our equal creation in natural rights under a providential God who is the author of the moral and physical laws of nature – underwrote both the constitutional arguments against slavery and the antislavery defense of the Constitution's compromises. James Wilson, at the Pennsylvania Ratifying Convention, noted that after 1808, Congress would have the explicit power to prohibit the international commerce in persons – a power not enjoyed by the national

[10] Max Farrand, ed., *Records of the Federal Convention* (New Haven, CT: Yale University Press, 1911), vol, 2, 370.
[11] US Constitution, Article 1, Section 9, Clause 1.
[12] Luther Martin, "Genuine Information" in Herbert Storing, ed., *The Complete Anti-Federalist* (Chicago: University of Chicago Press, 1981 [1788]), vol. 2, 63–71. Emphasis in original. See generally Bill Kaufmann, *Forgotten Founder, Drunken Prophet: The Life of Luther Martin* (Wilmington, DE: ISI Books, 2008).

government under the Articles of Confederation – and thus, he hoped, would lay "the foundation for banishing slavery out of this country."[13]

Living downstream from the American founding, we are heirs today to what King, in his most famous speech, referred to as the "promissory note" implicit in our Declaration of Independence and imperfectly reflected in our Constitution: that "all men, yes, black men as well as white men, would be guaranteed the unalienable rights of life, liberty, and the pursuit of happiness."[14] We have so taken to heart this founding aspiration that even our criticisms of the Republic's architects continue to be animated by the principles they professed. What seems obvious about the American founding today – that there was a deep tension between the principle of natural equality and the system of race-based chattel slavery – was also obvious to many in the founding era. That generation did not, however, pluck the beam from their own eye before they endeavored to remove the mote from the eye of King George. "That men should pray and fight for their own Freedom and yet keep others in Slavery," New York delegate to the Continental Congress, John Jay, lamented, "is certainly acting a very inconsistent as well as unjust and perhaps impious part."[15]

The Continental Congress nonetheless affirmed ideas in the Declaration of Independence that undermined, in principle, the institution of slavery: that all men are equally endowed by their Creator with natural rights to life, liberty, and the pursuit of happiness; that governments exist to secure these rights and derive their just powers from the consent of the governed; that it is the right of the people to organize the powers of government in a way that seems most likely to secure their safety and happiness. If those ideas are true, then slavery is a great moral evil and affront to natural justice. This is the premise that underlaid Jefferson's claim that he trembled for his country when he reflected that God's justice could not sleep forever. The author of natural justice, God "Almighty has no attribute which can take side with" those who would enslave another human being, Jefferson insisted.[16]

In his rough draft of the Declaration, before committee revisions and additions, Jefferson had written that it was a "sacred & undeniable" truth that "all men are created equal & independent" and "from that equal creation they derive rights inherent & inalienable."[17] In doing so, he did not advance any

[13] Jonathan Elliot, ed. *The Debates in the Several State Conventions on the Adoption of the Federal Constitution*, 5 vols. (Washington, DC: Jonathan Elliot, 1836–1845), vol. 2, 452.

[14] Martin Luther King Jr., "I Have a Dream" (speech delivered August 28, 1963). Accessed July 29, 2021, from https://avalon.law.yale.edu/20th_century/mlk01.asp

[15] "John Jay to Richard Price (September 27, 1785)," in Philip B. Kurland and Ralph Lerner, eds., *The Founder's Constitution* (Chicago: University of Chicago Press, 1987), vol. 1, 538.

[16] Thomas Jefferson, *Notes on the State of Virginia*, ed. William Peden, 2nd ed. (Chapel Hill: University of North Carolina Press, 1982), 163.

[17] "Jefferson's 'Original Rough Draught' of the Declaration of Independence." Accessed July 29, 2021, from https://founders.archives.gov/documents/Jefferson/01-01-02-0176-0004

novel or original idea. He was, as he would later claim, merely giving expression to the American mind, and it did not take long for those animating principles of the revolution, and of the American mind, to be put into the service of emancipation. Within a year of the signing of the Declaration of Independence, Prince Hall, a leader of the free black community in Boston, would file a petition with the Massachusetts legislature on behalf of "A Great Number of Blackes detained in a State of Slavery in the Bowels of a free & christian Country," asserting that "every principle" of the American Revolution "Pleads Stronger than A thousand arguments" in favor of freedom for the enslaved.[18]

In 1783, as the Treaty of Paris marked the end of the war, the state of Massachusetts abolished slavery by judicial decree – a significant indication of the revolutionary ethos. As the late Stanford historian Don Fehrenbacher observed, the

antislavery tendencies of the revolutionary period were not inconsiderable. State after state took steps to end the African slave trade. Abolition of slavery itself was achieved in New England and Pennsylvania, and it seemed only a matter of time in New York and New Jersey. Virginia in 1782 gave strong encouragement to private manumissions by removing earlier restrictions upon them, and both Maryland and Delaware subsequently followed her example. By the 1790s, abolition societies had appeared in every state from Virginia northward, with prominent men like Benjamin Franklin and John Jay in leading roles. And Congress in 1787 prohibited slavery in the Northwest Territory with scarcely a dissenting vote.[19]

And yet Fehrenbacher's last work, published posthumously and titled *The Slaveholding Republic*, detailed how US government policy was increasingly and consistently proslavery in the nineteenth century.[20] America's founding principles may have been arrayed against slavery, but American politics and law were not.

Aware of the ways in which nineteenth-century defenders of the institution of slavery had criticized and abandoned the principles of the Declaration – and knowing full well that the founders did not immediately realize the promise of their own avowed principles – Abraham Lincoln nonetheless made the Declaration central to his vision for America's future as he launched a campaign for the presidency and guided the country through the carnage of the Civil War. "All honor to Jefferson," Lincoln had written in an 1859 letter,

---

[18] "Petition for Freedom to the Massachusetts Council and the House of Representatives (January 13, 1777)," Jeremy Belknap Papers, Massachusetts Historical Society. Accessed March 3, 2022, from www.masshist.org/database/viewer.php?item_id=557
[19] Don E. Fehrenbacher, *Slavery, Law, & Politics: The Dred Scott Case in Historical Perspective* (New York: Oxford University Press, 1981), 8–9.
[20] See Don E. Fehrenbacher, *The Slaveholding Republic: An Account of the United States' Government's Relations to Slavery*, ed. Ward M. McAfee (New York: Oxford University Press, 2001).

– to the man who, in the concrete pressure of a struggle for national independence by a single people, had the coolness, forecast, and capacity to introduce into a merely revolutionary document, an abstract truth, applicable to all men and all times, and so to embalm it there, that to-day, and in all coming days, it shall be a rebuke and a stumbling-block to the very harbingers of re-appearing tyranny and oppression.[21]

The harbingers of reappearing tyranny and oppression included those confederates, such as Alexander Stephens, who recognized clearly that the principles of the founding were a bulwark against the rebel cause. "The prevailing ideas entertained by [Jefferson] and most of the leading statesman at the time of the formation of the old constitution," he said in his "Cornerstone Speech" delivered in Savannah on the eve of Civil War, "were that the enslavement of the African was in violation of the laws of nature; that it was wrong in principle, socially, morally, and politically," a conclusion they "rested upon the assumption on the equality of the races." In contrast, Stephens declared flatly that the new, confederate government "is founded upon exactly the opposite idea."[22] Against the confederate cornerstone of racial subordination, Lincoln pointed back to our founding principle of equality in natural rights and maintained that "nothing stamped with the divine image and likeness was sent into the world to be trodden on, and degraded, and imbruted by its fellows."[23]

The statesman and abolitionist orator Frederick Douglass righteously and rightfully denounced American hypocrisy but offered the same account of the wrong of slavery as Lincoln: that an enslaved person is "a moral and intellectual being" bearing "the image of God" and "possessing a soul, eternal and indestructible," and slavery is for this reason a "crime against God and man."[24] When invited to give a Fourth of July oration commemorating the signing of the Declaration of Independence, Douglass delivered a searing rebuke of the United States, and yet he nonetheless insisted that the principles of the Declaration were "saving principles." "Stand by those principles," he admonished his audience, "be true to them on all occasions, in all places, against all foes, and at whatever cost."[25] After the war, while some were still talking about schemes for black colonization or for the maintenance of a racially segregated and hierarchical civil society, Douglass envisioned a multiracial republic celebrating our "composite nationality" under a "Government founded upon justice, and

---

[21] Roy P. Basler, ed., *The Collected Works of Abraham Lincoln* (New Brunswick: Rutgers University Press, 1953), vol. 3, 376.

[22] Henry Cleveland, ed., *Alexander H. Stephens in Public and Private with Letters and Speeches* (Philadelphia: National Publishing Company, 1866), 721.

[23] Basler, *Collected Works*, vol. 2, 546.

[24] Frederick Douglass, *My Bondage and My Freedom* (Mineola, NY: Dover, 1969), 431, 445.

[25] Frederick Douglass, *Oration Delivered in Corinthian Hall, Rochester, by Frederick Douglass* (Rochester, NY: Lee, Mann, 1852), 9.

recognizing the equal rights of all men."[26] It was a bold vision built on the principles of natural equality and human dignity.

King's reference in his "I Have a Dream" speech to the Declaration as America's promissory note kept this vision in the American mind. Beginning with the dating in the biblical allusion of "five score years ago," King pointed his listeners to 1863, the year Lincoln began *his* most famous speech with the words, "four score and seven years ago." Lincoln, of course, was, in turn, pointing the country back to 1776, to the advent on the world stage of a "new nation, conceived in Liberty, and dedicated to the proposition that all men are created equal."[27] Lincoln's framing of the national narrative, and of the meaning of the war itself, around the principles of the Declaration was as much aspiration as it was plea, but it did underscore the real influence of the natural-law tradition in shaping American politics from the Declaration to the Civil War and beyond.

* * *

8.1 GOD AND NATURAL LAW ON THE EVE OF OUR SESQUICENTENNIAL

Looking back at the Declaration of Independence now, on the eve of our sesquicentennial, we can appreciate how much classical and Christian conceptions of natural law have shaped the broader American political tradition. Today, however, we live in a world that is very different than it was two and one-half centuries ago – a more secular age, a more skeptical age, a more fractured age. One of the most insightful efforts to distinguish our current epoch from the past is Charles Taylor's magisterial work, *A Secular Age*. Taylor sees a dramatic shift in consciousness from a time when belief in a transcendent reality and destiny was a given to our age in which faith is a choice. As a result, ours is a world in which public affairs and political organization are not in any meaningful sense – except perhaps as a historical vestige – "connected to, based on, guaranteed by some faith in, or adherence to God, or some notion of ultimate reality."[28]

Political liberalism in the late twentieth and now early twenty-first centuries has sought to bracket those questions of ultimate reality from public life. Such a world leaves little room for natural law as a guiding or framing public

[26] Frederick Douglass, "Composite Nation" (lecture in the Parker Fraternity Course, Boston, 1867). Accessed July 29, 2021, from http://hdl.loc.gov/loc.mss/mfd.22017
[27] Roy P. Basler, ed., *The Collected Works of Abraham Lincoln* (New Brunswick: Rutgers University Press, 1953), vol. 7, 23.
[28] Charles Taylor, *A Secular Age* (Cambridge, MA: Belknap Press, 2007), 1.

philosophy of public life. Yet the attempt to organize public affairs around a set of propositions that remain neutral with respect to questions of ultimate concern has been met with criticism from those in different ideological quarters who have come, in recent years, to reject liberalism root and branch.[29] For some, liberalism and its ideological and theological underpinnings are power structures that need to be dismantled and replaced; for others, liberalism represents a modern turn toward voluntarism and individualism, a path littered with destruction.

We teeter on this precipice with an insecure liberal tradition that is facing fundamental challenges from implacable ideological opponents, and chief among those challenges is a rejection of postwar liberalism's pretentions to metaphysical neutrality. Various moral and religious visions vie to replace the ostensibly neutral political liberalism that has dominated American politics for the last half century or more. Much of our progressive politics is now marked by a resurgent pre-Christian paganism that sees divinity as

fundamentally inside the world rather than outside it, that God or the gods or Being are ultimately part of nature rather than an external creator, and that meaning and morality and metaphysical experience are to be sought in a fuller communion with the immanent world rather than a leap toward the transcendent.[30]

Alongside this return to paganism is also the very different challenge to liberalism posed by resurgent forms of Christian nationalism and integralism, which seek to reintegrate those elements of spiritual and temporal authority – corresponding to immanent and transcendent concerns – that the liberal tradition tore asunder.[31] Both visions reject the modern liberal order wholesale, and, in their own way, both visions point to the failure of the twentieth-century secularization thesis and highlight the enduring relevance of political theology.[32]

---

[29] The most important such attempt is, of course, in John Rawls' theory of political liberalism and its attendant strictures on the kinds of reasons we may give one another when deliberating together as free and equal citizens of a pluralistic society. See, in particular, John Rawls, *Political Liberalism* (New York: Columbia University Press, 1993); John Rawls, "The Idea of Public Reason Revisited," *University of Chicago Law Review* 64(3)(1997): 765–807.

[30] Ross Douthat, "The Return of Paganism," *New York Times* (December 12, 2018). Accessed March 3, 2022, from www.nytimes.com/2018/12/12/opinion/christianity-paganism-america .html

[31] See, e.g., Edmund Walstein, "An Integralist Manifesto," *First Things* (October 2017). Accessed March 3, 2022, from www.firstthings.com/article/2017/10/an-integralist-manifesto

[32] Writing of theology and political philosophy, Eric Nelson notes that "even in today's secular age, it turns out to be surprisingly difficult to do one without simultaneously doing the other." See Eric Nelson, *The Theology of Liberalism* (Cambridge, MA: Belknap Press, 2019), xi.

8.2 THE ENDURING RELEVANCE OF POLITICAL THEOLOGY

One distinctive feature of human experience is that we search for greater-than-human sources of meaning and existence. This is arguably manifest across time and culture in our fundamental appetite or longing for meaning, which is apparent in art, poetry, and philosophy. Classical theistic natural lawyers have argued that the fundamental appetite or longing for full satisfaction of our desires is itself a sign that no created or temporal good can satisfy human beings' deepest longings, and that therefore there must be an uncreated good (God) that ultimately satisfies.[33] As C. S. Lewis explained, "If a transtemporal, transfinite good is our real destiny, then any other good on which our desire fixes must be in some degree fallacious, must bear at best only a symbolical relation to what will truly satisfy."[34] The experience of the desire for full satiation is a commonplace of the human experience. A skeptic might concede the reality of that experience but nonetheless dispute whether this desire corresponds to any real object. Considering this objection, Lewis replied:

Do what they will, then, we remain conscious of a desire which no natural happiness will satisfy. But is there any reason to suppose that reality offers any satisfaction to it? "Nor does the being hungry prove that we have bread." But I think it may be urged that this misses the point. A man's physical hunger does not prove that that man will get any bread; he may die of starvation on a raft in the Atlantic. But surely a man's hunger does prove that he comes of a race which repairs its body by eating and inhabits a world where eatable substances exist. In the same way, though I do not believe (I wish I did) that my desire for Paradise proves that I shall enjoy it, I think it a pretty good indication that such a thing exists and that some men will. A man may love a woman and not win her; but it would be very odd if the phenomenon called "falling in love" occurred in a sexless world.[35]

And yet, as Lewis points out, "almost all of our modern philosophies have been devised to convince us that the good of man is to be found on this earth."[36] Indeed, the idea of radical immanent fulfillment, of finding our only satisfaction and meaning in this temporal life, as Eric Voegelin observed, "grew rather slowly, in a long process that roughly may be called 'from humanism to enlightenment.'"[37]

One of the outstanding representatives of the modern transition toward radical immanence is Michel de Montaigne. As Benjamin and Jenna Storey have recently argued, Montaigne was massively influential in arguing for

---

[33] Thomas Aquinas, *Summa Theologica*, trans. Fathers of the English Dominican Province (Encyclopedia Britannica, 1952), I–II, 2.1–8.

[34] C. S. Lewis, *The Weight of Glory and Other Addresses* (New York: HarperCollins/HarperOne, 2001), 29.

[35] Ibid., 32–33.   [36] Ibid., 31.

[37] Eric Voegelin, *The New Science of Politics: An Introduction*, foreword by Dante Germino (Chicago: University of Chicago Press, 1987), 119.

"immanent contentment."[38] Montaigne did not dispute that the longing for full satiation was something "to which nature herself has disposed us," and yet he maintained that this natural disposition was a by-product of the human propensity to be anxious about the future.[39] While one can see similar accounts of the religious instinct or religious longing in other modern thinkers, this sort of critique talks past the classical and Christian natural-law traditions, which were not based on an anthropology that grounded the religious instinct in the mere emotion of fear.[40] On the classical view, fear is an appetitive movement in response to a perceived evil, the mere fact of which does not dislodge the classical Christian metaphysical and anthropological claims about the human longing for goodness. The classical idea was that the will is the sort of power that can only be fully satisfied by the universal, uncreated good – that is, by something transcendent rather than immanent.

According to this classical Christian anthropology, the modern turn toward immanence is not "secular" in the sense of nonreligious, precisely because we cannot avoid placing our fundamentally religious hopes for happiness in something, whether or not that something is external to this world. Aquinas made this Aristotelian and Christian point this way: "That in which a man rests as in his last end, is master of his affections, since he takes therefrom his entire rule of life. Hence of gluttons it is written (Philippians 3:19): 'Whose god is their belly': viz. because they place their last end in the pleasures of the belly."[41] In short, the teleological orientation of the will entails that we do not fail to place our last end in some object – and that object will take on a sacred character to us. In this sense, we are all religious.

The desire for immanent contentment is the defining attitude of immanentism, which itself can be traced from some medieval thinkers to various modern political religions and ideologies.[42] This attitude is characteristic of a world in which "we understand our lives as taking place within a self-sufficient immanent order," what Taylor calls the "immanent frame."[43] If classical Christian anthropology is correct, then this feature of modernity is not surprising. Man's deepest longings for full happiness are the heart of the religious instinct. It is longing that gives rise to angst rather than the vice versa. The idea of man as an irreducibly religious creature suggests that religion is therefore plenary to the human experience, because the desire and therefore quest for ultimate

[38] Benjamin Storey and Jenna Silber Storey, *Why We Are Restless: On the Modern Quest for Contentment* (Princeton and Oxford: Princeton University Press, 2021).
[39] Michel de Montaigne, *Essays of Montaigne*, trans. Charles Cotton, rev. William Carew Hazlett (New York: Edwin C. Hill, 1910), vol. 1, 85.
[40] Cf., e.g., Hobbes, *Leviathan*, ch. 12.   [41] Aquinas, *Summa Theologica*, I–II.1.5.
[42] For an argument that this is an expression of the Christian heresy of Gnosticism, which "overcame the uncertainty of faith by receding from transcendence and endowing man and his intra-mundane range of action with the meaning of eschatological fulfilment," see Voegelin, *The New Science of Politics*, 107–32.
[43] Taylor, *A Secular Age*, 543.

fulfillment is essential to human nature. The religious longing then will inevitably manifest itself through human placement of faith in some object, where faith is understood in the sense of "ultimate concern," to borrow Paul Tillich's helpful formulation.[44]

In his provocative study of paganism and Christianity in the ancient and modern worlds, Steven D. Smith has recently revived a version of this thesis, locating the source of the religious instinct in either the inclination to seek out meaning (per thinkers such as Viktor Frankl) or the human encounter with the sublime or the holy (per thinkers such as Rudolf Otto). Smith offers a weaker and more conciliatory version of the thesis than the one advanced by classical natural-law theorists. Because he worries that some people will find it insulting to suggest that they *really* are religious animals, even if they understand themselves as entirely nonreligious and unconsecrated, Smith therefore claims only that *many* human beings experience the need for meaning and/or the encounter with the sublime such that one will fail to understand social reality without taking it into account.[45]

Still (as even Smith seems to acknowledge), the *homo religiosus* thesis does not stand or fall on the subjective report of the skeptic, any more than the natural lawyer's thesis of a universally knowable and known set of basic moral principles stands or falls upon the subjective report of the sociopath. Even if there are people who do not experience the longing for full satisfaction, this would not disprove the *homo religiosus* thesis. To recall a passage from one of Jefferson's letters discussed in Chapter 2:

Some men are born without organs of sight, or of hearing, or without hands. Yet it would be wrong to say that man is born without these faculties, and sight, hearing, and hands may with truth enter into the general definition of man. The want or imperfection of the moral sense in some men, like the want or imperfection of the sense of sight and hearing in others, is no proof that it is a general characteristic of the species.[46]

In both cases, what Smith calls the "audacious" theological-philosophical anthropological claim is that human beings have a nature that is inclined toward objective goods, including the good of religion, which a person with a well-formed and properly functioning power of reason grasps. The desire or need to seek for meaning turns out to be an aspect of the basic appetite for full satisfaction, which in classical Christian metaphysics can only be given by the external Object, the Good Itself that at once can be encountered as holy/sublime and as imparting meaning to the whole of existence.

---

[44] Paul Tillich, *Dynamics of Faith* (New York: Perennial Classics, 2001), 1 ff.

[45] Steven D. Smith, *Pagans and Christians in the City: Culture Wars from the Tiber to the Potomac* (Grand Rapids, MI: William B. Eerdmans, 2018), 16–49. Smith also discusses the previously quoted passages from Lewis at 35–36.

[46] *The Papers of Thomas Jefferson*, ed. J. Jefferson Looney (Princeton: Princeton University Press, 2011), vol. 7, 414.

8.3 TWENTIETH-CENTURY TOTALITARIANISM

Paradoxically, some of the most powerful evidence for the "audacious" version of the *homo religiosus* thesis can be found amid the twentieth-century experiments in jettisoning God from polity. Consider the Bolshevik totalitarian regime, which sought to stamp out traditional Orthodox Christianity. The regime officially embraced scientific materialism, ridiculed the church and the faith, imposed various legal disabilities on the church, engaged in show trials and secret executions of clergy, and confiscated or destroyed church property. But the regime's strategy was not limited merely to destruction of its religious opponents. It also included a positive campaign to construct loyalty to the new regime through coopting religious longing and directing those longings from the transcendent to the immanent. As Michael Burleigh explains, the Bolsheviks, "while acknowledging a general religious instinct, described as a 'necessary illusion', sought to divert it from a transcendental God to worship of mankind and science. The essence of this faith was 'Man does not need God, he himself is God. Man is a God to man.'"[47]

Fascists also understood the power of the religious instinct and the importance of constructing new political religions. Mussolini put it this way: "Fascism is not only a party, it is a regime, it is not only a regime, but a faith, it is not only a faith, but a religion that is conquering the labouring masses of the Italian people."[48] Substantively, this meant that the regime adopted and transformed the trappings of the traditional church with its own public liturgy of rites and rituals that sought to breed sacral loyalty to a secular state. Burleigh's historical work corroborates Voegelin's judgment that communism and fascism were political religions that sought to bring heaven and earth together through political organization, what Voegelin in his memorable phrase said was an attempt to "immanentize the eschaton."

What Smith's work has provocatively suggested is that political religion did not die with the evident defeat of totalitarian ideologies of communism and fascism in the twentieth century. Rather, Smith argues, liberal democracy now flirts with the specter of paganism. As Smith explains, the pagan gods were "*part of* the world; they are creatures of time and space," in radical contrast to the Creator God of Judaism and Christianity, who was the Creator precisely because He was unlimited by matter, space, time, and so on. This is key to understanding Smith's thesis: he does not mean that late modernity is rediscovering faith in Zeus, Athena, and the rest of the gods of the pantheon. Rather, he argues that late modern progressive liberalism has increasingly adopted an immanentist faith that sacralizes (or resacralizes) this world. So, for example, the ancient pagan believed that the gods were present in and sanctified the sexual act. The modern pagan does not believe the god Eros is literally present,

---

[47] Michael Burleigh, *Sacred Causes* (New York: Harper Perennial, 2008), 42.   [48] Ibid., 56–57.

but he effectively ranks it as sacred because it takes on an architectonic centrality to his personal dignity, happiness, and ultimate concern.[49]

It is fruitful to juxtapose Smith's work both to that of political theorist Joshua Mitchell, who offers a similar insight with a distinct variation, and to the work of Andrew Whitehead and Samuel Perry, who document and analyze the rise of Christian nationalism in populist conservative politics. First, Mitchell contends that rather than a resurrected paganism, the characteristic doctrine of advanced progressive liberalism, that is, identity politics, trades in essentially Christian concepts such as sin, death, guilt, and innocence, but transforms them. In Mitchell's account of identity politics, the world is divided into two camps: those who by virtue of their race or sex are guilty transgressors and those who by virtue of their race or sex are innocent victims of oppression. Public life becomes "a religious venue for sacrificial offering."[50] In this immanentist inversion of the biblical narrative, there is no original sin, but there are original sinners; there is no redemption, but there is a constant need for repentance and reparation. Christian concepts and categories have been transformed and brought into everyday politics. The manifestation of identity politics at the popular level, cultural critics have noted, seems to be at root religious and even puritanical.[51]

By contrast, Whitehead and Perry draw our attention to the phenomenon in populist conservative politics of Christian nationalism, accentuated now in the age of Trump. Christian nationalism is a difficult concept to define with precision, but Whitehead and Perry emphasize its advocacy of national allegiance to an "almost ethnic" Christian cultural identity (rather than set of policies) that will secure divine blessings for the nation as a whole, a form of religious identity politics that appeals to a beleaguered cultural minority in the United States who perceive that their way of life is under siege.[52] Although Perry and Whitehead do not make this connection, one could argue that Christian nationalists, so understood, perceive that their culture and identity are under siege from the very identitarian and religious impulses of progressivism chronicled by Smith and Mitchell, respectively. These progressive and conservative populist movements feed on each other and metastasize together.

---

[49] For an account of how this feature of the modern self came to be, which argues Freud's account of sex as central to human identity and human happiness as genital pleasure was a turning point, see Carl R. Trueman, *The Rise and Triumph of the Modern Self: Cultural Amnesia, Expressive Individualism, and the Road to Sexual Revolution* (Wheaton, IL: Crossway, 2020).

[50] Joshua Mitchell, *American Awakening: Identity Politics and Other Afflictions of our Time* (New York: Encounter Books, 2020), preface, sect. 10.

[51] See, e.g., Andrew Sullivan, "Is Intersectionality a Religion?" *New York Magazine: Intelligencer* (March 10, 2017). Accessed July 15, 2021, from https://nymag.com/intelligencer/2017/03/is-intersectionality-a-religion.html?mid=twitter-share-di

[52] Andrew L. Whitehead and Samuel L. Perry, *Taking America Back for God: Christian Nationalism in the United States* (New York: Oxford University Press, 2020), 11.

Perry and Whitehead helpfully distinguish twenty-first century Christian nationalism from what they call "America's civil religious tradition" that is characterized by its appeals "to 'Providence,' the 'Creator,' or 'Nature's God'" and that advocates national "fairness, beneficence, and faithful stewardship if we are to retain our blessed inheritance."[53] That civil religion, we have argued, has historically been connected to the classical and Christian natural-law tradition, and it remains distinct from the cultural identity politics that now mark the twin specters of progressive identity politics and Christian nationalism. On Smith's and Mitchell's accounts, Americans are either apostate Christians who have embraced paganism or they are Christian heretics. Christian nationalists have responded to this, as the title of Whitehead and Perry's book suggests, by urging Christians to "take America back for God," but this taking back is understood as a reclaiming of cultural and political power for a specific identity group that occupies a shrinking part of the US political landscape.

What each account holds in common is an acknowledgement that, to a certain extent, the strife and polarization in contemporary politics is at root a conflict between political theologies. One cause and consequence of this civic strife is waning public confidence in liberalism evidenced by some of the recent and widely discussed narratives that trace America's ills to the classical liberal principles of the American founding itself.[54] The question, for these critics, is what to offer in its place, and at least some of those who draw a straight line from the American founding to American decline contend for a reintegration of church and state along medieval lines. Adrian Vermeule, one of the most prominent Roman Catholic integralists, argues, like Smith and Mitchell, that late modern liberalism is essentially a sacramental religion.[55] What is distinctive about the integralist response is its rejection of the classical liberal elements of the founding and its return to medieval Christian forms of polity. Beginning with the thesis that human beings long for a deeper satiation of desire than what liberalism can offer, Roman Catholic integralists argue that the state ought to cooperate with the Church and positively direct man toward his true final end. The state, in other words, must not feign neutrality on matters of ultimate concern but should instead aim to direct man to his transcendent good. The Roman Catholic version of integralism has been advocated by prominent legal and political theorists and widely discussed, but there have also been

---

[53] Ibid.
[54] See, e.g., Patrick Deneen, *Why Liberalism Failed* (New Haven, CT: Yale University Press, 2018); Michael Hanby, "The Birth of Liberal Order and the Death of God: A Reply to Robert Reilly's *America on Trial*," *New Polity* (February 2021), 54–85.
[55] See, e.g., Adrian Vermeule, "All Human Conflict Is Ultimately Theological," *Church Life Journal* (July 26, 2019). Accessed March 3, 2022, from https://churchlifejournal.nd.edu/art icles/all-human-conflict-is-ultimately-theological/; Adrian Vermeule, "Liturgy of Liberalism," *First Things* (January 2017). Accessed July 20, 2021, from www.firstthings.com/article/2017/ 01/liturgy-of-liberalism

undertheorized proposals for what might be called a kind of protestant integralism – something that is closely connected to the rise of Christian nationalism discussed previously and remains prominent in populist conservative politics rather than in academic circles.[56]

8.4 RECONSIDERING THE FOUNDERS' CLASSICAL NATURAL-LAW APPROACH TO RELIGION IN PUBLIC LIFE

A recovery of the classical and Christian elements in the founders' approach to religion – which grounds individual and corporate religious liberty in a prior duty to pursue the truth about God – provides an alternative to these twin pressures toward various forms of religious identity politics, on the one hand, and integralism, on the other. As is evident in the Declaration of Independence and across the founders' writings, natural rights were grounded in the laws of nature.[57] We noted in the previous chapter how James Wilson put this: "Order, proportion, and fitness pervade the universe. Around us, we see; within us, we feel; above us, we admire a rule, from which a deviation cannot, or should not, or will not be made."[58] This order, proceeding from God and known by human reason, is the natural law, and it is the transcendent criterion of the moral validity of all human laws. And as we saw in Chapter 1, Alexander Hamilton explained that "the deity, from the relations, we stand in, to himself and to each

---

[56] See Greg Forster, "A Protestant Integralism?" *Law & Liberty* (June 2, 2020). Accessed March 3, 2022, from https://lawliberty.org/book-review/a-protestant-integralism/ (reviewing Albert Mohler Jr., *The Gathering Storm: Secularism, Culture and the Church*). As a prominent example of a kind of undertheorized integralism enveloping conservative politics, consider the regional Jericho Marches that culminated in a rally in Washington, D.C., on December 12, 2020. That rally was designed to act out the biblical story of the Israelite march around the walled city of Jericho until Yahweh took down the walls and gave Israel victory. Featuring an ecumenical group of Jews and Christians, the rally positioned the United States as ancient Israel, President Trump and his supporters as Israel's remnant, and the rally as a call for divine intervention to allow President Trump to win the Electoral College vote on December 14.

[57] Some scholars claim that the phrase "law of nature" is modern, whereas the phrase "natural law" is classical. As one example, see James McClellan, *Joseph Story and the American Constitution: A Study in Political and Legal Thought* (Norman: University of Oklahoma Press, 1971). McClellan notes that Joseph Story used "the terms 'natural law' and 'law of nature' interchangeably and is unaware of the fact that the latter, which is a semantical innovation of the modern school, is wholly antagonistic toward traditional natural law" (73). But as we saw in Chapter 7, James Wilson explicitly divided "natural law" into the two subcategories of the "law of nature" and "law of nations" depending on the application of natural law to domestic or international law, respectively, and he was explicitly drawing on the classical tradition in doing so. What any author means by natural law or the law of nature must be inferred from usage and context, not simply from an oversimplified semantic division between classical and modern conceptions.

[58] James Wilson, *The Collected Works of James Wilson*, ed. Mark David Hall and Kermit L. Hall (Indianapolis, IN: Liberty Fund, 2007), vol. 1, 464.

other, has constituted an eternal and immutable law, which is, indispensably, obligatory upon all mankind, prior to any human institution whatever."[59]

We have also already seen in Chapter 2 how James Otis articulated the classical natural-law philosophical-theological anthropology of a divinely pedigreed, teleological nature with inclinations toward objective goods. Human beings share with other created things a range of natural inclinations in virtue of their vegetative and animal nature, but human beings also have distinctive inclinations in virtue of the capacity to reason. This was evidence of a hierarchical created order, with human beings situated at the top of the material order, by virtue of their capacity to reason. That capacity imparted moral dispositions, something that set human beings apart from the rest of creation. John Witherspoon explained: "[I]n man we have an example of what we see also every where else, viz. a beautiful and insensible gradation from one thing to another, so that the highest of the inferior is, as it were, connected and blended with the lowest of the superior class." In harmony with classical Christian natural law, Witherspoon contended that there are "instinctive propensities ... some of them intermixed with moral dispositions" that included inclinations toward goods distinctive to human nature.[60]

As we have noted throughout this book, some prominent scholars claim that the founders derived duties from rights in a radically individualistic, amoral state of nature. They argue that the founders assumed, in the spirit of Hobbism, that in a state of nature, persons have natural rights prior to any obligations, and that obligations are the mere creation of the social contract.[61] We have argued through this book that such narratives have the story backward. To take one example relevant to our discussion in this chapter, the founders believed the natural right to free exercise of religion was grounded in prior natural duties connected to the good of religion. Madison wrote that religion is antecedent to civil law; it is "the duty which we owe to our Creator and the manner of discharging it."[62] For Madison, the rights of conscience that the civil authority was bound to respect flowed from a prior duty to God that transcended civil competence and the fundamental equality of persons as natural-rights bearers. This prior duty grounded a fundamental feature of religious freedom: the equal right of every person to worship according to the dictates of his or her own conscience. Some of the founders harbored heterodox views of Christianity and shared Enlightenment skepticism of divine revelation while

[59] Alexander Hamilton, *The Farmer Refuted &c.* (February 23, 1775), Founders Online, National Archives. Accessed March 14, 2022, from https://founders.archives.gov/documents/Hamilton/01-01-02-0057

[60] John Witherspoon, *Lectures on Moral Philosophy* (Princeton: Princeton University Press, 1912), 6–8.

[61] See, e.g., Walter Berns, "Judicial Review and the Rights and Laws of Nature," *Supreme Court Review* (1982), 49.

[62] James Madison, *Writings*, ed. Jack N. Rakove (New York: Library of America, 1999), 30.

others held more recognizably orthodox Christian beliefs. Yet many of the widely shared political views of the time, as we have labored to demonstrate, rested on principles consonant with classical Christian natural-law theory, namely, that natural rights are tethered to the moral law and teleologically oriented toward genuine human flourishing.

Although the founders did not embrace liberal neutrality about the good life, they did deny to the civil authority – both federal and state – competence to coerce citizens to accept the state's judgment as to the content and meaning of the doctrines of divine revelation. Still, they widely shared the belief that religion was essential to the public good in a constitutional republic. Even the anticlerical and disestablishmentarian Jefferson rhetorically asked, "can the liberties of a nation be thought secure when we have removed their only firm basis, a conviction in the minds of the people that these liberties are of the gift of God?"[63] Jefferson, Madison, and their allies among religious dissenters such as the Baptists insisted that state establishments were actually corruptive of religion. Others in the founding era espoused a civic republican argument that the state had a role in supporting religion for its utilitarian value in promoting virtue. But even defenders of a plural establishment such as Patrick Henry maintained that church and state were institutionally and functionally separate and that the maintenance of religious exercise was primarily the purview of civil society. Virtually no founder wanted a *national* religious establishment, and even those who preferred nonestablishment at the state level conceded that states retained constitutional authority to establish or not establish a church locally under our federalist system.[64]

Most founders then agreed on a common set of principles: liberty of conscience, or the freedom of belief; free exercise, or the right to put those beliefs into practice; religious equality, or nondiscrimination; institutional separation of church and state; and disestablishment at the federal level.[65] George Washington spoke for most founders when he said he saw these principles as compatible with government encouragement and support for religion. As he put it in his Farewell Address,

Of all the dispositions and habits which lead to political prosperity, religion and morality are indispensable supports. In vain would that man claim the tribute of patriotism, who should labor to subvert these great pillars of human happiness, these firmest props of the duties of men and citizens. The mere politician, equally with the

---

[63] Thomas Jefferson, *Notes on the State of Virginia*, Query XVIII, in *The Selected Writings of Thomas Jefferson*, ed. Wayne Franklin (New York: W. W. Norton, 2010), 134.

[64] For a detailed state-by-state analysis of the role of religious arguments in the process of religious disestablishment, see Carl H. Esbeck and Jonathan J. Den Hartog, eds., *Disestablishment and Religious Dissent: Church-State Relations in the New American States, 1776–1833* (Columbia: University of Missouri Press, 2019).

[65] See John Witte Jr. and Joel A. Nichols, *Religion and the American Constitutional Experiment* (New York: Oxford University Press, 2016), 41–63.

pious man, ought to respect and to cherish them. A volume could not trace all their connections with private and public felicity. Let it simply be asked: Where is the security for property, for reputation, for life, if the sense of religious obligation desert the oaths which are the instruments of investigation in courts of justice? And let us with caution indulge the supposition that morality can be maintained without religion. Whatever may be conceded to the influence of refined education on minds of peculiar structure, reason and experience both forbid us to expect that national morality can prevail in exclusion of religious principle.[66]

Washington may have underspecified the good and natural duty of "religion" for both principled and pragmatic reasons. Not only was this position a deduction from natural-law and natural-rights philosophy, but it was also a recognition that the United States was in fact marked by a pluralism of publicly reasonable religious practices. The principles of liberty of conscience, nondiscrimination, institutional separation, federal disestablishment, and de facto pluralism provided the conditions for robust free exercise as well as social peace and civic unity. It made possible civic friendship among protestant sects and even between protestants and non-protestants. As Pope Leo XIII recounted a century later:

[A]t the very time when the popular suffrage placed the great Washington at the helm of the Republic, the first bishop was set by apostolic authority over the American Church. The well-known friendship and familiar intercourse which subsisted between these two men seems to be an evidence that the United States ought to be conjoined in concord and amity with the Catholic Church. And not without cause; for without morality the State cannot endure – a truth which that illustrious citizen of yours, whom We have just mentioned, with a keenness of insight worthy of his genius and statesmanship perceived and proclaimed.[67]

The upshot is that the founding understanding of the free exercise of religion was rooted in the precepts of natural law. The founders understood positive law to be grounded in the natural moral law, which included natural duties to God. As just one example, the North Carolina state ratifying convention echoed Madison's language: the manner of discharging the natural duty of religion was to be directed by "reason and conviction" rather than "force or violence."[68] The language of reason and conviction is important – it suggests both an objective and a subjective component that are not without some tension. Subjectively, religion must be an individual's own conscientious

[66] "George Washington, Farewell Address, 19 September 1796," Founders Online, National Archives. Accessed March 3, 2022, from https://founders.archives.gov/documents/Washington/99-01-02-00963
[67] *Longinqua*, Encyclical of Pope Leo XIII on Catholicism in the United States (1895). Accessed March 3, 2022, from www.vatican.va/content/leo-xiii/en/encyclicals/documents/hf_l-xiii_enc_06011895_longinqua.html
[68] *The Complete Bill of Rights: The Drafts, Debates, Sources, and Origins*, ed. Neil H. Cogan (New York: Oxford University Press, 1997), 12.

conviction. Objectively, reasonable pursuits of religion will abide by the precepts of natural law.

The immediate legal deductions from the dictates of natural law, such as criminal laws proscribing murder, theft, slander, and the like, were essential to the protection of natural rights and would set the standard of reasonable conduct to which diverse religious practitioners would be expected to adhere. In the same way, the positive law translated natural rights into the civil rights of persons and citizens. As Thomas G. West puts it, for the founders, securing protection against "intentional injuries to life, liberty, and property" was the "government's single most important domestic policy."[69] In other words, civil enactments reflective of the first precepts of natural law, and their enforcement, were the essential constituents of peace and good order.

Reinforcing just this idea, James Wilson, echoing Anglican theologian Richard Hooker, held that the natural law is the "mother of ... peace."[70] As Wilson explained further, it is not sufficient for the natural law to be promulgated by God to the consciences of men and women. The natural law must be translated into positive law with credible authoritative threats of sanction for their breach, because of the ineradicable spark of passion and therefore dangerous potential in man for evil:

Without laws, what would be the state of society? The more ingenious and artful the twolegged animal, man, is, the more dangerous he would become to his equals: his ingenuity would degenerate into cunning; and his art would be employed for the purposes of malice. He would be deprived of all the benefits and pleasures of peaceful and social life: he would become a prey to all the distractions of licentiousness and war.[71]

Wilson intimated here what Madison memorably stated: men are not angels. The founders thus accepted the axiom from classical Christian philosophy that human beings are dangerous when unruly passions are cut loose from reason (a disorder in the powers of the soul that the scholastics sometimes referred to under the general term "concupiscence"). Laws rooted in natural law and combined with credible threats of sanction for noncompliance are therefore the necessary supports of public peace and the antidote to licentiousness and war.

In this light, consider the proviso of the New York Constitution of 1777 (South Carolina's 1790 Constitution used similar language):

free exercise and enjoyment of religious profession and worship, without discrimination or preference, shall forever hereafter be allowed, within this State, to all mankind: *Provided*, That the liberty of conscience, hereby granted, shall not be so construed as

---

[69] Thomas G. West, *The Political Theory of the American Founding* (New York: Cambridge University Press, 2017), 151.
[70] *Collected Works of James Wilson*, vol. 1, 465.   [71] Ibid., 505; cf. 690, 704.

to excuse acts of licentiousness, or justify practices inconsistent with the peace or safety of this State.[72]

"Licentiousness" referred to disordered acts of will. In Shakespeare, for example, the licentious man makes his own will the "scope of justice."[73] Similarly, Locke distinguished between liberty, which was a condition of enjoyment of all of one's natural rights within the bounds of the moral law, and license, which equated liberty with power and which the founders associated with Hobbes.[74] For the founders, acts of licentiousness were behaviors flowing from unruly passions as opposed to "sober reason."[75] "Licentiousness" thus often referred to overt violations of precepts of natural law in disturbance of the peace as distinct from acts of ordered liberty. The term included a range of behaviors, such as rioting,[76] theft,[77] slander and libel,[78] trespasses of frontiersmen on people of other nations,[79] movements to break up states and form new ones,[80] and resistance to paying taxes on whiskey,[81] to name just some.[82] Blackstone included sexual activity outside of conjugal marriage as a form of licentiousness.[83]

[72] *The Complete Bill of Rights*, 26.
[73] William Shakespeare, *Timon of Athens* in *The Complete Works*, 2nd ed. (Oxford: Oxford University Press, 2005) act 5, sc. IV, 967.
[74] John Locke, *Two Treatises of Government*, 2nd treatise, ed. Peter Laslett (New York: Cambridge University Press, 1988), bk., II, ch. 2, para. 6. Cf. Hamilton, "The Farmer Refuted &c. [23 February] 1775."
[75] "The Farmer Refuted &c. [23 February] 1775," at n. 2.
[76] "Pennsylvania Assembly: Reply to the Governor (February 11, 1764)," Founders Online, National Archives. Accessed March 3, 2022, from https://founders.archives.gov/documents/Franklin/01-11-02-0013
[77] "To George Washington from Major General Philip Schuyler (August 29, 1776)," Founders Online, National Archives. Accessed March 3, 2022, from https://founders.archives.gov/documents/Washington/03-06-02-0134
[78] "From John Jay to Silas Deane (December 5, 1781)," Founders Online, National Archives. Accessed March 3, 2022, from https://founders.archives.gov/documents/Jay/01-02-02-0275
[79] "From James Madison to Richard Henry Lee (November 14, 1784)," Founders Online, National Archives. Accessed March 3, 2022, from https://founders.archives.gov/documents/Madison/01-09-02-0241
[80] "Abigail Adams to Thomas Jefferson (November 24, 1785)," Founders Online, National Archives. Accessed March 3, 2022, from https://founders.archives.gov/documents/Adams/04-06-02-0151
[81] "From John Adams to George Washington (November 22, 1794)," Founders Online, National Archives, *available at* https://founders.archives.gov/documents/Adams/99-02-02-1598
[82] Some forms of conduct identified as licentious were more controversial. For example, some believed that the "African slave trade" was a form of licentiousness. See "An Address from the Quakers to George Washington, the Senate, and the House of Representatives," *The Papers of George Washington 8 September 1789 – 15 January 1790*, ed. Dorothy Twohig (Charlottesville: University Press of Virginia, 1993), vol. 4, 265–69, at n, 1.
[83] William Blackstone, *Commentaries on the Laws of England in Four Books* (Philadelphia: J.B. Lippincott, 1893 [1753]), vol. 1, bks. I and II, 438.

Regarding the latter, the founders saw marriage as of a piece with their natural-law philosophy. In John Witherspoon's words, marriage is "part of natural law" and "holds a place of first importance in the social compact."[84] Hence, it was commonplace for the law to sanction behaviors destructive of marriage such as adultery. In New York, adultery was grounds for divorce, but New York sought to deter it by making it unlawful for the adulterer to remarry. There was opposition to this law – but notably the opponents made their protest in the name of chastity, believing that by punishing adulterers in this way they would simply provide incentives for adulterers to flout the marriage norm and engage in open licentiousness with a "pernicious influence on public morals."[85]

8.5 RELIGIOUS EXEMPTIONS AND THE RULE OF LAW

Given that they grounded religious freedom in the duties that arose from natural law, the founders rejected out of hand any notion that religious freedom – or other claims to autonomous liberty – could become a shield for exemption from laws regulating licentious conduct or laws promoting virtue.[86] If that happened, the natural right to religious freedom would then become twisted in subversion of the very precepts of natural law on which it was grounded. This does not mean that the founders were averse to any religious accommodations or exemptions but that those exemptions were either granted for behaviors that did not contravene fundamental moral norms or they were granted in a way that avoided subversion of the moral norm.

Take, for instance, Washington's example of the religious duty undergirding oaths to tell the truth in courts of law. The underlying moral norm here is the requirement to tell the truth, and the governmental has a compelling interest in sanctioning false testimony. Quakers often sought exemptions from oath swearing based on their interpretation of Christ's words on the subject, and indeed they were granted an exemption in Carolina in 1669. But the accommodation did not relieve them of the duty of truth telling in courts of law. Rather, they were "allowed to enter pledges in a book in lieu of swearing."[87] The founders incorporated this reasonable accommodation into the Constitution

---

[84] John Witherspoon, "Queries, and Answers Thereto, Respecting Marriage," *The American Museum, or Repository* (Philadelphia: Matthew Carey, 1788), vol. 4, 315–16. Quoted in West, *The Political Theory of the American Founding*, 222.

[85] "New York Assembly. Remarks on an Act Directing a Mode of Trial and Allowing of Divorces in Cases of Adultery (March 28, 1787)," Founders Online, National Archives. Accessed March 3, 2022, from https://founders.archives.gov/documents/Hamilton/01-04-02-0066

[86] See also Vincent Phillip Muñoz, "Two Concepts of Religious Liberty: The Natural Rights and Moral Autonomy Approaches to the Free Exercise of Religion," *American Political Science Review* 110(2) (2016): 369–81.

[87] Thomas J. Curry, *The First Freedoms: Church and State in America to the Passage of the First Amendment* (New York: Oxford University Press, 1987), 56.

itself for such conscientious objections – without forswearing the need to foster loyalty to the constitutional order – by allowing elected officials to bind themselves to uphold it "by Oath or Affirmation."[88]

The example of exemptions from military service confirms the point. Washington addressed the Quakers' desire for exemption from military service:

The liberty enjoyed by the People of these States, of worshipping Almighty God agreable [*sic*] to their Consciences, is not only among the choicest of their *Blessings*, but also of their *Rights* – While men perform their social Duties faithfully, they do all that Society or the State can with propriety demand or expect; and remain responsible only to their Maker for the Religion or modes of faith which they may prefer or profess.

Your principles & conduct are well known to me – and it is doing the People called Quakers no more than Justice to say, that (except their declining to share with others the burthen of the common defence) there is no Denomination among us who are more exemplary and useful Citizens.[89]

Clearly, Washington understood the natural right of free exercise of religion to be in essential harmony with the moral norm that all citizens must contribute their share to the common defense. As New York's constitution put the moral norm, "it is the Duty of every Man who enjoys the Protection of Society to be prepared and willing to defend it."[90] When state legislatures faced the reality that some conscientious objectors would rather die than fight, they sometimes accommodated them with an exemption, but the accommodation still required the exempted to shoulder a share of the burden of common defense through an alternative means. Hence, New Hampshire's Constitution provided, "No person who is conscientiously scrupulous about the lawfulness of bearing arms, shall be compelled thereto, provided he will pay an equivalent."[91]

We can draw a number of conclusions from the brief foregoing discussion of the founders' understanding of the duty of religion and corresponding right of religious freedom. First, it demonstrates that the founders did not establish constitutional protections for licentiousness, which they understood to be indulgence of the human will outside the bounds of the moral law. They were not voluntarists. Narratives of American decline, whatever their other merits, are thus incorrect to trace contemporary licentiousness to the founders' understanding of ordered liberty.

Second, one reason the founders rejected the full integration of church and state was to protect the good of religion and the natural duty of religious worship and corresponding natural right of religious liberty. Their emphasis on natural rights also prominently included the natural right of private

---

[88] US Constitution, Article VI.
[89] "From George Washington to the Society of Quakers (October 13, 1789)," Founders Online, National Archives. Accessed March 3, 2022, from https://founders.archives.gov/documents/Washington/05-04-02-0188
[90] *The Complete Bill of Rights*, 183.   [91] Ibid.

property, which led to a period of enormous material prosperity and economic growth,[92] but it was not merely material goods such as economic prosperity and private property rights that the founding stood for. Founding era natural-rights philosophy began with objective human goods and our duty to protect them, implying that government failure to respect natural rights was an offense against the dignity of human nature itself. The Declaration and other founding era sources clearly rooted the value and dignity of persons in a transcendent Creator, who was the source of value in the world, and apart from whom that world did not have value. Human dignity was and is, at bottom, a theological concept.[93]

The founders' affirmation of human dignity as rooted in and open to a transcendent source of value, which in turn imparts value on the created order, was fundamentally in harmony with classical Christianity. The separation of church and state was itself a consequence of the Christian desacralization of worldly government. In response to Pilate's inquiry, Jesus famously said, "My kingdom is not of this world." In light of the widespread ancient norm of theopolitics and sacralized kingship, such a statement was literally kingdom shaking.[94] The one whom Christians believed to be the King of Kings had inaugurated a spiritual kingdom that directed the fundamental longings of persons beyond earthly goods and toward a transtemporal and transfinite good. The corollary to this statement was at once Christ's establishment of a church, which would have care of souls, and Christ's acknowledgment of the authority of (even pagan) worldly governments: "Render unto Caesar what is Caesar's and unto God what is God's."[95]

In harmony with classical Christianity, the founders rejected sacralization of this world and, therefore, they rejected the sacralization of secular government. The transtemporal and transfinite good, and the way to its enjoyment,

---

[92] Deirdre McCloskey calls this the "Great Enrichment." See McCloskey, *Bourgeois Equality: How Ideas, not Capital or Institutions, Enriched the World* (Chicago: University of Chicago Press, 2016), xiv–xv, 5–13 (discussing the statistical evidence). For one recent celebration of this as a "secular event," see George Will, *The Conservative Sensibility* (New York: Hachette Books, 2019), ch. 5.

[93] See generally Larry Siedentop, *Inventing the Individual: The Origins of Western Liberalism* (Cambridge, MA: The Belknap Press, 2014); Kyle Harper, "Christianity and the Roots of Human Dignity in Late Antiquity," in *Christianity and Freedom, Volume 1: Historical Perspectives*, ed. Timothy Samuel Shah and Allen D. Hertzke (New York: Cambridge University Press, 2016), 123–48.

[94] "[S]acral kingship, prevalent in one or other form in cultures existing quite independently of one another right around the globe and in almost every historical era since the fourth millennium BCE, represents the nearest thing identifiable as a 'political,' or, better, theopolitical norm in the vast array of human societies studied by historians, anthropologists, and experts in comparative religion." Francis Oakley, *The Watershed of Modern Politics* (New Haven and London: Yale University Press, 2015), 129.

[95] See Matthew 22:21, Mark 12:17, and Luke 20:25.

Washington said in response to a group of Presbyterian ministers, was not the proper province of the federal government, but of the church:

To the guidance of the ministers of the gospel this important object is, perhaps, more properly committed – It will be your care to instruct the ignorant, and to reclaim the devious – and, in the progress of morality and science, to which our government will give every furtherance, we may confidently expect the advancement of true religion, and the completion of our happiness.[96]

In this context, the separation of church and state was a consequence of the desacralization of the state. In securing man's temporal good, however, the state needed the aid of flourishing and reasonable religious communities whose shared commitments buttressed republicanism. As we have already seen, Washington (and Hamilton, who drafted the Farewell Address) believed that republican government could not be sustained apart from religious principle, by which they envisioned a civil society full of multiple faith traditions affirming a shared belief in a providential, moralistic Creator who is the source of our natural duties and natural rights.

From the natural duty to worship God according to the dictates of conscience is derived an individual and corporate right to religious liberty. At the same time, as evident in Washington's letter to the Quakers, American political theology tolerated, but declined to affirm, a radical transcendentalism that would entirely eschew worldly government and its affairs as irredeemably corrupt in an attempt to build a high and impregnable wall sheltering the garden from the wilderness.[97] Yet as we have argued at length in this book, the founders also rejected modern Hobbist theories of unlimited state sovereignty that resacralized government and reintegrated church and state. In contrast both to a radical transendentalism that eschews state power and to a radical immanentism that embraces totalizing state power, the founders affirmed the goodness of, as well as the limited goods served by, a constitutional republic.

8.6 BETWEEN IDENTITY POLITICS AND INTEGRALISM

Smith, Mitchell, Whitehead and Perry, and others have already described and diagnosed contemporary identity politics in its various guises. Secular humanistic values have been sacralized and, for some, taken on a cultish devotion and a puritanical zeal to project one's own innocence while shaming and ostracizing dissenters, including those who espouse various brands of cultural conservatism. A related phenomenon is the political mobilization of Christian

---

[96] "From George Washington to the Presbyterian Ministers of Massachusetts and New Hampshire, 2 November 1789," *Founders Online*, National Archives. Accessed July 15, 2021, from https://founders.archives.gov/documents/Washington/05-04-02-0193

[97] "From George Washington to the Society of Quakers (October 13, 1789)."

cultural identity as one more identity group among others vying for political spoils. The overriding danger of this world of identity politics is its rejection of a common human nature and common standards of reason and judgment rooted in that nature. Without common standards of judgment rooted in a common human nature, these socially constructed groups can relate to each other only through assertions of will. To the extent that identity politics jettisons a transcendent Creator of a common human nature, there is no way in which persons with different social identities can relate to one another as natural equals. Immanentist identity politics therefore subverts all features of constitutional republicanism that rely on the premise of equal creation. In contrast, the transcendental vision and promise of the founders, represented and carried forward by Lincoln and King, provided a ground for the essential features of constitutional republicanism that flow from equal creation such as mutual recognition of equal rights, deliberative and temperate majoritarian politics, the bonds of loyalty forged through a shared past, common citizenship, and shared sacrifice for a common good.

Integralism presents a different challenge. While we are sympathetic with aspects of the critiques of contemporary liberalism associated with or adopted by integralists, those critiques often rest on a mistaken genealogy that conflates contemporary liberalism with the elements of Hobbism we have discussed throughout this book and then draws a direct line from contemporary Hobbism to founding era political thought. That move leads prominent integralists to overstate Hobbes' influence on Locke and Locke's influence on the founding while neglecting the providential constitution out of which the American union was created. In contrast with the commitments underlying identity politics, the integralists do offer a sound restatement of classical Christian theological anthropology. They affirm the Thomistic doctrine of twofold common good and the twofold final end of man as the metaphysical ground of the institutional distinction between church and state. In this scheme, the twofold beatitude of man (imperfect/perfect or temporal/eternal) corresponds to a twofold rule of man: state and church. The state or polity aims at imperfect beatitude, which includes fostering the practice of virtue and the bonds of justice and peace characteristic of the temporal common good. Meanwhile, perfect beatitude is available by grace and is administered by the ministers of Christ's Church. But integralists go further and infer an ideal of church–state relations in which the state ought to be the secular arm of the church. In response to modern theorists of sovereignty, integralists concede that sacral politics is unavoidable, and conclude that we ought to take our cues for how to do sacral politics from the thirteenth century rather than the eighteenth or the twenty-first.

Of course, from the Christian perspective, the state's purview of the temporal common good is metaphysically subordinate to the object of the church, but this claim does not necessitate a particular juridical form of church–state relations. Sectarian confessional states (which respect legitimate claims to free exercise) are, in our view, in principle within the ambit of prudence as a constitutional arrangement.[98] Prudence, however, would also admit (say) an Augustinian understanding of church–state relations that emphasizes existential humility about God's will for polity, a healthy skepticism of the competence of public officials, and state authority that is limited to a range of temporal goods.[99] Such a vision of civil authority would limit its purview to a subset of objects pertaining to the common good, which may turn out to be challenging enough for it to administer, for example, delivering the mails, protecting the shores from external threat, regulating commerce, and policing internal order. Such an Augustinian would doubt that a government that regularly fails to rationally deliberate on and pass a budget has the capacity to be a competent secular arm of the church.

In such an order, the state could still be seen as subservient to the church metaphysically, because it would foster the preconditions for the practice of the good of religion. On this view, a well-ordered state need not remain neutral with respect to genuine religion, as if such neutrality were possible. As in the broad approach of the founders outlined previously, the state might confess its public belief in a moralistic providential God while protecting an order of free exercise. In this way, it would remain cognizant of genuine but underspecified religion and the duty owed by individuals and society to God while accepting the state's incompetence to judge specific doctrines or modes of worship. It therefore would vigorously defend institutional and individual religious liberty in order to secure the good of religion. In our view, such an approach is in harmony with the classical natural-law duties pertaining to religion and, with relevance to the debate over integralism, also with the magisterial teaching in *Dignitatis Humanae*.[100]

---

[98] For an example of such a polity, see the 1937 Irish Constitution.

[99] See Kody W. Cooper, "Existential Humility and the Critique of Civil Religion in Augustine's Political Theology," *Augustine in a Time of Crisis* (Cham, Switzerland: Palgrave Macmillan, 2021).

[100] We think *Dignitatis Humanae* (*DH*) can be fairly seen as a development of doctrine, but we do not pretend to resolve the debate over its status relative to previous magisterial teaching. Integralists defend nineteenth-century papal teaching regarding the juridical norm of church–state relationships, citing encyclicals such as *Mirari Vos, Quanta Cura*, and *Immortale Dei*. We cannot comprehensively canvas the ways scholars have read *DH* in relation to these encyclicals, but we can briefly summarize some influential approaches. Some read *DH* as compatible/continuous with Leonine integralism; for example, Thomas Pink argues that it simply limits the *state of itself* to coerce in matters of religion; but it leaves intact the church's right of coercion of members of the church and the possibility of using the state as its secular arm. Others, such as Joseph Trabbic, argue that *DH* leaves intact the notion of confessional states as an ideal that is normative for Catholics. Some read it as contradictory to previous teaching and therefore in error (Marcel Lefebvre). And some read it as contradictory to Leonine teaching, but correcting it. These would emphasize that it is in the genre of authoritative nondefinitive teaching (this is the tier below de fide teachings (revealed truths in Bible; Christology, creeds, etc.), and teachings doctrina catolica "held definitively" (infallibility of the pope, ordination of

Integralists propose that Christians should support integration of church and state from within key positions of civil authority. The goal is to infiltrate government or exploit positions already held to mitigate the aggression of the dying liberal state, thereby imitating godly and clever biblical heroes who exploited fortuitous positions of power. As Adrian Vermeule articulates this view, the models for integralist politics are

> Joseph, Mordecai, Esther, and Daniel who in various ways exploit their providential ties to political incumbents with very different views, in order to protect their own views and the community who shares them. This is not the problem of doing evil to do good; none of these agents transgress the bounds of morality, although they act strategically within those bounds. What marks out these agents as distinctive is that they are fully engaged with and within the world of the imperium, and fully loyal to it – so long as there is no conflict with their ultimate commitments. There is no hint here of a "Benedict option" or a localist Deneen community.[101]

Vermeule thus suggests, contrary to the founders' vision of a more limited federal government apparatus, that the vast late modern administrative state ought to be embraced and turned to advance a conservative vision of the common good.[102]

It is one thing to say that, in the short term, Christians who find themselves in places of government authority ought to push and pull the levers of bureaucracy where the law permits, and to nudge things toward a sounder account the common good in areas where the federal government has already arrogated authority. Yet as long as we live under the US Constitution, it remains authoritative in virtue of the secondary sovereignty of the American people.[103] It therefore imposes obligations on citizens in both the short and long terms, and pursuit of the common good must work to shore up, rather than abandon, constitutionalism, not least because constitutionalism and the public political theology of the founding have the potential to foster approaches to social life that allow local communities to be animated by grace and oriented toward the

---

men, canonization of saints …). And that in this third tier there can be contradictions in teachings across time. For a helpful discussion, see Lawrence King, "The Authoritative Weight of Non-Definitive Magisterial Teaching" (dissertation. Catholic University of America, 2016). And then there is the reading of it as discontinuous with staunch integralism but *continuous in a broader sense* of being a development of doctrine to generate vigorous doctrine of religious liberty (e.g., John Courtney Murray, Ian Ker, Cardinal Avery Dulles).

[101] Adrian Vermeule, "Integration from Within," *American Affairs* II(1) (Spring 2018). Accessed July 20, 2021, from https://americanaffairsjournal.org/2018/02/integration-from-within/

[102] To take one example, however, Daniel does not seem to support this aspect of Vermeule's vision. Daniel's service to the House of Nebuchadnezzar can certainly be seen as serpentwise and dove innocent, but it was not aimed at taking over the Babylonian state from within. It was rather a service to authority under God while waiting on God to restore Israel and her freedom.

[103] See the discussion in Chapter 6.

transcendent good.[104] The founding does not necessitate a conflict between those immanent goods common to human nature and the hope of a transcendent good that will fully satisfy our longings. Rather, the founding reflects a collective prudential judgment about the application of principles that were common to the classical Christian natural-law tradition and that formed part of the providential constitution of the North American colonies in the eighteenth century.

The influential academic narrative that claims the roots of the American founding are ultimately Hobbist – because allegedly wedded to a voluntarist ontology of moral obligation, pantheist theology, and rejection of final causality – gets the story exactly wrong.[105] The founders were aware of those fundamentally important philosophical and theological questions associated with Hobbes, and, with very few exceptions, they rejected Hobbism by affirming moral realism rooted in the will and reason of a creating and providential God who holds nature in being and imbues nature with purposes that point, ultimately, toward an object of satisfaction that lies beyond nature. Fundamental principles of American politics and constitutionalism have roots in the classical and Christian past, including the notions of natural equality, natural rights, popular sovereignty, government by consent, and the right of resistance to tyrannical (and therefore unlawful) government.[106] These are the principles the delegates to the Continental Congress together affirmed under the "Laws of Nature and of Nature's God" with an appeal to the "Supreme Judge of the world" and a profession of "reliance on the protection of divine Providence" – highlighting, in that founding moment, the classical and Christian origins of American politics.

---

[104] For accounts of what such communities might look like, see Alasdair MacIntyre, *Dependent Rational Animals* (Chicago and La Salle, IL: Open Court, 2001), 119–46; Deneen, *Why Liberalism Failed*, 191–98.

[105] See Robert R. Reilly, *America on Trial: A Defense of the Founding* (San Francisco: Ignatius Press, 2020).

[106] Ibid. See also Paul R. DeHart, "Whose Social Contract? Hobbes versus Hooker and the Realist Contract Tradition," *The Catholic Social Science Review* 26 (2021): 3–21. Building on Reilly's argument, DeHart shows that some of the political ideas that some scholars consider distinctively "modern" – for example, natural equality in a state of nature, political authority residing in the people as a whole, and government powers derived from the consent of the governed – have roots in the Thomist tradition and especially in Hooker. DeHart and Reilly evidence from different angles that, as we have also argued, the fundamental lineaments of American political thought predate modern theorists such as Hobbes and Locke and are rooted rather in (and only coherent in light of) the classical Christian synthesis of the medieval period.

Index

Pantheism, Christian natural law distinguished, 4
Parry, Stanley, 180
Particular will, 160–61
Pascal, Blaise, 24, 160–62
Passive obedience, 109–11, 116–17
Patriarchalism, 90–93, 95–96
Patterson, William, 164
Paul (Saint)
  antecedent will versus consequent will, 160
  body analogy, 160, 162
  nonviolent civil disobedience and, 210
  on passive obedience, 109, 112
  on resistance, 114–15
Peace of Augsburg (1555), 158
Peace of Westphalia (1648), 158
Peace or War Memo (Beaumarchais), 144–45
Penn, William, 56–57
Pennsylvania
  abolition of slavery in, 215
  Constitution, 155, 174
Perry, Samuel, 223–24, 234
Peter of Auvergne, 48–49
Peter (Saint), 109, 117
Petition of Right to Charles I, 36
Physical laws of nature, 14
Pinckney, Charles, 164
Pink, Thomas, 236–37
Plato, 17–18, 154
Plymouth Charter, 103–4
Pocock, J.G.A., 61
Polarization, 224
Political liberalism, 218
Pontius Pilate, 116, 233
Popular sovereignty
  absence of, 171
  Articles of Confederation and, 165
  in Constitutional Convention, 164–65, 167–69
  Constitution and, 155–57, 177
  division of powers and, 169
  Hamilton on, 165, 168–69
  historicism and, 172
  individual versus collective sovereignty, 173–74
  Madison on, 164
  normative theory and, 171–72
  positivism and, 172
  post-independence period, in, 155
  preference utilitarianism and, 176
  Rousseau and, 163
  small states and, 165

  states as sovereigns for purposes of, 165, 168
  supermajoritarian procedures and, 175–77
  voluntarism and, 172
  Wilson on, 164–65
Positive law
  civil rights and, 229
  classical natural law and, 186
  criminal law and, 229
  social peace and, 229
  Wilson on, 229
Positivism
  parliamentary sovereignty and, 53
  popular sovereignty and, 172
  sovereignty and, 26–27
Preference utilitarianism, 176
Presbyterianism, 72, 205–6
Priestly, Joseph, 80
Princeton, Battle of, 135–36
Princeton University, 18–21, 45, 72
Prisoners of war, 134–35
Proclamation for Suppressing Rebellion and Sedition, 131
Proper authority, 100, 114
Property rights
  Aquinas on, 53
  Dickinson on, 57–58
  divine workmanship thesis and, 93–94
  extensionalist theory of, 92, 94
  Jefferson on, 89–90, 95–96
  Locke on, 53–54, 65, 90–94
  matriarchalism and, 92–93
  natural law and, 232–33
  Otis on, 53–54
  patriarchalism and, 90–93, 95–96
Protestantism, 191, 204–5, 228
Providential constitution, 183–85
  civil religion and, 212
  Constitution and, 184
  secondary sovereignty and, 184–85
  "We the People" and, 184
Providentialism
  generally, 122, 124, 152
  in American history, 123–24
  American Revolution and, 154
  Beaumarchais and, 148
  British cruelty viewed as confirming, 152–54
  classical natural law and, 124–25
  Constitutional Convention and, 166–67
  in Continental Congress, 125–27
  in counterintelligence, 136–40
  Deane and, 142, 146, 148
  in diplomacy, 140–50